the image and the witness
TRAUMA, MEMORY AND VISUAL CULTURE

Nonfictions is dedicated to expanding and deepening
the range of contemporary documentary studies.
It aims to engage in the theoretical conversation
about documentaries, open new areas of scholarship,
and recover lost or marginalised histories.

General Editor, Professor Brian Winston

the image and the witness

TRAUMA, MEMORY AND VISUAL CULTURE

Edited by Frances Guerin and Roger Hallas

 WALLFLOWER PRESS LONDON & NEW YORK

First published in Great Britain in 2007 by
Wallflower Press
6 Market Place, London W1W 8AF
www.wallflowerpress.co.uk

A catalogue record for this book is available from the British Library.

ISBN 978-1-905674-19-0 (pbk)
ISBN 978-1-905674-20-6 (hbk)

Book design by Elsa Mathern

Printed and bound in Poland; produced by Polslabook

Contents

Notes on Contributors

Matthias Christen is Fellow of the Swiss National Science Foundation at the Seminar für Filmwissenschaft der Freien Universität Berlin. He is the author of *To the End of the Line: Zu Formgeschichte und Semantik der Lebensreise* (1999) and a forthcoming book on the circus film. He has also published several articles about film and photography. He has taught at the universities of Constance, Zurich, Prague and Berlin, and is a curator of photographic exhibitions.

Stephanie Marlin-Curiel has taught at Emerson College and at New York University where she received her Ph.D. in Performance Studies in 2001. She has published several essays on cultural responses to the Truth and Reconciliation Commission and theatre for development in South Africa.

Davide Deriu has taught architectural history and theory at University College London. His main research interests are modern architecture, urbanism and visual culture. He has participated in international art and architecture exhibitions and is a regular contributor to the Italian monthly, *Il giornale dell'architettura*. His essays have been published in various books, including *Visual Culture and Tourism* (2003), *Endangered Cities* (2004) and *Imagining the City* (2005). He is currently completing a book on aerial photography and urban representations.

Marcy Goldberg is a consultant specialising in documentary film, and a freelance journalist and translator. She is a programmer at the international documentary film festival Visions du réel in Nyon. She teaches film studies at the Seminar für Filmwissenschaft of the University of Zurich and is currently writing a dissertation on contemporary Swiss cinema.

Frances Guerin teaches in the School of Drama, Film and Visual Arts at the University of Kent, Canterbury. She is the author of *In a Culture of Light: Cinema and Technology in 1920s Germany* (2005); and her articles have appeared in international journals, including *Cinema Journal, Screening the Past, Film and History* and *Cinema e Cie*. She is currently completing a book entitled *Through Amateur Eyes: Cinema and Photography from the Nazi Years*.

Karen J. Hall is Faculty Fellow in the Humanities at Syracuse University. An activist for peace and social justice, she is a member of the Syracuse Peace Council and dedicates her research and teaching to raising awareness in the US of the multitude costs and effects of militarism. She has published articles on war toys and first-person shooter video games, and is completing a book on Hasbro's GI Joe action figure entitled, *Yo Joe!: Playing with Global Imperialism*.

Roger Hallas is Assistant Professor of English at Syracuse University where he teaches courses on film studies, documentary media and visual culture. His articles have appeared in *Camera Obscura, Canadian Journal of Film Studies, Millennium Film Journal, Afterimage* and *The Scholar and the Feminist*. He is currently completing a book about witnessing AIDS in queer film and video.

Jonathan Kear is Senior Lecturer in History and Philosophy of Art at the University of Kent, Canterbury. He has published many articles on Paul Cezanne and on various aspects of nineteenth- and twentieth-century art and photography. He has also published a book and several articles on the French filmmaker Chris Marker. Currently he is completing a book on Paul Cezanne and working on another on Fantin Latour.

Camila Loew teaches contemporary literature and film in Barcelona. She belongs to a research group at the Universitat Pompeu Fabra on the discourse of war in twentieth-century literature and visual arts. She specialises in testimonial literature of the Holocaust. She has published articles on literature and film of the Holocaust and the Spanish Civil War, and on women's testimonies of the First World War. She is currently writing on the Spanish film director Pedro Almodóvar.

Devin Orgeron is Assistant Professor of Film Studies at North Carolina State University where he teaches courses such as Contemporary American Cinema, Cinematic Realism and International Cinema of the 1970s. His book-in-progress, *Motion Studies*, traces the cinema's longstanding interest in the subject of automobility. His writing has appeared in *CineAction, COIL, Film Quarterly, College Literature* and *Post Script*.

Marsha Orgeron is Assistant Professor of Film Studies at North Carolina State University where she teaches courses on American and international film history. Her research interests include movie fan culture in the studio era, amateur and educational films and independent filmmakers of the 1940s and 1950s. She has published articles in *Cinema Journal, American Literature, Quarterly Review of Film & Video, College Literature, COIL* and the *Canadian Review of American Studies*.

James Polchin holds a Ph.D. in American Studies from New York University. He has taught at Princeton University and the New School and currently teaches in the General Studies Program at New York University. He is completing a book on the history of violence and sexual panic.

Leshu Torchin is Lecturer in Film Studies at the University of St Andrews. Interest in media and advocacy fuels her dissertation, 'The Burden of Witnessing: Media and Mobilisation in the Age of Genocide', as well as her ongoing research. Her essays have appeared in *American Anthropologist*, *Tourist Studies* and *Cineaste*.

Tina Wasserman is Chair of the Visual and Critical Studies Department at the School of the Museum of Fine Arts, Boston/Tufts University. She has written numerous articles on film and visual culture in such journals as *Dialogue*, *C Magazine*, *Afterimage* and the *New Art Examiner*. She is currently working on a book on film and the uses of memory.

Guy Westwell is Senior Lecturer in Film Studies at London Metropolitan University. He is the author of *War Cinema: Hollywood on the Frontline* (2006) and is currently working on a book examining iconic American photographs and cultural memory.

Edlie L. Wong is Assistant Professor of English at Rutgers, the State University of New Jersey, where she teaches nineteenth-century African American and American literature. She is currently completing a book entitled *Fugitive and Foreigner: Cultures of Travel in the Black Atlantic, 1830–1865*.

Introduction

Frances Guerin and Roger Hallas

Images are not just a particular kind of sign, but something like an actor on the historical stage, a presence or character endowed with legendary status, a history that parallels and participates in the stories we tell ourselves about our own evolution from creatures 'made in the image' of a creator, to creatures who make themselves and their world in their own image.

W. J. T. MITCHELL

The art of witness … bids us to consider how a remembered image might gain new hold on our lives and actions.

KYO MACLEAR

Cultural studies abound with declarations and denunciations of our image-saturated contemporary world. Computer screens, video monitors and electronic billboards fill the social spaces of work, leisure and education. Television has become almost as fixed in public spaces as it has in our living rooms. Billboards and hoardings, magazines and advertisements tutor us in our consumer desire. The World Wide Web has taken over as our primary source of information. And where we find words – in newspapers and books or on the Internet – our eye is instantly drawn to the images to verify, convince or titillate us. However, what cultural studies often fail to acknowledge in their critique of the hegemony of the visual is that hand in hand with this popular attachment to the currency of images, we also treat them with an equally popular scepticism. For all our reliance on images, we never quite believe in their revelations. Despite the privilege given to the authority and presence of the image, it is, after all, just an image, a picture. It might be manipulated, biased in perspective: it does not fully reveal the truth of what it claims to represent. This scepticism has become even more pronounced in an age of greater technological sophistication when images can be generated without an original referent. How can we ever be confident that the image tells the truth when we live in a world where, however transparent images may appear, they are, in reality, 'opaque, distorting, arbitrary [mechanisms] of representation … [processes] of ideological mystification'?[1]

It is not only the production and proliferation of images that generate doubt about their veracity. Their modes of exhibition and circulation do little to build our confidence in their truth value. Images flicker past our eyes in a moment too ephemeral to allow us to test their substantiality: when we drive past them on the highway, as they fill our evenings in front of the television, as they punctuate the written text of a magazine or newspaper, and as we surf from site to site on the Internet. So many of the public images which make up our sensory environment are not trusted to be on display for more than a second or two. Their producers imagine that we will find them monotonous and superfluous, or that time might enable the kind of unsanctioned thinking that leads to unwanted questions and criticisms. There is usually no time to build a relationship with the image; if we are not in motion, then the image is designed to pass us by in an instant. Each image thus appears to ensure its own built-in obsolescence. As Susan Sontag notes, 'Image-glut keeps attention light, mobile, relatively indifferent to content. Image-flow precludes a privileged image.'[2] In keeping with the demands of capital, there is no time to discover, to reflect, to learn or to imagine in the presence of the image. Rather, the image is at its most stable when it is functional, goal oriented, silently reinforcing a textual discourse.

This iconoclasm that pervades the production, dissemination and philosophy of the image in the twenty-first century is nowhere more pronounced than it is in relation to images of traumatic historical events. In spite of the ubiquity of public images that witness such events, there is a persistent scepticism expressed toward their capacity to remember or redeem the experience of the traumatised victim. Similarly, images have been repeatedly deemed inadequate in the face of events understood to be too heinous to be represented. This is because, hitherto, images have been embraced for their mimetic promise, for their perceived ability to produce a representation which addresses the demand for evidence triggered by historical trauma. As Kyo Maclear asserts in her study of 'testimonial art' about the atomic bombing of Hiroshima and Nagasaki, the visual art of witnessing has long been 'tethered to criteria of accuracy and authenticity' that insist on an 'evidentiary necessity' as the principal function of such art.[3] And if, as trauma studies maintained in the last decades of the twentieth century, no representation can even begin to communicate the truth of the traumatic experience, then the mimetic image claims to represent what is, in fact, unrepresentable.

Consider, for example, the criticism levelled at the documentary photographs taken by Allied cameramen and photographers on liberation of the Nazi concentration camps in 1945.[4] These criticisms were founded on a resentment toward the image for its erasure of the humanity and integrity of both the survivors and the dead. These films and photographs may have shown the devastating physical consequences of the camp system on the bodies of its victims, but they did not even begin to approximate either the existential or metaphysical reality of the prisoners' debasement. Therefore the image fell short of what it claimed. And yet, the same images have subsequently found widespread circulation as documentary evidence of Nazi atrocity and evil in the concentration camps. Even though they were taken on liberation, when the Germans had abandoned the camps, the images are often held up as windows onto the horror of life *during* incarceration.[5]

Alternatively, the home-video images of Rodney King as he was beaten again and again by four white Los Angeles policemen in 1991 were elevated to an iconic status: they gave birth to a riot that arguably changed the face of race relations in the United States. And yet, the graphic depictions of police brutality were deemed not sufficiently authentic to hold the perpetrators responsible in the criminal court case. Despite the prosecutors' claims for the video's evidential status, the defence attorneys successfully argued that there was more to the event, more that the image did not, or chose not to see.[6] By stressing the limitations of the image, the defence was able to reframe the meaning of what the image actually captured. Thus, the brutal beating of King came to be seen by the jury as the necessary subjugation of a violent felon. In a widely discussed example from the Iraq War, the provocative digital pictures taken in 2004 of tortured Iraqis in the Abu Ghraib prison continue to be disseminated as evidence of US violence toward Iraqi prisoners.[7] While the proliferation of discourses on their subject testify to the many lessons of these images, the debate regarding their status continues with animation: Do they in fact constitute evidence of systematic torture by US forces? Are the images a form of propaganda that asserts cultural dominance or a despised strategy of added intimidation and humiliation to provoke the Arab prisoners to disclose information? Are they simple documents of the interrogation process? Or are they the perverse souvenirs of aberrant US military personnel, as the Pentagon claims?[8] On the one hand, all of these images are disseminated in abundance, and they carry political conviction way beyond their status as representation. On the other, like many public images of trauma, they also continue to be denigrated, dismissed, questioned and cast in doubt.

This popular scepticism towards the visual representation of historical trauma finds its intellectual correlate in the shared assumptions of two interdisciplinary formations that have profoundly influenced the contemporary course of the humanities: visual studies and trauma studies. Both formations developed partially in response to the poststructuralist critique of representation that understood the categories of truth and the real as effects of discourse, and therefore, as historical constructs.[9] Visual studies have taken up the task of historicising the role of the image and visual representation in modern regimes of truth and knowledge. Trauma studies have sought to redeem the category of the real by connecting it to the traumatic historical event, which presents itself precisely as a representational limit, and even a challenge to imagination itself.[10] Trauma studies thus offer poststructuralist theory a means to reintroduce a political and ethical stake in the representation of the real without regressing to the very notions of mimetic transparency that it has striven to overturn.[11] Trauma studies consistently return to an iconoclastic notion of the traumatic event as that which simultaneously demands urgent representation but shatters all potential frames of comprehension and reference. Likewise, in their elucidation of the power dynamics instantiated by the historical development of specific discursively constituted gazes, visual studies demonstrate an iconoclastic impulse to uncover and undo the power of the visual. Even redemptive accounts of the image and visual representation rely on the deconstruction, appropriation or resignification of existing historical modes of seeing. Such redemptive critical work can be found in a wide range of knowledge formations and aesthetic practices. For example, it can be located in the disciplinary crisis in anthropology, the playful postmodernism of New Queer Cinema, art history's institutional critique and the culture-jamming of Adbusters.[12]

While acknowledging the wider limitations and contradictions of bearing witness to historical trauma through visual media, the new scholarship collected in this volume resists the iconoclastic urge within both trauma studies and visual studies. The contributions move beyond a focus on the radical limitations and aporia of visual representation in the face of historical trauma. The individual chapters seek to locate the specific ways that the material image enables particular forms of agency in relation to various historical traumas across the globe. We do not see this agency as some kind of transcendental or essential power held by images, whether redemptive or pernicious, as though they were active agents outside their historical contexts of human production and reception. This type of essentialism of the image is pervasive in the moral panics swirling around media-effects discourses that treat images as monocausal agents of violent and destructive social behaviour.[13] Faith in an essential power of the image, such as we see in these moral panics, is likely to lead to an iconoclastic agenda similar to popular scepticism toward the image. As we discuss more extensively below, the agency of the material image upon which this collection focuses, is grounded in the performative (rather than constative) function of the act of bearing witness. Within the context of bearing witness, material images do not merely depict the historical world, they participate in its transformation.

The broad array of visual forms analysed in this book, including film, photography, painting, sculpture and digital interfaces, attests to the diverse possibilities to bear witness through the use of the material image. It thus contests the longstanding denigration of the image within trauma studies.[14] Collectively, the chapters of the book intervene in theoretical conceptions of the image and of the witness within visual studies, trauma studies and documentary studies. Accordingly, the scholarship brought together here offers an opportunity to connect theories, practices and contexts previously kept separate, and simultaneously, to diversify the conceptual frameworks for analysing practices of witnessing within visual culture. This introduction thus offers a conceptual orientation through the theoretical premises that ground the scholarship of the chapters.

The chapters that follow each illuminate how the image actually facilitates specific possibilities to bear witness to historical trauma rather than foreclose or compromise them. Thus, of critical importance to our conceptualisation of the role of the image in bearing witness are the uses to which it is put, and the contexts in which it is placed. The material image is relieved of the singular burden of veracity when it is seen within the much broader context of its reception and use. Moreover, the concept of the image as performative moves our understanding of it away from the all-too-common tendency toward iconoclasm. This shift away from an evaluation of the mimetic achievements (and failures) of the documentary image to produce evidence toward an interrogation of the language, processes and broader concerns of visual documentation extends the interest of documentary studies, most influentially

in the work of Bill Nichols and Michael Renov, in the analysis of rhetoric and poetics.[15] In the early 1990s documentary film studies shifted from a narrow focus on
questions of truth and referentiality in documentary film to a theoretical and historical
concern with its complex discursive construction. This shift has helped to propel the
intellectual expansion of documentary studies into a dynamic interdisciplinary field
that brings together film studies, performance studies, communication, rhetoric, philosophy, anthropology, history and art history. Of particular importance to documentary studies has been the field's commitment to historicise the development of the
documentary film in relation to other forms of non-fiction film. For example, documentary film is understood in its relation to actualities, amateur film, travelogues and
ethnographic film, as well as documentary practices in other media, such as radio,
television, photography, video art and digital media. Documentary practices are thus
increasingly understood and analysed in cross-media contexts.[16] As editors, we understand this book to be an important opportunity to further cross-pollinate critical
discourses on the documentary image.

In spite of the proliferation of discourses which continue to distrust the image,
artists, filmmakers, photojournalists and amateurs continue to produce a vast body
of images as a means to bear witness to historical trauma. It is not only images
themselves, but also exciting curatorial and publicity initiatives such as exhibitions,
public installations, film festivals, the World Wide Web, media activism and visual
archives of past traumatic events which are now at the forefront of efforts to memorialise, interrogate and at times create the individual and collective experiences of
these events. Despite the ambivalence shown toward the image in the public sphere
and scholarly discourse, photographic, filmic, electronic and digital images play an
increasingly important role in the formation of contemporary cultural imaginaries.
This volume emphatically acknowledges the centrality of images where they have
otherwise been eclipsed by various forms of scepticism. The representation of traumatic historical events thus becomes an extreme test case for ever-present questions about the ethical and political status of the image in the twenty-first century.

More than any other recent event, the 11 September terrorist attacks provoked a
revival in the urgent need to bring traumatic historical events into the collective imaginary. Images of all genres took up the responsibility to guide the shape of cultural
memory.[17] As an event that took place at the heart of the First World, an event that
was not distanced by the gulf of political, geographical, religious or social otherness,
the compulsion to bear witness to 11 September in and through images has become
ever-present in this first decade of the new millennium. Without privileging the 11
September terrorist attacks, they are nevertheless a prime example of a traumatic
historical event that was and continues to be witnessed through the image in all its
many forms. The repeated return within televisual representation of the event to the
video footage of the planes' initial impact and the collapse of the World Trade Center
embodied a form of traumatic repetition-compulsion as the medium struggled to
master and make sense of the event. Still photography subsequently played an even
greater role: through the personal photographs in missing persons' posters turned
ad hoc memorials on the streets of New York City; in the democratisation of the
medium's witnessing function in the *Here is New York* project that anonymously
mixed professional and amateur photographs of the event; and in the production of

several emblematic photographs, such as the raising of the flag by New York City fire-fighters. In turn, this image, like its precedent, Jack Rosenthal's famous Iwo Jima photograph, has subsequently provided the foundation for further images produced in other media, particularly murals and public statuary.

Even where language played a significant role in shaping the comprehension and experience of the event, such as the reference to 'Ground Zero' and '9/11', images often provided the necessary representational foundation for such terms to make sense or take hold. The photographic images of the World Trade Center site after the attack not only resonated with the images of total destruction from the Hiroshima and Nagasaki bombings (when the military slang term 'ground zero' first achieved popular usage), they also invoked a similar horrific absence of so many victims from the image, who were known in both cases to have been literally vaporised or turned to dust by the attack. The historical caesura implied by '9/11', the notion that the world was no longer the same after 11 September 2001, has consistently been underlined by recourse to the now highly fetishised images of the downtown skyline of New York City, both with and without the towers of the World Trade Center.

As Marianne Hirsch has pointed out, this widespread impulse to produce images as a means to bear witness to the event did not go unquestioned, even in the initial aftermath of the attacks.[18] Backed up by a public request from Mayor Rudolph Giuliani, policemen at the World Trade Center site initially urged visitors to refrain from taking photographs, citing both national security and the need to respect the victims. In this double rationale for such iconoclastic policies, we find the very paradox at the heart of our contemporary understanding of the image: it potentially offers invaluable knowledge of the event and, at the same time, it fails to do justice to the human magnitude of the traumatic event.[19]

SUSPICIOUS IMAGES

Contemporary suspicion toward the veracity of the image can in part be pinned to the ability of technology to reproduce images without an original referent. However, the mistrust of the image as witness to traumatic historical events is more complicated and more deep-rooted than the ontological status of photographic reproduction. It also has everything to do with the way images are interpreted and used. In turn, the dissemination and interpretation of images are inextricably linked to the philosophical and ethical issues at stake in the context of reception. To return to the Rodney King trial as an example, the 'failure' of the video images as evidence in the trial was built on a slow and insidious expropriation of the images from their narrative context as home video footage shot by George Holliday. They were slowed-down, stopped, reversed and re-narrativised to such an extent by the defence that the apparent mimeticism of image and event was eroded.

The ambivalence towards the truth status of images is also linked to the ever-changing definition of 'appropriate' and 'responsible' representation. When the Allied forces went into the camps and filmed the survivors as they walked around like skeletons, unable to speak for themselves, the resultant images were offensive, disrespectful and transgressed the integrity of the human subject. Ever since, doubt has been cast over the ability of the image to capture ethically the magnitude of the suffering of trauma victims. As John Durham Peters argues, since the end of the Second World War, the survivor-witness has been encouraged to take an active role in the narration of his or her own story.[20] The image has not been given precedence in this struggle to 'give voice', and according to Peters this is because seeing is a passive activity whereas saying is active. While Peters' distinction must be left open to debate – particularly given the control and dominance afforded to the one who looks within the psychoanalytic and poststructuralist discourses on which dominant concepts of witnessing are dependent – it is true that words are more frequently considered closer to the communication of feeling and experience. Words, particularly those of oral testimony, are still connected to the body of the sufferer while the material image implies a separation (spatial, temporal or both) from that which it captures. As we shall argue, however, this distinction does not cast an inauthenticity over the process of witnessing in which the material image engages. On the contrary, a number of the chapters in this volume illuminate how the physical materiality of the image is often the very basis of its capacity for involvement in bearing witness to past events.

The iconoclastic tendencies of literature on trauma, memory and the representation of traumatic historical events are often more salient than they are in the analysis of everyday images. To date, scholars have paid more attention to the written and spoken word as the most appropriate communicative forms for bearing witness to and remembering the suffering of the traumatised subject. The privilege given to both textual and oral testimony as witness to traumatic historical events can ultimately be traced back to the iconoclasm that pervades the history of Western philosophy.[21] But this iconoclasm among intellectuals is, perhaps most importantly, and more immediately, the legacy of some of the earliest circulated images of the Nazi Holocaust, namely those already mentioned, which were taken by Allied cameras on the liberation of the concentration camps. Much of the early scholarship on the documentation, representation and memorialisation of traumatic historical events has focused specifically on the genocide of the Nazi Holocaust.

The specifically visceral nature of the first published Holocaust images prompted a subsequent shift away from visual depictions of the suffering. Indeed, in the late 1950s and early 1960s when filmmakers, writers, scholars and theologians began to reflect on this dark moment of their recent past, the focus was on the implication of the Holocaust for human nature and destiny, religious and moral life.[22] It was not until the 1980s and 1990s that historians turned to the issue of representation, and in particular, the role of language, art and literature in the memorialisation of the Holocaust.[23] In the interests of minimising distortions which might lead to the erasure of the event, literary and textual representation was repeatedly deemed more honest, more responsible because it did not claim absolute, mimetic truth.[24] The autobiographical account was considered most authentic because it spoke or wrote from an individual and deeply personal experience that did not claim to represent the experience of all those who suffered.[25] Survivor testimony locates its truth value precisely in its subjectivity, in its production of embodied knowledge. Similarly, the victims of the Nazi Holocaust did not have the privilege of access to image production – what cameras and other image-producing materials they once had were typically confiscated by their captors. Thus, unlike the immediacy and first-hand nature of the oral and written accounts of the transportations, ghettos and death camps, the images were often taken by someone else, most commonly, perpetrators, collaborators and bystanders. Since 1945, it has repeatedly been the case that victims of genocide do not have access to the production of their own images.[26] Understandably, their journals and other writings, often hastily written on scrap paper which adds to their authenticity, have been annexed as the most profound evidence of their suffering.[27] For these reasons, images of traumatic events have been considered the viewpoint of those who speak on behalf of the silenced. In written and oral histories, as well as in psychoanalytical exchange, the survivor is understood to gain agency on several levels. The therapeutic aspect of bearing witness allows the traumatised victim to work through the experience of the trauma and hopefully be released, if only partially, from the compulsion which forces him or her to involuntarily and repeatedly relive the trauma. As a social act, testimony also permits the survivor to speak to a public, whether to condemn or accuse the perpetrator, to memorialise the suffering, or to teach as a warning against repetition. These circumstances and beliefs that spawned the birth of trauma studies in the late 1980s and early 1990s have had, we would argue, a lasting hold over the still burgeoning field.[28]

The iconoclastic impulse of trauma studies can only partly be explained by the scepticism towards the massively influential images taken at the liberation of the concentration camps in 1945. It is also deeply rooted in the history of iconoclasm in the philosophy of Western art. The attitude of distrust is born of a history of aesthetics which expects too much from the image. As cultural critics and philosophers have argued, the truth for which the nineteenth- and twentieth-century aesthetician looks is nowhere found in the image itself, but commonly determined in advance. As Michael Kelly has carefully detailed with regard to the work of philosophers from Hegel through Arthur Danto, philosophers repeatedly look to art as a blackboard for truth, expecting their independently conceived-in-advance notion of truth to be discovered by the viewer when face to face with the image.[29] And when the image disappoints, it quickly becomes shrouded in doubt, delegitimised in the interests of moving closer to aesthetic truth. While art continues the struggle to find meaning in the possibility of representation, philosophers continue to be disappointed with these efforts, bemoaning art's inability to locate the truth that philosophers claim to be its responsibility. In an extension of Kelly's argument, the perpetuation of the philosophical project of nineteenth- and twentieth-century aesthetics can thus be understood as dependent on a failure of the image. If the truth could be located in the image, the work of the aesthetician would become redundant.

This conception of an aesthetic pursuit of truth brings us necessarily back to the development of Western art, a development rooted in the religious function of the image as icon. The social and political role of the image as icon dates back to early Christian times when the image was bestowed with metaphysical power as not simply in the likeness of God and the Saints. Rather, people behaved to certain images as to the very abode of God. In the conventional use of religious icons, some of the earliest uses of images 'were kissed and venerated with bended knee … they were treated like personages who were being approached with personal supplications'.[30] The making visible of an invisible God, that is, the making visible and present of what is otherwise unrepresentable, has powerful ramifications for the conception of representing traumatic historical events. Like the absent God who is given human form in the figuration of medieval icons, images of cataclysmic historical events have come to imply the appearance and presence of the event itself.[31] It has become commonplace to accept that the ontology of the image claims an immediacy and presence at events, such that the image is remarkable for its likeness to the lived experience. Images are considered not simply to evoke the violence and trauma of the event, but to re-present it, to make it present again (and in some cases, consciously make it present for the very first time). An identical behaviour toward the image, founded on beliefs about the ontological status of the medieval icon, maintains that God is present in the image itself. At the same time, however, we must recognise that the image is only a likeness of God, that is, it has a spiritual similarity, but ultimately, the material image itself is not authentic. The truth exists in its likeness.

Across his work, W. J. T. Mitchell has convincingly demonstrated that, despite our avowed modernity, our fundamental relationship to the image and its pictorial manifestations has not changed from the Biblical era to the present. In his discussion of the Judeo-Christian tradition of taboos against graven images and idolatry, he writes: 'The true, literal image is the mental or spiritual one; the improper, derivative, figurative image is the material shape perceived by our senses, especially the eye.'[32] For the material image, the picture, is understood to be the copy, that which is bought and sold, rented and stolen, it is 'the image plus the support; it is the appearance of the immaterial image in a material medium'.[33] This contradictory impulse of, at one and the same time, a reverence toward the material image for its mimicry and a suspicion towards its status as mere formal presentation of an idea, resonates with our contemporary treatment of images when we see and understand them to lay claim to the 'real'. In an era of commodity culture dominated by the mass media, Mitchell offers countless examples of how the image is constantly being evaluated on the basis of its semblance or otherwise of the 'true form'. By extension, as Martin Jay points out, the task of the critic is inherently iconoclastic: it is to police and expose the false images.[34] This is nowhere more the case than with those images that speak the experience of a personal encounter with a traumatic past, a past that belongs to a now absent history.

In spite of these historical and cultural contradictions toward the image, as Hans Belting argues, history has also proven that the image is potentially the most convincing witness. Since medieval times, the image has been held, in the words of Belting, as 'representative or symbol of something that could be experienced only indirectly in the present, namely, the former and future presence of God in the life of humankind'.[35] Belting continues: 'the image reached into the immediate experience of God in past history and likewise ahead to a promised time to come'.[36] Echoing Walter Benjamin's comments about the auratic quality of the photographic image, Belting connects the function of the early Christian icon to more contemporary images: 'The authenticity inherent in a photo supports the claims of authentic appearance always raised by icons; the image was to give an impression of the person and to provide the experience of a personal encounter.'[37] Thus, in theoretical and practical terms, the image makes present that which is absent. But Belting is careful to argue that images do not merely *return* that which has become absent. He deploys the term 'iconic presence' to contend that images replace absence with a different kind of presence: '*Iconic presence* still maintains a body's absence and turns it into what must be called *visible absence*. Images live from the paradox that they perform *the presence of an absence* or vice versa.'[38] To reiterate, the image offers the experience of a personal encounter through such iconic presence and this experience is understood to be its most authentic moment. Far more so than words, images are still perceived to have a power and an agency to bring to life – to bring into a particular kind of presence.

BEARING WITNESS

The encounter with an other is central to any conception of bearing witness. For a witness to perform an act of bearing witness, she must address an other, a listener who consequently functions as a witness to the original witness. The act of bearing witness thus constitutes a specific form of address to an other. It occurs only in a framework of relationality, in which the testimonial act is itself witnessed by an other. This relationality between the survivor-witness and the listener-witness frames the act of bearing witness as a performative speech act. It is not a constative act, which would merely depict or report an event that takes place in the historical world. In its address to an other, whether a therapist, a jury or an audience, the performative act of bearing witness affirms the reality of the event witnessed. Moreover, it produces its 'truth' in the moment of testimonial enunciation. The nature of the truth produced by the testimonial act depends on the discursive and institutional context in which it functions. The act of bearing witness, of giving testimony, is most commonly performed within the juridical institution of the trial where the witness does not merely express or report an a priori truth to the jury; the legal truth of an event can only be produced in the moment of the witness's enunciation before the judge and jury. In being addressed by witnesses testifying to the truth of an event, the jury is given the responsibility, via the authoritative guidance of the judge and the rhetorical interpretation of attorneys, of coming to a verdict, of coming to a judgement in the face of the legal truth claims produced on the witness stand. Within certain religious traditions as well, the believer may bear witness to the truth of his faith, to the theological truth of an Absolute or of a specific divine order.[39] In such cases, the process of bearing witness is, of course, dependent on the presence of God, or rather, a god.

The most influential discursive context for shaping the kind of truth produced in the act of bearing witness to historical trauma is the psychoanalytic one. This body of knowledge has played a foundational role in the development of the interdisciplinary fields of both Holocaust studies and trauma studies. Shoshana Felman and Dori Laub's book *Testimony: Crises of Witnessing in Literature, Psychoanalysis, and History*, published in 1992, is one of the earliest and most influential attempts to develop a comprehensive psychoanalytic model of bearing witness to historical trauma.[40] Drawing on his practice as a psychoanalyst who has worked with numerous Holocaust survivors, Laub explains how massive trauma precludes its initial psychic registration at the moment it occurs. As a defence mechanism for self-preservation, the mind literally blocks the traumatised subject from actually experiencing the event at the time it occurs. The repressed trauma thus repeatedly returns to the survivor in the form of an involuntary acting out and living through the event that denies the survivor any control over her traumatic past. The therapeutic process thus provides the survivor-witness with a space in which she may begin the difficult process of narrativising the event. This process of bearing witness externalises the traumatic event as an experience that may be both told by survivor and heard by the listener *for the very first time*: 'The emergence of the narrative which is being listened to – and heard – is, therefore, the process and place wherein the cognizance, the "knowing" of the event is given birth to. The listener, therefore, is a party to the creation of knowledge de novo.'[41] Thus the act of bearing witness is not the communication of a truth that is already known, but its actual production through this performative act. In this process, the listener becomes a witness to the witness, not only facilitating the very possibility of testimony, but also subsequently, sharing its burden. That is to say, the listener assumes responsibility to perpetuate the imperative to bear witness to the historical trauma for the sake of collective memory.

Following Elie Wiesel's claim that testimony has become the literary mode par excellence of the post-Holocaust era, Felman parallels Laub's discussion of the witness's address to the listener in the psychoanalytic context with that of the writer's address to his reader in the mediated context of literature.[42] Like the psychoanalytic encounter of witness and listener, the one between writer and reader is an encounter that actually produces, in itself, a profound truth: 'a performative engagement between consciousness and history, a struggling act of readjustment between the integrative scope of words and the unintegrated impact of events'.[43] Drawing on her experience of teaching a graduate seminar on testimony in 1984, Felman comes to argue that testimonial literature thus provides a cultural space in which individual processes of working through historical trauma are mediated into collective ones. In the final weeks of the seminar, Felman showed her class two video testimonies from the Fortunoff Video Archive for Holocaust Testimonies at Yale University. After the screenings, her usually loquacious and eloquent students were speechless or inarticulate. In the days and weeks that followed, the students felt compelled to share with everyone around them the experience that they had undergone; at the same time they insisted on its unrepresentability and alienating uniqueness, for it had broken all frames of reference for them. Felman's subsequent challenge as a teacher was how to reintegrate the crisis, without foreclosing it, how to recontextualise the crisis within a transformed frame of reference. Although this crisis in her seminar was triggered by the introduction of images, Felman is wholly reticent to discuss the agency of the image in this crisis. Rather, she emphasises the shift from literary texts to 'raw document' of a historical and autobiographical nature: 'It seemed to me that added dimension of *the real* was, at this point, both relevant and necessary to the insight we were gaining into testimony.'[44] Felman thus treats the video image as a transparent document of the testimonial event, rather than a medium with its own potential dynamics of witnessing.[45] In this book, we take Felman's oversight of the image's role in the crisis experienced by her students as our cue to annex the specificity, and ultimate agency, of the image in the performative act of bearing witness to historical trauma.

Given that the scholarship on bearing witness is intricately interwoven with textual or oral representation, how then do we conceive of an image-based process of bearing witness? While the imaging technologies embedded in processes of surveillance, science and industrial production increasingly generate automatic images without a human agent, such images are not considered to bear witness to any specific event they happen to record. Rather, they are understood to provide evidentiary proof of the event. Jacques Derrida reminds us that bearing witness is not proving:

> Whoever bears witness does not bring a proof; he is someone whose experience, in principle singular and irreplaceable (even if it can be cross-checked with others to become proof, to become conclusive in a process of verification) comes to attest, precisely, that some 'thing' has been present to him.[46]

In the moment of testimony, the witness bears witness to the event by re-presenting it – in the sense of bringing it into presence – before his addressee. In the context of historical trauma, it is not only the addressee who experiences this re-presentation of the event for the very first time (having not been originally present to it). The act of bearing witness, more importantly, also allows the witness to bring into presence, to externalise, for the very first time, the event that has persistently haunted him.

As we have discussed earlier, the image has long been considered particularly apt in bringing into a form of presence that which is absent. As in the biblical and medieval context given to religious icons, the power of the image to bring into presence relies on the shared faith of its producer and its viewer. As Derrida insists, the act of bearing witness similarly occurs within the space of sworn faith: 'With this attestation, there is no other choice but to believe it or not believe it. Verification or transformation into proof, contesting in the name of "knowledge", belong to a foreign space.'[47] Thus, the image's role in the process of bearing witness can be seen to rely not upon a faith in the image's technological ability to furnish empirical evidence of the event, but upon a faith in the image's phenomenological capacity to bring the event into iconic presence and to mediate the intersubjective relations that ground the act of bearing witness. Since this understanding of the 'life' of the image in witnessing detaches the image from a singular imperative to produce documentary proof, it pertains to a wide range of images, not only photographically-based ones. In addition, the intersubjective relations generated by the presence of the image opens up a space for a witness who did not directly observe or participate in the traumatic historical event. This form of what might otherwise be thought of as 'secondary' or 'retrospective' witnessing is in fact primary to the collective cultural memory of traumatic historical events as it is conceived by a number of the contributors to this book.[48]

The Tuol Sleng Genocide Museum in Phnom Penh, Cambodia, an image of which we chose for the cover of this book, exemplifies the compelling use of images within such practices of secondary or retrospective witnessing. Established in 1980, the year after the fall of Pol Pot's regime, the museum inhabits the site of S-21, the Khmer Rouge's notorious secret prison where over 14,000 people suspected of treason were systematically interrogated, tortured and killed between 1975 and 1979.[49] Since no prisoner was ever released by the Khmer Rouge (and only seven survived), the identification photographs taken of each prisoner immediately on arrival at S-21 bear witness to the atrocity on several levels. As David Chandler indicates: 'Frozen by the lens, the prisoners stare out at their captors. Nearly twenty years later they are also regarding us. Their expressions ask their captors: "Who are you? Why am I here?" – and ask us: "Why did this happen? Why have we been killed?"[50] Installed in the museum as individualised enlargements and grid-like mass portraits, these photographs not only stand as historical documents of the Khmer Rouge's genocidal machine, but they also, and more importantly, open up an intersubjective space in which museum visitor encounters the iconic presence of the ultimate witness – the one who has not survived.[51]

IMAGES THAT WITNESS

Each of the chapters in the book demonstrates an awareness of the complex and often fraught search to locate or produce an image that may adequately, appropriately and authentically bear witness in the here and now to historical trauma. Similarly, the authors interrogate the problems and contradictions raised by the use of the image in the representations on which they focus. However, they do not do this as their ultimate goal, but rather, as the critical move that allows the images' specific forms of agency to come into view. Moreover, the contributions cohere around the understanding that individual and collective trauma are historically and culturally determined. While obviously indebted to the foundational scholarship of Holocaust studies in theorising the representation of historical trauma, this volume widens and diversifies that conceptual framework.

The individual chapters of the book focus particularly on largely overlooked or under-examined images from around the world. They address historical situations in Britain, Colombia, Japan, Vietnam, South Africa, Ukraine, Armenia, Spain, Germany, Poland, Switzerland and the United States in an effort to demonstrate that local, cultural and historical differences necessitate variable theoretical models for understanding the dynamics of collective trauma. The book's range of historical contexts is complemented by its attention to an equally broad array of material images: documentary films, experimental cinema, amateur film and photography, aerial photography, photojournalism, painting, sculpture, electronic art and internet sites. The intersection of these two indices of difference – the historical and the formal – constitutes the book's organising ethos. By bringing together a diverse range of visual media and historical contexts, this volume conceptualises the agency of the image in relation to historical trauma without reifying any single model of witnessing dynamics. We have organised the chapters of the book into conceptual clusters to allow for salient issues running through all the contributions to come to the fore. The sections are neither exclusive nor definitive frameworks for considering the scholarship in the book, but rather, heuristic aids to identify the cross-pollination of its concerns. For example, the fourth section highlights a concern with time and space in the narrativisation of trauma which can also be found in other chapters of the book. Nevertheless, temporal and spatial dynamics are writ large in the analyses of section four.

The book opens with a section on 'The Body of the Witness'. The body has a dual role in acts of bearing witness to traumatic historical events. First, historical trauma inflicts such physical devastation on human bodies that visualising these consequences of enormous violence has become a principal and necessary component of witnessing practices. However, as we have already discussed, the task of visualising the corporeal consequences of trauma is forever fraught with the risk of dehumanisation, especially in the context of bearing witness to death. Second, the act of bearing witness demands a certain *habeas corpus*. The testimony of the survivor-witness is dependent on her embodied presence at the moment of enunciation. No one can bear witness in her place. Thus, when acts of bearing witness to historical trauma are mediated through the material image, corporeal inscription of the witness often provides the foundation for both bringing the event into presence and establishing the intersubjective relations between the survivor-witness and the listener/viewer-witness. The three chapters in this section engage with both aspects of the body's significance.

Camila Loew's chapter on Catalan collective memory and the Holocaust examines *Memòria de l'infern* (2002), a book and exhibition project by the photographer-journalist team of Jordi Ribó and David Bassa, as well as the recent biography and documentary about the leftist photographer and concentration camp survivor, Francesc Boix. In her analysis of *Memòria de l'infern*, Loew illuminates how the carefully posed portraits of Catalan concentration camp survivors – whose testimony is also published in the book – produce a tension between the singularity of their experience and the articulation of their collectivity. Boix worked in the darkrooms of the *Erkennungsdienst* (Identification Service) at Mauthausen concentration camp and secretly copied thousands of identification photographs taken by the SS. Loew understands Boix as 'a witness to the witnesses' who recycled this archive of visual evidence and inverted the Nazi's use of the 'camera as weapon.' Roger Hallas's chapter approaches the question of embodiment by analysing Derek Jarman's final film, *Blue* (1993). Hallas elucidates how Jarman's experimental film about AIDS opens up the potential for a radical reconfiguration of the relation between witness and film spectator. Through its intertwining of what Michel Chion calls an *acousmêtre* (acousmatic voice) and Laura Marks's notion of experimental film's haptic visuality, *Blue* produces an intersubjective encounter for the spectator, grounded in the sensory experience of proximity and what Hallas calls 'corporeal implication'. In the visual absence of Jarman's ailing, dying body, the spectator's body becomes implicated in the process of bearing witness. Matthias Christen's chapter continues this concern with the sick and diseased body as it examines *Case History* (1999), Boris Mikhailov's book of photographs documenting the destitution and physical degradation of the homeless in Kharkov, Ukraine. *Case History* provides an almost encyclopaedic collection of physical disfigurations suffered by the homeless in post-Soviet society: smashed skulls, rotten teeth, infected genitals, scarred limbs and all manner of skin conditions. Christen argues that Mikhailov presents the exposed sick bodies of the contemporary homeless as the site where the memory of a traumatic history materialises. The body here serves as an allegory of social and economic malaise in post-Soviet Ukraine.

Turning to the other side of the intersubjective relation of witnessing, the second section of the book, 'Testimonial Interactivity', focuses on the active role of the spectator of visual culture in the dynamics of witnessing. All three chapters in this section address the concern with interactive forms of visual media in which the functions of the user and the player are redefining the concept of the spectator within certain areas of visual culture. In her analysis of *Truth Games* (1998) and *Can't For-*

get, Can't Remember (1999), Sue Williamson's interactive installations about South Africa's Truth and Reconciliation Commission, Stephanie Marlin-Curiel investigates what happens when individual and collective memory is translated as information and then recirculated through the sensory channels of digital media. As Marlin-Curiel explains, Williamson chooses the interactive medium of the CD-ROM as a means to illuminate how the Commission functioned as a mediatised live event to produce what she calls the 'collected' rather than fully 'collective' memory of apartheid. Through an interaction between spectator and digital image where the viewer selects decontextualised images and fragments of testimony from highly codified options, the installations self-consciously simulate the highly managed processes by which South African television and the press mediated the Commission as a national experience. The process of managing the collective memory of a national trauma through the possibilities of new media is also explored in Leshu Torchin's analysis of archival websites devoted to 'screen memories' of the Armenian genocide. According to Torchin, the visitor to these archival sites interacts literally and affectively with the representation of genocide in the interests of legal clarification, historical documentation and collective memory of a genocide that has hitherto been systematically denied. In the final chapter of the section, Karen Hall analyses the function of what she calls 'citizen training' within forms of US combat entertainment, such as the war film, video games and action figures. Hall locates an active spectator/player who is involved in the kind of pathological process of 'false witnessing' that Robert Jay Lifton identified in the wake of the Vietnam War. She argues that images such as the US combat film use vengeful violence to produce a displaced externalisation of the grief and pain suffered in the face of the traumatic experience of modern warfare. This process of false witness prepares viewers to understand history as a justification for the perpetration of future atrocity.

The third section on 'Second-hand Visions' examines acts of witnessing based on appropriation and re-use of found and archival images. Images which appropriate and expropriate existing visual representations of public trauma respond to the immense ethical responsibility which burdens the image. As discussed above, ethical responsibility to the integrity of the victim is one of the defining criteria of authentic witnessing to trauma. This is especially urgent when the sufferer is no longer able to speak. Thus, the one who carries the continued memory of suffering also carries the responsibility to do so in a manner that empathises with, rather than violates, the silent victim. In keeping with James Young's call for continued memory, the chapters in this section explicitly represent the experience of the act of remembering.[52] Frances Guerin attends to Gerhard Richter's recycling of German press images of the arrest, imprisonment and death of the leaders of the Baader-Meinhof group in his 1988 cycle of paintings, *18. Oktober 1977*. Guerin argues that, through strategies of re-presentation of photographs through the medium of painting, Richter blurs a number of boundaries – such as those between West German state institutions and the Baader-Meinhof revolutionaries – to effect an emotional, intellectual and physical confrontation with the gallery visitor. The confrontation leads, in turn, to the viewer's responsibility to remember and reconsider his memory of the civil unrest of the 'German Autumn'. In his analysis of Chris Marker's *Level 5* (1996), Jonathan Kear examines the tendency for experimental or avant-garde works to appropriate images with the goal of critically interrogating or challenging the meaning of the image in its original context. In returning to his avowed interest in the battle of Okinawa as one of the most significant, but historically neglected, events of the Second World War, Marker constructs what he calls a 'free replay' of Alain Resnais' *Hiroshima mon amour* (1959). Kear elucidates how *Level 5* uses the organising structure of gameplay to recuperate the memory of the battle of Okinawa from historical oblivion, while simultaneously foregrounding the limits to any such historical recuperation. Guy Westwell's chapter investigates the ideological contexts in which home movies taken by US soldiers during the Vietnam War have been reframed as authentic and privileged acts of public witnessing within contemporary US popular culture. Westwell contends that, at the time of their production, these amateur films facilitated a consistent disavowal of death and traumatic violence by imposing the ideological frame of the family and domestic space on the visual representation of the military experience of the war. This ideological framework was subsequently amplified when these amateur films were transferred to video and commercially released under the series title *Vietnam Home Movies* in the mid-1980s.

The chapters of the fourth section, titled 'Temporal and Spatial Displacements', engage with the necessary manipulation of time and space in the narrativisation of trauma. Following Freud, and in particular his insights in *Moses and Monotheism*, bearing witness to trauma is experienced at a distance from the traumatic event, beyond the limits of locatable time and space.[53] It has also been common for images involved in the process of bearing witness to emphasise the importance of returning to the site of original trauma. Claude Lanzmann's *Shoah* (1985) is exemplary in this regard when, in spite of its insistence on the inability to represent the horror of the Holocaust visually, the film maintains the possibility of the victim's renegotiation of the trauma through a return to the geographical location of genocidal violence. Either the victim or the camera returns to this now othered location. While it is not possible to recapture the temporal parameters of the original trauma, as Lanzmann would have it, the distance between then and now can be simultaneously effaced and maintained through an imaginative and intellectual process facilitated by the image. Through its role in the process of witnessing, the image enables such imaginative excursions between past, present and future, between the site of the original trauma (albeit usually repressed or absent) and the geographical, social and cultural locations of the spectator. While the trafficking between often disparate times, places and spaces is usually marked by ineffability and fluidity, the image functions to ground the process of witnessing, if only through its own formal dimensionality.

In her analysis of the film *Cooperation of Parts* (1987) and the video *History and Memory* (1991), Tina Wasserman follows Daniel Eisenberg and Rea Tajiri's respective searches, at the remove of a generation and a continental divide, for the memory of their parents' traumatic experiences of Nazi concentration camps and Japanese-American internment. Returning to the site of their parents' trauma allows Eisenberg and Tajiri to re-anchor their own 'unhinged memories' of historical trauma in lived experience and recorded images. However, the absence inscribed in such images of the present also reminds these artists precisely of the limits to such recuperative aspirations. Edlie Wong's chapter reflects upon Doris Salcedo's representation of the loss that besets Colombia's recent history of state and paramilitary violence.

Salcedo's sculpture and installations visualise the violent procedures of 'disappearance' by grafting ordinary household objects and furniture into material fetishes of the missing bodies of the disappeared. Wong reads Salcedo's work both as a practice of translation, in which testimony becomes visual object, and a complex process of temporal and spatial displacement, in which the once safe and private space of home that has been ruptured by state violence is resituated in the public space of the international art gallery. Davide Deriu argues that aerial photographs of ruined landscapes in the wake of the Second World War are involved in bearing witness to the trauma of destruction and for the continuation of memory. Deriu inverts the familiar argument – usually associated with the work of Ernst Jünger – that the distance and abstraction of aerial photographs of ruined landscapes underline the coldness and brutality of the eye that sees them.[54] Deriu emphasises their capacity to trigger historical consciousness – to provoke memory and deep empathy in the mind of the viewer.

The collection closes with 'Witnessing the Witness', three chapters on works dedicated to the self-reflective interrogation of the act of witnessing itself. James Polchin exposes the conundrum of the initial incarnations of 'Without Sanctuary', an exhibition of lynching photographs mounted in New York, Pittsburgh and Atlanta. Polchin demonstrates that in their anxiety to remain conscious of *how* we look at images of violence without replicating or underlining that same violence towards the victims, the exhibition increasingly nurtured a displacement of the image. Paradoxically the exhibition became, in the end, an ethical directive not to look, but to read and to listen to the contextual materials supplied by the curators to counter the racist gaze of the photographs. Marcy Goldberg's chapter introduces the work of the important Swiss documentarist, Richard Dindo, who is little known outside his own country. Dindo's primarily biographical films consistently stage performances of witnessing acts in the face of the traumatic event's absence and the camera's belatedness. Like Lanzmann, Dindo uses the image of the present with its simultaneous effect of presence and absence to prompt his viewers to imagine the traumatic event while recognising the incommensurable gap separating them from the event. In the final chapter of the book, Marsha and Devin Orgeron examine the films of Errol Morris for their performance of the process of witnessing the witness. Sometimes, as if in a hall of mirrors, Morris's viewer finds herself before films that witness witnesses to witnesses, where the camera also struggles for legitimacy as a witness to this process of witnessing. Ultimately, however, according to Orgeron and Orgeron, Morris questions the legitimacy of all witnesses and all cameras. In turn, the image is only witnessing when it is involved in the contingent and ephemeral dynamics of the intersubjective relationship between subject, spectator and producer of the image.

ACKNOWLEDGEMENTS

We would like to thank all those who generously supplied images and copyright permissions for the book, especially Maciej Dakowicz for the cover photograph. We are grateful to Steven Cohan for his sage advice throughout the editorial process. Along the way, Richard Allen, Matthew Fee, Jane Gaines, Randolph Lewis, Michael Renov, James Williams, Brian Winston and Patricia Zimmermann have also given us important guidance. We would also like to thank Yoram Allon at Wallflower Press for his strong commitment to the project, and for his congeniality throughout the publication process. And thanks too to Michele Combs for the comprehensive index. For its financial assistance in the publication of the book, we are grateful to the College of Arts and Sciences at Syracuse University. Finally, our sincerest and most important thanks goes to the contributors whose commitment to and enthusiasm for the project has sustained us. We are grateful to them for their inspiration.

Notes

1   On this notion of the inherent deception of images, see W. J. T. Mitchell (ed.), *The Language of Images* (Chicago: University of Chicago Press, 1980).

2   Susan Sontag, *Regarding the Pain of Others* (New York: Farrar, Strauss and Giroux, 2003), 106.

3   Kyo Maclear, *Beclouded Visions: Hiroshima-Nagasaki and the Art of Witness* (Albany: State University of New York Press, 1999), 23.

4   See the documentaries *A Painful Reminder* (Sidney Bernstein, 1985) and *Memory of the Camps* (Sergei Nolbandov, 1993). The most vehement criticism came with Claude Lanzmann's *Shoah* (1986), but the criticism began with Alain Resnais' *Nuit et Brouillard* (*Night and Fog*, 1955).

5   As Barbie Zelizer has argued, the broad symbolic function of these images was established right at their initial public circulation in 1945: 'The transformation of atrocity photos from definitive indices of certain actions to symbolic markers of the atrocity story had to do with a general and urgent need to make sense of what had happened.' *Remembering to Forget: Holocaust Memory Through the Camera's Eye* (Chicago: University of Chicago Press, 1998), 139.

6   On the manipulation of the George Holliday footage of Rodney King's beating, see Bill Nichols, *Blurred Boundaries: Questions of Meaning in Contemporary Culture* (Bloomington: Indiana University Press, 1994), 17–42.

7   On the continued effort to keep these images in circulation, see Seymour M. Hersh, 'Photographs from a Prison', in *Inconvenient Evidence: Iraqi Prison Photographs from Abu Ghraib* (New York: International Center of Photography, 2004), 7–10.

8   Ibid. See also Seymour M. Hersh, *Chain of Command: The Road from 9/11 to Abu Ghraib* (New York: HarperCollins, 2004); and Susan Brison, 'Torture, or "Good Old American Pornography"?', *Chronicle of Higher Education*, 4 June 2004, B10.

9   See Patrick H. Hutton, 'Michel Foucault: History as Counter-Memory', in *History as an Art of Memory* (Hanover: University Press of New England, 1993), 106–23.

10 See, for example, Gertrud Koch, 'The Aesthetic Transformation of the Image of the Unimaginable: Notes on Claude Lanzmann's *Shoah*', *October* 48 (Spring 1989): 15–24.

11 Ana Douglass and Thomas A. Vogler make this important connection in the introduction to their collection, *Witness and Memory: The Discourse of Trauma* (New York: Routledge, 2003), 5.

12 See respectively, Lucien Taylor (ed.), *Visualizing Theory: Selected Essays from V.A.R. 1990–1994* (New York: Routledge, 1993); Michele Aaron (ed.), *New Queer Cinema* (New Brunswick: Rutgers University Press, 2004); Douglas Crimp, *On the Museum's Ruins* (Cambridge, MA.: MIT Press, 1995); Naomi Klein, *No Logo* (New York: Picador, 2002).

13 A cycle of moral panics around the alleged 'media effects' of represented violence in popular cinema and video games have gripped industrialised societies for the past quarter century. See Martin Barker and Julian Petley (eds), *Ill Effects: The Media/Violence Debate* (London: Routledge, 2001).

14 As such, this volume contributes to an emergent body of scholarship that is beginning to investigate seriously the potential agency of the image in bearing witness to historical

trauma. See Kyo Maclear's *Beclouded Visions* and the essays collected by Barbie Zelizer in *Visual Culture and the Holocaust* (New Brunswick: Rutgers University Press, 2000).

15 See Bill Nichols, *Representing Reality: Issues and Concepts in Documentary* (Bloomington: Indiana University Press, 1991); and Michael Renov, 'Towards a Poetics of Documentary', in *Theorizing Documentary*, ed. Michael Renov (New York: Routledge, 1993), 12–36.

16 Visible Evidence, the annual international conference and book series published by University of Minnesota Press, is one of the salient indicators of this diversification of documentary studies. It brings together scholars from diverse disciplines working on a wide range of media.

17 See Marita Sturken, 'Memorializing Absence', in *Understanding September 11*, ed. Craig Calhoun (New York: New Press, 2002), 374–84.

18 Marianne Hirsch, 'I Took Pictures: September 2001 and Beyond', in *Trauma at Home: After 9/11*, ed. Judith Greenberg (Lincoln: University of Nebraska Press, 2003), 69–86.

19 Bill Nichols argues that documentary images' engagement with the issue of magnitude necessarily extends beyond the mere communication of an event's human scale or importance. Magnitude, for Nichols, involves our ethical relationship to the victims of historical trauma. It thus requires a 'politics of phenomenology, a recognition of the priority of experience not as a structure to bracket and describe but as the social ground or foundation for actual praxis'. *Representing Reality*, 232.

20 John Durham Peters, 'Witnessing', *Media, Culture and Society* 23 (2001): 707–11.

21 Scholars such as W. J. T. Mitchell and Martin Jay have written with conviction on the ubiquity of the privilege given to word over image throughout the history of Western thought. See W. J. T. Mitchell, *Iconology: Image, Text, Ideology* (Chicago: University of Chicago Press, 1986); and Martin Jay, *Downcast Eyes: The Denigration of Vision in Twentieth-Century Thought* (Berkeley: University of California Press, 1993).

22 One of the first works to take these steps toward representation of these momentous events was Elie Wiesel's *Night* (New York: Hill and Wang, 1960).

23 Central to this effort was the landmark Holocaust conference at the University of California, Los Angeles in 1990, the proceedings of which are collected in Saul Friedländer (ed.), *Probing the Limits of Representation: Nazism and the 'Final Solution'* (Cambridge: Harvard University Press, 1992).

24 It is interesting to note that fictional films and art works did not come under the same criticism as documentary. See, for example, Anton Kaes, *From Hitler to Heimat: The Return of History as Film* (Cambridge: Harvard University Press, 1989).

25 It is not only the work of autobiographical writers, such as Primo Levi and Charlotte Delbo, which has been the subject of searching appraisal of Holocaust testimony. The work of poets, such as Paul Celan and Dan Pagis, has played an equally significant role.

26 The contemporary significance of providing cameras to victims of human rights abuses is highlighted in Katerina Cizek and Peter Wintonick's documentary *Seeing is Believing: Handicams, Human Rights and the News* (2002). The documentary highlights how the value of images captured by activists are simultaneously under- and overestimated by a cynical and exploitive global news media.

27 There are many poignant examples of such writings. See, for example, Alan Adelson and Robert Lapides (eds), *Lodz Ghetto: A Community History told in Diaries, Journals and Documents* (New York: Penguin, 1989).

28 The work of Cathy Caruth, Linda Belau and Peter Ramadanovic offers striking examples of the scholarship being done in the field. Their anthologies and single-authored works build on that of Shoshana Felman and Dori Laub. See Cathy Caruth (ed.), *Trauma: Explorations in Memory* (Baltimore: Johns Hopkins University Press, 1995); Cathy Caruth, *Unclaimed Experience: Trauma, Narrative and History* (Baltimore: Johns Hopkins University Press, 1995): and Linda Belau and Peter Ramadanovic (eds), *Topologies of Trauma: Essays on the Limit of Knowledge and Memory* (New York: Other Press, 2002).

29 Michael Kelly, *Iconoclasm in Aesthetics* (Cambridge: Cambridge University Press, 2003).

30 Hans Belting, 'Introduction', in *Likeness and Presence: A History of the Image Before the*

Era of Art, trans. Edmund Jephcott (Chicago: University of Chicago Press, 1994), 6.

31 Cornelia Brink discusses the use of a handful of photographs as being elevated to the status of icons that are always quoted to speak of the Nazi Holocaust. See Cornelia Brink, 'Secular Icons: Looking at Photographs from Nazi Concentration Camps', *History and Memory* 12, no. 1 (Spring–Summer 2000): 135–50.

32 Mitchell, *Iconology*, 32.

33 W. J. T. Mitchell, 'The Surplus Value of Images', in *What Do Pictures Want?*, 85.

34 Martin Jay as cited in Mitchell, *What Do Pictures Want?*, 81.

35 Belting, 10.

36 Ibid., 11.

37 Ibid., 11.

38 Hans Belting, 'Image, Medium, Body: A New Approach to Iconology', *Critical Inquiry* 31 (Winter 2005), 312.

39 Many early Christians bore witness to the truth of their new faith through their very martyrdom. In fact, the etymological source of our modern word 'martyr' was a Greek term for witness, *martis*.

40 Shoshana Felman and Dori Laub, *Testimony: Crises of Witnessing in Literature, Psychoanalysis, and History* (New York: Routledge, 1992).

41 Ibid., 57.

42 Eli Wiesel, 'The Holocaust as a Literary Inspiration', in *Dimensions of the Holocaust* (Evanston, IL: Northwestern University Press, 1977), 9–13.

43 Felman and Laub, *Testimony*, 114.

44 Ibid., 42 (emphasis in original).

45 This reticence to address the function and impact of the moving image is similarly apparent in her chapter on *Shoah*, which she analyses principally in terms of the testimonies filmed, rather than for its significance as a cinematic mode of witnessing.

46 Jacques Derrida, '"A Self-Unsealing Poetic Text": Poetics and Politics of Witnessing', in *Revenge of the Aesthetic: The Place of Literature in Theory Today*, ed. Michael Clark (Berkeley: University of California Press, 2000), 190.

47 Ibid., 194.

48 For elaboration of these concepts, see Dora Apel, *Memory Effects: The Holocaust and the Art of Secondary Witnessing* (New Brunswick: Rutgers University Press, 2002); Andrea Liss, *Trespassing Through Shadows: Memory, Photography and the Holocaust* (Minneapolis: University of Minnesota Press, 1998); and Marianne Hirsch, 'Surviving Images: Holocaust Photographs and the Work of Postmemory', in *Visual Culture and the Holocaust*, ed. Barbie Zelizer, 215–46.

49 David Chandler provides a comprehensive history of the prison in his book *Voices from S-21: Terror and History in Pol Pot's Secret Prison* (Berkeley: University of California Press, 2000).

50 David Chandler, "The Pathology of Terror in Pol Pot's Cambodia," in *The Killing Fields*, ed. Chris Riley and Douglas Niven (Santa Fe: Twin Palms Press, 1996), 102.

51 Rithy Panh's documentary *S-21: The Khmer Rouge Killing Machine* (2002) makes significant use of these photographs as well as prison survivor Vann Nath's paintings to stage a testimonial encounter between survivors, perpetrators and the executed within the very space of the former prison.

52 James Young, *At Memory's Edge: After-Images of the Holocaust in Contemporary Art and Architecture* (New Haven: Yale University Press, 2000), 7.

53 Cathy Caruth's *Unclaimed Experience* develops an extensive reading of Freud's *Moses and Monotheism* as the basis for her conception of trauma studies.

54 Ernst Jünger, 'War and Photography', *New German Critique* 59 (1993): 24–6.

PART I | THE BODY OF THE WITNESS

1. Portraits of Presence: Excavating Traumatic Identity in Contemporary Catalan Testimonies

Camila Loew

REDISCOVERING MEMORY IN CONTEMPORARY CATALONIA

Several thousand Catalans were victims of the Nazi Holocaust, and yet very few Catalan testimonies, whether as fiction or non-fiction, were ever written. This is in contrast with the production of written and visual works on the Holocaust that have continued to be produced in Europe and North America for well over half a century. After the liberation of the Nazi concentration camps in 1945, when the survivors were encouraged finally to return home, the Republican Catalans still had to face decades of exile, marginalisation and silence. They remained 'stateless' and, as a consequence, also nameless and faceless for the next thirty years.[1]

The scarcity of Holocaust-related publications in Catalonia and Spain is but one of many silences of the forty-year Franco regime. Through fierce censorship and manipulation of public discourse, the dictatorship not only obliterated Spain's own history, but also managed to divorce Spain's past from the rest of European history. As historian Rosa Torán points out, the myth of Spanish neutrality during the Second World War permitted Franco's Spain to 'forget' important events that other European countries took pains to deal with and build into their own national histories after 1945. The end of the Franco regime in 1975 gave way to the possibility to uncover and thereby rediscover cultural and historical memory, and to talk about the events that had been effaced from the country's historical discourse.

In this chapter, I analyse attempts to give these forgotten witnesses back their right to a name and a face through the practice of portraiture, and specifically, the photographs of Jordi Ribó and Francesc Boix. I have chosen to work with portraits for two reasons. First, portraiture is a mode of representation that aims to remove silenced subjects from anonymity and to restore the meaning and significance of the *individual*. The portrait, notes Max Kozloff, 'set[s] apart this person or that from all others as a proper subject for viewing'.[2] Second, if portraits are able to grant an identity to the individual subjects they capture, in doing so, the function of photographic portraiture is doubled. Moreover, as Allan Sekula argues, the system of representation defined by modern portraiture is both 'honorific' (in the tradition of painted portraits and their ceremonial presentation of the self) and 'repressive' (due to the indexical, criminological use of photographic portraits that dates back to the late-nineteenth century). In this sense, portraits can be read as not only representing individual persons, but also defining 'a generalized look, a typology'.[3] The individuality that portraits evoke becomes one of repetition when the subjects are objectified into mere instances of a group. It thus becomes possible to observe a constant tension between the individual and the collective in the practice of portraiture. I describe how portraiture functions in both these ways in the works here analysed: they both grant a personal, exceptional stance to each witness and at the same time construct a collective identity when the shared aspect of these extreme, exceptional stories take part in the portrayer's attempt to shape a collective memory.

I also consider portraits within the broader framework of visual representation. Today, a broad range of images have become incorporated into the ways we represent and understand the past: in the new perspectives adopted by contemporary historians, images are 'read' alongside literary texts and oral testimonies for their historical insights into the past.[4] This embrace of the image as a historical document, rather than just as visual evidence, encourages us to see histories from different perspectives. The work of the two photographers that I examine in this chapter offers precisely this kind of new perspective, namely the history of the Holocaust from a Catalan perspective.[5] *Memòria de l'infern* (*Memory of Hell*), published by Edicions 62 in 2002, represents a collaborative project between photographer Jordi Ribó and journalist David Bassa, and as such unites the three forms that historian Peter Burke notes are responsible for broadening the range of evidence used in historical discourse: oral history (the testimonies of Catalan survivors of the Nazi camps), images (Ribó's portraits of the survivors) and literature (Bassa's own narrative framing and reworking of the testimonies). The other project considered here is the rediscovery of Francesc Boix, a Catalan photographer who worked in the *Erkennungsdienst* (Identification Service) at Mauthausen concentration camp from January 1941 until the camp's liberation in 1945, and became the only Catalan and Spaniard to testify at the Nuremberg trials. Two recent works recall Boix's singular experience in order to give a face, a name and a heroic story to a man whose work, sixty years after the war, remains largely unknown: Catalan filmmaker Llorenç Soler's documentary film *Francisco Boix, un fotógrafo en el infierno* (*Francisco Boix, a Photographer in Hell*, 2000), and Benito Bermejo's book *Francisco Boix, el fotógrafo de Mauthausen* (*Francisco Boix, a Photographer of Mauthausen*, 2002). Both the book and the film present and re-present Boix's biography and his photographs of Mauthausen.

Over three thousand Republicans born in Catalonia were deported to Nazi concentration camps. Approximately two thousand of them died in Nazi captivity, and most of them, although not all, in Mauthausen. The first in-depth research into this forgotten chapter of Catalan history was Montserrat Roig's groundbreaking and emblematic book, *Els Catalans als camps Nazis* (*The Catalans at the Nazi Camps*).[6] Commissioned in 1973 by a Catalan publishing house based in Paris, the book was first published in 1977, only two years after Franco's death. Roig's study serves as a starting point and inspiration for many of the authors who would later take on the task of historical recuperation. The publication date of Roig's book coincides with the return of some of the exiled Republicans to Spain and Catalonia. For the first time, the unknown resisters, victims and survivors were beginning to have a face, and thus an image: their pictures began to appear in the printed press and on television. Other international events covered by the mass media, such as Klaus Barbie's arrest and the television series *Holocaust*, occurred at approximately the same time. Together, these media events awoke public awareness to a history that for the first time was being presented as part of the Catalan people's own past.

When describing her project in 1974, Roig used a concrete image to describe the function of journalists, artists and writers: she said their task was 'to shed light on the dark zones of the collective memory of our people'.[7] Roig presents her book as if the text functioned as a *monument*, an official memorial site for the forgotten survivors.[8] Without denying the experience of all Republican Spaniards, Roig felt that the Catalan experience warranted its own representation, in the belief that '*els nostres deportats*' (our deported) could only begin to deal with the trauma of their deportation once their individual memories were restored to the collective memory of the Catalan people.[9] Needless to say, she believed that it was not only the survivors who needed to face that traumatic past. Roig's efforts to help survivors voice their memories were clearly aimed at awakening contemporary Catalans to a forgotten chapter of their past.

In spite of its success, Roig's book did not reach institutionalisation at the time of its release. It has only been very recently, more than two decades into democracy, that the theme of the Republican victims of the Holocaust has received the public attention it warrants. This is slowly happening through the publication of testimonies, historical essays, journalism and fiction, as well as in classrooms and other official institutions.[10] However, the difference is not only due to distribution and reception; as already stated, visual representation is playing an ever greater role in both historical discourse and collective memory.

Roig included visual evidence in *Els Catalans*; she used both photographs from the Boix collection that were taken inside the camps by the Nazis and others taken after liberation. In addition, the book included images such as maps of the camps drawn by survivors, facsimiles of letters and official lists of prisoners. The textual silence in relation to the images is impossible to overlook. The images in the book are neither referred to nor commented upon; they are merely inserted into the midst of the book. It is difficult to imagine that Roig conceived of the images as mere 'illustrations' of the collective trauma described in detail in the text. As documentary pieces of evidence, she perhaps assumed that the images were as 'objective' as the numerical statistics that appear in appendices of the book. Or perhaps she believed that their shocking content was self-eloquent enough in itself, as an archive of horror, a form of what Ernst van Alphen calls 'bare realism'. For van Alphen, such bare realism is a representational effect that responds to the moral imperative imposed by Holocaust remembrance; it tries to convey a sense of historical reality in a seemingly objective way by erasing the intrusion of the subject or medium of representation.[11] Thus Roig ensures that the images are not impinged upon by distracting elements. Indeed, Roig's preferred strategy is common to other works of historical fiction that insist on neither words nor images being overwhelmed by the other. Each is left to function according to its own logic.[12] In this sense, the images function in the same way as the long lists of deported Catalans included in the book: they show that the population of almost every single city, town and village of Catalonia was affected by the Holocaust. These lists also recall those compiled by the Red Cross after the war, lists that helped relatives to find out if family members had survived. In this case, the lists are calling out to the citizens of every single town in Catalonia to acknowledge their own status as victims of the Holocaust. Similarly, because the images do not function as mere illustration of the texts, they have a significance far beyond the specific limits of the trauma represented in the text.

MEMÒRIA DE L'INFERN: RENOVATING ROIG'S PROJECT

As if in commemoration of the twenty-fifth anniversary of Roig's book and the tenth anniversary of her death, Bassa and Ribó accepted Roig's open invitation to future generations to continue delving into the stories of the witnesses and survivors of the Nazi camps. Memòria de l'infern was thus conceived as a continuation of Roig's work. Quoting from her opening paragraph on the absolute lack of information on the story of the Catalans deported to the Nazi camps, Bassa states that Memòria de l'infern could have begun the exact same way: 'The story of the reality of the Catalans who were deported to the Nazi death camps is still, sadly, news today … Although twenty-five years have gone by since Roig wrote these words, today it is – unfortunately – as necessary as ever to remember them.'[13]

The main aspect that seems to unite Bassa and Ribó's work to that of their predecessor is the relation between personal, individual memory and collective memory. As we have seen, Roig's main aim was to prove that there were a significant number of individual survivor stories of Republican Catalans, enough to grant a collective status and even to give the Catalan people a defining aspect of their identity. The retrieval of the forgotten survivors in Roig's work aimed not only to show exceptional stories of resistance, but also, to construct a collective image of the Catalan people as a marginal, persecuted culture based on resistance to domination.

This same tension between the individual and the collective can be observed in Bassa and Ribó's project. Two and a half decades later, these young Catalans still felt the need to construct an image of Catalan culture and history that is defined by persecution and resistance. Yet, Bassa and Ribó's project is more than a follow-up to Els Catalans als camps nazis; it also defines its own aims and tone. Although they might agree on the still urgent need to give a voice to those who were unjustly silenced for too long, Bassa and Ribó's commemoration of the witnesses is very different from Roig's tribute in the 1970s. The differences can be attributed to the recent developments in historiography that focus on the everyday as opposed to grand scale histories. Similarly, the differences between Roig and Bassa's textual style and tone are linked to the increasing validation of oral history as a mode of historical representation and enquiry. Significantly, the more impersonal, factual history that defines Roig's text is presented in *Memòria de l'infern* as a group of explanatory footnotes that the author introduces at his discretion. Thus, for Bassa, public history is a footnote, always secondary to the witness's narrative.

Although both Roig's original work and Bassa and Ribo's recent publication use personal interviews with survivors as the primary source, there are significant differences in the ways they relate to and present this material.[14] By transforming the original first-person testimonies into third-person narration, Roig uses her own authorial voice to represent the personal interviews with survivors to reconstruct the details of life in the concentration camps which in the 1970s were still largely unknown to her readership. Bassa and Ribó claim, however, that they let the survivors speak for themselves (we shall question whether this is achieved). Whereas *Els Catalans* includes a significant number of statistics, lists and a comprehensive bibliography, *Memòria de l'infern* focuses on the witnesses 'in person', through its foregrounding of portraits and personal memories. For this reason, writes Bassa, 'there is no bibliography at the end of this book. It wouldn't make sense'.[15]

One of the main differences between Roig's book and Bassa and Ribó's project reveals itself through the use of visual material. The images of *Memòria de l'infern* do not picture the explicit, almost voyeuristic horror one could expect to find in a book on Holocaust testimonies. In Ribó and Bassa's book, a very closed frame, natural illumination is used to focus on the faces and the hands of the twenty-one Holocaust survivors – now senior citizens – who are the main characters of the 21 corresponding chapters. The reader is thus visually persuaded to imagine the same face fifty years before as each witness recalls his or her tale of suffering and resistance. In each black-and-white portrait, the deep creases in the skin and the bright eyes, emphasised by the dark background, induce contrast and emotion. The visual depth of the facial wrinkles and the dilated pupils is a correlative of how deep into memory they are delving. Similarly, the creases ask us to return to *l'infern* and back again as the portrait holds up the picture of hell before our eyes. By placing each portrait on the page before the commencement of the relevant

Figure 1: Jordi Ribó, *Portrait of Josep Egea i Pujante*, 2002. The witnesses symbolise collective trauma through formal repetition. In each portrait, the witnesses literally bear the weight of the heavy memories they hold inside. Courtesy of the artist.

Figure 2: Jordi Ribó, *Portrait of Antoni Ibern i Eroles*, 2002. The visual depth of the facial wrinkles and the dilated pupils are a correlative of how deep into memory the witnesses are delving. Courtesy of the artist.

chapter, the authors frame the narratives with the image of the present-day survivor to stress his or her prominence in the narrative that follows.

A close reading of text and images shows that they are far from being, as Bassa suggests, fragments of twenty-one possible novels. The imprint of the book's authors is clearly visible, not only in the testimonial chapters, but also in the portraits that accompany them. A form as apparently 'neutral' or 'accurate' as the portrait is in fact never free of symbolic value. Through conventional aspects such as posture, gesture or props, 'what portraits record is not social reality so much as social illusions, not ordinary life but special performance'.[16] Accordingly, Ribó's portraits do more than just represent the faces of the Catalan witnesses. Contemporary portraiture theory stresses the double interpretation of portraits: they are simultaneously an expression of *subjectivity*, as well as an *objectification* of the portrayed. Whereas popular characterisation of portraiture foregrounds uniqueness and exceptionality, one must bear in mind that portraits have also been used since the nineteenth century as an indexical inventory of the human species.[17]

Bassa and Ribó claim to represent these ordinary individuals as subjects with unique stories and identities, and yet, one discovers objectifying operations within their work that turn these portraits of individuals into repeated instances of an archival inventory. Accordingly, the symbolic constructions of the portraits in *Memòria de l'infern* are visual correlates to similar textual strategies inscribed in the testimonies. Although Bassa, the 'transcriber' of the narratives, and Ribó, the author of the portraits, both attempt to present the witnesses as naturally and neutrally as possible – Bassa through the maintenance of the simple syntax found in personal testimony and Ribó through the photographs' natural lighting, shading and framing – certain strategies lead us to interpret and 'frame' the portraits as symbolic, and thus belonging to constructed narratives. The portraits place their subjects uncomfortably somewhere between the singular instance of their exceptional experience and their attribution as a representation of the collective. On one hand, they are individuals thanks to the fact that each can tell and recover his or her own story. On the other, they symbolise a collective trauma due to the formal repetition in each photograph.

Simultaneous with the book's publication, the portraits of *Memòria de l'infern* were exhibited in the Museu de Granollers in the town of Granollers, Barcelona in Spring 2002. On the main commercial street of the town, the outside bustle was in sharp contrast to the small museum's cold, grey naked walls. The twenty-one portraits hung from iron wires from the ceiling and formed a circle. The faces of the 'twenty grandfathers and one grandmother' were located facing outwards, towards the external area of the circle and towards the windows facing the town's centre. Enclosed, or trapped, within the circle of portraits was a mass of entangled barbed wire. It was as if the survivors were turning their backs on this metonym of their imprisonment, or perhaps, the barbed wire represented the memories contained behind their faces, within their minds. Spotlights focused on the portraits, which cast their shadow both on the mass of barbed wire, as well as on the cold cement floor. The layout of the portraits engaged with the tension between inside and outside, on both an individual and a collective level. On one hand, the barbed wire represented the 'internalised' trauma behind the faces of the witnesses; on the other, the layout stood as a spatial articulation of the 'externalised' status of these once stateless

Catalan Republicans. Similarly, given the magnitude of the trauma suffered by the witnesses, all distinction between inside and outside is forever turned inside out, a confusion literalised in the installation.

In the introduction to *Memòria de l'infern* Bassa explains the process of the portraits' production. The photo session always took place halfway through the interview that became the narrative of each chapter. The 'austere, natural portraits, taken without flash, always in search of the natural light source of the room, which was usually the window or balcony' were conceived of as a pause between memories, a return to the present that gave momentary solace and relief to the witness. The witness was able to relax in front of the camera because 'for a while, he or she didn't have to keep digging up the darkness of sixty years ago'.[18] Bassa and Ribó deliberately scheduled the interviews so that the middle of the interview coincided with the brightest moment of the day. Ribó wanted as much light as possible to be directed towards the interviewee's face, particularly the eyes, which is why he used dark backgrounds.[19] There is an aesthetic tension between the plain black background – perceived as an abstraction of the moment of sitting – and its actual embedding in the testimonial process, shot at the moment and site of the act of bearing witness. This interplay between light and darkness is an important element in the photographer's representation of the witnesses. Ribó captures each survivor in a deliberate posture: in each portrait, the hands are shown near the face, as if they are literally 'holding' the head to physically bear the weight of the heavy memories that reside inside: 'Bodily expression and frame of mind, always present through the hands, were the next aim of the portraits. Eyes and hands, body and soul, hell and present.'[20] The eyes of the witnesses also acquire a regularity in all the portraits: the dark, dilated pupils that correspond to the 'darkness' or obscurity of their memories are accentuated by the lighting which, in turn, is manipulated to make the sitter seem teary-eyed. The use of lighting also gives the witness a look that makes them appear as if looking off into space, or perhaps far away in time.

These images of the witnesses acquire another meaning which requires a more active role on the spectator's part. This particular meaning is based on a previous knowledge of the typical mug shots taken of the prisoners on arrival in the Identification Service at each concentration camp. Similarly, the tattoo on Josep Jornet's right biceps is privileged by Ribó in his portrait, perhaps in an allusion to another tattoo that we know he has, but remains unseen. Even in the mug shots of the Boix collection, some of the young Republicans, not yet aware of the horrors that awaited them, could not help but to venture a smile. In contrast, of all the many portraits taken of each survivor, Bassa and Ribó chose to use those in which the survivors' expressions are grave. It is as though the hope they once had, a hope that helped them keep resisting, is countered by the tragedy they would go on to tell.

Figure 3: Jordi Ribó, *Portrait of Josep Jornet i Navarro*, 2002. Photographer Ribó privileges the tattoo as an allusion to another tattoo the viewer is left to imagine. Courtesy of the artist.

In order to comprehend the authors' need for coherent closure, one must bear in mind that the ultimate aim of this project is rooted not in the past but in the present. The past may come forth through narrative 'images' of past events, such as the ekphrastic descriptions, but there is an underlying tension between that re-presentation and the fact that, as in Claude Lanzmann's *Shoah* (1985), we can only visualise images of the witnesses in the present. To overcome this potential contradiction, we are offered in a film like *Shoah* 'an insight into the complexity of the relation between history and witnessing' rather than just a simple view of the past.[21] Bassa and Ribó focus on the trauma of the past and its disruption to identity, as it is understood from the present moment of the portrait as an act of witnessing. In order to help their audience of younger generations to acknowledge that identity, and to identify with their subjects, the authors of *Memòria de l'infern* stress the common aspects among the witnesses in both portraits and testimonial narratives. In this sense, Bassa and Ribó not only make an inventory of survivors, as a form of 'bare realism', that promises the presence of the past, a promise that can never be fulfilled, but they also re-invent the identity of the sitters.

The creation of identity is simultaneously operated by the brief texts that accompany the portraits in the form of captions in the exhibit and catalogue. They are biographical details stating concise, factual information regarding the survivors' past and present lives: place of birth, occupation before deportation, circumstances of deportation and liberation, where they lived and what they were doing at the time the interview and photo session took place. Also, Bassa and Ribó make a point to mention the names of the children and grandchildren of each survivor – emphasised when Bassa and Ribó call them '*avis*' (grandparents) in their prologue to the book and the catalogue. The aim of this objective data is apparently to establish a link with the younger generations, who have lost touch with this part of their people's history. Bassa and Ribó are thus attempting to remind Catalan citizens of their own past, and present the Holocaust as a part of Catalonia's own cultural patrimony. Thus, this major event in the Western world becomes relevant to Catalonia's own particular history, and Catalan history is situated within the broader international frame of European history. While Roig felt the need to insist on the regional cultural aspects of her fellow Catalans when she was working at the beginning of democracy in Spain, Bassa and Ribó are arguably struggling to place Catalonia and its people on the map of Europe. Bassa and Ribó's gesture befits their historical moment: the continuing expansion of the European Union, a political and economic infrastructure in which regional culture and identity must work hard to assert its significance. For Catalonia, this struggle is twice as urgent as it must assert its identity first within the context of the national, and again, within the transnational.

This process of identity formation is performed through the portraits by making them seem as natural as possible. In opposition to the testimonial narratives, which in their extremity undermine the correspondence to present reality, the images stress precisely that correspondence: the faces of these people are not those of exceptional heroes, but rather, of ordinary citizens. When Catalan schoolchildren visit the exhibit they are compelled to imagine the faces of these witnesses as similar to those of their own grandparents. This mode of viewing encourages the children to imagine that this is their story too. The younger generation are therefore permitted to ask new questions in relation to their own cultural and national identity. They can now say 'thank you for letting us, the young ones, see that all of this cruelty took place not so far away'.[22]

FRANCESC BOIX: WITNESS TO THE WITNESS

Photography was an important administrative tool in the organisation and running of the Nazi death camps. Mug shots were taken by the Identification Service upon prisoners' arrival. Prisoners working in the construction of the camps were carefully documented, as were prisoners who were killed 'trying to escape'. Similarly, the many medical experiments were documented as a part of their 'scientific' findings.[23] The documentary photographs of the camps were primarily taken by the perpetrators; taking pictures became a part of the Nazi project of dehumanisation. As Sybil Milton argues: 'Their sadistic voyeurism led to the crassest violations of the victims' privacy; even the most personal moments of death and dying were no longer respected'.[24] According to the declarations at the Dachau trial of SS-Oberscharführer Paul Ricken, director of the Mauthausen *Erkennungsdienst* from 1940 to 1944, it was the duty of the Identification Service to photograph SS portraits, inmates' portraits, executions, suicides, accidents, medical issues and various other events.[25]

Boix's portraiture and self-portraiture, as well as the recently reconstructed narrative 'portrait' of Boix's life and work, seek to counter the Nazi project of dehumanisation and annihilation of the subject. Whereas Bassa and Ribó's work of the latter stresses a search for and construction of a notion of identity based on repetition and integration, in Boix's work we find an urge to restore the portrayed with exceptionality and uniqueness. Recent scholarly and documentary works recuperate Barcelona-born Francesc Boix's biography and work to retell his story as that of a true hero. Boix has been cast as an individual Republican Catalan who risked his life so that the history of fascist oppression and genocide would not be erased as it had been in Spain, but revealed and given the possibility to shed light on history. This work of recuperation was carried out through the images of historical evidence. Bermejo's book *Francisco Boix, el fotógrafo de Mauthausen* and Soler's documentary *Francesc Boix, un fotógrafo en el infierno* strive to give back to Mauthausen inmate 5185 precisely what he risked his life for: an image of a face, with a set of eyes and a name.[26] In contrast to Bassa and Ribó's project, the Boix biographies are focused entirely on the exceptionality of the individual.

Before deportation, Boix was already an experienced photographer. As a teenager, he served as a correspondent for the Communist publication *Juliol* during the Spanish Civil War. Thanks to this skill, he was assigned a privileged position in Mauthausen in the *Erkennungsdienst* in 1941. Boix's main task at Mauthausen was to develop the photographs taken by Ricken with the camp's Leica camera. Because he was aware of the potential value of these images, Boix was able to smuggle thousands of images out of Mauthausen with the help of the Poschacher Kommando, a group of young inmates who had permission to leave the camp. Following liberation of the camps in 1945, Boix recovered the photographs.

Sybil Milton speaks of the dual meaning of the 'camera as a weapon' in the Holocaust: it was a weapon of aggression used by the killers and then subsequently a weapon of retribution exploited by the liberators. In the latter sense, the narrator of Soler's film describes how the Republican Spaniards bore arms during the first days after their liberation from Mauthausen. This same moment is signalled as the first time Boix was able to seize the same Leica camera as his own weapon. The same camera would be his weapon in his fight against the perpetrators of fascism, a fight which would continue until the end of his life.

A consideration of the various moments in Boix's life story brings to the foreground the many notions implied in the concept of witnessing. Boix was a witness to the Nazi camp system in several ways. As an inmate of Mauthausen, he was an eyewitness to the Nazi horrors. His work in the Identification Service and later as a photographer of the liberation, made Boix a witness to the witnesses. He also served as legal witness at the trials of Nuremberg and Dachau. Even in these courts of law, Boix was not limited to the witness stand: he was also an official photographer of the Dachau trials for *Regards*, the French news magazine. This complex layering of Boix as witness to the Nazi concentration camps places his images at the centre of the cultural of memory that nurtures an identity for Catalan and Spanish survivors of the Holocaust.

In the first days of chaotic freedom, Boix used his self-portrait to make himself the official photographer of liberated Mauthausen. One such self-portrait shows him with the camera case hanging around his neck, with a handmade armband pronouncing his self-appointed position: the English inscription on the armband reads 'Spanish War reporter – war photographer'. Boix stayed on in Mauthausen for one month witnessing the scenes of the immediate liberation. Among the most well-known and reprinted of his photos are images of mountains of corpses, of barely human survivors, of the Spanish inmates preparing a welcome sign for the Allied troops and of the destruction of the imperial eagle that crowned the entrance gate to the camp.[27]

A particularly noteworthy illustration of the power of self-imaging is revealed by one of the photographs taken during the interrogation of the dying Franz Ziereis, the SS-Kommandant of Mauthausen. This captivating series creates a *mise-en-abîme* of photographs and the taking of photographs: Boix's camera captures the captor's capture. In one particular photo of the series, Boix could not resist the temptation to include himself as witness to this historical moment of testimony: at this moment Ziereis was himself 'on the witness stand'. The image shows a somewhat content Boix looking down on the dying Ziereis, while in the foreground we can see the back of someone transcribing the Kommandant's declarations. This written act of legal testimony is thus privileged within the visual image. Although Boix's head is cut off in the photo, it is he, not Ziereis, who occupies most of the frame. In addition, Boix appears to show off his armband in the photograph, thus legitimating his status as both photographer and witness.

Boix is a witness in many senses: he *saw* the scene of Ziereis' capture, he *experienced* the liberation of the camps and he also *created* a historical document. Moreover, Boix not only asserts his own identity as a complex and multivalent witness in the self-portraits (as the photographed and photographing photographer), he likewise places the spectator in a privileged position. The direct address of the self-portrait locates us, the spectators, in the same place as Boix, a witness to the witnesses. There is here a play on a double, simultaneous operation of enticing and distancing spectators to the scene, to the moment of witnessing. On one hand, as spectators we are involved as we are led to view the exact place from where Boix stood, watched and witnessed. In this self-portrait Boix is captured witnessing as Ziereis bears witness; thus the spectator also becomes a witness to the witness to the witness. On the other hand, the operation contains a distancing device: by addressing himself and his camera directly, the medium of photography as an agent of intervention is revealed. Thus, as spectators, we are reminded how truly removed from the actual events we actually are.

Many of Boix's photographs were reprinted widely in the immediate post-war period, particularly by *Regards*. But the profusion of such images made Boix's name begin to disappear; many photos did not even credit his authorship or refer to his story. His heroic feat in risking his life to save these visual testimonies for posterity was mostly forgotten, even though he had played an important role as a witness in the Nuremberg trials. At the trials he had testified to the authenticity of the photographs that documented mass murders, many of which he himself had developed in Mauthausen.[28] In Boix's authentication of these images of extreme horror, the traditional idea of 'seeing is believing' is upheld even though the evidence is removed in time and space through the photograph: photographs become as trustworthy as the naked eye. Perhaps in events as traumatic as these all scepticism for the agency of the image is necessarily left aside. At the Nuremberg trials, Boix's declaration was based not only on what he had seen in the camps with his own eyes, but also on things that he saw solely in the photos he had developed in the Identification Service, including the presence of certain people at the camp (such as Albert Speer). The president of the court was careful to point out, however, that the jury did not want to hear about details that Boix himself had not seen with his own eyes.[29] It is noteworthy that while Boix here believes unreservedly and unswervingly in the transparency of the photographic image, the jury in court was less convinced. It only gave credence to the images present in Boix's own visual memories, and disregarded the material evidence of the events he declared to have seen captured on film.

In Bermejo's book and Soler's film, many of the same images are used to reconstruct the story of Boix's life, which came to an early end in 1951. Particularly noteworthy is Bermejo's inclusion of images of Boix's own notes on the back of each photo. Boix made these inscriptions after liberation, once he had recovered the photos. The images of the notes create yet another layer of witnessing: a number of the photos would have been impossible to interpret without Boix's guiding words as an expert witness. One such example is the disturbing self-portrait of Ricken, an automatic photo taken in 1942, in which Ricken lies on the ground wearing a suit and tie, apparently dead but in fact only imitating the corpses of inmates whom he photographed himself, following their death through supposed 'escape attempts'. This disconcerting image would be almost impossible to comprehend if it were not for Boix's explanatory note written on the back.

Among the most provocative of Boix's photographs in Bermejo's book is a series of portraits of fellow inmates taken after liberation that bear striking similarity to the mug shots made by the SS Identification Service. For these photos, Boix used the material that was still available to him in the Identification Service after liberation. The similarity is so strong that, on several occasions, they have been credited as identification photos taken by the SS themselves.[30] Why did Boix purposely choose to re-construct the typical mug shots of the Identification Service? Boix's use of the identi-fication photograph taken after liberation exploits portraiture's ambivalent oscillation between the honorific and the repressive. Similarly, Boix's portraits subvert the Nazi strategies of repression through the image. The Nazi mug shots were the epitome of the image as repressive mode of organisation that de-individualised and transformed the human subject into an object for categorisation. Boix's portraits reverse the de-humanised gaze of the *Erkennungsdienst* mug shots when they honorifically restore the individual's subjectivity through their very articulation as portraits.

The role of photographic portraiture to the recovery of Catalan Holocaust memory finds powerful resonance in Kozloff's suggestion that 'sitters for portraits appear as people auditioning for parts in their own lives'.[31] Here identity becomes performative, constructed through the act of portraiture. Bassa and Ribó design an archive of survi-vors' portraits, and stress the common aspects of twenty-one faces and twenty-one stories in order to unify them into a single portrait of a people with a common story. Yet Francesc Boix used the 'camera as a weapon' in order to give names and faces to those who had just survived the Nazi project of annihilation of identity. Likewise, both Bermejo and Soler retrieve Boix's figure from oblivion, and reconstruct his story as the story of a heroic individual who risked his life to rescue the visual evidence that would bear witness to the tragedy of the concentration camps. Boix is portrayed as one of the 7,200 Spanish victims of the Nazis, but also singled out as a witness who fought to make the tragedy of all the victims of the Holocaust known to the rest of the world and to posterity. Both Bermejo and Soler chose to retell Boix's story fifty years after the events, at a time in which the memory of the Holocaust is being revised in contemporary Spain.

A portrait can be imagined as the bearer of an entire story, a narrative that speaks of the moment of witnessing through its silences. The silences can be recaptured and revamped in different moments and for different purposes, in order to tell its story anew, and convey a new identity to the sitter. This story and this identity are always already inherent to the portrayer's intentions, as well as the spectator's in-terpretation. In *Memòria de l'infern*, the narratives of these portraits are shaped by Bassa and Ribó; Boix's story has been reconstructed by Bermejo and Soler. In both cases, the recuperation of the images of these witnesses to extreme horror per-mits the portrayers to bring the complexities of a traumatic past to a present which is still in the making. The circulation of portraits and their narratives becomes part of a process that operates not only as a retrieval of a forgotten past, but also as the configuration of an identity for the present. The portraits discussed here thus play a complex role; I have attempted to show that they can be read not only as transparent images of witnesses to traumatic past events, but also that a closer analysis – through which, in turn, the spectator also comes into a status or degree of witnessing – reveals the portrayers' intentions and preoccupations as witnesses to those witnesses. In this way, we can speak of moments of witnessing; due to the interplay between the photographed, the photographer and the spectator (as well as the texts and contexts that frame the image), the image of the witness can be re-newed to serve a transformed context. In contemporary Catalonia, re-presenting the witnesses of the Nazi concentration camps becomes a way to approach a national identity of mourning and memory. By introducing the witnesses of fifty years before, the works of Soler, Bermejo, Bassa and Ribó not only take us back to the darkest chapters of the twentieth century; they also bring with them the issues of memory and commemoration, identity and identification, and force us to constantly come back to the complex questions witnessing entails.

Notes

1　The status of the Republican refugees in France was described as 'stateless' by Spanish Minister of Foreign Affairs Serrano Suñer in conversation with his German counterpart, Baron von Ribbentropp, in 1940.

2　Max Kozloff, *Lone Visions, Crowded Frames* (Albuquerque: University of New Mexico Press, 1994), 24.

3　Allan Sekula, 'The Body and the Archive', *October* 39 (1987): 6–7.

4　Peter Burke, *Eyewitnessing: The Uses of Images as Historical Evidence* (London: Reaktion Books, 2001), 9.

5　Other recent publications include Carles Torner, *Shoah. Una pedagogia de la memòria* (Barcelona: Proa, 2002); Rosa Torán, *Vida y mort dels republicans als camps Nazis* (Barcelona: Proa, 2002); Rosa Torán and Margarida Sales, *Crònica gráfica d'un camp de concentració: Mauthausen* (Barcelona: Museu d'Història de Catalunya, 2002); David Serrano's interview with survivor Francesc Comellas, *Un català a Mauthausen. El testimoni de Francesc Comellas* (Barcelona: Pòrtic, 2001); and Vicenç Villatoro's novel *Memòria del traïdor* (Barcelona: Edicions 62, 1996). Art Spiegelman's *Maus* was also translated into Catalan by Edicions l'Inreyés in 2003.

6　In fiction, Mauthausen survivor Joaquim Amat-Piniella's epic novel *K. L. Reich* is probably the first effort by a Catalan to represent in writing the experience of a Catalan Republican in the Holocaust. Written in exile in Andorra in 1945, *K. L. Reich* was not published in Catalan until 1963. The complete original text did not see the light until 2001, published posthumously by Edicions 62.

7　Montserrat Roig, *Els Catalans als camps Nazis* (Barcelona: Edicions 62, 1995), 5.

8　Montserrat Roig, *Noche y niebla. Los catalanes en los campos Nazis* (Barcelona: Península, 1978), 242.

9　Ibid., 350.

10　A similar phenomenon is occurring in relation to the Spanish Civil War. More than a quarter of a century has gone by since the end of the dictatorship, and even though the Civil War has been an ever-present theme for decades, publishing houses are only now recovering the long-silenced stories. See, for example, Javier Cercas' novel *Soldados de Salamina* (Barcelona: Tusquets Editores, 2001).

11　Ernst van Alphen, *Caught by History: Holocaust Effects in Contemporary Art, Literature, and Theory* (Stanford: Stanford University Press, 1997), 112.

12　See, for example, W. G. Sebald, *The Emigrants* (London: Harvill Press, 1996), in which family photographs accompany, but do not illustrate, the stories of exile and loss experienced by four different Holocaust survivors.

13　David Bassa and Jordi Ribó, *Memòria de l'infern* (Barcelona: Edicions 62, 2002), 23–5.

14　One variation is marked by the time gone by between the events themselves and their retrieval through memory; fifty years after the events, Bassa and Ribó were able to interview 21 survivors, while Roig, 25 years earlier, had talked to four dozen.

15　Bassa and Ribó, 26.

16　Burke, 28.

17　See Sekula.

18　Bassa and Ribó, 22–3.

19　Often, in the absence of other material, the photographers used their T-shirts as background.

20 Bassa and Ribó, 23.

21 Shoshana Felman and Dori Laub, *Testimony. Crises of Witnessing in Literature, Psychoanalysis, and History* (New York: Routledge, 1992), 205.

22 Copied by the author from the visitors' book of the exhibition.

23 Sybil Milton, 'Photography as Evidence of the Holocaust', *History of Photography* 23, no. 4 (1999): 303.

24 Sybil Milton, 'Documentary Photography and the Holocaust', *Simon Wiesenthal Center Annual* 1 (1984), 49.

25 Benito Bermejo, *Francisco Boix, el fotógrafo de Mauthausen* (Barcelona: RBA, 2001), 107.

26 The film won prizes at the San Francisco International Film Festival, the Festival International du Film d'Histoire (Pesca, France), the Bienal de Cine Científico de Zaragoza (sección humanidades) and the Festival de Cine Español de Málaga. It was also selected as a finalist at the International Emmy Awards.

27 As Bermejo states in his book on Boix, the evidence suggests that Boix had these photos with him when he travelled from Mauthausen to Paris in 1945. Nowadays these documents are dispersed; they can be seen mostly in archives in France such as the Amicale de Mauthausen or the Fédération National de Déportés, Internés, Résistants et Patriotes in Paris. Most of the original negatives were lost. Many of the most emblematic photos published shortly after liberation were incorrectly attributed.

28 Boix was called to the stand on 28 and 29 January 1946 by Charles Dubost, who represented the French Republic. On the stand, he declared the authenticity of the images that testified to the mass murders, many of which he himself had developed in Mauthausen. Both Montserrat Roig and Benito Bermejo include a literal transcription of Boix's testimony in their books.

29 Bermejo, 213.

30 Bermejo, 238.

31 Kozloff, 30.

2. Sound, Image and the Corporeal Implication of Witnessing in Derek Jarman's *Blue*

Roger Hallas

The physical nature of film necessarily makes an incision or cut between the body and the voice. Then the cinema does its best to restitch the two together at the seam.

MICHEL CHION

In the pandemonium of image
I present you with the universal Blue
Blue an open door to soul
An infinite possibility
Becoming tangible

DEREK JARMAN

The act of bearing witness presupposes the logic of *habeas corpus* – you must have the body.[1] The witness must be present at the site and the moment of testimony's enunciation. To speak or mediate through an other risks the disqualifying charge of hearsay. Reading Paul Celan's famously enigmatic line, 'no one bears witness for the witness', Shoshana Felman underlines the solitary appointment of the witness: 'Since testimony cannot be simply relayed, repeated or reported by another without losing its function as testimony, the burden of the witness – in spite of his or her alignment with other witnesses – is a radically unique, non-interchangeable and solitary burden.'[2]

The medium of film, however, allows for the testimonial act to be preserved beyond its moment of enunciation, and the reproducibility of the medium permits a broad dissemination of the testimonial address. But since cinema mediates through a temporal deferment and spatial displacement, films dedicated to the act of bearing witness necessarily rely on techniques which enhance the impression of a witness's presence before the viewer. The documentary convention of the talking head is, without doubt, the principal technique to serve such a function. The witness addresses an off-screen interlocutor or even the camera directly, but the presence of these entities comes to be disavowed since they serve as the future viewer's proxy, his/her cipher. During the screening, the viewer takes up the position of this cipher, and thus, experiences the witness's address as directed to him/her, an address that apparently takes place in the present. Even when the dynamics of bearing witness are mediated through less explicit identificatory processes, such as they are in Claude Lanzmann's *Shoah* (1985), what remains paramount for an impression of presence to hold is the corporeal inscription of the witness in the film's sound and image.[3]

It is for this reason that Derek Jarman's *Blue* (1993) proves such an intriguing and provocative work. Jarman bears witness to his own AIDS-related illness and mortality in what Patrizio Lombardo has called 'the most bodyless film ever produced'.[4] We never see Jarman (and only hear his voice once) during the film, since *Blue* performs a radical visual ascesis by removing all images from the frame. For the film's entire 76-minute duration, the screen is filled only with a luminous monochrome blue, while the soundtrack incorporates a complex audio mix of poetic and testimonial spoken text, music, song and sound effects. Created during the final years of his life, at a time when Jarman was struggling with the onset of AIDS-related blindness, the film both visualises blindness on its monochrome screen and thematises it in the spoken script. The image and the word thus come together in *Blue* to explore the boundaries of visuality itself. As the film's spoken script asks at one point: 'If I lose my sight, will my vision be halved?' Time and again in the film, Jarman prioritises the visual imagination over the physical realm of perception as the ethical space in which the act of bearing witness to AIDS can most effectively take place. *Blue* thus rejects the conventional visual components of cinema that render its impression of reality: cinematography, editing and *mise-en-scène*. The film image not only denies any sensuous or material figuration of the witness's body, it also negates the profilmic itself (the time-space in front of the camera). In fact, *Blue* is one of those rare analogue films made without a camera, for the monochrome blue was produced photochemically in a film lab.[5]

The film's provocative visual form has prompted many critics to frame it as an integral part of avant-garde cinema's long-standing iconoclastic dedication to what William Wees has termed 'a fuller and much more revealing *visualization of sight*'.[6] This tradition has pursued a modernist self-reflexivity around the cinematic apparatus, challenging the perspectivist tradition of the photographic camera in the service of liberating the spectator's vision, of forging new relations between seeing and knowing the world. Noting Jarman's rejection of cinematic language, Paul Julian Smith contends that in *Blue* we are 'thrown back on the cinematic apparatus itself, on the projection of light onto a screen and our own physical presence before it'.[7] The chromatic constancy of the blue screen also prompts us to notice the scratches and nicks on the celluloid, distinct reminders of its historical materiality. Chris

Darke argues furthermore that the soundtrack, especially the film's spoken script, transfers the responsibility of visualisation from the filmmaker to the spectator: 'The soundtrack works to spark the spectator's own images off the silent blue canvas: this is a film that takes place as much in the spectator's head as it does onscreen – "an infinite possibility becoming tangible", as Jarman puts it in one of the monologues.'[8] In this sense, *Blue* draws on the visual aspects of radio as a medium: it stimulates the mind's eye to imagine images rather than have the eye perceive them physically. Indeed, the ascetic denial of sensually perceptible images provides the very stimulus for the rich visual imagination of *Blue*. But it is more than a 'radio film' such as Walter Ruttmann's *Weekend* (1930), because the spectator's experience of his/her own visual perception of the film's projection is crucial to the stimulation of his/her mind's eye.[9] By attending to the significance of the film spectator's embodied perception and cognition, Smith and Darke demonstrate how *Blue* is not in fact the 'most body-less film' that Lombardo claims it to be. Although the film's spectators are denied any explicit figuration of the witness's body on the screen, they do however become distinctly aware of their own body in the theatre during the screening of the film. The body of the witness that has disappeared from the screen returns through the corporeal experience of the spectator. This chapter examines how sound and image are deployed in *Blue* to implicate the body of its spectator in the act of bearing witness to AIDS. This process of what I call 'corporeal implication' allows the film's spectator to become a witness to AIDS through a simultaneously visceral and imaginative encounter with Jarman's subjectivity.

HYBRID ORIGINS

The idiosyncratic characteristics of Jarman's final film owe much to its long genesis. Dedicated to an imagistic rather than narrative mode of filmmaking with little commercial appeal, Jarman struggled throughout his filmmaking career to secure funding for his projects. The first trace of the work's conception is to be found in one of Jarman's notebooks from 1974 with the tantalising, but enigmatic phrase, 'the blue film for Yves Klein'.[10] Jarman had long been fascinated with Klein and his work. Like many of the other artists, filmmakers and writers, such as Caravaggio, Pasolini and Genet, from whom Jarman drew inspiration, Klein provided not only an influential body of work, but also, and perhaps more importantly, an artistic and public life with which Jarman could identify. It was the kind of public life that he would borrow for the performance of his own public life as an artist.[11] Thus, the subsequent shift in the project from a biography of Klein to a personal and frequently autobiographical exploration of AIDS appears less a displacement or rupture and more an intelligible conceptual development, a more complete identification with Klein.

In the late 1950s Klein began to produce a series of monochrome paintings. Derived from specially developed luminous pigment, Klein's paint was applied uniformly with a roller. By rejecting the paintbrush, Klein gestured to a radical evacuation of artistic expression in the material trace of the paint. By 1958, Klein narrowed his monochrome interest to one colour: blue. In a masterful gesture of artistic self-promotion, Klein adopted a particular hue of ultramarine blue and branded it with his name: I.K.B. (International Klein Blue). Appropriating the notion of 'a blue period' *à la*

Picasso and evacuating the colour of its expressive function, Klein celebrated blue for what he believed to be its status beyond the signifying dimensions of other colours.[12] Gaston Bachelard's claim that blue offers poetic knowledge which precedes rational knowledge was profoundly influential on Klein, who often quoted a line from the French critic as a testimonial for his own art: 'First there is nothing, then there is a deep nothing, then there is a blue depth.'[13] Klein himself stressed that even in its most material and concrete associations, namely the sea and the sky, blue signified 'the most *abstract* aspects of tangible and visible nature'.[14] Through his monochrome blue canvases, Klein strove to de-objectify the work of art.[15] As art historian Sidra Stich notes about Klein's use of blue,

> This is then a realm in which imagination thrives without images; it is a realm of solitude, transparency and dematerialization that prospers within and by means of effacement. It is therefore a realm of nothingness that is, however, alive with possibility.[16]

Throughout the spoken script of *Blue*, Jarman invokes notions of blue that draw heavily from Klein's conception of the colour. The film script invokes 'the fathomless blue of Bliss' as 'an infinite possibility becoming tangible'.

Jarman's idea for 'the blue film for Yves Klein' only materialised into a concrete project in 1987. Following the success of his film *Caravaggio* (1986), Jarman began to build a funding proposal for an experimental biography of Klein, tentatively titled *International Blue*. Jarman described the project as 'a film without compunction or narrative existing only for an idea'.[17] Funding discussions with Sony dried up after the company realised that Jarman remained committed to a radically anti-narrative film. The project resurfaced in 1991, but not as a film. Titled *Symphonie Monotone*, after Klein's famous single note symphony, the event functioned as a pre-screening performance before a special AIDS benefit premiere of Jarman's film *The Garden* (1990).[18] A film loop of one of Klein's blue monochromes owned by the Tate Gallery was projected onto the cinema screen while Jarman and the actress Tilda Swinton, dressed in blue, sat at a table on the stage running their moistened fingers around the rims of wine glasses and reading Jarman's personal and poetic reflections on the colour blue. Musicians sat at the front of the theatre playing an ethereal score by contemporary British composer Simon Fisher Turner. From time to time, a young boy would run out into the audience and hand out blue and gold painted stones to the audience.[19] Jarman was simultaneously researching and writing a book of reflections on colour that he would subsequently publish as *Chroma* (1994). Typical of Jarman's writing style, the book draws together a montage of philosophical reflections, historical anecdotes and personal memories centred around the colours of the spectrum. Although most of the chapters included recent memories and journal entries dealing with Jarman's illness, it was the chapter on blue that most fully explored such experience. This chapter subsequently became the foundation for the film script of *Blue*.

The filmed loop of Klein's painting was replaced by a 35mm film strip of luminous blue generated within a film lab once Jarman's producer, James Mackay, finally secured the majority of funding for the film in 1992 from Channel Four, the Arts Council of Great Britain, Brian Eno and Japanese producer Takashi Asai. The blue image was no longer a photographic image of an object in the spatio-temporality of the historical world, albeit an abstract image. It now existed only as a non-representational colour field generated through the alchemy of modern film technology.[20] Mackay secured completion funds for the production from BBC Radio Three, which facilitated the simultaneous broadcast of *Blue* on British public radio and national television.[21] Coinciding with the theatrical release of *Blue* in the UK, the film script was published as a book and the soundtrack released on compact disc. Mackay also planned a special CD-ROM version of *Blue*, but lack of funding prevented it from being completed.[22]

Clearly this history of the work's genesis challenges any attempt to privilege the origin and status of the work as quintessentially cinematic. This hardly seems surprising when we consider that throughout his career Jarman self-identified as a painter and an artist far more than as a filmmaker, despite the critical and popular perception of him as first and foremost a filmmaker. *Blue* not only emerged from, but was also disseminated in multiple media forms, including live performance, film, television, radio, a book, a book chapter, a sound recording and, at least conceptually, a CD-ROM. Each of these media offers a different opportunity to mediate the act of bearing witness. Each produces a varying dynamic of reception and can render the impression of the witness's presence through often starkly differing means. Live performance and cinema for instance rely heavily on the visual presentation of bodies in front of their audiences, even though cinema functions through a paradoxical presence/absence of such bodies.[23] Radio privileges the auditory qualities of the voice and its presentation within an intimate acoustic space, whereas books articulate presence through a linguistic understanding of 'voice' that is tied to structures of address and discursive register. However, none of the manifestations of *Blue* signified uniquely through a single medium. They each implied a relationship to one another. For example, the performers in the live performance *Symphonie Monotone* acted as both a corporeal supplement or excess to the abstract monochrome film and as a bridge closing the gap between the spectator and the screen. While the film screen lacked the impression of corporeal presence the performative aspects of the event 'filled in' that absence of represented bodies with live ones in the auditorium. *Blue* is certainly a work of cinema, but it is also far more than that. This multiplicity frames the ways the film produces meaning, thus suggesting that it need not necessarily be understood as either quintessentially cinematic or as a self-reflexive critique of the cinematic apparatus. The film's hybrid origins indicate how its visual iconoclasm cannot be understood outside of a consideration of the complex dynamics between sound, word and image, especially those borrowed and adapted from other media.

THE ACOUSMATIC WITNESS

Jarman's application of the monochrome screen in *Blue* resonates with other works of queer film and video from the 1990s that turned to visual iconoclasm as means to challenge the instrumental vision of dominant AIDS representation. For example, Marlon Riggs' performative portrait, *Je ne regrette rien (No Regret)* (1992), a video portrait of five black gay men living with AIDS, employs various forms of black video mattes that obscure its testifying bodies in an exploration of the cultural and social dynamics of HIV disclosure. Similarly, Jonathan Horowitz's video installation, *Countdown* (1995), challenges the sentimental pedagogy of Jonathan Demme's *Philadelphia* (1993) by blocking virtually the entire image track of the original film with white mattes imprinted with transparent ascending numbers. Yann Beauvais' ironically-titled video *Still Life* (1997) disavows the image altogether in favour of texts about AIDS from media reporting, public policy documents and cultural criticism that perpetually scroll across the screen in different directions.

The visual iconoclasm of such works specifically targets what Simon Watney has called 'the spectacle of AIDS', the dominant regime of AIDS representation that has historically pathologised HIV-infected people through the visual discourses of techno-science and social documentary.[24] The stigma of AIDS in the developed world has been perpetuated through disciplinary mechanisms of visuality, whether it be the iconography of emaciated dying bodies, the drive to identify HIV-infected individuals or the perception of Karposi Sarcoma lesions as signs of 'sexual abomination'. The iconoclasm of the videos by Riggs, Horowitz and Beauvais relies precisely on the production of an abstract anti-spectacle, an anti-spectacle forged in the destruction of the reassuring fullness and depth of the profilmic image. Visuality is, for them, a perilous realm, fully implicated in the social abjection and pathology of HIV-infected bodies. The spoken script of *Blue* indeed acknowledges at several points its own iconoclastic impulse in the face of the visuality of AIDS:

> For accustomed to believing in image, an absolute idea of value, his world had forgotten the command of essence: Thou Shall Not Create Unto Thyself Any Graven Image, although you know the task is to fill the page. From the bottom of your heart, pray to be released from image.

As Peter Schwenger notes, the injunction against the image in this passage is paired with an implicit command to write.[25] It is not the screen, nor the canvas, that is filled, but the page. Language in *Blue* not only facilitates the means by which to bear witness, to construct a testimonial address to an other, it also serves as the form through which the witnessing body may be imagined. In combining an abstract monochrome image track with a rich and multilayered soundtrack structured around verbal performance, Jarman inverts the hegemony of image over sound that has shaped the history of both popular narrative and experimental cinema.[26] Film sound theorist Michel Chion argues that the very notion of the 'soundtrack' misleadingly implies an autonomy to the perception of sound during film spectatorship: 'A film's aural elements are not received as an autonomous unit. They are immediately analyzed and distributed in the spectator's perceptual apparatus according to the relation each bears to what the spectator sees at the time.'[27] In what Chion calls 'an instantaneous perceptual triage', many aspects of film sound are merely 'swallowed up' in the image's false depth, often in the service of enhancing a conventional narrative film's realistic impression of spatio-temporality.[28] *Blue* shatters this conventional 'triage' by denying the image track figuration and rendering its impression of spatial depth as either infinite or zero. The blue screen presents itself as either pure surface or a depthless void, neither of which provide suitable perceptual anchors for sound, and in particular, for the voice.[29]

The unanchored, seemingly disembodied quality of the voice functions as a particular and idiosyncratic example of what Chion calls the 'acousmêtre', the speaker who cannot be seen.[30] While certain modern media, like radio, the phonograph and the telephone, rely completely on 'acousmatic listening', cinema has been able, since the arrival of sound film, to explore the tension between seeing and not seeing the source of a voice or other sound. A film spectator may frequently oscillate between such visualised and acousmatic listening during the course of a film. Chion points out that the placement of the loudspeaker behind the cinema screen produces a specific perplexity in the spectator's perception of an acousmêtre during the film: 'For the spectator, then, the filmic acousmêtre is offscreen, outside the image, and at the same time *in* the image ... It's as if the voice were wandering along the surface, at once inside and outside, seeking a place to settle.'[31] *Blue* complicates these dynamics by denying any figuration or perspectival depth and breadth to the image. There is therefore simply no place on the screen where the voice can be located.

Citing the voice of God and the maternal voice as its precedents, Chion finds significant power in the film acousmêtre: 'The acousmêtre has only to show itself – for the person speaking to inscribe his or her body inside the frame, in the visual field – for it to lose its power, omniscience and (obviously) ubiquity.'[32] During the first ten to fifteen minutes of *Blue*, film spectators may well anticipate the imminent appearance of the witness's body within the film frame – and with it, a reassuring phenomenological relation to the witness – but eventually they submit either to their own boredom or to the obstinacy of the film's visual abstraction. Or, as John Paul Ricco argues about the film, 'one is never free from the sense that a visual accompaniment to the audio has gone missing.'[33] The image track of the film could present the body, but it resolutely does not.[34] To understand why the film refuses to visualise the witness's body on the screen we need to examine more closely how the film's language and its spoken performance allow that same body to be imagined.

CORPOREAL IMPLICATION

The spoken script of *Blue* engenders an elaborate collage of different themes, discourses and modes of address. While it frequently journeys into poetic and philosophical ruminations on the colour blue, often through a mythical boy character called Blue, the film's script consistently returns to the subject of the body and the ravage inflicted upon it by AIDS: 'I have a sinking feeling in my stomach. I feel defeated. My mind bright as a button but my body falling apart – a naked light bulb in a dark and ruined room.' *Blue* records in great detail the painful and arduous treatment that Jarman undergoes to fight the cytomegalovirus (CMV) which is gradually blinding him: 'The shattering bright light of the eye specialist's camera leaves that empty sky blue afterimage ... The process is a torture, but the result, stable eyesight, worth the price and the twelve pills I have to take a day.' The address of the spoken script shifts from such first-person testimony to the impersonal pharmaceutical small print of the drugs Jarman is taking, or to his doctor's diagnosis: 'The white flashes you are experiencing in your eyes are common when the retina is damaged.' After reading out the over forty possible side effects of the CMV treatment drug DHPG, which include its proven capability as a carcinogen, the spoken voice sarcastically parrots the advice at the end of the small print on the packaging: 'If you are concerned about any of the above side-effects, or if you would like any further information, please ask your doctor.'

The script spoken across the film is read by four different voices, Jarman regulars: Nigel Terry and John Quentin, occasionally Tilda Swinton, and for one brief, compelling passage, by Jarman himself. Rather than suggest a polyphonic or heteroglossic structure, these voices imply a subtle diffusion of the author's voice. We hear no overlapping or dialectic engagement between these distinct voices; they each enunciate as part of an ongoing monologue that is passed from one voice to the next. Moreover, these shifts in voice follow no apparent pattern or logic, whether thematic, discursive or affective. The often sudden shifts in the spoken script between different emotional states – despair, anger, sadness, black humour and acceptance – bear out the experience of discontinuity and radical unpredictability that people living with AIDS have time and again articulated. As listeners of *Blue*, we thus come to feel a distinct tension between this relative coherence to the testimonial subjectivity of the script – its 'voice' – and the multiple layers of differentiation that begin with the four voices who perform it.

Those familiar with Jarman's other films and his books will recognise, however, several aspects of *Blue* as continuities within his oeuvre. First, all three of the actors who Jarman used in the film – Terry, Quentin and Swinton – had become closely associated by 1993 with his film oeuvre as members of his informal ensemble. Since Jarman's films had consistently been framed (by both himself and his critics) as personal visions, the use of his 'ensemble' actors in his last film ensured that the performance of the testimonial script through several voices could disperse, but not completely dissipate the subjectivity articulated in *Blue*. Second, the complex collage-like script of *Blue* follows the free-flowing and digressive, non-linear structure of his books *Dancing Ledge* (1984), *The Last of England* (1987), *Modern Nature* (1991), and *At Your Own Risk: A Saint's Testament* (1992), all of which drew heavily from the content and form of his personal journals.

The specific techniques of sound recording in *Blue* also play an important role in determining how the film's 'voice' is articulated, and how it is subsequently perceived by the audience. All of the different voices are closely miked, creating a sense of intimacy between the speaking voice and the listening spectator that is similar to the auditory dynamics of radio listening. In *Blue*, we thus sense virtually no distance between the voice and our ears. At certain points, the voice even whispers the script. Close-miking also reduces reverberation, the sonic quality that situates a voice in space. This recording technique renders a strong impression of aural presence to the voice, hinders the perception of distance, and thus closes up any identifiable space that would facilitate the clear delineation between speaker and listener. Chion argues that this technique, what he calls 'the I-voice', structures the spectator's identification in a particular manner: 'All you have to do is add reverb in the mix to manipulate an I-voice; the *embracing* and *complicit* quality of the I-voice becomes *embraced* and *distanced*. It is no longer a subject with which the spectator identifies, but rather an object-voice, perceived as a body anchored in space.'[35] To hear the difference in aural quality between these two modes, one need only compare the soundtrack of the film *Blue* to the live recording of the Rome performance of *Blue* in July 1993. In the Rome recording, the specific sound quality of the live performers' voices anchors their bodies in a specific space.[36]

By liberating the speaking voice from its body through both visual and aural dis-embodiment, *Blue* produces the effect of corporeal implication in the spectator: 'The voice makes us feel in our body the vibration of the body of the other.'[37] This visceral, mimetic component to the spectatorial experience of *Blue* generates a potential transformation in the dynamics of bearing witness to AIDS. The film's visual and aural techniques negate the space in which a stable phenomenological relationship between the listener/spectator and the person with AIDS may be constructed. In foreclosing my ability to imagine the body of the person with AIDS 'out there', and thus, as wholly other, I come to witness the witness through my very own body. The body of the other, the witness's body is implicated in my own.

HAPTIC VISUALITY

The profound significance of such corporeal implication cannot be underestimated during an epidemic in which people living with HIV or AIDS have consistently been subject to the spatial techniques of abjection, including pathology, social isolation, quarantine and even incarceration. Cultural hysteria about the presumed contagion of the retrovirus has demanded that HIV-infected bodies be contained at a 'safe dis-tance'. But at a safe distance from whom? As cultural critics such as Simon Watney have contended, the ideological construct in popular AIDS discourses of a hetero-normative 'general population' is produced precisely through the identification of its abject, the bodies of presumed 'risk groups' such as gay and bisexual men, IV drug users and sex workers.[38] The mass-mediated spectacle of AIDS has performed this particular ideological task; the media has relied heavily on forms of instrumental and disciplinary vision to present and represent the abject bodies of the always suspect, potential harbingers of disease.

Blue reverses the visual attention of the spectacle of AIDS from the body with AIDS out *there* back onto the spectator's own body right *here* before the blue screen. I felt this transformative moment during the very first time I saw the film at Film Fo-rum in New York City in 1994. Sitting in the movie theatre gazing at the monochrome blue screen, I gradually began to pay attention, like Paul Julian Smith, to my own presence within the cinematic apparatus, to my phenomenological encounter with a screen of reflected blue light.[39] And the object of my gaze continually spilled over be-yond the edges of the screen. Blue light seeped out of the rectangular frame and into the space of the theatre, bathing the normally darkened space of the theatre's seats in diffuse illumination. In the blue light in which Jarman's body, the witness's body, remained unfigured, the spectator's body, my own body, now became visible. I had begun to notice my own seated body in the blue aura around me. Such diffusion of light threatened to absorb the distance between spectator and screen, putting at risk my very ability to grasp precisely the object of my visual perception. Was I looking at a screen or merely, and incredibly, at light? On one hand, the rectangle of light on the screen resisted definitive perceptual identification as either a frame (delimiting two-dimensional space) or an aperture (opening up to infinite space).[40] This ambiguity snagged my visual perception in that impossible gap between surface and depth. If, on the other hand, I was looking at light, then I was already looking at both nothing and everything. It was thus my own body which emerged as the surest presence to be sensed by my own visual perception. I could see myself engaged in the act of seeing at the same time that I felt myself losing control of it.

This embodied spectatorship engendered by *Blue* operates through the combination of seeing and hearing. The spectator's vision is denied an external body on the screen to either misrecognise in the phantasmatic process of identification or to repudiate through a disidentification with it as an abject other. The monochrome screen reflects back merely light, bathing the spectator's body in an illumination that arouses the perception of his/her own embodiment. Vision in this instance relies less on the spectator's perceived distance from the world and its otherness than on his/her felt incorporation within it. Hearing similarly frames the spectator's relation to otherness in terms of proximity and corporeal implication. The film's employment of the aural I-voice produces a perception of such closeness to the ear that the boundary between inside and outside the spectator's body seems to dissolve as he/she listens and watches. Light and sound envelop him/her in a space-diminishing embrace.

We may comprehend these particular spectatorial dynamics in terms of what Laura Marks has called haptic visuality.[41] Drawing from the work of nineteenth-century art historian Aloïs Riegl, Marks distinguishes two modes of visuality: optical and haptic. On one hand, optical visuality relies on a separation between the viewing subject and the world, thus allowing the former to distinguish the latter as distinct objective forms in deep space. This is how we conventionally think of seeing in an everyday capacity. However, we must be aware that it is also the foundation of instrumental and disciplinary modes of seeing. Haptic visuality, on the other hand, posits a relationship of proximity and contact (rather than distance) between the viewing subject and the world; it allows our eyes to function like organs of touch. Haptic visuality presupposes a different mode of seeing, one that tends to move over the surface of the world and its objects, rather than focus on specific objects or bodies situated in deep space. Marks draws such distinctions to explain how works of diasporic and exilic filmmaking, such as Rea Tajiri's *History and Memory* (1991) and Mona Hatoum's *Measures of Distance* (1988), come to represent experience and memory. The haptic visuality engendered by such 'intercultural cinema' facilitates the representation of cultural difference through embodied knowledge rather than through the rational, disciplinary epistemologies of Western modernity.[42]

Although not a work of intercultural cinema in the sense proposed by Marks, *Blue* certainly does invoke the dynamics of haptic visuality when it bears witness to the filmmaker's experience of AIDS by rejecting the disciplinary gaze of the spectacle of AIDS. In fact, the ways in which Marks describes the spectatorial dynamics of haptic visuality in intercultural cinema could equally be applied to *Blue*: 'The works I propose to call haptic invite a look that moves on the surface plane of the screen for some time before the viewer realizes what she or he is beholding. Such images resolve into figuration only gradually, if at all.'[43] In its process of displacing the body of the witness from the screen to the auditorium, *Blue* takes this ambivalent relationship to figuration to an extreme. Spectators are suspended in the simultaneous contemplation of the material surface of the projected image and the infinite depth of the representational image. As our eyes graze across the screen, we come to detect in the monochrome frame the minor scratches and marks that accrue on the film print as it is repeatedly projected. Marks understands such attention to the film's materiality to be a major distinction between optical and haptic visuality: 'While optical perception privileges the representational power of the image, haptic perception privileges the material presence of the image.'[44] In *Blue*, that material presence is dual: both the monochrome rectangle of reflected blue light on the screen and the diffuse blue light that bathes the auditorium. When our eyes attempt to sustain an optical perception of the monochrome image in *Blue* – to focus on it as representation – we gradually succumb to the perceptual effects of continuously gazing at a homogenous visual field, the phenomenon known as the Ganzfeld effect: 'It is as if the mind cannot endure pure ground, but must always play figures against it, if only those of its own erratic physical vision. So, irregular movements of the eye produce a sense of irregularities in the perceived field, which are then interpreted by the mind's eye as images.'[45] Degrees of visual figuration in the image thus arise in *Blue* from the physical qualities of both the film itself and the spectator's own act of seeing.

Of course, these dynamics do not function in isolation from the film's use of sound. The film's spoken words and non-verbal sounds generate a complex array of synesthetic effects that allow *Blue* to figure the lived experience of AIDS in ways that resist optical visuality. This resistance to the optical is at the core of Jarman's radical call to the spectator as witness because with it are rejected the risks of pathologisation and abjection.[46] Such synesthesia abets the process of corporeal implication that allows the viewer to become a witness to the witness with HIV/AIDS.

'AN INFINITE POSSIBILITY BECOMING TANGIBLE'

Jarman's film-script for *Blue* abounds not only in rich sets of literary imagery but also in poetic language that continually fuses the senses of seeing and hearing. For example, in an early passage of the script (read by John Quentin), Jarman posits his own subjectivity through the metaphorical figuration of an empty, sunlit room filled with the echo of voices:

I fill this room with the echo of many voices
Who passed time here
Voices unlocked from the blue of the long dried paint
The sun comes and floods this empty room
I call it my room
My room has welcomed many summers
Embraced laughter and tears
Can it fill itself with your laughter
Each word a sunbeam
Glancing in the light
This is the song of My Room
(*in whispers*) David. Howard. Graham. David. Paul. Terry…
(*repeated refrain*) Blue stretches, yawns and is awake.
(*simultaneously in whispers*) David. Terry. Paul. Howard. Graham…
Blue.[47]

This passage figures Jarman's remembrance of individual friends and lovers who have died of AIDS as, at once, rays of light and echoed voices, unlocked from the 'long dried paint' of death. Each metaphor is imbricated in the other: 'Each word a sunbeam/Glancing in the light.' The synesthetic effect is here enhanced by the musical score which introduces sharp, high-note percussive rings that evoke such glinting rays of sunlight. This accompanying music and the sound effects of summertime (birdsong, buzzing insects and a trickling stream) do not provide an aural anchor so that the audience may situate John Quentin's voice in an objective spatio-temporality. Like the closely miked 'I-voice', these accompanying sounds are presented as interior, as the subjective sensations of memory.

In imagining Jarman's subjectivity through the image of the empty room, the film not only implies the psychological and physiological toll of an impending death brought about by AIDS, but it also suggests how subjectivity is filled with the traces of other subjectivities who have 'passed time' in it. Jarman cannot bear witness to his own experience of AIDS without also remembering those close friends who have died before him. This is not merely an ethical commitment to speak on behalf of those who have already been silenced by death. The knowledge of their painful fate haunts Jarman's experience of illness and mortality with the anticipation of his own as he follows their path.[48] This passage of the film-script resuscitates hope, however, by awakening the mythical boy Blue, the film's embodiment of infinite possibility in the face of death.

By figuring subjectivity *as a space* that is filled by the presence and effect of other subjectivities, rather than as something existing *in a space* that renders its differentiation from other subjectivities, *Blue* suggests new possibilities for shaping the intersubjective encounter at the heart of the act of bearing witness. The film clearly rejects conventional means for mediating acts of bearing witness in cinema, such as the talking head or the observational mode of documentary. Jarman rejected the optical visuality that allows such conventions to generate a strong visual impression of the witness's presence in the deep space of the image. He preferred the haptic visuality that implicates the viewer's own body in the dynamics of bearing witness through an audio-visual medium like cinema. The power of the film lies in the embodied spectatorship it generates, 'in the infinite possibility becoming tangible'. The interaction of the film's visual asceticism with its acousmatic qualities enables the viewer to experience the subjectivity of the witness 'passing time' in his/her own embodied subjectivity. The intersubjective encounter in which the listener/viewer becomes a witness to the witness comes to occur within bodies rather than between them – a significant achievement in the context of the widespread stigmatisation and abjection of people with HIV/AIDS.

Author's note: This chapter benefited enormously from Frances Guerin's critical guidance. I would also like to thank my colleagues in the English Department's faculty writing group at Syracuse University for their insightful feedback on a crucial draft. I would like to express my deepest gratitude to Matthew Fee, whose loving support and savvy advice have sustained me throughout this whole book project.

the image and the witness

Notes

1   Latin translation taken from *The Concise Oxford Dictionary of Current English* (Oxford: Oxford University Press, 1990), 529.

2   Shoshana Felman and Dori Laub, *Testimony: Crises of Witnessing in Literature, Psychoanalysis, and History* (New York: Routledge, 1992), 3.

3   In *Shoah*, the viewer's relationship to the witness on the screen is complicated by two important aspects of film: Lanzmann's avowed presence both on- and off-camera during the interviews and the layers of interpreting and subtitling needed in light of the multiplicity of languages spoken by the film's subjects. Both aspects have a self-reflexive effect, not only making us more aware that we are watching an act of bearing witness, but also pushing us to contemplate the testimonial dynamics displayed on the screen.

4   Patrizio Lombardo, 'Cruellement bleu', *Critical Quarterly* 36, no. 1 (Spring 1994): 133.

5   Experimental cinema has a long tradition of 'cameraless' filmmaking, most notably the work of Stan Brakhage, Len Lye, Oskar Fischinger and Man Ray. Digital film technology has, however, now made 'cameraless' film production also prevalent in mainstream cinema.

6   William Wees, *Light Moving in Time: Studies in the Visual Aesthetics of Avant-Garde Film* (Berkeley: University of California Press, 1992), 54 (emphasis added).

7   Paul Julian Smith, 'Blue and the Outer Limits', *Sight and Sound* 3, no. 10 (October 1993): 19.

8   Chris Darke, '*Blue*', *Sight and Sound* 3, no. 10 (October 1993): 41. Darke thus connects *Blue* to structuralist filmmaking like Hollis Frampton's *Hapax Legomena II: Poetic Justice* (1972), in which filmed pages of a rudimentary script displace the responsibility of visualisation from the filmmaker onto the viewer.

9   Walter Ruttmann's 12-minute audio montage combines the sounds, speech fragments and silence of a Berlin weekend during the Weimar period.

10 Biographer Tony Peake suggests the 1974 Klein exhibit at the Tate Gallery as the probable catalyst. See Tony Peake, *Derek Jarman* (London: Little, Brown, 1999), 196.

11 By 1993, when *Blue* was first shown, Jarman had become arguably the most prominent public figure living with AIDS in the UK. I analyse the paradoxical dynamics between Jarman's deliberately performed 'AIDS stardom' and the visual iconoclasm of *Blue* in my book, *Reframing Bodies: AIDS, Bearing Witness and the Queer Moving Image* (Durham: Duke University Press, forthcoming).

12 Jarman's *Blue* reaffirms Klein's notion with the line, 'Blue transcends the solemn geography of human limits.'

13 Quoted in Sidra Stich, *Yves Klein* (Ostfildern: Cantz, 1994), 77.

14 Ibid. 78. Blue has also historically been the most tangible colour in an economic sense due to the rarity and expense of premodern blue pigments like *lapis lazuli*. Since their use in commissioned artwork constituted an act of conspicuous consumption, these pigments came to function as materialist fetishes, as much abstract as representational. Jarman imaginatively engages with this history of *lapis lazuli* in the spoken script of *Blue*. For an extensive material history of the colour blue, see Michel Pastoureau, *Blue: The History of a Color* (Princeton: Princeton University Press, 2001).

15 In his de-objectifying use of blue, Klein ironically appropriated a colour long-prized not only for its economic value, but also for its symbolic significance in Western art. Since the late Middle Ages, blue has been associated with the melancholy of the Virgin Mary. See Pastoureau, *Blue*, 49–84.

16 Stich, *Yves Klein*, 78.

17 Quoted in Peake, *Derek Jarman*, 398.

18 After a second performance in London, the event travelled internationally, but without Jarman, to generate the kind of cultural interest that would facilitate the eventual funding of the film.

19 As the two most expensive materials available to the artist in the late Middle Ages and the Renaissance, *lapis lazuli* and gold leaf were frequently combined in commissioned works

of art.

20 Jarman shared Klein's intense passion for alchemy which is present in many of his films. Peake traces the origins of Jarman's early interest in alchemy to his research on sixteenth-century alchemists which he carried out as set designer for Ken Russell's *The Devils* (1971). See Peake, *Derek Jarman*, 190–2.

21 Radio listeners were invited to send in for a blue postcard if they decided not to watch *Blue* simultaneously on television. This was perhaps a sly reference on Jarman's part to Klein's famous postcard invitations to a double show he put at the Iris Clert and Collette Allendy galleries in 1957. Although Klein painted over all the stamps with International Klein Blue, the French postal system franked and processed all the postcards.

22 The CD-ROM was to include the film along with Jarman's previously unreleased Super-8 films, materials from the live performances, video interviews with principal participants, the complete script, HIV-prevention information and a segment entitled 'the Void' which would invite participants into an interactive exploration of *Blue* where they could potentially manipulate sound and image.

23 Christian Metz, *The Imaginary Signifier: Psychoanalysis and the Cinema*, trans. Celia Britton, Annwyl Williams, Ben Brewster and Alfred Guzzetti (Bloomington: Indiana University Press, 1982), 43.

24 Simon Watney, 'The Spectacle of AIDS', in *AIDS: Cultural Analysis/Cultural Activism*, ed. Douglas Crimp (Cambridge, MA: MIT Press, 1998), 78.

25 Peter Schwenger, 'Derek Jarman and the Colour of the Mind's Eye', *University of Toronto Quarterly* 65, no. 2 (Spring 1996): 421.

26 Although the history of experimental cinema has produced key champions of sound, including Dziga Vertov, Hollis Frampton and Michael Snow, it has been largely dominated until quite recently by filmmakers who have been dedicated to what Melissa Ragona dubs 'the phenomenal purity of visual experience'. See her article, 'Hidden Noise: Strategies of Sound Montage in the Films of Hollis Frampton', *October* 109 (Summer 2004): 96–118.

27 Michel Chion, *The Voice in Cinema*, trans. Claudia Gorbman (New York: Columbia University Press, 1999), 3.

28 Although it is grounded in the consideration of narrative cinema, Chion's theorisation of film sound remains pertinent for analysing experimental film since the history of the latter cannot be understood outside of its dialectical relationship to narrative film, which, as the dominant mode of cinema, has historically shaped the habits and assumptions of film spectatorship.

29 This ambiguous perceptual status of the blue screen has also led me to avoid using the term 'voice-over' to describe the spoken script in *Blue*. A voice-over implies a phenomenological separation from the spatio-temporality figured on the screen, *over* which it may speak. This applies to narrative, documentary and even much experimental cinema. Such conventional relations between sound and image are deliberately absent from *Blue*.

30 Chion uses the example of Fritz Lang's Dr Mabuse in *Das Testament des Dr. Mabuse* (*The Testament of Dr Mabuse*, 1932) who is the voice of an absent, yet omniscient body, ultimately revealed to be no more than a microphone behind a screen. In this way, Mabuse is literally a metaphor for cinema. See Chion, *The Voice in Cinema*, 17–29.

31 Ibid., 23.

32 Ibid., 27.

33 John Paul Ricco, *The Logic of the Lure* (Chicago: University of Chicago Press, 2002), 47.

34 This refusal is at the heart of what Ricco calls 'a disappeared aesthetics' in *Blue*, which 'visualizes nothing but a potentiality or a preference to not-visualize, and thereby points to the ethical-political dimensions of visuality itself'. Ibid., 42.

35 Chion, *The Voice in Cinema*, 51.

36 *Live Blue Roma (The Archaeology of Sound)*, Mute Records, 1995.

37 Chion, *The Voice in Cinema*, 53.

38 Watney, 'The Spectacle of AIDS', 72.

39 Smith, 'Blue and the Outer Limits', 19.

40 In this sense, watching *Blue* mirrors the experience of encountering one of James Turrell's light installations. See Frances Richard, 'James Turrell and the Nonvicarious Sublime', in *On the Sublime: Mark Rothko, Yves Klein and James Turrell* (Berlin: Deutsche Guggenheim, 2001), 87–103.

41 Laura U. Marks, *The Skin of the Film: Intercultural Cinema, Embodiment, and the Senses* (Durham: Duke University Press, 2000), 162.

42 Marks explains the concept of 'intercultural cinema' in the following terms: '"Intercultural" means that a work is not the property of one culture, but mediates in at least two directions. It accounts for the encounter between different cultural organisations of knowledge, which is one of the sources of intercultural cinema's synthesis of new forms of expression and new kinds of knowledge' (*The Skin of the Film*, 7).

43 Ibid., 162–3.

44 Ibid., 163.

45 Schwenger, 'Colour of the Mind's Eye', 420.

46 Marks discusses synesthesia as another significant dynamic in intercultural cinema. See Marks, *The Skin of the Film*, 213.

47 I have transcribed these words from the film since the published film script omits the whispered refrain of names from this section of the script.

48 The trope of 'walking out of life' recurs several times in the script.

3. Symbolic Bodies, Real Pain: Post-Soviet History, Boris Mikhailov and the Impasse of Documentary Photography

Matthias Christen

The act of tearing down and dismantling statues of political leaders marks a turning point in history, one which most often proves to be final for the power represented by the monument. Since the desecrated bodies are mere effigies, their dismember-ment, however violent, will hardly be liable to have traumatic effects, except per-haps on those who firmly believed in whatever the inanimate bulk of stone or iron represented. Rebels and conquerors alike are desperate for pictures of this kind of destructive act precisely for their symbolic potency. Images of shattered statues and paintings torn apart provide relief after a long period of oppression and testify to the superiority of the new power over the old, which is no longer in a position to protect its symbols from the power of its enemies. This is why the US military brought in an armoured recovery vehicle to help insurgent Iraqis topple a monumental statue of Saddam Hussein in the centre of Baghdad during the second Iraq War, while the dictator himself continued to elude their urgent attempts to seize him in person.[1]

Falling statues are an alluring subject matter for even the most impartial photog-rapher. They allow the photographer to condense a complex historical process, the outcome and causes of which cannot yet be assessed, into a comprehensible visual emblem the meaning of which seems available for anyone to see. The symbolic power of such photographs is so overwhelming that they do not actually have to depict real historical events at all. Thus, Magnum photographer Josef Koudelka's image of a gigantic dismembered statute of Lenin peacefully floating down the Dan-ube river became an emblem for the waning of Soviet communism. Its emblematic status arose despite the fact that the picture was taken as part of a documentary on the making of *Ulysses' Gaze* (1994), a fictional feature film about the Balkans by the Greek director Theo Angelopoulos.[2]

Photographs such as Koudelka's are likely to recall the crucial role played by symbolic bodies in the public representation and maintenance of power in the Soviet Union, as in any other totalitarian regime.[3] For well over two decades, Ukrainian photographer Boris Mikhailov (born 1938) commented critically on what he called the Soviet 'experiment' and the imagery it produced before he went on to document its final failure in the early 1990s. In the preface to *By the Ground*, the first of several series of photographs originating during the 1990s, Mikhailov states: 'In view of the fact that we are at a turning point in history, I decided to make a documentary of the situation.'[4] Unlike many news photographers, Mikhailov in his own documentary work never relies on symbolic images such as those described. In *Case History*, his most controversial book to date, which represents the downfall of the former Soviet empire, Mikhailov instead investigates the overall historical changes on a personal, almost private level.[5] In a series of more than four hundred colour photographs, he portrays homeless people in the streets of his hometown Kharkov and the truly miserable conditions in which they live. By its title alone, the book indicates an understanding of history quite contrary to the one reified in symbolic monuments. Accordingly, history as documented by Mikhailov is less a single, abstract process than a wealth of individual destinies, however typical they may be within a broader context.[6] It is less what people do than what they suffer, and above all, it is not about inanimate symbolic bodies, but rather, about sentient real bodies.

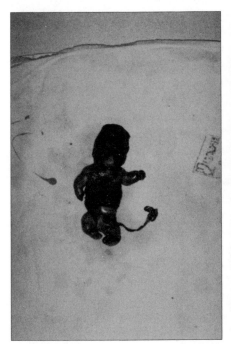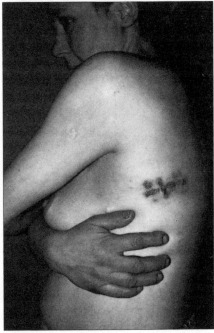

Figure 1: Boris Mikhailov, *Case History* (Zurich and New York: Scalo, 1999), 404/405. Courtesy of the artist/ Scalo Verlag.

The homeless people portrayed by Mikhailov experience history, or to be more specific, the downfall of the Soviet Union, as a trauma in that it physically endangers their lives, and is beyond what they can cope with. In Mikhailov's photography, the consequences of the empire's demise are made visible on the bodies of his subjects. As in the Greek etymology of the word, trauma appears in these images precisely as a physical wound. In keeping with the clinical meaning of its title, *Case History* displays an almost encyclopaedic array of pathological disfigurations: smashed skulls, swollen bellies, teeth rotting away, infected genitals, limbs covered with scars, scabs and all manner of dermatological diseases. On what is perhaps the book's most unsettling double-page, Mikhailov induces the twinned sights of a badly stitched, discoloured scar on a female's back and an aborted foetus (figure 1). According to the clinical definition, traumas cause, above all, severe psychological disorders such as anxieties or involuntary memories.[7] However, in Mikhailov's *Case History* everything is turned inside out. Whatever psychopathological effects it may have, the traumatic experience of homeless people in Kharkov affects their bodies first of all. At least this is what the photographer gets to see through the lens of his camera. To Mikhailov, the sick body is the site where the memory of a traumatic history materialises.

In as much as Mikhailov represents the historical process of the Soviet Union's decay in the physical ruin of its former subjects, there is also a symbolic moment to his pictures. This becomes even more apparent when on rare occasion emblems of the bygone power emerge, such as in the portrait of a middle aged man who has Lenin's stylised features tattooed on his chest (figure 2). There is an undercurrent of tension between the private, almost intimate setting within which the photograph has been taken – the man seems to be at home as he sits on a bed and reveals himself naked to the camera – and the political world, represented by the emblematic tattoo. The emblem of the old political power is indelibly fixed on the subject's skin, and thus continues to interfere with his private life. Even though it has passed away quite some time ago, this power continues to assert its hold on the living. The obvious discrepancy between Lenin's determined look and the man's rather poor physical condition – his eyes heavy from drinking too much alcohol, his penis studded with ulcers – engenders in the photograph's observer the sentiment that a once mighty power has collapsed once and for all. Yet, unlike in the more popular type of photojournalism depicting dismembered statues, the effigy of the political leader on the chest is inseparable from the subject's private

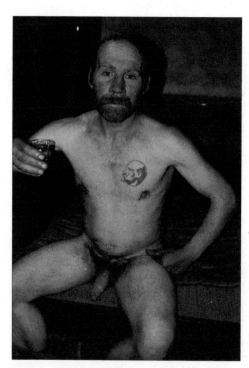

Figure 2: Boris Mikhailov, *Case History* (Zurich and New York: Scalo, 1999), 242. Courtesy of the artist/Scalo Verlag.

the image and the witness

destiny: as a tattoo it forms an almost organic part of the man's body. It is a real living body, not a mere symbolic one, which in this particular instance, experiences what such massive historical change entails. Whereas Lenin's image, on the contrary, seems to be unaffected by what the man has gone through since he had it tattooed on his chest, no doubt under more favourable circumstances. Thus, while looking at the photograph, we cannot contemplate the emblematic head of Lenin and what has become of his political legacy without simultaneously noticing that the subject's penis is badly infected. Whatever symbolic value Mikhailov's picture may bear, due to the iconic character of photography, there is no way around acknowledging that the individual portrayed is physically suffering from what has happened in the aftermath of the empire's demise. There is no doubt that he is seriously ill like so many other models in *Case History*.[8]

In order to enhance the strange physical quality of his pictures, Mikhailov repeatedly asked his homeless models to undress and pose naked in front of the camera. Nakedness has played a crucial role in Mikhailov's work ever since the late 1960s. It was a key part of a photographic aesthetic which privileged the individual and his or her private longings over the political system and its ideological constraints. The larger part of Mikhailov's photographic work during this time focused on Soviet citizens' private lives, their homes and leisure activities, such as dancing, sports or family trips to the beach.[9] In this context, nakedness amounted to a privacy which managed to elude political control. Thus, depicting nudity assumed a subversive character, especially since pictures of naked bodies were banned by the political authorities from public display and from all official distribution. Mikhailov himself became a victim of legal restraints imposed on what was officially considered pornography. When nude photographs of his wife were found in his home by the Soviet secret service, Mikhailov lost his job as an engineer with a Kharkov-based camera factory.[10]

Aside from the law on so-called pornography, there existed similar ones on 'spying activity' and 'biased collecting of information'. These laws prohibited photographers to take pictures 'from higher than the second floor, the areas of railways, stations, military objects, at enterprises, near enterprises, at any organisation, without special permission', as well as 'photos which brought into disrepute the Soviet power, the Soviet way of life'.[11] Governmental prohibitions such as these considerably restricted photographic practice in public as well as private life. Significantly, they also resulted in a lack of visual evidence for vast stretches of Soviet history. Thus, as Mikhailov points out in the preface to *Case History*, one of the worst periods of Ukrainian history, the great famine in the 1930s which claimed millions of casualties, went largely undocumented. One of Mikhailov's primary reasons to document the lives of the homeless was the prevention of such loss of visual memory.[12] The role of nakedness within Mikhailov's oeuvre, however, changes along with the larger historical circumstances. In contrast to the beautiful sensual bodies in the artist's earlier pictures from the Soviet period, in *Case History*, the models' bodies, which have been disfigured by illness and violence, testify to the misery endured since the downfall of the Soviet Union. While up to the 1980s, nakedness betokened a privacy that evaded control by the contemporaneous political system, it now proves that, in its demise, this system finally managed to penetrate the privacy of some of its most vulnerable former subjects. With all their bruises exposed, the homeless bodies in *Case History* become bodies of evidence by which an essentially traumatic history gains an almost palpable presence. To Mikhailov, showing his models naked is the ultimate photographic means to authenticate physically their position as victims of the social disaster which ensued after the fall of Soviet communism.

When the book was published in 1999 its representation of nakedness triggered animated discussion on how far photographers should be allowed to go in depicting human misery.[13] The fact that Mikhailov made his models undress seemed to expose them to a situation even more shameful than the one they already find themselves in as homeless people. Criticism grew even fiercer when Mikhailov, who claims to have worked in a 'documentary' way, declared that he paid his models to pose naked in front of the camera and that most of them were not in a position to turn down his offer.[14] This avowal seemed to confirm age-old suspicions, voiced repeatedly since the 1970s by critics such as Susan Sontag, Martha Rosler and Allan Sekula, in a major debate on documentary photography and its capacity to bear witness.[15] In taking pictures of less fortunate people, these critics contended, photographers most often did nothing other than double the victimisation that their subjects had already suffered. And instead of trying to improve the situation by drawing the public's attention to other people's misery they had merely exploited their suffering, whether for professional ambition, profit or bare curiosity.[16] Within this critical frame of reference, paying poor people for photographs of their naked bodies, as Mikhailov does, amounts to exploitation, if not pornography or prostitution. Moreover, both of these phenomena are linked to the deteriorating economic conditions in former Communist countries.

While these arguments touched on the photographer's moral integrity, others aimed at the different ways that images were circulated and received. According to the critics, whatever the photographer's intentions, the pictures tend to lose political poignancy and moral value as the distance between their subjects and recipients grows in time and space. A viewer who is familiar with the subject's social world, and who may even know him or her personally, might easily be moved to help. Yet, to a more distant observer, the person depicted may as well be a mere symbol, a symbol which stands for an abstract and remote malaise. The more symbolic a body becomes, the more it is dissociated from the individual and the personal fate 'behind' the image. Bodies of flesh and blood turn into purely symbolic figures. For the historically and geographically distant viewer, the two become interchangeable.[17]

The various forms of image exhibition and distribution are often liable to widen that gap. When images are shown in galleries or museums, aesthetic aspects easily prevail over the depicted subject matter. The gallery visitor's attention might shift from the subject of a picture to its author. Instead of compassion, the images instil admiration for the photographer's artistic dexterity, especially when there is no personal or cultural bond between subject and viewer. Critics such as Rosler or Abigail Solomon-Godeau fear that the processes of mass media distribution also stymie the personal involvement of the documentary viewer. For the more images compete for the public's attention, the more likely they are to turn into spectacular sights. As honest as the photographer's intentions may have been, his pictures end up serving the curiosity of a mass-media audience, less and less able to cope with the surfeit of photographic images. This situation has led to what French critic Luc Boltanksi calls a 'crisis of pity'.[18] Consequently, the spectator of documentary photography has also become an object of critical concern over the last few years. In an essay entitled 'Regarding the Pain of Others', Susan Sontag imputes to the viewer an innate 'tropism' toward 'regarding the pain of others'.[19] For Sontag, this tropism perfectly matches the photographer's inclination to exploit the misery of his subjects.

The discussions regarding the problems of documentary photography reached their most profound level when focused on the photographic apparatus itself.[20] According to the modern monocular system of a single-point vanishing perspective, the camera technically rearranges reality. Doing this, as Solomon-Godeau states, the camera assigns a 'position of visual mastery' to the spectator rather than the powerless subjects depicted. This imbalance of power inevitably results in a 'complicity of representational structures in a variety of ideological formations that will always impose a point of view independent of the personal politics of a photographer and the particular intention of the work'.[21]

All of these doubts regarding documentary photography eventually converge into one: documentary testifies to almost everything. To the moral flaws of its authors as well as their artistry, to the spectators' voyeurism and even to the delusive ideological power of the photographic medium. In short, the documentary photograph testifies to everything other than what it actually depicts. Whatever happens in front of the camera, the photograph cannot be accepted as a reliable witness. As radical as this critique may be, it must be accepted that professional photographers take a highly precarious stance as 'secondary' witnesses towards human tragedies. The photographic subject is not in a position to bear witness through documenting her own fate. This inability is part of her status as a victim. The homeless of Kharkov, for instance, are not only lacking the necessary technical means to take their own photographs, let alone the distribution systems to make them publicly accessible. They are kept busy meeting more urgent needs such as acquiring food, clothing and shelter. To these homeless people, discursive contexts which would allow them to bear witness in a more self-determined way through legal, therapeutic and cultural means are almost completely foreclosed. The only chance they have to testify is through their bodies.

In contrast, photographers such as Mikhailov have all the technical means they need at their disposal. The photographer as intermediary establishes the relation to an audience that is essential to the process of bearing witness. Without the photographer as intermediary there would probably be no testimony. Yet it is unusual for the photographer to experience personally what his subjects went through. Moreover, he no doubt makes them feel even more uncomfortable when taking their photograph, and thus victimising them once again. Therefore, even if one does not subscribe to the radical critique of Rosler and others, a basic 'moral paradox' which bears heavily on the photographic practice must be acknowledged.[22] In order to take pictures and to solicit the public's attention and compassion, photographers usually have to intrude into their subjects' private lives. Photographers do them wrong while hoping that the images will eventually turn out to be in the subjects' interest. Though morally highly-charged, the photographer's work aims to bring about some sort of relief to their subjects, and ultimately to put an end to the misery depicted by bringing it to the attention of an unknowing audience. In Christian Frei's documentary portrait *War Photographer* (2001), Magnum photographer James Nachtwey reports a situation typical of the kind of moral dilemma in which news photographers have frequently found themselves. During the Balkan wars, Nachtwey repeatedly documented how family members buried relatives who had fallen victim to the war. He did so even though he was well aware of the fact that funerals are commonly considered a private event, an event to which no strangers, and certainly no photographers, are given access. Pictures of the kind Nachtwey took at funerals during war time would hardly cause the intended effect to stir the viewer's compassion if it were made salient that the people depicted were somehow disturbed by the photographer's presence. Thus, whatever reminds the spectator of the photographer's intrusive professional behaviour is usually avoided or concealed deliberately, be it on site by the photographer himself or during the subsequent process of editing. This maintains a mutual agreement between photographer and spectator that images, like windows, grant an unmediated view on what is going on 'out there'.[23] People gesturing at the photographer or staring at the camera would inevitably spoil the illusion. Thus, they are usually pictured as completely absorbed by the situation and the emotions they are experiencing.

While the critique of documentary photography starting in the 1970s never really managed to reform photographic practice thoroughly, it nevertheless set standards by which documentary work is still discussed and judged. According to these standards, paying for pictures and staging scenes, as Mikhailov has done for *Case History*, undoubtedly qualifies as an ultimate threat to the images' testimonial value, as well as to the photographer's moral credibility. That Mikhailov claims to have worked in a documentary, almost journalistic manner notwithstanding, the outcome in this respect seems to be less documentary than an assault on documentary photography, its taboos and its ethical standards.

Parallel to this ongoing theoretical debate, photographers such as Rosler and Sekula have tried since the 1970s to reform classical documentary practice. They developed 'a number of mediating (or distancing) strategies, or discursive devices (juxtapositions, textual anchorage, dialogical modes, serialised imagery, appropriation, pastiche, hiding oneself in the studio, changing profession)' in order 'to mark conscious distance to the idea of photographic transparency'.[24] Mikhailov follows however a contrary strategy in *Case History*. While the work of photographers such as Rosler were dedicated to creating an appropriate relationship between image and subject, rather than emphasising the emotional impact pictures have on their viewers, the images gathered in *Case History* directly assault the onlookers' sensitivity. They do this by bringing the viewer face to face with the misery of the photographic subject in the most seemingly unmediated of ways. Mikhailov's photographs are consciously aimed at provoking disgust and repulsion. Due to the viscerality of these two emotional responses, the viewer achieves an emotional recognition of the physical suffering of the sitter from afar. Instead of building up a distance between the sitter and the viewer by mediating aesthetic devices, Mikhailov violently overcomes whatever barriers the viewer might have erected in an attempt to ward off distressing experiences and protect her psychological balance. Indeed, the naked, violated bodies in *Case History* display something bewildering, even repulsive. Most often, Mikhailov does not portray his models completely naked. He has them just lower their pants so that their dirty underwear is still visible, as in the portrait of a half-undressed couple leaning on a birch (figure 3).[25] The images thus recall scenes from police raids or from war where people's pants are stripped down in order to render them totally defenceless and to break all resistance through humiliation. In the couple's portrait, the setting is likewise shaming and degrading, a fact that is acknowledged by the man's embarrassed look.

Through this deliberate exposure of his models to a humiliating gaze, Mikhailov assigns an awkward position to the viewer. The unease stirred up by these photographs is further underlined by the fact that the majority of viewers will most certainly live under far better conditions than the subjects of these photographs. Unlike Mikhailov's pictures dating from the Soviet period, these photographs are

Figure 3: Boris Mikhailov, *Case History* (Zurich and New York: Scalo, 1999), 193. Courtesy of the artist/Scalo Verlag.

no longer intended to be shown in private circles alone, among the photographer's friends and fellow artists, the forums for 'unofficial photography' during the Soviet era.[26] *Case History* is published by Scalo, an international art publisher based in Zurich and New York, and the works have been exhibited by major European and Northern American galleries and museums. Thus, the images of *Case History* address the much broader audience of the international book and art market.

When Mikhailov started his documentation of the Soviet Union's final collapse in the early 1990s, there were already clear signs of the degree of decline still to

Figure 4: Boris Mikhailov, *By the Ground* (Cologne: Oktagon Verlag, 1999), unpaged. Courtesy of the artist.

come in the streets of Kharkov.[27] Yet, as captured in the format of the panoramic camera which Mikhailov was using at the time, the first victims of economic change still remained part of a broader social world with its daily routines still functioning (figure 4). The slumped, most probably drunk man to the right is physically supported by the bold pillar which, together with its counterpart on the left, is framing the scenery. Even though the subjects were vulnerable to their social circumstances, they appeared to be cushioned by the images' aesthetic composition. A brownish tint added to the originally black and white prints in *By the Ground* contributes to the sense of historical remoteness which is instilled by the large panoramic format. Thus, Mikhailov's documentary of post-Soviet life in its early stages is more about a period of Eastern European history already gone than it is about life in the aftermath of socialism's demise.[28]

Case History, on the contrary, allows no such aloofness on the part of its on-looker. In terms of photographic genres, *Case History* introduces a transition from land- and cityscapes to portraits. Mikhailov moves close to his subjects, singles out individuals or small groups, and more often than not he has them look directly into his camera. While in the previous series, the citizens of Kharkov faded into their urban surroundings, the homeless now address the viewer directly. Brought into the foreground, the subjects' faces and bodies engage the audience on a more personal level and elicit a strong empathic response. This is achieved through involuntarily evolving processes such as affective mimicry, facial feedback and emotional con-tagion.[29] In addition, the film stock brings out in full colour whatever marks their lives have inflicted on their bodies.[30] In *By the Ground* (1996) and *At Dusk* (1996), Mikhailov's two previous books dedicated to post-Soviet street life in Kharkov, the toning, alongside the pictures' obvious technical flaws such as scratches, blotches, and fluffs occasionally blur the view of what happened in front of the camera. These material flaws helped mitigate the emotional impact of the images. However, the im-ages in *Case History* are processed and printed in a technically perfect way. Thus, lit-erally everything lies open to close scrutiny. Quite often, Mikhailov photographs the same person again and again, zooming in from a master-shot to particularly horrific pathological details, using a flash whenever necessary. The high technical standards as well as the transparency this enables make these images even more paradoxical, since these technical possibilities are part of an economic progress which reached Mikhailov's hometown after the collapse of socialism and, indeed, doomed many of its inhabitants to their brutal poverty.[31]

While *Case History* invokes the idea of photographic transparency through its aesthetic choices, the fact that many of the pictures are apparently staged seems at first rather contradictory. This is particularly so because nothing is done to hide that the models are posing. On the contrary, Mikhailov occasionally has them sing and dance in front of the camera, thereby underlining the theatricality of their poses. This heightening to outright theatricality serves first of all to point out the tension that always exists in documentary photography between topicality and its aesthetic aspects. In *Case History* there is, however, no need to fear what most concerns critics of documentary photography: that the pictures' referentiality and whatever the photographer originally wanted to achieve is lost once they are perceived as aesthetic artefacts. As for the woman offering an apple to a man (see figure 3), one cannot help but see haggard bodies, food and dirty underwear rather than a well-arranged scene representing Man's Fall under the primordial tree of knowledge.[32] With every new role or pose Mikhailov makes his subjects adopt, it becomes clearer that the usual distinction between actor and role, and the concomitant comfort of this distinction for the viewer, is erased. Thus, the viewer is robbed of another possibility to establish a distance between herself and the subject of the pictures when she looks at them as mere art works or as skilfully composed photographs.

The impact of the individual picture on its viewer, based as it is on the subject matter and aesthetic, is consciously intensified by Mikhailov's choice to publish his works in book form. Although the viewership for a photographic book is far fewer than that of other kinds of mass media, such as newspapers, magazines or even television, books do usually grant their authors more freedom to present a greater number of pictures and to have more control over the selection and editing of images. Unlike newspapers and magazines, there is no additional material to divert the viewer's attention. Topic and style notwithstanding, *Case History* will leave a lasting impression on its reader due to the sheer number of images. The book gathers more than 450 photographs in as many pages. The sequence of the images resonates with how post-traumatic stress disorders evolve and affect victims' memory. Simulating the repetitive haunting experienced in post-traumatic stress disorder, the viewers of *Case History* are denied the opportunity to pass over and subsequently forget what has aggressively confronted them on the page. While in more ephemeral media,

Figure 5: Boris Mikhailov, *Case History* (Zurich and New York: Scalo, 1999), 465. Courtesy of the artist/Scalo Verlag.

images of disaster usually engage the audience's attention only for a short period of time before their subjects recede into anonymity and vanish, Mikhailov's models appear repeatedly throughout the book, sometimes separated from the first instance by dozens of pages.[33] Their reappearance signals the passing of historical time such that the social circumstances will have worsened in the space between the pages of *Case History*. A young woman, for instance, who is first portrayed naked in a private room that suggests she is making her living as a prostitute, returns towards the end of the book, where she is seen undressing in a snowy landscape (figure 5). The woman has obviously lost her home since she was last photographed. In other words, *Case History* is not only about the trauma suffered by its subjects in the wake of the Soviet Union's demise, but the book also consciously tries to convey a kind of assaultive, traumatising experience itself. Just as the homeless have involuntarily come to testify for the decline of post-Soviet society, Mikhailov's book makes its viewer a forced witness by assaulting him again and again, willing or not, with the most atrocious sights.[34]

While the viewer grows more compassionate and increasingly attached to the models' personal history each time they reappear, he inevitably ends up in an emotional dilemma because photographs such as the one of the young woman also instil a feeling of unease. The viewer cannot help but ask: for whom else should she expose her naked body, despite the bitter cold, in an open and unprotected space, if not for an onlooker? The viewer may not be responsible for what happened to the people depicted by the photograph. Yet it is for the viewer that the model undergoes the humiliating process of undressing and exposing her naked body stained by illness, violence, poverty and age. The theatrical set-up leaves the viewer with no choice but to regard himself the addressee of whatever he sees. Mikhailov renounces the mutual agreement between viewer and photographer so typical of documentary photography when he deliberately brings to the fore the role played by both parties in photography as a communicative act. Directly addressed as they are by the theatrical set-up, the photograph's viewers are no longer allowed to consider the events in the image as happening somewhere 'out there', irrespective of whether anyone is watching. Whatever the spectators of conventional documentary representation happen to witness from their emblematic window onto the world, they may ease themselves by the thought that it is not set up on their behalf, that nobody is hurt just because they are watching. Their status as witnesses therefore always remains somewhat accidental. In *Case History*, however, the photographs were obviously taken for no other reason than to be seen. In addition to the suffering caused by economic malaise, Mikhailov's models undergo a good deal of humiliation precisely because they are photographed.

Mikhailov is no less clear however about his own stance as a photographer. He occasionally makes the unusual move of presenting himself before the camera, to become a subject of the photograph himself.[35] He not only poses naked in front of the camera as his models do. In a very awkward turn, a picture actually shows him at work in an ethically ambiguous gesture, intruding into the private sphere of one of his models (figure 6). The image depicts the photographer aiming his camera at the crutch of a young woman who is posing half naked in front of him with her pants lowered. Mikhailov's making himself visible does not serve to reduce the gap between model and photographer. Instead, it stresses the transaction-

Figure 6: Boris Mikhailov, *Case History* (Zurich and New York: Scalo, 1999), 421. Courtesy of the artist/Scalo Verlag.

the image and the witness

al aspect at the core of documentary photographic practice, with its trespassing and constant negotiation between unequal partners. Emphasising the photographic economy, Mikhailov addresses the viewer as an integral part of this morally ambiguous process. So, whatever emotional response the pictures solicit, there is an inevitable sense of ethical malaise instilled in the viewer.

Mikhailov's long experience of image manipulation at the hands of political authorities caused him, in contrast to many Western documentary photographers, to never really trust in images as true and 'innocent' documents. Yet, however ambivalent Mikhailov may be about the practice of documentary photography and its shortcomings, in *Case History* he never goes so far as to doubt the general ability of photographic images to bear witness. As strongly conceptual as *Case History* may be in its status as a visual treatise on the impasse of documentary photography, the book nevertheless relies heavily on the 'transparency' of its pictures. The strong emotional impact on the viewer is achieved precisely because of the indexical relation the images have with their subjects. Every emotional response the photographs provoke – be it shock, disgust or compassion – is tied up with the viewer's belief that it is real people who are shown, just as the pain is real. Similarly, the viewer is not under the delusion that the models in these photographs can simply slip back into a more comfortable life after having been photographed. This is why Mikhailov is so obsessed with homeless bodies and their decay throughout *Case History*.

The dismembered statue of Lenin, which is peacefully floating down the Danube in Josef Koudelka's photograph, may ultimately convey a similar message. Like Koudelka's statue, the bodies in Mikhailov's images represent a once strong body politic that has fallen into a state of disintegration. In *Case History* however, this process makes itself felt through the living, sentient bodies of those people who have suffered through such political disintegration. It thus elicits spectator empathy in a way that merely symbolic bodies never would be able to. The contentious fact that the pictures are set up does not abolish their testimonial value. Instead, the model's wilful posing brings out the ways that images are produced and received in the exchange between subject, photographer and audience, all with their own conflicting interests. Within this setting, bearing witness is no longer just a question of images and their veridical reliability. It is a highly-mediated process which entails hardships and irresolvable ethical problems on every level. Mikhailov's insistence on photography's operational aspects belongs to the book's most disturbing and shocking features, for there have been pictures of comparably gruesome content in the history of documentary photography that have not provoked a similar critical outrage.

Mikhailov's photographs are wont to cause traumatic effects due to their constant denial of the viewer's agency to assert a protective psychological distance between herself and the subject of the photograph – to merely stand behind the window and watch. Moreover, these images stir feelings of shame and guilt due to their aesthetic construction. Through these strategies, *Case History* ultimately aims for the single goal of anchoring history in the viewer's vivid memory. Mikhailov's *Case History* is not about the dead monuments of a reified history, indeed, it is not even really about photographic images. Above all, the book is about people who suffer and those who have the responsibility to remember that by every means possible.

Notes

1 Typical of the entwinement of symbols and power, one of the major collections of pictures documenting the iconoclastic rage of Iraqis can be found on a website which is financially supported by manufacturers of US flags and flagpoles: Online. Available <http://kholamon.tripod.com/sh/saddam2.html> (accessed 22 August 2003).

2 See Josef Koudelka, *Periplanissis: Following Ulysses' Gaze* (Thessaloniki: Organisation for the Cultural Capital of Europe Thessaloniki, 1996) and *Magnum Degrees* (London: Phaidon, 2000), 4–5.

3 See similar images by Magnum photographers Gueorgui Pinkhassov and Ferdinando Scianna in *Magnum Degrees*, 71 and 92–3.

4 Boris Mikhailov, *By the Ground* (Cologne: Oktagon Verlag, 1996), 7.

5 Boris Mikhailov, *Case History* (Zurich and New York: Scalo, 1999). The pictures were shot during 1997 and 1998, a time when, as Mikhailov puts it, 'devastation had stopped', but alongside the wealthy, a second hitherto unknown class had emerged: the homeless (see Mikhailov, *Case History*, 4).

6 See the definition of 'case history' in *Webster's Third New International Dictionary*: '1. a record of an individual's personal and family history and environment for use in analyzing his cause or as an instructive illustration of a type.'

7 See Scott R. Vrana, 'Post-traumatic Stress', in *International Encyclopedia of Psychology*, vol. III, eds Frank Northen Magill, Jaclyn Rodriguez and Lindsey Turner (London, Chicago: Fitzroy Dearborn Publishers, 1996), 1258–61; and *Development and Psychopathology* 10, 4 (Fall 1998), special issue 'Risk, Trauma, and Memory'.

8 Several of them reportedly died within two months after he had begun his work on the series. See Mikhailov's statement in *Case History*, 36.

9 See the so-called 'Private Series', part of which is published in *Boris Michajlov*, ed. Brigitte Kölle (Stuttgart: Oktagon, 1995), 41–7; the series 'Dance', shot in Kharkov and Moscow in 1978 (published in *Boris Mikhailov: The Hasselblad Award 2000* (Goteborg and Zurich: Hasselblad Center, and Scalo, 2000)), and 'Salt Lake', dating from the mid-1990s (Gottingen: Steidl and Pace/MacGill Gallery, 2002). See as well Mikhailov's statements in *Äussere Ruhe* (Dusseldorf: Richter Verlag, 2000), 82–3; and *Case History*, 7.

10 'The Aesthetic of Imperfect Knowledge: Brigitte Kölle in Conversation with Boris Mikhaylov', in Kölle, *Boris Michajlov* 17, and Gilda Williams, *Boris Mikhailov* 55 (London: Phaidon, 2001), 6–7.

11 Mikhailov, *Case History*, 7.

12 Ibid., 6–7.

13 See the audience response reported by Anne von der Heiden and Inka Schube in the catalogue to the major retrospective dedicated to Mikhailov's work by the Fotomuseum Winterthur in Switzerland: Urs Stahel (ed.), *Boris Mikhailov: A Retrospective/eine Retrospektive* (Zurich: Scalo, 2003), 154–7 and 170–2.

14 See Mikhailov's preface to *Case History*.

15 Susan Sontag, *On Photography* (New York: Dell Publishing, 1977); Martha Rosler, 'In, Around, and Afterthoughts (On Documentary Photography)', originally published in 1981, reprinted in *The Contest of Meaning*, ed. Richard Bolton (Cambridge, MA: MIT Press, 1989), 303–41; Allan Sekula, 'Dismantling Modernism: Reinventing Documentary', (1978), reprinted in Allan Sekula, *Photography Against the Grain* (Halifax: The Press of Nova Scotia College of Art and Design, 1985), 53–76; and Abigail Solomon-Godeau, 'Who Is Speaking Thus? Some Questions about Documentary Photography', in Abigail Solomon-Godeau, *Photography at the Dock: Essays on Photographic History, Institutions, and Practices* (Minneapolis: University of Minnesota Press, 1994), 169–83, 299–302.

16 For the history of documentary photography and its reformist agenda see Solomon-Godeau, *Photography at the Dock*.

17 Dorothea Lange's famous 'Migrant Mother' in this respect became an archetype: while the model's social and economic conditions hardly improved over the years, her image became

a photographic icon applied to different purposes in all sorts of contexts.

18 Luc Boltanksi, *Distant Suffering: Morality, Media and Politics* (Cambridge: Cambridge University Press, 1999), xvi.

19 Susan Sontag, *Regarding the Pain of Others* (New York: Farrar, Strauss, and Giroux, 2003), 97.

20 See Solomon-Godeau, *Photography at the Dock*, 180–2.

21 Ibid., 182.

22 Max Kozloff, 'Photojournalism and Malaise', (1985) in Max Kozloff, *Lone Visions, Crowded Frames: Essays on Photography* (Albuquerque: University of New Mexico Press, 1994), 160–9.

23 The highly influential metaphor has been coined by MoMA's late curator of photography John Szarkowski in his seminal essay *Mirrors and Windows: American Photography since 1960* (New York: The Museum of Modern Art, 1978).

24 See Jan-Erik Lundström, 'Real Stories', in the catalogue to the eponymous exhibition *Real Stories: Revisions in Documentary and Narrative Photography* (Odense: Museet for Fotokunst and Forlaget Brandts Klædefabrik, 1993), 2–10, 7–8

25 See *Case History*, 14, 31, 101, 190–3, 254–6, 361–3, 421, 465.

26 On how 'unofficial' photography was being circulated in the Soviet Union, see Ekatarina Degot, 'Unfinished Dissertation: Phenomenology of Socialism', in *Mikhailov: A Retrospective*, 102–5, as well as Diane Neumaier (ed.), *Beyond Memory: Soviet Nonconformist Photography and Photo-Related Works of Art* (New Brunswick: Rutgers University Press, 2004).

27 See *By the Ground* (1991; published 1996) and *At Dusk* (1994) (Köln: Oktagon Verlag, 1996).

28 See *By the Ground*, 7: 'My method of embedding a series of photos in layers of time, i.e. triggering parallel, photohistorical associations, makes the viewer feel that my compatriots are now simultaneously living in different, past times … The brown-colouring is also of "nostalgic" origin, and is also related to the depth of memories.'

29 Over the last years, cognitive studies have added a great deal to the understanding of how the optical distance between viewer and subject affects the former's emotional response to the image. See Carl Plantinga, 'The Scene of Empathy and the Human Face on Film', in *Passionate Views: Film, Cognition, and Emotion*, eds Carl Plantinga and Greg M. Smith (Baltimore: Johns Hopkins University Press, 1999). Although Plantinga's findings refer to fiction films, they hold true to a good extent for documentary photography as well.

30 Due to its ideological connotations, colour has always played a significant role in Mikhailov's work, even when the photographs were originally made on black and white stock. Adding colour to black and white pictures by tinting them partially or totally was a way of appropriating a public space by artistic means which otherwise was perceived as grey or dominated by the (different) range of colours, mainly red, used by the regime to display its ubiquitous power. See *Äussere Ruhe*, esp. 8, 50, 70–1 and the so-called 'Red' series (1968–75) of which different parts are published in *Mikhailov: A Retrospective*, 32–41, and in Kölle, 27–39. Having accomplished *By the Ground* (toned brown) and *At Dusk* (toned blue), Mikhailov originally planned for a third, conclusive series toned pink, a colour which by 1997/98 seemed no longer appropriate to the worsening situation. That is how *Case History* came to replace the final, more optimistic pink series.

31 This is why Mikhailov conceives of his colour photographs – in a significantly close association of image and subject – as a kind of 'rash on the ill body'. See *Case History*, 10.

32 Nonetheless, critics felt reminded of patterns from Christian iconography when the book first appeared. See Anne von der Heiden, 'Von dem, was der Fall ist: Case History von Boris Mikhailov', *Kunstforum International* 153 (June–March 2001): 117–31; and Anne von der Heiden, 'Consumatum est? Case History by Boris Mikhailov', in *Mikhailov: A Retrospective*, 170–2.

33 See, for instance, the man with the Lenin-tattoo on his chest: *Case History*, 234–5, 239, 242–50, 307–15, 317, 431–4. What the series loses in extent and editorial consistency when shown in museums or galleries is made up to some degree by the scale to which the

individual prints are enlarged, some of which attain almost life-size (125cm x 185cm). Thus, the emotional impact the pictures have on a museum's visitor might match that of the one on a viewer of the book, though the effect is caused by different aesthetic means.

34 People suffering from post-traumatic stress disorders, in the clinical sense of the word, do not necessarily have to have been themselves victims of a threat to life and limb. Witnessing such events affecting others may also suffice to provoke similar symptoms. See Vrana, 'Post-traumatic Stress', 1258.

35 See *Case History*, 128, 431, 434.

PART II | TESTIMONIAL INTERACTIVITY

4. Re-collecting the Collective: Mediatised Memory and the South African Truth and Reconciliation Commission

Stephanie Marlin-Curiel

Two years after the first South African democratic elections in 1994, the national and international public witnessed the hearings of the Truth and Reconciliation Commission (TRC). For the South African television-viewing public, the drama of the hearings was experienced collectively as a rite of transition to democracy. With 'victims' and 'perpetrators' cast in the leading roles, everyone else became the audience. 'Everyone else' included bystanders of apartheid who had benefited from an unjust system; activists in the struggle against apartheid who did not directly perpetrate or suffer from gross human rights violations; and hordes of local and foreign researchers and journalists.

We audience members found ourselves in a morally ambiguous position, unsure of what we were expected to do with what we had heard and seen. As witnesses, we were called upon to be profoundly affected by a survivor's testimony, and to remark upon our transformation. In such circumstances, we must, as Dori Laub writes, 'bear witness to the process of witnessing'.[1] In addition, we take on a 'response-ability': first to respond to the witness, and then, to those around us in a way that reflects our process of witnessing, and effects change in others. The change can take the form of consciousness-raising or social action. And yet, rather than bearing witness to our own internal struggles, we often bear witness instead to others' experiences, bypassing our own psychological processes. This may be due to the relative difficulty of representing one's own trauma of witnessing, or because our trauma of witnessing is incommensurate with the magnitude of the survivor's trauma. At the TRC, the media helped to turn public attention away from the audience's experience, by focusing on that of the witnesses, reinforcing a scenography of spectacle rather than a participatory and transformative ritual. The TRC was broadcast to mass audiences as a spectacle of nation-building. Witnesses and cases became woven into a collective memory framed in 'truth', 'reconciliation' and political transition to be consumed as a symbol of 'new South African' citizenship. The mediatised manufacture of collective memory compromised the response-ability of witnessing and the TRC's aim of restorative justice for victims. What were we responsible for and what does it mean to bear witness? Because the audience's role as witnesses was never delineated by the TRC, the postmodern thinkers among us felt responsible for criticising the TRC's grand narrative and the use of highly unstable terms such as 'truth' and 'reconciliation'. Journalists felt responsible for creating dramatic headlines and sound-bites to ensure the broadest possible impact on the public. Others felt they could be responsible as consumers by following the process, knowing the names and faces, feeling the appropriate empathy or condemnation, and becoming enlightened new South Africans or foreign sympathisers.

The limitations that these responses place on witnessing are reflected in the work of South African artist Sue Williamson. In her series of interactive panels entitled *Truth Games* (1998) and her CD-ROM installation *Can't Forget, Can't Remember* (2000), Williamson draws from her experience as a journalist, intellectual and anti-

Figure 1: Sue Williamson, *Tony Yengeni – "wet bag' torture – Jeff Benzien* from *Truth Games*, 1998. Photo by Wayne Oosthuizen. Courtesy of the artist.

the image and the witness

apartheid activist to demonstrate the ambiguous role of audiences as consumers, critics and witnesses. Both pieces are constructed from media images and testimonial excerpts from the TRC. They offer the viewer the opportunity to manipulate fragments of testimony and media images of both victims and perpetrators, or 'accusers' and 'defenders', as Williamson renames them. In the *Truth Games* panels, media images of an 'accuser' and 'defender' flank an image of 'the event' in a triptych configuration. The images are cropped and enlarged to life size so that the gaze and body language of the witnesses can express the emotional life of the story.[2] Placed in the middle, the event panel reminds us that the memory of the event binds victim and perpetrator, as much as it divides them. The horizontal plastic slats that hold the testimonial excerpts present multiple meanings. They evoke prison bars reminding us of the criminality of the event. Psychologically, they imply that the original event is only partially captured by memory. Even more immediately, they look like Venetian blinds that invite and discourage voyeuristic consumption. Sliding panels with testimonial sound-bites excerpted from the hearings tantalise the viewer with the interactive possibility to cover up and uncover 'the truth' (figure 1). When uncovering the 'truth' by sliding the words off the central 'event' panel, the viewer obscures the images of 'accuser' or 'defender', leaving no one responsible and no one to bear witness to the event now exposed in the middle panel.

The approach in *Truth Games* is elaborated and channelled through the senses in the CD-ROM installation *Can't Forget, Can't Remember*. Fragmented testimony floats across screens filled with still media images from the TRC hearings (figure 2). The space is further enlivened by an original musical score beginning with organic, primordial breathing and developing into a rhythmic punctuated sound like an electronic monitor sending a code blue emergency alarm. The sinewy metallic undertone of the score simultaneously evokes a range of associations: the human body; technologically regimented institutions such as the hospital and the prison; as well as the computerised medium through which we experience the work.[3] Within this environment, images of accuser and defender are layered on

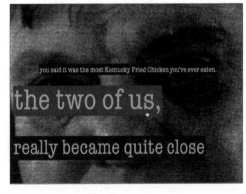

Figure 2: Sue Williamson, *Can't Forget, Can't Remember* (detail), 2000. Interactive video projection; video still. Courtesy of the artist.

top of each other in fragments and the viewer clicks the mouse to peel back the fragments gradually revealing the face underneath. Clicking on the floating testimonial excerpts freezes them momentarily while the viewer listens to the recorded testimonial excerpts as they were spoken at the hearings.

As we experience these works, we cannot help feeling uncomfortable with our participation in manipulating 'the truth'. In *Truth Games* we violently slice heads in half with the sliding testimonial fragments, and force words down the throats of victims or perpetrators. In *Can't Forget, Can't Remember* we dissolve and reconstitute the faces of victims and perpetrators, and torment victims with the infinite repetition of painful testimony. To gain an understanding of our role as the TRC's media-consuming audience discomfort proves more productive than complacent consumerism or disingenuous sympathy.

MEDIA AND MIMICRY

Williamson not only places us in the role of the media consumer, but also helps us to understand precisely what the product is that we are consuming. In these works, Williamson draws her material and methodology from the media in order to cast suspicion on it. She mimics the media's selectivity by emphasising the most dramatic and high-profile cases, and demonstrates how the journalist's craft can be used to manipulate meaning.

Out of thousands of cases, *Truth Games* covered twelve of the most well-known. This number was further edited down to just two representative cases in *Can't Forget, Can't Remember*. The TRC was a mediatised live event, meaning that the liveness of the event – the tears, the anguished cries, the 'spontaneous' apologies and moments of reconciliation – would acquire cultural currency once 'captured' by the media. Therefore, the live event was crafted specifically in anticipation of its repetitions in the media.[4] This pertained not only to the placement of cameras and the 'preparation' of testimony, but to the selection of stories that would bear relation to already familiar events in the history of the struggle against apartheid. Despite the mandate to obtain as 'complete a picture as possible of the nature, causes, and extent of gross violations of human rights of the past', the TRC's selection process began with the solicitation of specific witnesses from the general masses.[5] The TRC displayed posters with timelines of certain historical events that were being written into official history for the first time, but had already been ingrained in the psyches of those active in the struggle. People were encouraged to come forward and to tell their stories in relation to such tragic losses of life beginning with the Sharpeville massacre in 1960, and continuing with the Soweto uprising, the Church Street bomb, the Trojan Horse incident, the Bisho killings and the St James Church massacre, among others, up until the first democratic elections in 1994. Statement-takers went to people's homes with a form containing a 'narrative' section where the statement-taker took down the words as they were spoken, and a 'facts' section, where the important details to be corroborated were filled in. Many times, investigators had to jog the memories of witnesses with historical dates and locations.[6] From these, the TRC chose stories that the committee felt were representative of those events, images and stories that would become part of the nation's new collective memory.

The media helped to shape which stories became representative by emphasising the most dramatic moments. Media cameras focused on stories with maximum affect. For instance, Antjie Krog, a radio reporter covering the TRC, recalls a typically graphic piece of testimony in her book, *Country of My Skull*:

'I saw the severed hand of a black activist in a bottle at a Port Elizabeth police station. The police told me it was a baboon's hand. They said to me: "Look here, this is the bottled hand of a Communist." But I know that Sicelo Mhlawuli, one of the Cradock Four, was buried with his hand missing.' This is a perfect sound bite. (How quickly our language changes – fantastic testimony, sexy subject, nice audible crying...).[7]

The more graphic the testimony, the more memorable it is. But the media also had to be wary of hitting a saturation level in terms of public attention and openness. As community radio advocate John Van Zyl noted in 1997, just one year into the hearings: 'Already there is the question of the moral fatigue that will inevitably set in towards the end of the life of the TRC. The last victims giving testimony at the end of two years must be accorded the same respect as the first.'[8] As the TRC television broadcasts decreased from daily live coverage to weekly narrated summaries, the limited spots put extra demands on selecting those cases that would ensure a devoted audience.

While Williamson's exposure of media techniques delivers a critique, it is also practical. She faced similar limitations of resources, gallery space, public interest and marketability. By her own account, the limited mental and emotional capacity of the South African art audience in part drove her to choose not to introduce new material in the form of untold or fleetingly covered stories. Instead, she intended to start from a popular point of view by using mostly images with which people were already familiar.[9] Her twelve *Truth Games* panels featured only the most prominent of the TRC testimonies: Winnie Mandela's murder conspiracy against a member of her 'soccer league' suspected of spying; the murder of American Fulbright scholar Amy Biehl who was dragged out of her car and stabbed to death by black Pan Africanist Congress activists while driving through a black township; the beating to death of Black Consciousness leader, Steve Biko; the St James Church massacre; the Church Street bombing; the amnesty hearing of notorious torturer, Jeffrey Benzien; the poisoning of Simphiwo Mtimkulu; the murders by the security police's death squad, *Vlakplaas*, of the political activists known as the Gugulethu Seven and the Cradock Four; the murder of activist David Webster; the murder of former Mozambican president Samora Machel, shot outside his house in Johannesburg; and Afrika Hlapo's amnesty hearing for taking part in the mob riot in which two men, George Beeton and Frederick Casper Jansen, were stoned and burned to death. *Can't Forget, Can't Remember* explores the amnesty hearings of security policeman and infamous torturer Jeffrey Benzien and those of Gcinikhaya Makoma, Bassie Mkhumbuzi and Thobela Mlambisa, the perpetrators of the St James Church massacre. In both of these hearings, victims publicly excavated the perpetrators' memories. In the St James Church massacre, a group from the Azanian People's Liberation Army (APLA), the military wing of the Pan Africanist Congress, stormed the St James Anglican Church firing guns, killing eleven people and wounding fifty.

Jeffrey Benzien's hearing was one of the most famous hearings for its flagrant inversion of justice and its dramatic staging. In a shocking and tense confrontation, Tony Yengeni, who had been one of Benzien's victims, requested that Benzien demonstrate his wet bag torture technique on a volunteer from the audience. In the same hearing, Ashley Forbes, another one of Benzien's victims, also confronted his torturer to try to get him to admit to the heinous and inhuman way he was treated. To every accusation, Benzien kept claiming not to remember. In *Can't Forget, Can't Remember*, the line, 'I can't remember it correctly, Sir, but I will concede, I may have said it', floats repeatedly across the screen, offering itself to be remembered. Benzien, however, seemed only to remember several other moments in his relationship with Forbes and taunted him with these memories during the hearing. Even more painful for Forbes than having to witness the demonstration of his torture was to be overshadowed within Benzien's narrative of their 'intimate' relationship. *Can't Forget, Can't Remember* reflects Benzien's and Forbes's intimate relationship by fracturing their images into squares and laying them out like woven fabric or a checkerboard across the screen. You can click squares to complete Benzien's image or Forbes's image only to watch them fracture all over again. Benzien's account of their relationship is summarised in just a few quotes: 'You said it was the most Kentucky Fried chicken you had ever eaten'; 'The two of us really became quite close' (see figure 2). Forbes's accusations also float between Benzien's lines in an attempt to disrupt Benzien's version of events: 'Do you remember that when the wet bag method was used…?'; 'pulled over my head and suffocated?'; 'somebody inserted a metal rod into my anus and shocked me?'

In these works, Williamson uses a journalist's economy of words for the greatest impact and an artist's technique of capitalising on the performativity of the medium, remixing and recombining to bring out essences of character, mood or pattern. In only these very few lines, we see a glimpse of the sick and twisted relationship between torturer and tortured. Ultimately, Benzien's not remembering was attributed to post-traumatic stress disorder and his amnesty application was granted despite the condition of full disclosure not having been met. Forbes was the tortured, and yet, he remembered vividly. Against the TRC's intention to collect truth and memory for public record, this hearing's pattern of remembering and not remembering, the performative repetition of torture techniques that substituted for narrative recounting, and the granting of amnesty in the absence of full disclosure shrieked with vicious irony.

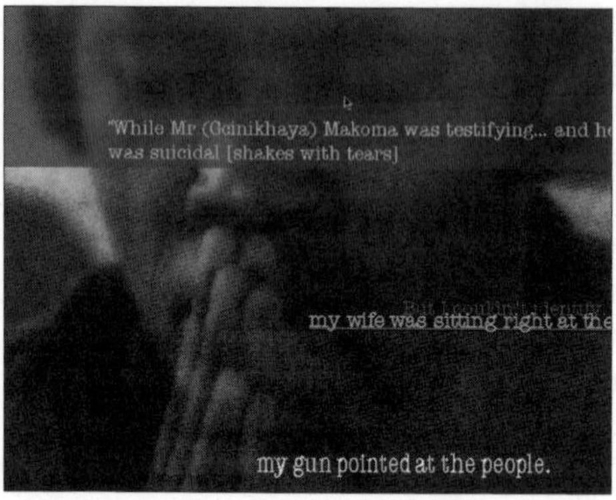

Figure 3: Sue Williamson, *Can't Forget, Can't Remember* (detail), 2000. Interactive video projection; video still. Courtesy of the artist.

The St James Church massacre hearing was also famous for the confrontation between the victim and perpetrator. Williamson cleverly captures the linguistic reversals and the way in which one truth substitutes for another. She chooses to include Dawie Ackerman's lines, 'he talked about his tortures and that he was suicidal, I could identify with that', 'this is the first opportunity we've had to look each other in the eye', with Mr Makoma's line, 'I do remember that I fired some shots but I could not identify'. These lines are full of double meanings when tightly framed in Williamson's composition. Rather than identifying the person who may have killed his wife as one might expect an accuser to do, Ackerman identifies *with* the person who may have killed his wife. Victim and perpetrator 'look each other in the eye'. Makoma's eyes are called attention to in this phrase, and yet he could not see well enough during the shootings to identify wheth-

the image and the witness

er or not it was Ackerman's wife he shot. Then considering Ackerman's identification with the perpetrator, the phrase also resonates as 'look each other in the I'.

In both *Truth Games* and *Can't Forget, Can't Remember*, Williamson invites viewers to identify alternately, and at times simultaneously, with victim and perpetrator, frustrating the inclination of bystander audiences to identify with victims. While inviting viewers to explore their identification with the witnesses and their understanding of the story, she nevertheless traps them in a hall of mirrors. Possibilities exist for recombination and juxtaposition, but there is no opportunity to escape the repetition of the carefully selected testimonial excerpts and media images. The interactive element is circular, self-contained and self-referential. As such, it also lends itself to the condition of denial. The interactive dimension of the work encourages viewers to see or hear what they want to, cover up what they do not. Williamson's choice to use famous hearings and highly edited testimonial fragments can be seen as journalistic gestures, but her alliance with the media is made fragile by her artistic techniques. In *Truth Games*, faces are enlarged so you can look into the eyes of witnesses. Pixels are exposed as if inviting us to find a smoother surface of skin underneath. Lines are excerpted in their different fonts and sizes, seeming to imbue printed letters with volume and timbre, which she finally does in earnest in *Can't Forget, Can't Remember*.

Can't Forget, Can't Remember does offer greater potential than *Truth Games* for spectators to be witnesses, to be psychologically affected and to be aware, even in control, of how they are affected by the testimony as spoken by the witnesses. *Can't Forget, Can't Remember* operates on similar principles to *Truth Games*, but offers a much more sensory, and thus, embodied experience. We respond to the work more emotionally than intellectually. The mobile and highly suggestive fragments of *Truth Games* cannot prepare us for the impact of audible voice in *Can't Forget, Can't Remember*, collected from recordings of the hearings with the accompanying score by Arnold Erasmus. Installed in a private room in the gallery space with amplified audio and projected images, the work allows for a visceral experience of envelopment that would not have been possible had the artist chosen to mass produce and market the work on CD-ROM (figure 4).[10] The audible testimonial fragments bombard, bewilder and shock the viewer as if they were being heard for the first time,

Figure 4: Sue Williamson (with technical assistance from Tracy Gander), *Can't Forget, Can't Remember*, 2000. Installation at Joao Ferreira Gallery, Cape Town, South Africa. Courtesy of the artist.

and yet the fragmentation and randomness of the phrases makes them feel as if they are jumbled and confused memories from the past. While the rigid structure of the *Truth Games* panels which only slide to the right or left hold few possibilities for recombination, the CD-ROM offers the viewer the chance to repeat the lines as many times as she clicks, and in any order. The cursor becomes the instrument of a game, a musical composition or a punishment. You make yourself listen to the phrases again and again, enhancing their power by repetition, elision or layering, until they feel like voices in your own head.

In both these works, Williamson shows our susceptibility to the media's frozen images and flashy headlines, and invites us to try to look beyond them. She seems to want us to experience the people behind the newsprint, and yet, of course, we only see ourselves. We are given the opportunity to witness our own process of witnessing through the medium of art and news media. As we animate the images of victim and perpetrator, we are aware of reducing their otherness to objecthood only to bring them back to life as projections of our own consciences. Is it possible, under these conditions to still fulfil our response-ability as witnesses?

TRUTH IN(TER)VENTIONS

In the two works, Williamson not only makes us aware of the malleability of truth in memory and representation, but she also points us toward the ambiguities of truth as an operational requirement for amnesty and for the 'restoration of the human and civil dignity of victims'.[11] Again, she masks her critique in mimicry. The selection of the St James Church massacre hearing and the Jeffrey Benzien hearings reflect the balanced, non-racial image of the South African collective memory that both the TRC and the media tried to project. In one instance, the perpetrator was black, and in the other, white. Both cases represented the TRC's intention to bring victim and perpetrator together in dialogue as a first step toward reconciliation. In the one case, there was forgiveness and in the other there was not. Williamson uses these two famous cases to show us the ways in which they contradict the standards of truth, reconciliation and restorative justice that the TRC hoped to achieve. Although the final report defined four different kinds of truth, three of which were not dependent on facts as such, its initial public relations campaign to encourage victims and perpetrators to come forward and testify did not contain these varying definitions.[12] Instead, its slogan, 'Truth: the Road to Reconciliation', implied that a singular notion of truth would be applied to the process. Moreover, early discussions of the TRC emphasised the idea that reconciliation was dependent on facing the past in its 'truth and reality'.[13] In 1993, the National Executive Committee (NEC) of the African National Congress (ANC) proposed the idea of a Truth Commission with the following rationale:

> It is because we believe that there must be full disclosure and accountability that the NEC has proposed that a truth commission be set up to investigate all abuses that have flowed from the policy of apartheid. Instead of self-indemnity, we need the whole truth, so that all the victims of disappearances, murder, torture and dirty tricks or their families know what happened.[14]

the image and the witness

It was hoped that the public acknowledgement of factual truth about the past would lead to healing and the 'restoration of the dignity of victims', as well as to social transformation and the development of a human rights culture in South Africa.[15] In highlighting these cases where amnesty was awarded, not on the basis of a disclosure of truth, but on an apparent inability to access truth, Williamson prompts viewers of Truth Games and Can't Forget, Can't Remember to reconsider the meaning of truth and its place in the work of the TRC.[16]

In another intervention, Williamson appears to extend the TRC philosophy of even-handedness by changing the TRC language from 'victim' and 'perpetrator' to 'accuser' and 'defender'. Behind this veil, however, she engineers the transformation of the victim not just into a survivor, but into an agent actively seeking justice. While the terms 'accuser' and 'defender' return agency to both bodies, the violent act meanwhile remains conditional and unrecognised. Its existence is completely dependent on the performance of public accusation rather than the private suffering of the victim. This becomes more troublesome when we realise that the person who accuses still has the burden of proving that the act happened, whereas the burden of proof is much lighter for the 'victim' and has usually been met before the case goes public. The terms 'victim' and 'perpetrator', however, objectify the body as an evidentiary site of violence and limit the scope of public acknowledgement to the violent act committed, rather than to their personal and political lives prior and following the act. Whatever their limitations and potentialities, 'perpetrator' and 'victim', or its preferred alternative, 'survivor', are terms from the discourse of witnessing. Their purpose is to acknowledge suffering. To change them puts suffering into question.

As valid as Williamson's interventions are as critiques of victimhood, truth and spectatorship, her methods and our own participation in them become a cause for concern. As spectators, our search for our own truth in the maze of media images and sound-bites feels manipulative and exploitative as much as it restores our role as participants in the TRC process.

MEMORY AND THE WITNESS: THE COLLECTIVE AND THE COLLECTED

Williamson's works bear witness less to the suffering of the survivors than to the loss of their humanity in the manipulations and misrepresentations of the media and the TRC. Ana Douglass and Thomas A. Vogler have argued that the artist as witness is frequently dedicated to engendering a critical rupture in representation.[17] And following Allen Feldman, we can further recognise the violence done by the systematic molding, translation and commodification of witnesses and witness testimony within the quasi-legal setting of the TRC, the media, and textual and artistic renderings such as Williamson's.[18] The violence of these processes is no more vividly described than by Yazir Henry who testified before the TRC:

> The lack of sensitivity with which my story was treated once it left the confines of that space and became part of the public domain was immediately apparent – my face and the story of my life were flashed across the country, on television, in newspapers, magazines and books, and often out of context. It was out of my control and done without my permission. Although my family

and I made some efforts to stop this, it became clear that the TRC had neither the time nor the logistical capacity to honor or protect the space it gave me in which to bear my soul and tell my story.[19]

Williamson seems less concerned with condemning the violence of the media than with redeeming the media by reorienting our relationship to it and its subjects. These works want us to find it in ourselves to look closely at faces and listen to the words of our fellow human beings. And yet, to do this we must give in to a world of simulation and we must abandon all illusions of the real. It is a shift that we witness in these works.

While our experience does offer us the opportunity to make these words and images part of our own psyche and to wrestle with how they feel inside our heads, ultimately we are still responding to the medium more than we are to the content of the testimonial narrative. Williamson's work may suggest that 'mediatized witnessing' is our only option.[20] As Douglass and Vogler note, 'now ... we have a much more immediately materialized history, one that can even be fabricated and recorded on the spot by the modern media – making history come before collective memory rather than after'.[21] If collective memory is 'the sum of a collection of separate but similar individual experiences over time', then the mediatised version is generalised, summarised and synthesised within the same historical moment into a marketable and consumable format.[22] It is thus becoming increasingly impossible to 'project the illusion that things still happen, that events exist, that there are still stories to tell, in a situation in which the uniqueness and irrevocability of private destinies and of individuality itself seem to have evaporated'.[23]

To what extent then are those whose stories are collected present in the collective and to what degree have they given consent to their own evaporation? My discomfort with such an acute fascination and postmodern engagement with media as media is based in this context less on a need to recover the original event or to recuperate the injured bodies of the collected. It is, rather, based on a concern for the future. The erasure of the body through technology produces a forgetting about the living. Witness-survivors have not only suffered in the past, but will continue to suffer if we, the witnesses of the witnesses do not take on the second stage of witnessing, the response-ability of ensuring that we act to reverse our own complicity in producing conditions of suffering. Judith Herman writes that the first principle of recovery is the 'empowerment of the survivor ... no intervention that takes power away from the survivor can possibly foster her recovery'.[24] Also integral to recovery from trauma is the construction of narrative and the reintegration of the witness into the community.[25] The process of mediating collective memory, however, wrenches agency away from witnesses. They are dis-integrated, rather than reintegrated.

Mediatised collective memory lends itself more readily to an economy of consumption where we can 'buy into' the new South Africa, rather than individual, social and political transformation. The TRC manufactured 'new South African-ness' by saturating the public with the newly 'collected' official history. The careful selection and management of public testimony insured that the public itself was defined by its exclusion from speaking roles at the hearings. This was a public who had lived through apartheid, but whose stories did not qualify to be legitimised as official history, and thus many people were left with no way in this process to perform their citizenship as new South Africans. This fosters the desire for memory in those who do not possess the 'right' memories.

As Natalie Zemon Davis and Randolph Starn observe, collective memory often functions as 'a substitute, surrogate or consolation for something that is missing'.[26] This understanding recalls Freud's theory of screen memories in which one memory is often constructed in order to hide or substitute for an event that the subject does not want to remember or face. The screen memory is not necessarily a complete fiction but is distorted in such a way as to link itself with the repressed elements of a past event or present situation. Citizens who were not active in combating apartheid or who are currently doing little to improve lives disadvantaged by apartheid might have reason to repress such thoughts and take on other people's legitimised stories as a screen memory.

Williamson herself should not be categorised as a bystander but her artworks seem intended for and reached mainly bystander audiences; those who did not know 'the truth' first-hand and could afford to question its relevance. They were exhibited in galleries in white neighbourhoods and metropolitan centres, reaching, by and large, an elite white audience within South Africa and abroad.[27] An act of soul searching is important for all South Africans, as well as for those agents and beneficiaries beyond South Africa's borders. If these works do not provoke the kind of soul searching that dredges up our own culpability, however, they do facilitate an awareness of our desire for truth and memory. And yet, for all their refusal to oblige spectators with easy access to 'the truth', these works simultaneously create an opportunity for appropriation and manipulation of screen memories, memories that suppress our sense of responsibility for the past and future.

The lives of those who have been irreparably damaged cannot ethically be disintegrated within a critique of rationality or a celebration of the postmodern. For living survivors, learning factual truths, such as who killed their loved one or where the body was buried, was extremely important. To the public, these truths were largely lumped together into a forceful, collected and mediated memory. Collective memory is a long-term process that evolves over time and should not be an end in itself, serving only to provide group or national identity. Freshly collected memory, rather, should provoke an ethical reckoning with our consciences and the social reality we share with the collected. Mediated testimony may still be transformative, but only if we face our response-ability to the collected as present and living, rather than mediated and past.

Notes

1   Dori Laub and Shoshana Felman, *Testimony: Crisis of Witnessing in Literature, Psychoanalysis and History* (New York: Routledge, 1992), 75.
2   Sue Williamson, interview with the author, Cape Town, 5 January 1999.
3   It brings to my mind images from William Kentridge's animated film *History of the Main Complaint* (1994), repeated in his 2004 staging of Monteverdi's *Ulysses*, depicting a sick man in bed with doctors surrounding him as a metaphor for the sickness that ails South African society.

4   For a comprehensive argument on the contemporary mutual dependency of live and me-diatised performance, see Philip Auslander, *Liveness: Performance in a Mediatized Culture* (New York: Routledge, 1999).

5   South African Truth and Reconciliation Commission, Promotion of National Unity and Rec-onciliation Act No. 34 of 1995. Online. Available <http://www.truth.org.za/legal/act9534.htm> (accessed 20 May 2001).

6   Lars Buur, 'Monumental History: Visibility and Invisibility in the Work of the South African Truth and Reconciliation Commission', paper presented at 'The TRC: Commissioning the Past', University of the Witwatersrand, Johannesburg, 11–14 June 1999. Online. Available <http://www.trcresearch.org.za/papers99/buur.pdf> (accessed 29 June 2004).

7   Antjie Krog, *Country of My Skull* (Johannesburg: Random House, 1998), 32.

8   John Van Zyl, 'Human Rights and Wrongs', *Rhodes Journalism Review* 14 (1997): 12.

9   Williamson, interview with the author, Cape Town, 5 January 1999.

10 Ibid.

11 *Promotion of National Unity and Reconciliation Act* (1995).

12 The report defines four different kinds of truth: factual or forensic truth; personal or narra-tive truth; social or 'dialogue' truth; and healing and restorative truth. The report supplies complex definitions of each. In brief, factual or forensic truth was based both on individual personal testimony and also 'broader patterns of gross human rights violations'. Personal or narrative truth referred to the recognition and 'validation of the individual subjective experi-ences of people who had previously been silenced or voiceless'. Social or 'dialogue' truth referred to the 'truth of experience that is established through interaction, discussion and debate', and healing and restorative truth referred to 'the kind of truth that places facts and what they mean within the context of human relationships – both amongst citizens and between the state and its citizens'. Republic of South Africa. Truth and Reconciliation Com-mission, *Truth and Reconciliation Commission of South Africa Report* (1998), vol. 1, chap. 5, pars 29–45.

13 Alex Boraine, *A Country Unmasked: Inside South Africa's Truth and Reconciliation Commis-sion*, (Oxford: Oxford University Press, 2000), 32.

14 NEC member Kadar Asmal cited in Boraine, *A Country Unmasked*, 12.

15 Willie Esterhuyse, 'Truth as a Trigger for Transformation: From Apartheid Injustice to Trans-formational Justice', in *Looking Back, Reaching Forward: Reflections on the Truth and Rec-onciliation Commission of South Africa*, eds Charles Villa-Vicencioa and Wilhelm Verwoerd (Cape Town and London: University of Cape Town Press and Zed Books, 2000), 144–54.

16 For further information on the 'technologies of truth' and the evolution of the idea over the course of the Commission, see Richard Wilson, *The Politics of Truth and Reconciliation in South Africa: Legitimizing the Post-Apartheid State* (Cambridge: Cambridge University Press, 2001), 33–61.

17 Speaking of Picasso's *Guernica*, Ana Douglass and Thomas A. Vogler write, 'The power of artistic "witness" in that work is not due to Picasso's Spanish blood (i.e. authenticating a legitimate connection to the victims) or to a literal representation of the events. Rather, it is the disruption of conventional modes of representation – the visual rhetoric of rupture.' Ana Douglass and Thomas A. Vogler, 'Introduction', in *Witness and Memory: The Discourse of Trauma*, eds Ana Douglass and Thomas A. Vogler (New York: Routledge, 2003), 33.

18 Allen Feldman, 'Memory Theaters, Virtual Witnessing and the Trauma-Aesthetic', *Biogra-phy* 27, no. 1 (2004): 164.

19 Yazir Henry, 'Where Healing Begins', in *Looking Back, Reaching Forward*, 169.

20 Douglass and Vogler, *Witness and Memory*, 9.

21 Ibid., 17.

22 Ibid.

23 Frederic Jameson quoted in ibid., 12.

24 Judith Herman, *Trauma and Recovery: The Aftermath of Violence from Domestic Abuse to Political Terror* (New York: Basic Books, 1992), 133.

25 Ibid., 3.

26 Natalie Zemon Davis and Randolph Starn, 'Introduction', *Representations* 26 (1989): 3.
27 At the Grahamstown 1999 National Arts Festival, Williamson's *Truth Games* did hang in a venue that is technically considered to be located in the township. However, based on my two visits to the exhibition during the festival I would say this did not significantly increase the audience for the work as the gallery was empty on both occasions.

5. Since We Forgot: Remembrance and Recognition of the Armenian Genocide in Virtual Archives

Leshu Torchin

On the eve of the invasion of Poland, Hitler exhorted his troops to kill without mercy and justified this charge with the question: 'Who still talks nowadays of the annihilation of the Armenians?' This question is repeatedly invoked in Armenian Genocide scholarship and commemorations. The popularity of the citation is hardly surprising since it recognises the past massacres of the Armenians to be continuous with genocide, while it also conjures the present-day failure to remember, and the moral repercussions of such failure. The Holocaust becomes possible because this past genocide has transpired without legal or political consequence, vanishing into the ether of amnesia and indifference. Hitler's question not only mandates memory, but also offers instruction as to its maintenance: animate and commemorate the past through the diligent attention of the present. In effect, to remember is not merely to relate a traumatic historical event, but to engage in an ethical act in the present for the sake of the future. It is to accommodate the directive of 'never again'.

The ethical charge of remembrance extends to the Armenian Genocide, where testimonies relate and reclaim collective trauma in order to save a history that is threatened by erasure. These memory projects are frequently placed in the service of political action, mostly in the struggle for official recognition. In recent years, the Internet has enabled and expanded upon these projects of remembrance and recognition, allowing online archives to bear witness to a traumatic past with several goals in mind: first, to recuperate a forgotten history; and second, to activate publics in the service of genocide recognition, a process that shapes memory according to both the cultural and the legal idioms of genocide. This combination of goals transforms these virtual archives into a claim about genocide that throws into relief its own articulation as governed by events and images that postdate the genocide. The pernicious legacy of amnesia not only imparts a moral force onto memory claims but also structures them so that the Armenian Genocide is remembered as forgotten. Additionally, the genocide claims of these memorial productions draw on an iconographic archive of recognised genocide, specifically the Holocaust, whose visualisation has contributed to a potent 'genocide imaginary'. Filtering the memory of the Armenian Genocide through the lens of the Holocaust, as in the case of Hitler's quotation, contributes to the claim that, not only should these events be remembered, but they should be remembered and recognised as genocide.

This chapter examines the virtual archives of a forgotten genocide for their work in transforming a memory long governed by amnesia and denial into a political project for achieving official genocide recognition. I analyse how this process exploits the visual strategies and interface enabled by the Internet as a new medium. Although this discussion holds broad implications for our understanding of the relationship between visual culture and the creation of morally and politically engaged global publics, these virtual archives frequently address an Armenian diasporic public. The particularity of the address specifically seeks to animate a sense of loss and to exact recuperation not only from the crime of genocide – and its forgetting – but also from the traumatic fracturing of a once united people. These archives are thus digital manifestations of what Anahid Kassabian and David Kazanjian call the *hai tahd* (Armenian cause) genre in Armenian discourse, which seeks 'conclusive and restitutive judgement on a legal and moral injustice' while producing 'a transnational Armenian identity based in the shared experience of genocide'.[1]

THE TESTIMONY OF ARCHIVES

The online archives I consider here make use of Internet technology to accumulate and present photographs, textual information, documentary clips, news items and the video testimony of survivors. These sites include the institutionally situated endeavours of the Armenian National Institute (ANI) and the exhibit designed by the Armenian Library and Museum of America (ALMA). This particular exhibit is hosted by the University of Minnesota Center for Holocaust and Genocide Studies site (CHGS-UMN). My discussion also addresses extra-institutional projects, such as that from the Museum of Amnesia, which responded to the exclusion of the Armenian Genocide from the Simon Wiesenthal Center's Museum of Tolerance. More individual efforts, such as those presented in TheForgotten.org, Genocide1915.info, Armenian Genocide 1915 (now defunct) and Raffi Kojian's genocide pages on his remarkable compilation of all things Armenian on Cilicia.com, which he has called his 'Virtual Armenia' are also included. In consistently supplying links to each other, these sites produce a mutual reinforcement, not to mention a high ranking on a Google search through a phenomenon known as 'Google bombing'.[2] Although the sites primarily focus on the act of producing remembrance through visual media, they mobilise their technology to activate a responsive spectator and to direct the engaged spectator to other sites of information and action. In this manner, these sites serve a testimonial function.

The testimonial process implicates both speaker and listener in that its specific scenario produces a community conducive to both listening and responding. Shoshana Felman writes: 'To testify is thus not merely to narrate, but to commit oneself, and one's narrative, to others ... to take responsibility for the truth of an occurrence.'[3] Meg McLagan applies this understanding to the human rights arena, where testimonials 'construct audiences as virtual witnesses, a subject position that implies responsibility for the suffering of others'. This audience, in turn, becomes a 'witnessing public', a term that refers not only to the role of this virtual witness as listener or spectator, but also as potential actor within a political or social sphere.[4]

Although testimony has largely been understood in narrative terms, visual media have played crucial roles in forming witnessing publics. Jeffrey Shandler expands Hans Kellner's argument that imagining the Holocaust is actively tied to creating a reader who recognises the event, to argue for the formative role of film, television and photography in the production of the Holocaust imaginary and its spectator.[5] Underpinning the use of these images is a belief in the transformative power of these images – that they confer legibility onto the baffling scope of atrocity and that they invoke an ethical change in the spectator. However, these visual media technologies are not transparent conduits for information, but constitutive elements in the production of testimony. In as much as these photographic images rely on their mimetic capacity to encourage the sense of authenticity and transparent witnessing that complement their evidentiary claims, they are, nonetheless, dependent on formal strategies to give meaning to the horror in the frame, meaning that makes ethical demands upon the spectator.

Virtual archives draw upon this framework of testimony in realising their potential for animating memory, hailing publics and forging political transformation. In the denial-laden case of the Armenian Genocide, visual representation of suffering meets the evidentiary demand because it produces the affective engagement that moves an audience. These virtual archives explicitly invite the visitor to take responsibility for the truth of the occurrence of the extermination. Moreover, the interactive possibilities of the Internet amplify the experience of the testimonial encounter, heightening the notion of exchange and the expectations placed on the visitor. In fact, while the image rests at the centre of this analysis, much of the information presented is textual, indicating the still logocentric nature of the Internet. However, it would be a mistake to ignore how this text, when placed on the screen medium, takes on visual and even aural components. The layout of information serves to direct the visitor, in that icons or single words not only summon attention and provide immediate information but also serve as links to further sources. The hypertext link makes clear the availability of information beyond that currently in view. Dragging the cursor across the screen can reveal the evidence of a link embedded in text, or animate a picture, or instigate a sound. 'This is the new rhetoric of interactivity', explains Lev Manovich, 'we get convinced not by listening/watching a prepared message but by actively working with the data: reorganising it, uncovering the connections, becoming aware of correlations.'[6] The virtual archive invites the participant to dig and recover the past, in effect, making the plea for an active witnessing public during the moment of the initial encounter, rather than after it.

the image and the witness

WHY REMEMBER?

In the Ottoman Empire during the First World War, the Committee of Union and Progress (CUP), better known as the Young Turks, promoted a tenet of pan-Turkanism in the establishment of a Turkish nation. Because the population of this new nation was imagined as exclusively Turkic, the state developed and administered a plan to remove the Armenian population. The CUP launched an aggressive campaign between 1915 and 1918 against the Armenian people who were subject to torture, massacre, rape, starvation and deportation. These acts of violence have been seen as a culmination of the persecution and violence initiated by Sultan Abdul Hamid during the 1890s in atrocities known as the Hamidian Massacres. While the Young Turk conspirators fled the nation after the war, the violence continued to be carried out until 1923 by Turkish Nationalists who opposed the CUP, but held to the same ideology of national ethnic exclusivity. It is estimated that one and a half million Armenians perished. These atrocities are considered by many to be genocide, and, in fact, these very acts occasioned the first use of the term 'crimes against humanity' in the joint response offered by Russia, France and Britain in May 1915.[7]

Such a response may be ascribed to the degree of attention the Armenians' plight received at this time courtesy of the many developing information technologies. Photographs illustrated the reports in weekly magazines and published testimonies, while film became a potent force in publicising these remote events. Near East Relief (NER), a mission-based relief organisation, found film to be particularly useful in its information and fundraising campaigns. *Ravished Armenia* (1919), a coproduction of NER, and early film pioneer Col. William Selig, was an adaptation of the published testimony of 17-year-old survivor Aurora Mardiganian and screened in both popular venues and at fundraising campaigns. The relative success of this film excited the possibilities of film activism, and for years to come NER used films to depict their organisation's work and the conditions they sought to alleviate.[8]

Despite this media spotlight on the 'Starving Armenians', active denial soon set in. Young Turk leader Talaat Pasha refuted claims of bureaucratic killing, ascribing the mass death to Armenian bandits and local officials.[9] In the United States, previous efforts to bring attention to the misdeeds were supplanted by a desire to maintain strategic alliances in the face of an oncoming war. Yet the repercussions of this denial extended beyond the repudiation of potential criminal charges to a plan to erase Armenians from the cultural landscape of Turkey. As early as 1920, with the rise of the Kemalist government, the Turkish general Kiazim Karabekir declared that in Turkey, 'there has been neither an Armenia nor a territory inhabited by Armenians'.[10] The erosion of the Armenian presence, both physical and cultural, became part of the Turkish state's monolithic nationalism. Taner Akçam argues that the Turkish national origin myth revolves around the image of a self-reliant, secular and anti-imperialist state bearing a unified ethnic and cultural identity. The very memory of the Armenian Genocide constitutes a threat to this mythology. The erasure of all things Armenian, which includes the memory of the genocide, has become a constitutive aspect of the Turkish state.[11] Anush Hovanissian describes such acts as 'cultural genocide', whereby state policy seeks to produce a new Turkish nation. The new nation is founded on the elimination of the cultural presence of Armenians by attributing Armenian history, literature and art to Turks. In addition, physical objects, such as monuments and churches, are allowed to decay, further expunging Armenian culture.

This denial expanded the arena of violence from the physical to the cultural, making the landscape of visual and material culture a new and charged battleground for memory. When *The Forty Days of Musa Dagh* (1933), Franz Werfel's popular novel of Armenian resistance during the massacres, was optioned by Metro-Goldwyn-Mayer in 1934, the Turkish Ambassador, Münir Ertegün Bey, informed the US State Department that the production of this film could have unfortunate repercussions on diplomatic relations with Turkey and other sympathetic nations. As the State Department brought pressure upon the Hays Office to quash the film, letter writing and print media campaigns launched by the Embassy threatened an international boycott of not only all MGM films, but American films altogether. Production on the film ceased immediately.[12] The failure of this film has been viewed not only as evidence of the Turkish endeavour to silence this memory, but stands out as a point where one can recognise the possibilities of cultural intervention, both for remembering and forgetting on an international as well as a national level.

The case of *The Forty Days of Musa Dagh* articulates both the international and historical scope of this ongoing denial and the way that visual culture offers a significant battleground for memory. Yet, in this case, the emancipatory potential is tempered by the dictates of larger state and commercial concerns that maintain a wilful amnesia regarding the genocide. This silence is by no means benign. Although prosecuting the perpetrators and offering reparations to victims are no longer viable options, repercussions linger in the psychic domain. Forcible silence forecloses on the possibility of emotional recuperation, allowing traumatic memory to take the place of mourning.[13] And if, as Andreas Huyssen proposes, national identity is predicated on cultural or collective memory, then this assault on remembrance can become an assault on the formation of a communal identity.[14] Such refusal to 'talk about the annihilation of the Armenians' not only risks the likelihood of future genocide, as the uptake of the Hitler quote suggests, but it also amplifies and maintains the Armenian Genocide.

CREATIVE STRATEGIES FOR MEMORIALISATION

In framing the denial as a sustained assault on the Armenian people, one where Armenians remain subject to the rules of the perpetrator, Richard Hovanissian identifies and advocates creative strategies for memorialisation.[15] Unlike Holocaust denial, which is continually contested through international political, legal and cultural structures, the institutional denial about the Armenian Genocide is broad and deep. It thus serves as a principal motivation in the creation of archives and memorials in such quasi-democratised spaces as the Internet. Even as the liberating potential is limited to communities of privilege that are wired and with access to computers and computer knowledge, the new technology has nonetheless opened up a sphere in which voices from the periphery can contribute fully to the discourse on genocide and its remembrance. The fact that many of these sites are produced by individuals rather than institutions indicates the degree to which the Internet has become a fertile ground for the kind of cultural activism in which, according to Faye Ginsburg, silenced people use media to respond to 'the structures of power that have erased or distorted their interests and realities'.[16] The spatial aspects of the medium further contribute to this potential by marshalling information from disparate sources – the displays on ANI, for example, draw from archives and collections ranging from the US to Britain to Russia – and then redistributing the information to dispersed on-line publics.[17] The independent producer of a virtual archive can then perpetuate the spread of information by dispersing the centralised and often inaccessible work of material archives. The reach of virtual space, across time and space, and the limited regard for institutional membership extends the reach of the archive, making it a use-ful locus of recovering forgotten memory for dispersed publics.

While the extension of the archive into democratised spaces excites the pos-sibilities of recuperation, it is necessary to remember that this presentation is not transparent. It is ensconced in formal and aesthetic practices, most of which post-date the event they represent. I refer to contemporary concerns about amnesia, the relationship of the Holocaust to genocide imaginaries and the interactive possibilities of the Internet. This recognition serves not to dispute the fact of the events, but to call attention to the way the images of these archives are deployed to call up memory for very specific purposes: to recuperate a public and to activate this public into a recognition project.

Formed in response to the omission of the Armenian Genocide in the Museum of Tolerance at the Simon Wiesenthal Center in Los Angeles, the Museum of Amnesia takes up the Internet as a space to provide information of a genocide absented from an influential institutional collection. More notably, the name and the primary image one encounters on the site underscore this absence. Upon arriving at the site, the viewer is greeted with a large blue bottle embossed with a label that reads 'Museum of Amnesia'. The shape and colour of the image recall the cobalt blue bottles of milk of magnesia, which prom-ise relief for an upset stomach. The asso-nance of the words amnesia and magne-sia enforces the connection and playfully declares this site's role as an antidote. The label on the bottle promises to cure 'curatorial oversight' and, like many a me-dicinal label it notes: 'If symptoms persist consult www.museumofamnesia.org.' The site constructs historical amnesia as a pathology to be redressed through this alternative venue. The playfulness persists in the online gift shop selling mu-seum souvenirs, a practice that simultaneously parodies and exploits the institutional production of material memory.

Figure 1: Homepage logo for the online Museum of Amnesia. Courtesy of the Museum of Amnesia (www.museumofanmesia.org) and CafePress.com.

The play of memory and forgetting manifests in the visitor interface with the pages on the site. To the right of the bottle stands a block of text with words published in hypertext, suggesting links to more sources of information. Yet it is not clear where one may find this exhibition. However, by dragging the mouse across the empty part of the page on the left side, hypertext links appear, and clicking on them transports the site visitor to the exhibition information.[18] Exploration over the blank white page of this site yields a hidden history that is excavated by the accidental or intentional effort of the visitor. The nature of the exhibition is embodied in its presentation, whereby what was invisible becomes visible with the visitor's movement of the cursor. This gesture calls to attention the ways in which Internet engagement may recall the lost and hidden histories while conversely revealing how readily a loss of interest can result in the disappearance or invisibility of the topic. Remembrance is predicated on forgetting.

Amnesia is also central to the website TheForgotten.org. Apart from the clear implications of its name, the site offers a Flash animation introduction; although this introduction can be skipped, the loading time is brief, even for a dial-up connection, and it begins before the visitor can opt to skip the animation and go directly to the home page.[19] Unidentified traditional Armenian music plays, and a man's whisper in Armenian names the date, 24 April 1915, the official day of remembrance for the Armenian Genocide. His whisper presents a history that is articulated yet distant. The animation itself offers a montage of image and text. After the first appearance of the date, a photographic negative of an emaciated refugee, possibly a corpse, flashes on the screen for less than a second; its momentary appearance provides a simultaneous affirmation and disappearance of the history it represents. The duration of the image makes its full understanding difficult, while the inverse quality of the negative further compounds the image's obscurity. A quotation from Armin T. Wegner's well-known testimony of the genocide appears as an archival recognition of death and devastation. Another negative image appears depicting a mass of Armenian deportees. As quickly as it appears, it fades. The next piece of text fades in: 'The Armenian Genocide' on the first line with the subtitle 'History does not fade away' on the second. Within a second's time, the subtitle fades, leaving a textual affirmation of the Armenian Genocide in the form of an indelible title on the screen, while a succession of images of corpses flash by, evidence of the starvation and violence that transpired. Each gesture simultaneously affirms the presence of a history while articulating its evanescence, even in the face of photographs and testimonial accounts. Like the Museum of Amnesia, the recuperation of memory enabled by the site's Flash introduction is forever yoked to and predicated upon the act of forgetting.

This oscillation between memory and loss animates a sense of trauma over the loss of a community at the turn of the century, and the extension of the loss through denial and silence. From both clinical and cultural perspectives, trauma is understood as 'an event not fully experienced at the time of its occurrence [that] thus repeatedly returns to haunt the psyches of its victims'.[20] Research on combat and domestic trauma characterises these recollections as fragmentary, as flashes of images without the context of the narrative of the fully restored memory.[21] Although this aesthetic of disjointed and shattered memory presents a continuing challenge to the field of Holocaust representation, particularly around the issue of representing the unrepresentability of its horror, it has nevertheless found a receptive medium in the Internet. This compatibility comes due to the Internet's capacity for Flash animation, the QuickTime movie and even the casual animation of its digital interface. In the case of TheForgotten.org, fragmented images flash on the screen, their only context is given by the murmurs of the Armenian voice-over and text that informs us of genocide and one man's witness to the horror. The images flash too quickly for us to apprehend thoroughly, to look at carefully and to master them. Unlike the QuickTime movie, there is no visible function in Flash animation to allow one to freeze the image for unlimited inspection. Moreover, the images appear on a smaller rectangular screen within the web browser (itself not necessarily inhabiting the full screen of the computer), thus invoking distance at the very moment the display suggests presence.[22] Vivian Sobchack remarks upon the immediate nostalgia generated by such plug-in media, noting their function as 'reliquaries' that 'preserve and cherish' the ephemera as souvenir, or talisman against inevitable forgetting.[23] At the Museum of Amnesia, one encounters blank space, the site of suppression and repression, but finds that a careless move of the cursor brings text onto the page. While here there is more control – one may keep the text on the page to read – the dialectic evoked is similar to that of trauma: the space that seems to be devoid of memory harbours a veiled shock.

Within the clinical context, the stages of recovery from trauma include a reconstruction of the traumatic narrative, an act that 'reclaim[s] the patient's earlier history in order to "recreate the flow" of the patient's life and restore a sense of continuity with the past'.[24] TheForgotten.org works to accomplish a similar goal. After the initial manifestation of trauma, the visitor is transported to a menu page full of context and narrative documentation, including a timeline of events, Wegner's photographs (taken from ANI's website), a clip from the ABC-TV news on the Armenian Genocide and a series of survivor video testimonies. Following the flashes of elusive and buried images of trauma, the site ushers the visitor into a place of more secure images with text boards that restore a narrative order onto the history, enabling a relatively enduring connection with the past. The virtual archives can be understood to transform Freud's 'screen memory' – a process of displacement where a memory is created to veil the psyche from the trauma – into Faye Ginsburg's inversion of the term's meaning: screen media are deployed to recuperate collective memories and histories that have been obscured from view.[25] The archival function of these new media asserts both the memory of the genocide and its importance in the face of institutional denial. The trauma is evoked then as prelude to the recovery.

WITNESSING PUBLICS AND THE GENOCIDE CLAIM

These virtual archives hail a transnational Armenian public into the community of remembrance with unmatched access to archival materials. They also offer the possibility of prolonged and repeated viewing. The suggestion of community is also made explicit on many sites, as they invite responses on message boards (where even combat with a denier can have bonding value), occasions to sign petitions or, for Internet producers, the option to join the Armenian Genocide Union of Sites (AGUS). The genocide page of Cilicia.com welcomes the visitor with the regularly updated statement of how many years, months and days since the genocide that 'we' have been waiting for an apology. The use of the first-person plural here invites the visitor into this community of memory and outrage. Cilicia.com not only offers links to written testimonies of survivors but asks visitors to contribute their own, a request that assumes Armenian heritage on the part of the visitor. A testimonial community thus develops online through the project of commemoration.

When the project of memory turns to the greater project of recognition, the virtual archives expand their potential witnesses to the Armenian public. Here, the expressions of loss and amnesia are yoked to ethical claims that hail a broader, transnational public committed to the official recognition of the genocide as genocide. ALMA's online exhibit, 'The Armenians: Shadows of a Forgotten Genocide', hosted by the CHGS-UMN website, presents a justification for continued memory, by opening with a mention of the genocidal campaign in Kosovo, attributing its existence to the 'continued success of the Armenian genocide'. Predicated on the failure of prosecution, reparations or official recognition, this success 'provides a welcome inspiration for others to copy'. The presentation of the text enhances the claim by presenting these words on a white square with edges made jagged to resemble a torn piece of paper, a fragment of the past once lost, but recovered for this crucial contemporary purpose. The threat to the memory of the Armenian Genocide represented by the torn paper image is extended to a threat to the present; the return of memory repairs not only the Armenian public, but other threatened publics as well.

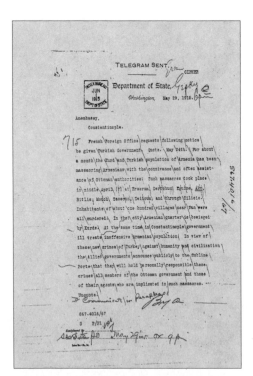

Figure 2: France, Great Britain and Russia Joint Declaration of 24th May 1915. Copyright Armenian National Institute (www.armenian-genocide.org).

The strategy of presenting textual evidence as visual document appears on other archival sites to grant both affective heft and legitimacy. Cilicia.com offers access to the full text of Western news reports from 1915–19 that covers the slaughter and the deportations. ANI offers multiple documents chronicling the stated intentions of the Young Turk administration as well the responses of the witnessing states. Language contributes to the production of the genocide claim, as these virtual archives post multiple documents that refer to plans to exterminate and systematically deport whole populations. Most notably, among the collection on ANI is the 1915 joint declaration of Britain, France and Russia, which declared these events to be crimes against humanity, a crime that would first be applied in international law at the Nuremberg Trials. Such charged language strives to meet the burden of evidence determined by the terms of the 1948 UN Genocide Convention.

the image and the witness

The evidentiary claims are supported by the appearance of these documents. The *New York Times* reports posted on Cilicia.com present the iconic logo, as if to confer further institutional legitimacy. ANI's archival texts are accessible through the 'Sample Documents' menu where documents are posted as both text (html) and image (gif). These documents bear signatures, marks of pens, the letterhead of the state and stamps of receipt. As images, they bear not only the text that supplies the information, but the marks of their exchange and the institutions of their circulation. The secrecy of this campaign and the hidden qualities of the Armenian Genocide are called into question, as the receipt and transmission of official forms of testimony are rendered visible on these pages.

THE GENOCIDAL IMAGINARY

While documentation can support the evidentiary burden of the genocide claim, it is the deployment of the Holocaust imaginary that renders the Armenian atrocities culturally legible as genocide, and thus bolsters the genocide claim. Photographs in print media and newsreels in the cinema brought the images of the Holocaust before a public, while in an unprecedented move, films, such as the US Department of Defense's *Nazi Concentration Camps* (1945), were used in the Nuremberg Trials to visualise the new charge of crimes against humanity. Since then, the images of emaciated bodies, mounds of corpses, barbed wire and box cars – images that saturated the public, political and juridical arenas – have crystallised into a set of universalised symbols for the Holocaust, functioning as a kind of genocidal imaginary. These images provide an interpretive frame through which other genocides are produced and understood. While this mode of seeing and remembering genocide through a set of universalised symbols threatens to flatten the complexities of a specific event and potentially neutralise response to contemporary atrocities, it may supply a strategic mode for invoking claims to genocide.[26] In effect, images refer to other images, but far from spiralling into a postmodern relativism where meaning evaporates in favour of simulacra, they can offer an on-the-ground strategy for action. Typically, the complexities of history can impede such political moves. Filtering the reports and photographs of the Armenian atrocities through the genocidal imaginary of the Holocaust authorises the claims of prior genocide and promotes moral engagement with the testimony of the archives.

Although ANI offers more extensive selections of photographs, most sites rely on the repetition and highlighting of certain recognisable images. The site Genocide1915.info presents the visitor with a page of thumbnail images of mass burials, mass deportations, human remains and emaciated Armenians, living and dead. In one image, bodies are neatly lined up in a row by the side of the road; and in another, men with and without shovels, arrange rows of bodies in a newly-dug trench, images that evoke Nazi concentration camp burials. As if doubting the affective or evidentiary capacity of these images, the site producers emboss them with legends to emphasise scope ('There were 1.5 Million') or assign blame ('Turks were here'). The slipperiness of the image in bearing witness becomes clear only when we realise that the mass burial photograph in question actually comes from the *Graphic* (London) in 1895. It is, in fact, photographic evidence of the earlier Hamidian massacres which, although devastating, were not actually part of the Armenian Genocide.

This slipperiness underscores the value of iconicity in the politics of claims-making. The repetition of Holocaust iconography continues across the sites allowing the visible evidence of the Armenian tragedy to be filtered through a lens of acknowledged genocide. The images that flash in the introductory animation of TheForgotten.org depict masses of deportees and emaciated corpses. The images that emphasise scope soon give way to individual suffering: in one picture, a young boy squats, swathed only in a blanket as he looks into a ditch where a naked, gaunt corpse lies splayed; in another, the corpses of two boys, collapsed in the desert with bandaged feet, recall both fallen bodies and images of gangrenous limbs that appear in *Nazi Concentration Camps*, but are perhaps more familiar from Alain Resnais' repurpose of them in *Nuit et Brouillard* (*Night and Fog*, 1955). The bodies in many of these cases lie strewn across the ground or framed by shallow graves, evoking the images of the camps at the liberation, where bodies were photographed en masse and individually.[27] The evidence of atrocity seems clear, and yet it is the Holocaust that supplies the contextual frame for comprehension.

Icons are put to use as portals to mass evidence on the Armenian National Committee site, where images instead of words offer links to further information. John Elder's photograph of an Armenian refugee, an emaciated young man with a shorn head who looks straight into the camera, directs the visitor to a synopsis of the genocide. The choice of a refugee with a shorn head, particularly when faced with those wearing clothing associated with a more 'Eastern' appearance, suggests a strategic affiliation with more familiar images, images that invoke the Nazi concentration-camp survivor. Furthermore, the decontextualised nudity directs the spectator to a body that bears the traces of the trauma, as does the shocking appearance of the 'walking skeleton' of the camp survivor. In another link, Hitler becomes a doorway to significant quotations. He supplies both acknowledgement and a sense of genocidal likeness, his model for ruthlessness predicated on the success of the Armenian Genocide. The use of image as link enforces its meaning, suggesting a direct relationship between the icon and the conditions it has come to represent. While certain words invoke the legal codes of genocide, and while documents are fetishised for their evidentiary status, it is the image of the document, whether scanned or reproduced to mimic the look of the report, that grants heft to the truth of the claim in virtual space.

In one case, the photographer as well as his photographs function as associative devices. ANI, TheForgotten.org and other sites not only post the photographs of Armin T. Wegner, but his biography as well. These biographies note that Wegner documented the conditions of the Armenian deportation camps and investigated the massacres in the Ottoman Empire as part of his social advocacy work, a legacy that resulted in his later efforts on behalf of European Jewry. This biography places these two profound human rights catastrophes on a single continuum. Wegner personifies the connection between the Armenian Genocide and the Holocaust just as his photographs animate the bond.

Although the Holocaust may dominate the genocidal imaginary, other events are brought into these images courtesy of a developing context in the age of genocide. Many of Wegner's and Elder's photographs offer pictures of women in refugee camps, and carrying children across the desert. Figures are draped in robes and cloths, heads are covered to shield from the sun, as they either walk in groups down dusty paths, or convene in tented camps. Such images draw on frames of suffering produced in the coverage of famine, and are now associated with the present-day genocides of Bosnia, Rwanda and Sudan. These contemporary genocides have continually emphasised displacement and refugee status as characteristics of genocide and ethnic cleansing. While the photographs of decapitated Armenians and collected skulls evoke the displays found in early footage of concentration camp liberation, they also recall the displays of skulls in the memorials to the Cambodian and Rwandan genocides.[28] Although these arrangements and readings threaten to efface the specificity of the past depicted, this interpretive frame confers a status of genocide on the Armenian atrocities. The image facilitates the process of claims-making.

ANIMATING THE STATIC IMAGINARY: *WORLD NEWS TONIGHT*

These sites house not only textual information and photographs but streaming video that transmits survivor testimonies and portions of documentaries. Notably, on both TheForgotten.org and Genocide1915.info, there is a commemorative segment from *ABC World News Tonight*, which was originally broadcast on 24 April 1999. This short segment animates the text and images presented on many of the sites, translating them into a 5-minute narrative that is consumable, economical and laden with authoritative and affective capital. Moreover its context of news reportage suggests this event as a present-day concern, thereby conferring urgency within the format, even though the segment is no longer live television. Peter Jennings opens this segment with a report from the *New York Times* of a community in danger, suffering intensive privations and horrors. 'Does this sound like the ethnic cleansing in Kosovo?' he asks. But, in fact, he refers to an event over eighty years past, a 'forgotten genocide'. This association reappears later in the segment as he charges the viewer to 'look at what is happening now to the ethnic Albanians in Kosovo', as images of crowds of Kosovars trail down a street, 'and you can follow a line that leads finally here'. Upon the word 'here', the images of present-day deportations dissolve into black and white images of the deportations of Armenians, the shape and direction of the lines preserved. The graphic match ensures the preservation of the historical line connecting the Armenian Genocide, the Holocaust and the ethnic cleansing in Kosovo. This filmic strategy and Jennings' later command to follow the line forward to Hitler's quote ensure the place of these events on a continuum of genocide.

Although the segment is officially entitled 'The Armenian Massacres', it is saturated with verbal and iconic gestures that support a genocide claim, including an opening montage with a crowd carrying flags evocative of Nazi demonstrations and a boxcar filled with people. The combination of charged terminology and images from an equally charged genocidal imaginary provide the operating structure of this segment. Jennings describes 'the Armenian Holocaust', calling Talaat Pasha 'the Turkish Hitler', while corpses in rows take over the screen. At another point, Jennings calls the caves where many Armenians found death by fire 'primitive gas chambers'. When Jennings acknowledges this event as genocide, the image of bodies lined up at the side of the road punctuates his observation. Throughout a historian's explanation of a Turkish plan for extermination executed through massacres and deportations, pictures of skeletal corpses, masses of refugees, boxcars and the familiar emaciated young man of Elder's photograph appear. Linguistic and iconic resonance combine to form a morally-charged appeal to recognise genocide.

The reliance on iconicity is underscored by the sheer repetition of images, not only from site to site, or site to segment, but within the single segment. The young man in Elder's image, who appears on so many sites, makes an appearance. And a skeletal corpse of a woman, her two children dead beside her, is twice used. The image is arresting because it transposes a familiar image of motherhood onto a scene of abjection. Her frail body specifically evokes the infamous photograph of a mother's corpse from Bergen-Belsen, even as it offers a broader graphic similarity to the atrocity images taken in the concentration camps on liberation. While there are many images of the dead to accommodate the claims within the narration, it is the 1895 photograph from the Hamidian massacres that appears most frequently. To prevent apparent repetition, the image is often divided into sections, allowing close-ups to offer repetition of iconic and useful images. Upon Jennings' reference to 'primitive gas chambers' the entire wide-shot photograph is presented. The repetition does not speak to the dearth of images, but this photograph's iconic appeal, its economic delivery of mass death for each frame of the narrative. Moreover, the iconic appeal overtakes the demand for accurate attribution; the provenance of the photographs is not addressed except for a brief mention of Wegner's participation.

The segment functions as an economising device, presenting survivor testimony, historian commentary and archival photographs in the service of a narrative authorised and made topical by the institutional aegis of *World News Tonight*. The Internet threatens degradation of video quality (the video is reduced and jerky), yet does not necessarily degrade the impact of a segment that relies on the static photograph rather than video. Similarly, the Internet images demand, as icons, more graphic resonance than denotative precision.

ACTIVATING THE CLAIM

Underpinning the discussion of a claims-making process is the assumption of mobilisation, the translation of memory into action. And these virtual archives support this translation of claim into action. On a general level, the medium itself produces an active reader as visitors are invited to click on icons or words for more information.[29] However, these sites deliberately engage the visitor, not only in an extended visit into the site or other archives, but into a community of concern for the Armenian Genocide. Hailed by the affective and evidentiary appeal of the genocide imaginary, witnessing publics are directed to sites that seek official recognition of the Armenian Genocide enacted through state legislation. For example, TheForgotten.org offers a link that reads: 'Will you allow history to be rewritten? Take action.' A click on that option leads the visitor to the ANCA action alert site.

Clicking for justice can seem an absurd proposition, an activity that is potentially disengaged from the emotional signification described above. However, the affective appeal that prolongs engagement, combined with new grassroots possibilities in cyberspace, may lend themselves to the action necessary for restoring cultural memory in a public realm. International jurisprudence is no longer possible but restoration of cultural memory is, and it is this goal that is sought in the political arena of official recognition. The ANCA Action Alert page offers cases of ongoing denial followed by an update of activities that support the recognition cause, specifically the activation of an Armenian Genocide Resolution. In the case of the American-based ANCA, the battle is fought in the House of Representatives and the Senate, and so the site updates visitors about present motions as well as instructions on how to act. This includes template letters, web faxes and a congressional directory to facilitate addressing the correspondence. The efficacy of the fight for justice remains to be determined.[30] Nevertheless, the Internet has the ability to lay out information, make affective appeals in both word and image, connect the visitor to more information on the topic or to connect the visitor to an opportunity for immediate action.[31]

The interactive dimension of the Internet invites the idea of extended engagement and enacts the notion of testimony as encounter where the listener/spectator is called to take responsibility for what she or he has heard, seen or read. This potential for action may lie within the medium, but it is the image that facilitates the engagement by contributing to the claims-making process. Photographs are deployed as evidence, but the evidence is given shape and legibility through an engagement with icons culled from the genocidal imaginary. This strategy combines evidence, affect and the terminology of genocide not only to restore a forgotten history, but rather, to remember it specifically as genocide.

Notes

1   Anahid Kassabian and David Kazanjian, 'Melancholic Memories and Manic Politics: Feminism, Documentary, and the Armenian Diaspora', in *Feminism and Documentary*, eds Diane Waldman and Janet Walker (Minneapolis: University of Minnesota Press, 1999), 204–5.

2   In 2001, Adam Mathes discovered that Google listed its search results in terms of page rankings determined by an algorithm sensitive to the number of links to that site. Higher number of links, or links supplied by pages with high rankings, improved the success of return. Google's uniqueness lies in the fact that the search results do not necessarily contain the keywords sought, but were linked to by other pages using these key words. If a site were to supply a link using the phrase 'Armenian Genocide', this would figure into Google's calculation of page ranking. In response to this discovery, Mathes coined the term 'Google bombing', a method by which blogging circles or other Internet publishers enhance the popularity of a site by supplying a link and using a particular and shared search term. See Adam Mathes, 'Google Bombing', *Über.nu.* 6 April 2001. Online. Available <http://uber.nu/2001/04/06/> (accessed 15 December 2003).

3   Shoshana Felman and Dori Laub, *Testimony: Crises of Witnessing in Literature, Psychoanalysis, and History* (London and New York: Routledge, 1991), 204.

4   Meg McLagan, 'Human Rights, Testimony, and Transnational Publicity', *The Scholar and Feminist Online* 2, no. 1 (Summer 2003). Online. Available <http://www.barnard.columbia.edu/sfonline/ps/mclagan.htm> (accessed 15 December 2003).

5   Jeffrey Shandler, *While America Watches: Televising the Holocaust* (New York: Oxford University Press, 1999).

6   Lev Manovich, 'Generation Flash'. Online. Available <http://www.manovich.net> (accessed 15 December 2003).

7   Vahakn N. Dadrian, *The History of the Armenian Genocide: Ethnic Conflict from the Bal-*

kans to Anatolia to the Caucasus, 6th edn. (New York and Oxford: Berghahn Books, 2003); Richard G. Hovanissian, 'Etiology and Sequelae of the Armenian Genocide', in *Genocide: Conceptual and Historical Dimensions*, ed. George J. Andreopoulos (Philadelphia: University of Pennsylvania Press, 1994), 111–40; and Peter Balakian, *The Burning Tigris: A History of International Human Rights and Forgotten Heroes* (New York: HarperCollins, 2003).

8 Their titles include *Alice in Hungerland, Seeing is Believing, Constructive Forces* and *What the Flag Saw* among many others (all produced from 1921–23). For the history of *Ravished Armenia*, see Anthony Slide, *Ravished Armenia and the Story of Aurora Mardiganian* (Lanham, MD and London: Scarecrow Press, 1997); for the history of Near East Relief, see James L. Barton, *The Story of Near East Relief (1915–1930): An Interpretation* (New York: MacMillan, 1930).

9 Balakian, *The Burning Tigris*, 374.

10 Cited in Balakian, *The Burning Tigris*, 375.

11 Taner Akçam, 'The Genocide of the Armenians and the Silence of the Turks', in *Studies in Comparative Genocide*, ed. Levon Chorbajian and George Shirinian (London: Macmillan, 1999), 125–46.

12 Edward Minasian, '*The Forty Years of Musa Dagh*: The Film That was Denied', *Journal of Armenian Studies* 3, nos 1–2 (1986–87): 121–31. *The Forty Days of Musa Dagh* was finally produced and released in 1982, but the epic scope and the distribution were extremely limited. The novel's publishers were also subject to certain pressures, although they were by no means as extreme as the campaign against the film. If anything, this suggests the disproportionate valuation of the image over the word.

13 Atom Egoyan's film about the memory of the Armenian Genocide, *Ararat* (2001), highlights the insidious effects of silence and forgetting on individual and collective levels.

14 Andreas Huyssen, *Twilight Memories: Marking Time in a Culture of Amnesia* (New York and London: Routledge, 1995), 12.

15 Richard Hovanissian, 'Eighty Years: Memory Against Forgetting', in *Problems of Genocide*: proceedings of the International Conference on 'Problems of Genocide', 21–23 April 1995, National Academy of Sciences, Yerevan, Republic of Armenia (Cambridge, MA and Toronto: Zoryan Institute, 1997).

16 Faye Ginsburg, Lila Abu-Lughod and Brian Larkin, 'Introduction', in *Media Worlds: Anthropology on New Terrain* (Berkeley: University of California Press, 2002), 7.

17 Rouben Paul Adalian, 'Finding the Words', in *Pioneers of Genocide Studies*, eds Samuel Totten and Steven Leonard Jacobs (New Brunswick: Transaction, 2002), 14.

18 As of 27 September 2005, the site functions mostly as a cyberary (a host of links to other resources).

19 Before encountering the Flash introduction, the visitor is offered a choice of languages: French, English, Russian, Spanish, Turkish, Italian and German, an indication of the dispersed and international nature of the intended audience. Curiously, the visitor is not offered the opportunity to enter an Armenian version of the site.

20 Michael Rothberg, *Traumatic Realism: The Demands of Holocaust Representation* (Minneapolis: University of Minnesota Press, 2000), 12.

21 Judith Herman, *Trauma and Recovery: The Aftermath of Violence – From Domestic Abuse To Political Terror* (New York: Basic Books, 1992).

22 Like much Flash animation, the introduction to TheForgotten.org site also borrows heavily from the genre of the movie trailer, with its rapid montage of titles, quotations and images. The rectangular shape of the frame even evokes a widescreen ratio.

23 Vivian Sobchack, 'Nostalgia for a Digital Object: Regrets on the Quickening of QuickTime', *Millennium Film Journal* 34 (Fall 1999): 4–5.

24 Herman, *Trauma and Recovery*, 176.

25 Faye Ginsburg, 'Screen Memories: Resignifying the Traditional in Indigenous Media', in *Media Worlds*, 40.

26 Barbie Zelizer makes this argument about the risks of such universalised symbols in *Remembering to Forget: Holocaust Memory Through the Camera's Eye* (Chicago and London:

University of Chicago Press, 1998).

27 In the photographic representation of both the Holocaust and the Armenian genocide, close-ups enable a more direct view of the physical body whose scars testify to unseen abuse, while wide shots emphasise the scope associated with genocide.

28 To emphasise such connections, the erstwhile site Armenian Genocide1915.info posted the reflection of a reporter in the *Daily Telegraph* (UK) that reads: 'Piles of Armenian skulls are reminiscent of the exhibitions of Khmer Rouge terror in Cambodia. Lines of Armenians on the move through Turkey under armed guard look similar to scenes in the Balkans in the Nineties.' Marcus Warren, 'The Horror that the World Wants to Forget', *Daily Telegraph*, 27 January 2001.

29 Fred Ritchin, 'Witnessing and the Web: An Argument for a New Photojournalism' *Pixel-Press*. Online. Available <http://www.pixelpress.org/contents/essays_fs.html> (accessed 15 December 2003).

30 Action is perceivable on an anecdotal level. *The Chronicle of Higher Education* reported in August 2000 that the Turkish government has threatened Microsoft with 'serious reprisals' unless all mention of the Armenian Genocide was removed from the Microsoft Encarta entries on 'Armenia' and 'Genocide.' In turn, Microsoft demanded its authors edit the entries. Reports were posted on the ANCA and Human Rights Action-Armenia sites summarising the *Chronicle* article. See Jeff Sharlet, 'The Other Side of Genocide', *Chronicle of Higher Education*, 18 August 2000, A20.

31 Klaus Marre, 'Grassroots growing fast in cyberspace; Web adds pressure on US lawmakers', *The Hill*, 15 October 2003.

Digital References

Armenian Genocide 1915: http://15levels.com/24.April/index-a.html
Armenian Genocide-Cilicia: http://www.cilicia.com/armo10.html
Armenian National Committee of America, Action Alert Page: http://www.anca.org/anca/actionalerts.asp?aaID=17
Armenian National Institute: http://www.ani.org
The Armenians: Shadows of a Forgotten Genocide: http://www.chgs.umn.edu/Histories_Narratives_Documen/The_Armenians/the_armenians.html
TheForgotten.org: http://www.theforgotten.org
Genocide1915.info: http:// www.armeniangenocide.cjb.net / http://www.genocide1915.info
Human Rights Action-Armenia: http://www.hr-action.org/armenia/
(all accessed 15 December 2003)

6. False Witness: Combat Entertainment and Citizen Training in the United States

Karen J. Hall

In the opening scene of Ron Kovic's filmic biography, *Born on the Fourth of July* (Oliver Stone, 1989), two boys dressed in jeans, T-shirts and military helmets sweep through a ravine with their weapons poised to fire. Suspense builds as the camera suggests movement on the ridge of the ravine. Suddenly, dirt clods fly at the two boys. The camera cuts back and forth from a high-angle shot of the attack (boys throwing dirt and shouting, 'Ronnie's dead!') to an overhead shot of Ron Kovic lying on the ground with dirt falling in his face repeating over and over as he vehemently shakes his head, 'No, I'm not! No, I'm not!' The scene captures what for many sub-urban boys in the 1950s was standard war play.

Millions of boys performed these Hollywood-inspired war scenes in the years between the end of the Second World War and the US involvement in Vietnam; their play was a rehearsal for a style of manhood instilled with a mythical national history and a sense of self inflated by aggressive militaristic posturing. In the same historical moment that out-going President Eisenhower was warning the United States of the dangers that the increasing power of the military-industrial complex would bring to the nation, toy manufacturers were, for the first time, recognising children as a viable audience on which to spend marketing dollars. Mattel spent half a million dollars on television spots promoting its Burp Gun, a realistic plastic model of a Second World War machine gun used by troops in the Pacific. This was only the beginning of the marriage between toy marketing and television. The union would bring powerful changes to the toy industry and the play practices of future generations of children, and it is significant that one of the first toys advertised was a war toy. The sum spent on this campaign alone represented the equivalent of half of the industry's annual expenditure on advertising. One million Burp Guns were sold in just one month. Demand so far exceeded supply that President Eisenhower himself had to write directly to Mattel to request a Burp Gun for a grandchild's Christmas gift.[1]

Although war-related toys had been marketed for children before Mattel's Burp Gun, this product was at the forefront of the developing synergy between toys, film and the US military. Once children began to expect realistic replica war equipment, home-made and self-made props would become less fashionable and acceptable. Children learned to expect and ask for accurate reproductions of the military equipment they saw in the movies. Marketing strategies increasingly made use of stills from popular films to sell war toys, the most famous being Hasbro's GI Joe who reportedly took his name from *The Story of GI Joe* (William Wellman, 1945), and whose promotional material drew on popular war films of the day, especially *The Longest Day* (Ken Annakin, Andrew Marton and Bernhard Wicki, 1962). Encouraged by toy commercials and packaging to act out scenes from films, a generation of soldiers took out some of their anger on John Wayne. Having mimicked Wayne's bravado and war stance as boys, these soldiers learned quickly in combat how false and dangerous war heroics could be. No doubt the men's sense of betrayal was in part fuelled by a sense that their own naïve ignorance was also to blame.

Children had little guidance for their war play. As was the case in the immediate post-war years, a relatively small number of citizens today gain actual combat experience and, for those soldiers who do, there are cultural as well as personal prohibitions against sharing these experiences upon return home. Therefore, media representations are the main place in which citizens learn about war. Combat entertainment is responsible for generating American culture's ability to imagine and articulate its war story, and, even more intimately coercive, for training citizens in how they will feel about war. For, as Ronald Reagan claimed, 'it is the motion picture that shows all of us not only how we look and sound but – more important – how we feel'.[2] Combat-related entertainment is a major thoroughfare for the transmission of the ideology of militarised imperialism into the bodies and emotions of individual subjects, training citizens in what the power of the nation should feel like in their bodies.

Deployed on the home front, the force lines of the Hollywood combat film act as a domestic technology of war, introducing militarised values and behaviours into the lives of citizens. Such films entertain and train the US citizen body in codes of patriotic conduct, training consumers to stand, walk, talk and hold the posture of leadership.[3] When entertainment technology capable of producing such a direct physical and emotional response is linked to concerns of national security, citizens literally pay to consume the ideological mechanisms that prepare them to be citizens of US empire. Melodramatic representations of losses, as discussed below, inflame consumer patriotism. Viewing war on screen works to produce a society in which the common citizen is a vengeful and voyeuristic bystander.[4] Those who consume war entertainment are trained to expect that any harm done to the US or its interests will be answered with swift and awesome force against any and all perceived as the enemy. Immediate revenge is an essential element in the process of what Robert Jay Lifton has called 'false witness'. The distance at which US consumers learn to experience war trains them to watch as others do the dirty work of killing.

DEFINING THE FALSE WITNESS

Robert Jay Lifton developed his definition of false witness from his work with US Vietnam War combat veterans. It became a common practice in this war, even for chaplains, to yoke the killing of enemy soldiers with the act of memorialising fallen comrades. Rather than be psychologically and spiritually present to the loss of their fellow soldiers, and to the grief that this loss caused, soldiers externalised their grief and transmogrified it into killing rage. Atrocities, even on the scale of those committed at My Lai, could be justified in the perpetrators' minds when they framed the murders they committed as a just response to the deaths of their comrades. False witness in this military context presumes to offer testimony for the combat deaths of comrades in the form of acts of revenge killing.

Oliver Stone calls attention to the phenomenon of false witness in *Platoon* (1986). On 1 January 1968, 'just another day', as Chris Taylor describes it, the platoon discovers a bunker complex. While investigating the area, Sandy detonates a mine left as a booby trap, killing himself and another soldier. Taylor sees Sgt. Barnes sitting alone in silence, disturbed by these deaths; however, Barnes appears more angry than contemplative and neither man speaks to the other. A short time later the platoon finds another of their members, Manny, tied to a tree with barbed wire, his throat cut and a piece of Viet Cong propaganda displayed from his neck. Before the camera shows Manny, the shot travels slowly from left to right, panning across a line of soldiers staring, some in shock, others in anger, at Manny's body. The camera then rests on Manny's dead body before it tracks, again slowly, from right to left, showing the rest of the platoon's reaction and ending with a long take of Barnes, who comments, 'Those motherfuckers.' The men observe the remains of his death, and their response is the fury of vengeance, not the grief of witness.

The well-known village atrocity scene then follows. Chris Taylor's voice-over narration informs viewers that 'the village, which may have been there for a thousand years, didn't know we were coming that day. If they had, they would have run. Barnes was at the eye of our rage and through him we would set things right again … That day, we loved him.' The soldiers storm through the village killing livestock and threatening the inhabitants. Taylor joins the fury, shooting at the foot of a one-legged Vietnamese man, making him 'dance'. Bunny then ends the dance by bashing the man's head in with his rifle butt. Bunny directly relates the soldiers' behaviour in the village to their anger over the deaths of their three comrades: before killing the Vietnamese man, he says, 'You just cryin' your little hearts out about Sandy and Sal and Manny.' Surveying the dead man and the elderly woman who was hiding with him whom Bunny has also killed, Bunny says, 'She probably cut Manny's throat.' The deaths of these villagers along with the destruction of their homes and the rape of some of their young girls function for the platoon as direct and immediate payback for the lives of their fellow soldiers. It does not matter that these particular Vietnamese people had nothing to do with Sal, Sandy or Manny's deaths. The men fictionalise all the connection they need in order to rationalise their violence to themselves. In a war purportedly fought to stop the spread of communism and promote the spread of democracy, this mode of vigilante justice is a particularly undemocratic and 'unAmerican' norm to establish.

Whereas the Vietnam War films of the 1980s and 1990s depict wartime revenge killing in a way that induces the moral judgement of their audience, the typical Second World War combat film works to standardise the process of false witness as a national norm. The opening scenes of *Bataan* (Tay Garnett, 1943) emphasises Japanese atrocity with a long sequence of shots that show Philippine villagers and US service people fleeing a Japanese air attack. The Japanese strafe these defenceless people with bullets and drop bombs on them. The camera emotionalises their plight, showing close-ups of the dead and wounded. The harm the film's small unit of men can inflict on the Japanese is justified by the violence depicted at the film's beginning. Even the most naïve, 'all-American' character, Purckett (Robert Walker), feels the righteousness of revenge, and he voices his enthusiasm, not once, but three times 'to get me a Jap and know that I hit him'. In *Bataan* and every other Second World War film that treats the same events of 7 December 1941 as an unjust and cowardly attack, cinematic representation works to normalise revenge killing as a justifiable, ethical and patriotic response to attacks by an enemy.

When the process of false witness is transferred from the combat front to entertainment venues, a cultural value and expectation is taught that military force must be used to defend any attack on the US. False witness, in this context, entails the observation of one's fellow citizens at the moment of their violent death. Whereas bearing witness is conventionally understood to allow the traumatised victim to *work through* the experience of the trauma, US war entertainment shapes the consumer audience as the traumatised victim primed for a vengeful *acting out*. Their countrymen are dead and can tell no tales. They have now experienced the jarring, enraging iconic vision of their deaths and are morally and physically primed for the experience of release that only an image of the murder of the enemy can bring. Thus observation justifies the observation of vengeance, most often in numbers far greater than the deaths which initially triggered the violent revenge. Neither the deaths of the enemy nor the act of killing itself help to integrate the physical and emotional experience of loss with the realities of history, place or social power. Rather than facilitate the healthy acceptance and closure of an event in history, acts of false witness create cycles of violence that block any release from the compulsions which force the victim/viewer to involuntarily and repeatedly relive the trauma. The design of false witness guarantees the continuation of militarised violence and the consensus of the US citizen body. Subjects are trained to remember moments of violence – often of mythic proportion, such as the Alamo, Pearl Harbor and 9/11 – but remain ignorant of the complex set of actions and relations that instigated these events. In this way, memories are confined to the events that serve the interests of the state. History is reduced to a series of iconic images.

LAST STAND ICONOGRAPHY

The modern combat film developed out of the 1940s-era war film that attempted to inspire audiences with the spectacle of modern warfare and the courageous sacrifices made by common citizens. Frequently, especially when dealing with the war in the Pacific, this meant scripting the war and the loss of American lives through the conventions of the last stand narrative. The structure of the last stand narrative emphasises US losses; enemies are represented as generic, objectified waves of violence. However, the last stand defenders are so few in number that audiences have the opportunity to learn their names, histories and motivations, and to identify with their cause and valour. Films like *Wake Island* (John Farrow, 1942) and *Bataan* assert the righteous heroics of 'our' men in the early and uncertain days of the war in the Pacific.[5] Despite the fact that all twelve of the men in Dane's unit are killed in *Bataan*, patriotic certainty is coupled with the righteous posture of the grossly out-numbered unit's defence against the attack of a ruthless enemy to give audiences a narrative formula with which to understand the war in the Pacific. Like the fight at the Alamo, the fight in the Pacific was a rear-guard action in which soldiers were necessarily sacrificed to buy time so that their comrades could prepare for a return to the territory lost in the early days of the war.

It is necessary for soldiers, and the citizens who support them, to feel they are victims of the enemies' violence, rather than the perpetrators of violence. Narratives of history such as *Bataan, Wake Island, Guadalcanal Diary* (Lewis Seiler, 1943) and *They Were Expendable* (John Ford, 1945) emphasise the moments when the US suffered attacks. These narratives help to turn perpetrators into victims, creating a role reversal which is one of the most ideologically significant inversions enacted by the combat film. Harm done to 'our boys' is unjustifiable and calls for immediate revenge, the primary response of false witnessing. Thus, in *Bataan* Sgt. Dane sprays a hail of bullets at the enemy even as he stands in his own grave, and in *Wake Island* Major Caton wires his superiors to 'Send us more Japs!' even as his death is immi-nent. US wartime audiences were clearly meant to be inspired by the fighting spirit these characters displayed and to feel assured at the end of *They Were Expendable* that when Lt. Brickley and Lt. Ryan return to the Philippines with more information, better strategies and more resources, US forces will bring defeat even more crush-ing to the Japanese than they brought to the US.

The last stand narrative structure of the combat film testifies to the fact that, although the US may not win every battle, its cause is morally just, and that more brave men will return to finish what the slaughtered innocents began. Japan's 'sneak' attack on Pearl Harbor epitomised the alleged treachery of the enemy in the Pacific War. Hollywood has re-staged these events so often that 7 December 1941 has become a filmic icon. The date is a shortcut reference to the enemy's deceit-ful savagery, US innocence and suffering, and the narrative's next event. Whether audiences hear the date on the radio as in *Fighting Sullivans* (Lloyd Bacon, 1944), or see an actual calendar page as in *From Here to Eternity* (Fred Zinnemann, 1953), US viewers know that family ties will be supplanted by national obligation and young men will either rush to recruiting stations or be deployed overseas. Surface details and icons would continue to accumulate once the war ended and world politics re-aligned in the Cold War, but the central assertion that GIs and the US as a nation were the innocent young underdogs fighting a savage enemy would be used to as-sert the moral legibility of the US in using force. US coverage of the events of 9/11 and the days following helped to blot out the United States' role as perpetrator of imperial injustice around the globe, and to frame the citizens of empire as power-less victims at the mercy of a cowardly and savage enemy.[6] Last stand iconography, such as the New York City firemen's re-staging of the flag raising on Iwo Jima, and last stand narratives, referenced indirectly by President George W. Bush's use of the discourse of the Old West, the originary site of the last stand, in his 'Wanted dead or alive' comments worked to authorise US force. At least, it worked among the nation's own citizens to substantiate the use of the term 'war' in the opening day's of the US 'war on terror'.[7]

Countless combat films have immortalised similar historical moments from the American war story, and toy manufacturers have given children the raw materials to interact with the icons of history that Hollywood has constructed. In an increasingly media-influenced children's culture, toys that emerge from their packaging with a pre-set narrative are more successful in the market place. In the mid-1950s, the Marx toy company released an Alamo playset enabling children to recreate the original American last stand. Now predominantly of interest to vintage toy collectors, these playsets still circulate and have been re-released in commemorative anniversary editions. Sets that depict the flag raising on Iwo Jima are available, and when Hasbro serendipitously released a GI Joe fire fighter for the Christmas toy-buying season that followed the 11 September 2001 attack on the World Trade Center, they made it possible for millions of GI Joe fans of all ages to create their own dioramas of the fire fighters' re-staging of the Iwo Jima flag raising. Creating war culture that narratively connects these events serves to establish their shared categorisation in the American war story. This grouping ideologically reinforces the Bush administration's claims that the current war on terror is as justified and necessary as these previous wars. This is despite interpretations of the rules and laws of the UN Charter, Universal Declaration of Human Rights, Geneva Conventions and the Nuremburg Principles which suggest differently.[8]

Re-enacting the scenes children view in other media serves to equate play with collecting. Invention and inquiry are drained from children's play when collecting becomes the primary activity their toys invite. Toy sets sold separately or as modular universes such as Star Wars, Spiral Zone figures and vehicles, Lego military sets and GI Joe dolls train children's desires toward acquiring objects rather than seeking out toys that augment creative activity, further strengthening the influence media narratives have in children's lives.

Media influences, predominantly in the form of films, television programmes and marketing forces have taken the positive aspects of generation out of war play. Consuming images synergistically feeds the consumption of products, and trains children in how to put those products to use via imitation rather than creation. Taking up Jean Piaget's assertion that play is not imitation, Nancy Carlsson-Paige and Diane E. Levin argue that the driving force for children's play is internal.[9] Although play involves the child's attempts to fit into reality and to conform to and replicate the external world, play is dominated by the children's interpretation and transformation of external events, not merely their replication. When the drive to play is externalised and play narratives and control are taken away from children, play activity, if indeed it can still even qualify as play, is far less supportive of social and ethical development. Thus the combat entertainment industry and its media marketing profoundly influence the possibilities for children's war play, even when toy producers do not offend consumer sensibilities. Ever Sparkle Industrial Co. Ltd did offend, however, when it released Forward Command Post during the 2002 toy-buying season.[10] This bombed out dollhouse came complete with 75 pieces, including a toy soldier, toy weapons, American flag, furniture, ammunition and fuel drums. It is difficult to think of what play narrative this toy set could support other than the embattled last stand defence. Children need only imagine or collect the waves of enemy soldiers attacking their one brave US fighter to be off and running inside the last stand narrative of the mythical American war story.

The following question and answer sequence from the website for Educators for Social Responsibility makes evident the issue of children's play patterns: 'During wars some students become focused on the excitement of "smashing the enemy" and begin to make revenge a more prominent theme of their writing, drawing, and play. Acknowledge that many people, including many adults, share those thoughts. When children see adults, particularly adults in power, modelling these kinds of responses, they often follow suit. Empathising with the underlying feelings and helping students clarify what is important to them (that justice be done, for example) can be helpful.'[11] Neither playsets, nor media, nor adults can dictate the modes of children's play, but all three do present children with a narrowed playing field. These forces encourage children to inhabit a mythical American history predisposed to imagining the US soldier as the victim of unjust violence. The toys and packaging encourage children to use the cover art, films and television shows to imitate iconic American history.

Children's play serves to bring iconic history into lived experience. However, because history has been mythologised, the absence that US war entertainment, and by extension children's war play, brings into presence has no material referent. War play based on war entertainment and marketing is mimetic, but the text it brings to life is counterfeit. Playing within these scripts of mythologised history aligns children forcefully, and physically, with the elements necessary to the practice of false witness. They have learned to focus their attentions and emotions not on the Other in war narrative, but on the Self, experiencing the pain of initial defeat and the power of ultimate victory. Finally, such scripts work to overwrite children's tendency to create their own play scripts.

PLAYING AT WAR AND LEARNING TO WITNESS

All war play is not made equal. Children can learn and rehearse important lessons about power, loss and violence in their war play. They can experiment safely with their responses to risk and fear. They can practice skills of communication across power imbalances. Additionally, war play can be an accessible space for social interaction. The rules of war play do not have to be worked out from scratch. Children can skip over much of the awkwardness of meeting new children and inventing activities in which all can participate. Because it is a widespread play narrative, war play can efficiently offer children a shared imaginative space in which to meet and interact. Whether war play includes child-sized weapons or miniature soldiers, the activities of drawing of sides, negotiating how long toys and children must remain outside of the play when they are 'killed' and maintaining the acceptable level of play force and speed all encourage children to learn through communication and activity.

However, the increasingly preset narrative quality to war play can also be a disadvantage to healthy play dynamics. The basic conventions of war play are so dominant that the rules of engagement read like a familiar rule book: 'It was an unbreakable rule that the "good guys" (most often Americans) couldn't win too easily – they must first be repulsed with heavy losses, then return to win the day in a struggle that would leave almost every soldier on both sides dead.' Children's war play teaches them that Americans always win, that they begin wars as 'plucky underdogs' who 'always return and conquer. No *Bataan* without a *Back to Bataan*.'[12] When war play is overly scripted, children do not learn the practices of communication and negotiation such play should ideally offer. They can be intellectually stunted as well when their war play and the toys sold to accompany it constrain the scope of questions children learn to ask about the realities and effects of war. The Iwo Jima playset encourages children to line up their 24 US marines and 24 Japanese soldiers for a fight to the death and a dramatic flag-raising, but because the set and the narrative that comes with it seems complete, certainly it matches what they have seen in the media and heard from adults, they do not ask questions outside this iconic version of history. Who controlled the island before the war? Who controlled it after the war? Did people live there? What happened to them? Any such questions are blocked out by the dominant war narrative focused on the US soldiers and their sacrifices.

Play is not a unidirectional cultural force: culture-making and the transmission of values, beliefs and expected behaviour not only takes place from older to younger generations, but also from younger to older. Children imitate the actions of adults in their play, and as the media representations of the 1980s demonstrated, adults also imitate the behaviours of children. Although cultural practices of false witness were conveyed unidirectionally from adults to children when children imitated Hollywood films, when these children grew up, they brought with them into adulthood childish notions about masculinity, size and power. During this era, male heroes were represented as ultra-inflated and superhuman, conveying a form of cultural puerilism.[13] The larger the Hollywood hero/man became, the more dangerous was the boy inside. These trends prompted Robin Wood to characterise the films of New Hollywood as children's films for adults.[14] The state of US masculinity was problematic enough when it took the form of the cartoon-character manhood portrayed by Sylvester Stallone and Arnold Schwarzenegger. Schwarzenegger was featured in three prehistoric narratives (twice as Conan the Barbarian and once as Kalidor in *Red Sonja* (Richard Fleischer, 1985). He played a macho cop or a wronged killer in three more films (*Raw Deal* (John Irvin, 1986), *Running Man* (Paul Michael Glaser, 1987) and *Red Heat* (Walter Hill, 1988)). And he was featured on both sides of the human/alien divide playing a super killing robot from the future in *Terminator* (James Cameron, 1984), and super commando alien hunter in *Predator* (John McTiernan, 1987). Stallone's character roles were similarly inflated during this period. Of his thirteen films made during the 1980s, his roles as Rocky and John Rambo are the most famous and clearest example of the overgrown, emotionally immature boy-man archetype. This masculine performance became far more dangerous when the United States' self-image as a righteously innocent adolescent stepped off the silver screen and into the sands of the Middle East in the first US Gulf War. Whether the soldiers themselves mimicked these screen idols or the news industry borrowed their storylines, the parallels between the two caused Lynda Boose to characterise the media representations of US masculinity during the 1991 Gulf War period as 'wanton boys, killing for their sport'.[15] The cross-fertilisation that has taken place between adult political culture and children's popular culture, especially in the realm of representations of war and warriors, functions to reformulate the play of childhood and the seriousness of adulthood. As the century came to a close, both children and adults had access to far more coercive and powerful toys as video games and their military equivalents replaced the once dominant plastic toy models. Contemporary events are encouraging and facilitating the collaborative relationship between the military industry and the toy and game industries. This was made very clear in the 2003 US war in Iraq in which soldiers went into battle with weapons modelled after toys, and toy companies watched developments in the war as they planned new products for the 2004 holiday season. The Dragon Eye remote-controlled reconnais-sance air vehicle used by the Marines in Iraq can be launched with a bungee cord just as the toy planes that inspired it are launched. The soon-to-be deployed Dragon Run-ner is a remote-controlled truck which soldiers will guide using a keypad modelled after Sony's PlayStation 2 game control. Moreover, Sony, the makers of PlayStation, acted immediately after the start of the Iraq war on 20 March 2003 by registering to patent the phrase 'Shock and Awe' for use as the title of a future game release.[16]

Boose's description of the media representations of US soldiers in the first Iraq war as wanton boys is equally apt for media representations of the second US war in Iraq. Just one of the many dozens of news reports that fit such a narrative of US soldiers came in September 2004 when these words from the mortar team for Capt. Kirk Mayfield's Phantoms were published in international and independent news sources: 'Building's gone. I got my kills, I'm coming down. I just love my job.' A British journalist embedded in Fallujah clearly sees the dynamics of false witness at work in the US war on Iraq as he notes that 'for many American soldiers the opportu-nity to avenge dead friends by taking a life was a moment of sheer exhilaration'.[17] It is little wonder that when soldiers in the heat of battle respond to killing in this manner, journalists and cultural critics compare war to a video game. In much the same way that damaging narratives of false witness and revenge have infiltrated children's play spaces, equally dangerous play behaviours associated with children's video game play have entered war zones. The migration of these narratives and behaviours is killing soldiers, civilians and the moral integrity of the US nation.

ANIMATING THE BACK STORY

Too often, the response to a consumer environment saturated with militarism and representations of false witness is to call for bans on products, or at the very least, to prohibit one's own children from interacting with such media.[18] But a 'No War Toys' policy is not powerful enough to address these cultural forces. The process of educating consumers of all ages to integrate violent images and entertainment dif-ferently into their lives is far slower than bans or prohibitions, but it would be a more positive and lasting solution.

What is so poignant about the opening scene of Born on the Fourth of July is seeing Kovic lying on the ground shouting that he is not dead while knowing what the outcome of his war career will be. He will suffer the weight of guilt caused by his killing of a Vietnamese family and one of his own men, and a body paralysed from the chest down. Outcomes such as these are rarely represented in US war entertainment, and consumers cannot provide moral witness for histories that they and the cultural industry they support refuse to acknowledge. US consumers and citizens have for too long accepted iconic history in their entertainment and their history books. Likewise, they have ignored warnings that the democratic process would likely be corrupted by the military-industrial complex. The synergy between US domestic life and militarism is so dangerously united that it is discussed even in children's films, with Joe Dante's *Small Soldiers* (1998) being the best example. As a result, US consumers cannot responsibly plead they have played no part in the perpetuation of militarism, false witness and the historical amnesia iconic history has created within the US.

The negative effects of this cultural and political reality could begin to be addressed if combat spectacle was the catalyst for a rejuvenation of consumers' ethical relationship to the implications of violence, rather than for a false witnessing. Combat spectacle could induce the 'shock of traumatic sight [that] reveals at the heart of human subjectivity not so much an epistemological, but rather what can be defined as an *ethical* relation to the real'.[19] Although combat spectacle has the potential to 'cut us off as knowers from what our bodies tell us about the world and suffering', war entertainment of all types also has the potential to awaken spectators' awareness of history in its fullest contexts.[20]

Sharing historical narratives of war requires that adults engage children in discussion regarding their war play in age-appropriate manners. Even better is for adults to join children's war play. Jim Muir relates in 'Hallowed Ground' how he, his brother and his father placed a broken Joe in a shoebox and buried it in the backyard. Over the next fifteen years, family pets and numerous GI Joes were buried in this plot.[21] Burying toys killed in action gives adults and children the opportunity to discuss the realities of war, remembrance and ritual. Children's play activity in this case mirrors the physical and emotional results of war in a child-appropriate manner. Destruction is not followed by replay but instead by a recognition of loss. Play that includes irretrievable loss in war narratives also invites the opportunity to rework the rules of war play with children to reflect historical reality: when toy soldiers are killed, we have a funeral and these toys do not return to life, they stay dead as would their human equivalent. Letting children discover that destruction is not fun in their own time and place is one way to encourage them to opt for imaginative play narratives that do not involve death and destruction.

Ultimately, the best way to change our relationship to war is to interact with it more not less, but in different ways. As long as war play continues to rely on US war entertainment for narrativisation, US military characters will hold centre stage. Viewers and players alike will then admit the trauma of their experience into their imaginations and muscles. The spectacle of combat focalised through the eyes of US military personnel continues to lead audiences to enact false witness, to answer violence with a vengeful and amplified measure of violence. But it is at the level of domestic play that combat spectacle can be countered, that a material referent can be offered which will reference the losses felt by the victims of US military force. US citizens do not have the direct power to write military policy, but they can help younger generations re-narrativise the scripts of war and witness. In so doing, US citizens will begin to weaken the chain of violence to which false witness has committed their nation.

Notes

1   Tom Engelhardt, *The End of Victory Culture: Cold War America and the Disillusioning of a Generation* (New York: HarperCollins, 1995), 148.

2   Quoted in Michael Rogin, *Ronald Reagan, the Movie* (Berkeley: University of California Press, 1987), 3.

3   J. David Slocum offers for a thoughtful analysis of how individual films as well as the institution of cinema socialise and regulate individual behaviour. See his article, 'Cinema and the Civilizing Process: Rethinking Violence in the World War II Combat Film', *Cinema Journal* 44, no. 3 (2005): 35–63.

4   My notion of the vengeful and voyeuristic bystander draws from the work of Robert Jay Lifton who has described the late twentieth century in the US as the age of the bystander: 'We are bystanders in connection with violence, war, even genocide depicted on our television screens, and with just about any form of suffering, so readily conveyed to us by our media – whether of starvation in Africa, murder and rape in Kosovo, or inner-city killings or drug deaths in this country.' Robert Jay Lifton and Greg Mitchell, *Who Owns Death? Capital Punishment, the American Conscience, and the End of Executions* (New York: HarperCollins, 2000), 168.

5   The ongoing scripting of Second World War battles as being last stand defences intimately connected to the American identity as the victimised underdog is evident in the 2003 television documentary *Wake Island: Alamo of the Pacific*, directed by Craig Haffner and written by Martin Gillam.

6   One of the clearest examples of popular entertainment's fostering of the process of false witness is country singer Toby Keith's 9/11 tribute song, 'Courtesy of the Red, White and Blue (The Angry American)': 'And you'll be sorry that you messed with the US of A / 'Cause we'll put a boot up your ass – It's the American way.'

7   Michael White and Lucy Ward, 'Blair distances UK from "dead or alive" claim', *Guardian*, 19 September 2001. Available <http://www.guardian.co.uk/wtccrash/story/0,1300,554256,00.html> (accessed 25 October 2006).

8   'September 11 and Its Aftermath', *Crimes of War Project*. Available <http://www.crimesofwar.org/expert/attack-main.html> (accessed 25 October 2006).

9   Nancy Carlsson-Paige and Diane E. Levin, *Who's Calling the Shots? How to Respond Effectively to Children's Fascination with War Play and War Toys* (Philadelphia: New Society Publishers, 1990).

10 Krista Foss, 'All I Want for Christmas is a Bombed-Out Dollhouse', *Common Dreams Newscenter*. Available <http://www.commondreams.org/views02/1123-01.htm> (accessed 25 October 2006).

11 Educators for Social Responsibility, 'Special Projects: World Events: Healing: Talking With Children'. Available <http://www.esrnational.org/guide.htm#revenge> (accessed 25 October 2006).

12 D. G. Green, 'Toy Soldiers and Wargames', *Dissent* 32 (1985): 115–16.

13 See Susan Jeffords, *Hard Bodies: Hollywood Masculinity in the Reagan Era* (New Brunswick: Rutgers University Press, 1994).

14 See Robin Wood, *Hollywood from Vietnam to Reagan* (New York: Columbia University Press, 1986), especially chapter 8.

15 Lynda E. Boose, 'Techno-Muscularity and the "Boy Eternal": From the Quagmire to the Gulf', in *Gendering War Talk*, eds Miriam Cooke and Angela Woollacott (Princeton: Princeton University Press, 1993), 100.

16 Julia Day, 'Sony to Cash in on Iraq with "Shock and Awe" Game', *Guardian Newspapers*

Limited. Available <http://media.guardian.co.uk/marketingandpr/story/0,7494,933239,00. html> (accessed 28 August 2003).

17 Toby Harnden, 'I got my kills ... I just love my job', *Daily Telegraph* (London), 9 November 2004.

18 Concerned consumers have called for bans on a wide variety of media promoting violence. From comic books to video games to plastic toys, the sentiment expressed in Code Pink's website is a familiar one: 'Every holiday season manufacturers prey on our children with pro-war propaganda disguised as innocent toys. Don't let your child be a victim of G.I. Joe!' Although the organisation offers more recommendations than a simple ban on war toys, they do not discuss the possibility that war play could and should be remade in children's and society's interest. 'Say No To War Toys', *Code Pink: Women for Peace.* Available <http://www.codepink4peace.org/article.php?list=type&type=96> (accessed 25 October 2006).

19 Cathy Caruth, 'Traumatic Awakenings' in *Violence, Identity, and Self-Determination*, ed. Hent deVries and Samuel Weber (Stanford: Stanford University Press, 1997), 209.

20 William Andrew Myers, '"Severed Heads": Susan Griffin's Account of War, Detachment, and Denial', in *Bringing Home Peace: Feminism, Violence, and Nature*, eds Karen Warner and Duane Cady (Bloomington: Indiana University Press, 1996), 109.

21 Joe Bodnarchuk, 'Childhood Memories', *Headquarters Quarterly.* Available <http://www.bodnarchuk.com/headquarters_quarterly/magazine.html> (accessed 28 August 2003).

PART III | SECOND HAND VISIONS

7. The Grey Space Between: Gerhard Richter's *18. Oktober 1977*

Frances Guerin

On Tuesday 18 October 1977 Andreas Baader, Gudrun Ensslin and Jan-Carl Raspe, three members of West Germany's urban guerrilla organisation, the *Rote Armee Faktion* (Red Army Faction/RAF), or Baader-Meinhof group, as they were later known, were found dead in their cells in Stammheim prison.[1] Gerhard Richter took the date of these deaths as the impetus and the title for a cycle of fifteen blurred 'photo-paintings'.[2] The date of the cycle's execution and public exhibition is as important to German history as that which gives it its title. In 1988, Germany was on the cusp of uncertainty: the borders that defined post-war Germany were about to crumble. As the geographical, political and cultural borders embodied by the Berlin Wall began to collapse the following year, responses to Richter's cycle pointed to its transgression of another set of borders: the works engaged in the increasingly vocal doubts about official versions of post-war German history.[3] They cast a shadow over the histories that have been written in the space between these two landmark events in post-war Germany. The intransigence of distinctions between the guilty and the innocent, perpetrators and victims, and the past and the present were the subject of an animated public and scholarly debate in West Germany during the 1980s known as the *Historikerstreit* (the historians' dispute).[4] These debates focused primarily on the legacies of Nazism in Adenauer and post-Adenauer Germany. Richter's paintings, however, shift focus to address the space between the 1970s and the late 1980s. Nevertheless, *18. Oktober 1977* responds to the call in its midst for images to represent, interrogate and remember the ongoing individual and collective responsibility to history, no matter how distant it may appear. In turn, all of these issues are played out on the surface of the paintings in *18.Oktober 1977*.

The works in the cycle explore through erasure: they define a set of dichotomies and then proceed to diffuse them. One of the most significant distinctions lies between the RAF revolutionaries as criminals and the institutions of the state as upholders of social order. As we move through the cycle, we also recognise the fallibility of the distinction between the public narratives of official history and those of the emotional lives of individuals. Furthermore, the lines between life and death, between the artist and the state, between museum visitor as viewer and the paintings as viewed are all blurred, even dissolved in the moment of viewing. Behind the challenge to otherwise clear demarcations lie two of Richter's signature formal concerns: an exploration of the interface between photography and painting, and the space – both physical and narrative – between the paintings as they hang on the pristine white walls of the gallery. All of these strategies amount to the most profound space-between, namely, the spectatorial space carved out by the cycle in the process of its viewing, in its engagement with a spectator. The grey space-between established in the works' surface articulations produces a fundamentally destabilising viewing experience. This experience is characterised by a simultaneous invitation to an emotional engagement of each individual viewer and a withholding of all such possibility, a withholding that ultimately guarantees an intellectual involvement with the paintings. This complex process ultimately forces the German museum-goer to recognise her need to keep searching for a place from which to remember and rethink her relationship to German history and its representation.

The disquiet stirred in the viewer by the paintings is central to the status of *18. Oktober 1977* as an agent in the process of bearing witness to the events of the German past. According to established definitions of witnessing, in particular, those reliant on the influential theories of Dori Laub and Shoshana Felman, a painting cannot be a witness. For Laub and Felman, the visual object is always a medium and never an agent in the act of bearing witness. The image is understood only to mediate the intersubjective relation between survivor-witness and the listener/viewer-witness. However, in this chapter, I want to make a more radical argument. Namely, I imbue the works in *18. Oktober 1977* with an agency: I argue that they are directly involved in an intersubjective relationship that serves to articulate a process of bearing witness.

I base this notion of the image as agent on the provocative, though self-consciously equivocal, thinking of W. J. T. Mitchell in his recent book, *What Do Pictures Want?*[5] Mitchell insists that he does not want to personify pictures, but rather, that as viewers, spectators and consumers of images, we see them, criticise them, appropriate them and replicate them as though they were animated. We give them the power of vivification. When asked if he really believes that images, for example, have desires and 'want things', Mitchell responds, 'No, I don't believe it. But we cannot ignore that human beings (including myself) insist on talking and behaving as if they *did* believe it.'[6] Richter's representations are not actual witnesses of the Baader-Meinhof deaths. But in our active dialectical involvement in the process of viewing the cycle, the paintings can be approached as agents in an intersubjective process of witnessing. As Mitchell would have it, we ask questions of them, we project our desires onto them, they seduce us 'to feel and act in specific ways?'[7] Specifically, the surface sensitivities of Richter's paintings entice us to enter into a relationship with them. The physically, emotionally and intellectually active viewer, and especially the German viewer, gives them the power of involvement in the revivification of history. Through the feints of their surface ambiguities, through their opening up of a series of grey spaces-between, these paintings become 'lifelike' and history becomes re-energised – witnessed – in the intersubjective process of reception.

By 1988, attention had shifted away from the social turmoil caused by the RAF in West Germany during the 1970s. Consideration of these past events and their significance for the German state was nowhere to be found in the vociferous celebrations of reunification that dominated the political, social and cultural landscape of Germany in 1989. Richter's paintings provoke, unsettle and remind their contemporaries that the highly-charged events of the late 1960s and 1970s are central to their own social revolution. Like the process of exchange between the analysand and the analyst, who facilitates the former's recovery of deep memory, these paintings engage in a process of witnessing through their three-way interaction with viewers and the represented past. As agents in the process of bearing witness, the paintings agitate their viewer and re-expose the not-yet-worked-through collective traumas of the German past. In this chapter, I argue that the paintings in *18. Oktober 1977* revive these otherwise repressed traumas in the minds of their viewers. To reiterate, this process is begun in the nebulous grey space that is exposed when otherwise independent discourses begin to bleed into one another.[8] Moreover, it is a grey space that commences in the sensuous and aesthetic qualities of these monochrome images.

Lastly, of critical importance to the emotional effect and intellectual insight of the paintings in the process of bearing witness is that they be experienced in non-linear narrative possibilities. All of the individual paintings of *18. Oktober 1977* are self-contained and able to be viewed in isolation. However, they also make sense in their narrative progression beginning with a portrait of Ulrike Meinhof, through images of arrest, incarceration, an image of Baader's cell and record player (which concealed the gun he used for suicide), death, autopsy and funeral. Within this narrative of temporal progression, some works also fall into clusters in diptych and triptych formations. Because the museum visitor's experience of the cycle is inflected by the order in which individual paintings are viewed, it is also enlightening to explore the possible non-linear paths through the cycle. Thus the cycle creates different sets of meanings depending on the order in which the paintings are experienced.

The Baader-Meinhof group wrought havoc on the post-war status quo of West Germany in the late 1960s and 1970s. From the arson of two Frankfurt department stores in October 1968 to the kidnapping and slaying of Mercedes-Benz executive Hans Martin Schleyer in September 1977, and the hijacking of a Lufthansa jet a few weeks later, the young radicals spawned a civil conflict that reverberated through all levels of West German government and a range of capitalist institutions, including the West German press.[9] Images of the Baader-Meinhof littered the popular press – television, newspapers, right- and left-wing publications – and they came to be labelled 'the number one enemy of the State'.[10] Wanted posters covered in mug shots offering rewards for information on the whereabouts of these *Anarchistische Gewalttäter* (Anarchist Violent Criminals) were pasted on every available surface across the country.[11] Images of the revolutionaries claimed to capture the violence, aggression and injustice of their actions. The members of the Baader-Meinhof group were represented as dangerous, irrational and out of control. This image of danger and uncontainable otherness is the convention that Richter's paintings most obviously question.[12]

One of the most familiar press images is the often replayed fragment of news footage depicting the arrest of Baader, Raspe and Holger Meins on 1 June 1972 outside a Frankfurt garage. The footage exemplifies the official agencies' construction of the group.[13] Having appeared as instructed at the entrance of the garage in their underwear, the resistant Raspe and Meins are dragged one at a time, past the combat tank brought in as back up, into the thin crowd of policemen, press and general public gathered on the streets. Baader stands fully clothed at the entrance to the garage and, after being shot in the torso, his still struggling weight is carried to an ambulance. The three individuals are furious at the injustice of their treatment. As they kick, writhe and scream in protest, their near-naked or seriously wounded bodies are flanked by perfectly composed, silent policemen, their uniforms unruffled and their faces expressionless. The image is framed alternately from above and at street level when the camera follows the police-escorted prisoners, always keeping the body of the young radical in centre-frame. The irrepressible anger and apparent hysteria of Baader, Raspe and Meins is emphasised as much by the unswerving composure of the police as it is by the jerky, hand-held movements of the camera that films the captured. As they scream and thrash their bodies in an attempt to break free, the revolutionaries are filmed to appear like dangerous lunatics, wholly other to the human bystanders.

Two of the earliest images of *18. Oktober 1977* are based on photographic stills produced from this press footage. Like all of the paintings in the cycle, *Arrest 1 (Festnahme 1)* and *Arrest 2 (Festnahme 2)* mimic the aspect ratio of snapshot photographs. Although both are oil on canvas and at 92 x 126.5cm are significantly larger than snapshots, the paintings explore the medium and semantics of the press photograph.[14] Through the works' attention to the medium of painting, the two images also interrogate the intersection of photography and painting. And where painting and photography meet, we find Richter's most devastating claim regarding the failure of both media to mimetically depict the reality of that which they see. In turn, this failure becomes the ground on which the viewer is invited to confront her own assumptions about that reality, the ground on which the historical trauma is brought back to life. Thus, Richter refuses to dichotomise the photographic representation and that of his paintings. Rather, he uses the discrepancies between the two media to find a common ground. And he discovers this common ground to be fraught with epistemological uncertainty.

The negotiation of the space between painting and photography begins on the surface of the painting. It begins with the application of Richter's steel grey palette to the blur of his brushstroke. Richter describes grey as the mediator, the space in-between, the uncertain, the ill-defined. The colour is, he says, 'the welcome and only possible equivalent for indifference, non-commitment, absence of opinion, absence of shape'.[15] Richter's grey transforms the black and white intensities in high-contrast press photography of the period. The source photographs of paintings such as *Arrest 1* and *2* found in the illustrated press were high-contrast black and white images that claimed to capture the objectivity of actual events. Richter's re-painted version of the same scene is consciously grey and hazy. It appears uncertain of its status as objective or otherwise. Together with the blurring of the painted surface, the shift to grey encourages the viewer to question the veracity of the image. We puzzle over what we see in the painting and, by association, what the source photograph saw.

All of the *18. Oktober 1977* paintings use the same aesthetic strategies as the *Arrest* diptych to bring us physically closer to the images, then to distance us from their content. The austere grey, the blur, the physical distance of the events from the high-angle perspective of the point of view all remove the events from our grasp; they render them cold and distant. The blurred grey rejects the clarity of a press photograph, renders it out of focus, a mistake. Thus, the re-painting appropriates the press photograph's distant point of view to indicate that the photographs and paintings meet in the mutual prohibition of their access to reality. In their appropriation and manipulation of the parameters of photography – aspect ratio, colour, contrast, perspective and focus – the paintings in the cycle offer a critique of the photograph's representational truth claim.

Arrest 1 and *2* are almost identical, but only almost. Although they are of identical dimension, they show two different scenes. This inclusion of multiple yet individually discrete images contributes to the paintings' further departure from the reality they claim to depict. The strategy refers to the mass reproducibility of the photograph and, in particular, the mass reproduction of the source press photograph. The repetition also calls attention to the photograph's spurious claim to objectivity. No matter how many times a photograph is reproduced, it can only ever approximate what it represents. The slight differentiation in each repetition of Richter's paintings reminds us of this. Of course, the same could be said of Richter's paintings: they do not come any closer to the truth of the photograph's subject matter. They are, after all, representations of representations; as removed from the historical events as the distance from which they depict. However, unlike the photographic versions, images such as the *Arrest* diptych do not claim to access the truth, or to offer a definitive vision. Above and beyond the challenge to the veracity of the press photograph, *18. Oktober 1977* refuses both its own basic truth claims, and also those of painting more broadly. The paintings' representational elusiveness and their blurring of the distinctions between photography and painting form the foundation for a much deeper truth: the viewer's active involvement in the process of rekindling the otherwise buried historical trauma.

PUBLIC HISTORY AND INDIVIDUAL LIFE

The relationship of scepticism between painting and photography, and between historical events and their representation, provides the vacillating platform on which Richter interrogates the distinction between public history – the Baader-Meinhof as they conceive of themselves and are conceived of by state-sanctioned institutions – and their fate as individuals. The cycle challenges the viewer to negotiate the tension between these two irreconcilable narratives through a provocation of both historical awareness and emotional engagement. In turn, two simultaneous responses merge to encourage the viewer to remember the events of 18 October 1977, and to question their official representation. In particular, while the source photographs announce the closure or finality of the historical events they depict, so Richter brings the event back to life through a focus on the individual. More specifically, like many of the late 1980s representations of the 1970s 'German Autumn', the paintings only give the appearance of offering access to the desires and emotions of the represented individuals. Because as soon as the invitation is extended, it is retracted. In turn, this stopping short of what the paintings portend to provide prompts an intellectual engagement. This process is key to the revivification of memories of broader historical events in the mind of the viewer.[16] Once again, what remains unique about Richter's paintings is the use of paint and the painted surface to reiterate the historical 'space between' that is examined in their representation.

Figure 1: Gerhard Richter, *Hanged (Erhängte)* from 'October 18, 1977' (1988). New York, Museum of Modern Art (MoMA).

Hanged (*Erhängte*) (figure 1) is one of five single images in the cycle. It depicts the disturbing scene of Gudrun Ensslin hanged in her cell. Due to the intensity of the blurring, we are unsure of the identity of the corpse. If we are aware of the historical details, then we will know that it is Ensslin who was found 'hanged' in her cell on the morning of 18 October 1977. However, the date of the cycle's title is designed to confuse rather than clarify, and it would be misleading to identify the corpse on the basis of this information alone.[17] Nevertheless, identification of the individual is not what is at stake in *Hanged*. Indeed, the inability to identify and individualise the corpse is perhaps the point. For unlike the sensationalism of the full-frontal, black and white press image from which *Hanged* is drawn, the blur of Richter's painting, the lack of distinction between figure and ground, and the placement of the body in the recess of the image all protect Ensslin's corpse from the ogling eyes of the viewer. Simultaneously, these aesthetic elements ensure the continued effort of the viewer to search for clarity and meaning. The blurring guarantees a sustained engagement with the painting which is, in turn, the basis of the painting's involvement in the process of bearing witness. Ensslin's body was found hidden behind a woollen blanket in the window alcove. When the image appeared in the magazine weekly *Stern*, her body was depicted in a full-length, full-frontal shot in which all but the window frame behind her and the ground beneath her feet was cropped away.[18] A tape measure ran the length of her body in a gesture of scientific rationalisation. Richter recoups Ensslin's 'privacy' when he safely sequesters the corpse behind the surface of the brushstroke, the blurred surface of the image. He also places the figure well into the background of the image.

the image and the witness

The identity of the body may be hidden in the depths of the painting, behind the brushstroke, but the viewer is drawn into the painting, the cell and Ensslin's silence through the use of light and composition. Richter frames the figure through an exaggeration of the blanket, which is now a black curtain to the left of the image, and the bright white of the wall that runs along the right side of the frame. With almost half the vertical space of the image being consumed by this inner framing device, the relative boldness of the black and white elements guides our vision towards the vertical, seemingly elongated, blurred grey figure in the centre. Even though the image is blurred, the framing device ensures that there is little else in the image to distract us from the figure. While the aesthetic manipulation of the grey painted surface repeats Ensslin's seclusion in death behind the curtain, Richter simultaneously invites us to peer through the frame of Ensslin's room into the space of her death. The blurring also entices us physically closer to the painting as we step forward to see behind the veil-like haze of the blurred surface. Nevertheless, the closer we go, the less we can see of the figure and the more the image dissolves into the abstraction of paint on a canvas. Like the dots of a printed-press photograph, the medium of paint is reduced, at close range, to abstract lines, shades and forms on Richter's canvas. Thus, *Hanged* withholds the information and knowledge that is claimed through clarity of detail by the photographic reproduction on which it is based. To borrow Mitchell's rhetoric, this is a painting that wants simultaneously to be seen and to be left alone.[19]

The press image emphasises information that confirms the event has indisputably taken place; it has been documented for the historical record and now belongs to the past. *Hanged* is concerned to reopen the historical record, to revive the event in its various forms of representation, and to explore the brutality and isolation of Ensslin's death. *Hanged* does more than repeat the coldness of the photographic representation in the popular press. Through obscuring the image, denying access to Ensslin's corpse, the painting asks the viewer to acknowledge representation (both photographic and painted) as a transgression of the space of an individual's death. Specifically, she was an individual forced to die isolated from a world that insisted on littering every possible surface in the pubic eye with her face. *Hanged* thus provokes the viewer to recall an image and an historical event that had otherwise been laid to rest by a press photograph when it claimed the last word. Richter's painting unfixes the past by clouding it in aesthetic and historical uncertainty. *Hanged* explores the tension between the official desire to resolve and close the door on events of the past, and the urgency to keep this ephemeral moment alive in the public imagination. By doing so, it generates an intersubjective relationship with the viewer, which is at the heart of a process of bearing witness to the past.

Images such as the *Confrontation* (*Gegenüberstellung*) triptych of Gudrun Ensslin (figures 2–4) as she poses for a line-up exaggerate this tension between public history and individual experience even further. Through the interrogation of the space between these irreconcilable narratives, the paintings are involved in the creation of a space that enables the viewer to move beyond a confrontation with an unresolved history to a recognition of her own implication in this same historical narrative. All of the same compositional strategies are used in *Confrontation* to draw attention to the facial expressions and bodily disposition of Ensslin's figure. However, this time Ensslin is identifiable and her gestures are legible. When the minutiae of these gestures

Figures 2 and 3: Gerhard Richter, *Confrontation 1 (Gegenüberstellung 1)* from 'October 18, 1977' (1988). New York, Museum of Modern Art (MoMA).

and emotions are revealed by the painting, the physical, psychological and emotional relationship between figure and viewer becomes unsettling. In the same moment that we are drawn toward Ensslin's physical being and engage with the privacy of her emotions, we are confronted with the revolutionary as a reflection of our own selves. She is no longer simply the anonymous captive of the source photograph who brought about civil chaos and suffered the consequences. In *Confrontation*, Richter paints an emotionally alive individual who is also entrapped by social and political institutions. As viewers of this triptych, we not only observe, but we are seduced into the space of Ensslin's entrapment. And, as I shall argue, thanks to the discursive qualities of the painting, we become implicated in her plight.

The source photographs for *Confrontation* were taken as Ensslin entered the Stammheim courthouse having been out of the public eye for a month while in captivity. Like the successive images of a film sequence, in *Confrontation* Ensslin is paraded in her prison garb before our inquisitive eyes. Here Richter introduces another set of interstices, namely the space between the paintings, to undermine the fixity of our position as viewer and Ensslin and her representation as viewed. Somewhere between the first and the second *Confrontation* paintings the individual is brought into the spotlight. The first painting is not only blurred, but the contrast between the black of Ensslin's shirt and the white skin of her neck, and again, between the background and her dull prison attire is muted. Due to the blur of the painted surface, in the first of these three identically-sized paintings, we are unable to determine if Ensslin is smiling or surprised, quietly contemplative or suspicious of the eyes that watch her. The middle image shows Ensslin's face so alive that we can feel the brightness of her surprised eyes. While in the first painting her left shoulder is in the process of turning to the viewer, in the second, her body is all but squared within the frame. It is as though she has recognised someone in the crowd, and now, she looks directly at the viewer. Despite the blur to the left side of her face, and the

the image and the witness

Figure 4: Gerhard Richter, *Confrontation 3*
(Gegenüberstellung 3) from 'October 18, 1977' (1988).
New York, Museum of Modern Art (MoMA).

uncertainty it engenders, Ensslin's animated expression touches us because it is directed towards, and perhaps intended for, us. An alteration in the lighting, the distinction of Ensslin's figure from the background and the relative clarity and softness of her face allow her to motion towards the front of the image, away from the wall against which she is pinned in the first *Confrontation*. Thus, across the space of the first and second paintings, Ensslin is physically and emotionally opened up to the viewer.

In the third painting, Ensslin's body has once again turned away from the viewer, her head is bowed, and although her mouth is now without signs of tension, perhaps even with the remnants of a smile, her emotions are once again out of reach. Ensslin's figure is now in a three-quarter length as opposed to head-and-shoulders composition. Her profiled face now shines under a much harsher, colder light and her prison dress, shadow and background merge into a dark middling grey. The physical and emotional retreat, or refusal, of *Confrontation* leads us through painfully private emotional states of the prisoner. Of course, it is not that we are really engaged with the emotional life of Ensslin, but once again, this is the feint of Richter's painted representation of a photograph that invites us to participate in its narratives. Through this process, the triptych also protects Ensslin's vulnerability; it always keeps her slightly ambiguous, her feelings are never quite tactile because they are only ever a painted appearance. The paintings watch the figure move towards us, away from us, open her gestures out to us, and then retract the invitation to connect to them. In turn, the viewer's identification and sustained engagement with Ensslin as emotive individual through the narrative played out across the gallery wall stimulates his own involvement in the larger historical narrative. Through engaging us in this direct encounter with the individual Ensslin, the triptych sets in motion a process of witnessing the historical trauma. It forces us to recognise our role in and responsibility to the historical past of which Ensslin was a central public media figure.

Ultimately, however, the viewer can never fully identify with Ensslin as she is presented in *Confrontation*. As Richter says, there is nothing private or individual about the RAF members; they are no more than the sensational public image that the media created of them.[20] Their images function like those of film stars when they give the impression of psychological and emotional depth, while all the time representing a generic public image representative of an idea, an illusion. This does not absolve our responsibility, but on the contrary, it underlines it. We are thrust into a space between the well-rehearsed public history of the RAF leader as criminal and an affective recognition of Richter's narration of Ensslin as a psychologically complex individual with whom we strive to connect. As we shift between identification with the painted figure as a real historical person and recognition of her image as a construction of the press, we are drawn ever deeper into the revivification of the history of which she is a protagonist and in which we are consequently implicated. Thus the 'confrontation' of the triptych's title might be understood as the image's confrontation with the viewer to assume the responsibility for the continuing urgency to keep these narratives alive.

ARCHIVES OF THE STATE AND THE ARTIST

18. Oktober 1977's scrutiny of the spaces between official institutional representations of the RAF and those which challenge these representations extends to an interrogation of the unstable relationship between the handling of the photographic images by the German State and by Richter himself. This layer of analysis is formed when the paintings work with and against the use, dissemination and storage of the source photographs for official purposes.

In a gesture of fear and simultaneous fascination with the power of the photograph's presumed potential for anarchy, thanks to both its potent subject and its inherent reproducibility, the police-commissioned photographs of the RAF were carefully archived out of public sight. The Baader-Meinhof members were subjected to the same processes of possession, domination and de-individualisation that has been the fate of all modern social deviants when they were photographed for identification purposes. In turn, the photographs were themselves sorted and classified in an attempt to stymie their desire to cause social unrest. RAF activities continued in the wake of the Stammheim deaths. There was unprecedented controversy and political scandal surrounding the deaths due to the possibility that the state had perpetrated murder. The brighter the spotlight shone on images of the Baader-Meinhof deaths by the press, the more intense the public indignation. Social order was consequently sought through the systematisation of reproducible images which were threatening to proliferate uncontrollably. With the photographs archived away, the threat was erased, or at least hidden from view. Similar to the obsessive organisation and cataloguing of identification photographs pioneered by late nineteenth-century police forces, the public prosecutor's office in Stuttgart reduced the official photographs taken at the time of the RAF deaths to abstract, quantifiable objects when it placed them in an archive.[21] Like so many sensitive documents that harbour the potential to expose vulnerability and culpability in official ranks, the RAF photographs were, according to Robert Storr, all but inaccessible to the public.[22]

While Richter challenges the objectivity of the photographs through blurring, the handling of the source images by the public prosecutor's office would have us believe in their mimetic credibility. When placed in an archive that took the form of a locked filing cabinet, the images were defined and legitimated as objective documents which could potentially prove a crime. The fear of and need to master the perpetrator-revolutionary as social aberration is here transferred onto the photographs that depict him or her. As modern idolators, the German officials who commanded ownership of these images appeared not only to believe in the indexicality of the photographic image, but to equate the image with the subject.[23] Unwittingly, such acts of archival hoarding elevate the image and its subject to the status of fetish. These practices remind us of the conservation of old graven images to protect against their power.[24] These precious objects had to be hidden away, somewhere safe, where the represented enemy culture could not wreak the havoc it promised. *18. Oktober 1977* resists this desire to fetishise the image when, as illustrated here, the paintings oscillate between various incompatible, yet interdependent, discourses: painting and photography, life and death, public history and individual experience. And in their act of resistance, the images open up the space in which the viewer is called to revivify her memory of this chapter of German history. And in the grey zone of the space-between, history must be remembered, confronted and engaged if the traumas it generated are not to be repeated in the future. Thus, when they enter into the discourse on the handling of their source photographs, Richter's images ignite a relationship with their viewer that leads to the witnessing of history. However, Richter's paintings simultaneously replicate the same cycle of archival classification and mastery over the image and what it depicts. Each of the images in *18. Oktober 1977* is drawn from *Atlas*, Richter's own continually evolving photographic archive.[25] Since the early 1960s, Richter has continued to compile both found and self-generated photographs into what amounts to a *catalogue raisonné* of the world seen through Richter's eyes. The images range from landscapes and family portraits, through pornography, press photographs and Holocaust images. Some are carefully staged, while others appear to be taken on a whim. Irrespective of aesthetic quality, all of them are meticulously ordered, systematised, according to how Gerhard Richter sees. It is not an order that is apparent to all. Richter's system is, in the end, subjective. Just as the museum visitor is on the precipice of grasping the logic of Richter's selection and ordering of the photographs in *Atlas*, the criteria are changed. An image that does not belong appears, the one we expect to see is removed or the seemingly logical order is disrupted in some other way. As much as *Atlas* imitates systems of categorisation and mnemonic logic, it also performs its failure to do so.[26] Thus, Richter's archival processes plunge his works into yet another grey space of ineffability. They are practices for classifying and containing the aleatory events of history in all its guises. Simultaneously, his work always stops short of containing, thus exercising control over the images it accommodates.

The paintings of *18. Oktober 1977* underline this conundrum. On the most obvious level, the fifteen appropriated photographs on which the *18. Oktober 1977* cycle is based are now absent from the archive of *Atlas*. Their absence rewrites the narrative of *Atlas* from which they are plucked. In their new context of *18. Oktober 1977*, the reworked, painted images rewrite the narrative of the historical events at Stammheim prison. Although *Atlas* incorporates approximately one hundred photographs of the Baader-Meinhof deaths, *18. Oktober 1977* includes only fifteen. Thus, the painted images are three times appropriated: first in pre-production from the official public discourse, second in production from the photographic medium into painting, and third, for the purposes of exhibition they are appropriated from *Atlas*. Through this three-fold appropriation, Richter distances the images still further from the spectacle identifiable in their press and police contexts. Similarly, his readiness to reorganise his own archive draws attention to the authorities' policy not to disturb theirs.

Richter also gives each image a temporality that it otherwise does not have in its official capacity within a news article, or as forensic evidence. The mass media and official institutions use the image to convey information, information that is typologised, organised according to the categorical separators of a filing cabinet. Richter uses the same images both to indict this mode of communication, and to offer a more tentative, less easily accessed, less instantaneous knowledge. The knowledge offered by the paintings is acquired gradually through an interaction with the image on the part of the viewer as she contemplates the individual lives of the revolutionaries as victims. In effect, we recognise our own humanity in the inner, emotional life of each RAF member. As we watch ourselves attempting to master the image, we are simultaneously humbled before it, forced to recognise our own culpability in its objectification. This complex process of interaction with the depicted figures, with individual painted photographs, and with the space-between, keeps this traumatic historical moment and its representation alive and urgent in the viewer's mind. The image as witness therefore stirs a self-awareness in the viewer of *18. Oktober 1977*, and provokes a revivification of complex events that, today, tend to be relegated to a completed chapter in Germany's history.

THE PRESS, THE STATE AND THE MUSEUM OF MODERN ART

Richter's images as agents in the process of bearing witness do not stop here. Indeed, they continue to fall deeper into the discursive modes of power and knowledge that they critique. Richter is adamant that the cycle not be broken up, that it remain unique and coherent.[27] Similarly, he stipulated that it be sold to a museum, that the cycle cannot be adequately housed or exhibited by a private art gallery. When it was finally purchased by New York's Museum of Modern Art in 1995, the irony of Richter's directives became even more accentuated. The chosen fifteen images appropriated from the archive of *Atlas* became housed in one of the world's most revered cultural institutions. Thus, the sale of *18. Oktober 1977* placed the images back in the hands of a capitalist institution that engages in comparable practices of objectification to those the images seek to vilify. As a museum, MoMA is no less committed to the business of commodifying images than is the German illustrated press. The museum is driven by economic imperatives and cultural practices that offer images as objects for aesthetic appreciation, often setting up the limits of interpretation. In exhibitions, the direction and shape of museum visitors' responses are carefully molded through the autocratic organisation of the works into a univocal narrative. The fact that Richter chose MoMA, rather than any other museum, to be the owner of *18. Oktober 1977* underscores the transformation of the paintings from agents in the process of bearing witness to that of cultural commodification. As is widely acknowledged in the art historical and museum world, MoMA imparts an unrivalled economic and cultural value to those works it sanctions through inclusion in its collection.

MoMA included *18. Oktober 1977* in its 2002 retrospective of Richter's oeuvre, which was organised according to the chronology of his career. The MoMA exhibition placed *18. Oktober 1977* and other works in the service of a narrative about Richter the artistic genius. The museum gave no more information about the paintings than the titles and dates of execution. The historical circumstances of the works' production and consumption, the contradictory social discourses out of which they grew, and the historical events to which they refer were not available. American visitors' only chance of learning of these historical discourses came when their path through the exhibition terminated in the bookshop. Thus, like the West German popular press in the 1970s, MoMA exploited the historical images as objects in the interests of promoting its own narrative of cultural dominance. In addition to the economic benefits of the exhibition, it was designed to promote the development of Gerhard Richter as the great contemporary European painter. For all the differences between their strategies of display, both the museum and the popular press strip the image of its connection to its social and historical roots.

In their new context for an American audience, the paintings raise still more questions, and are even more elusive. Despite their apparent pragmatism, the titles are chosen to create imprecision rather than clarity around the deaths. *Arrest (Festnahme)*, *Confrontation (Gegenüberstellung)* and *Hanged (Erhängte)* all introduce uncertainty into the images: Who is arrested? Someone just outside the images? Perhaps it is the scene before the camera that is arrested? And in *Hanged*, is Ensslin hanged or does she hang herself? Similar questions could be asked of *Confrontation*. Where is the confrontation? Is it between the represented figure and the viewer? Between the law and the individual? Or, as I have claimed, between painting and viewer. The title of the cycle as a whole shows equal ambivalence toward its apparent specificity. Why 18 October 1977 when not all of the paintings represent events that took place on this date? *Youth Portrait (Jugendbildnis)*, a portrait of Meinhof that opens the cycle, is painted from a photograph taken in 1970. The arrests represented in *Arrest* took place in 1972, and Ulrike Meinhof whose displayed corpse is the content of another triptych, *Dead (Tote)*, died on 9 May 1976. Dates are used to confuse rather than clarify or identify images, while titles are given to the paintings as though to quell the urge to archive or organise on the museum wall, yet all the time resisting this possibility. This irresolute use of titles first appropriates and then undercuts the impulse to rationalise that lies behind the preservation of images. *18. Oktober 1977* thus points the finger at the museum as another institutional archive, a cultural companion to the West German State.

Richter's sale of *18. Oktober 1977* to MoMA for US$3 million in 1995 successfully commodified the images in a manner that, for all the differences, reminds us of the source context of the German illustrated press.[28] The paintings had been on loan to the Museum for Modern Art in Frankfurt and Richter suddenly sold them without informing the Frankfurt Museum. There was understandable public outrage in Germany over the decision. The German press and art world objected: it was equivalent to selling a part of German history. *Frankfurter Allgemeine Zeitung* reported that these paintings represented the trauma of a still unresolved period of history. Indeed, the German response to the sale legitimates my claim for the image as agent in the revivification of historical events in the mind of the spectator. The press argued that by selling them, Richter removed a critical focus for the continued ideological struggle over German history and its memory.[29] And we cannot ignore that Richter was in full control of the sale, thus placing himself as complicit in the processes of decontextualisation. For MoMA, *18. Oktober 1977* was an important late twentieth-century artwork. Its purchase signaled 'a serious attempt to strengthen its collection of post-war European art'.[30] On the one hand, the ambiguity and inconclusiveness that enables the paintings to bring history alive is erased by the new narrative which casts them as exemplary works of 'post-war European art'; after all, how can an American audience engage in a critique of the representation of historical events for which it is given no context? On the other, Richter's sale and MoMA's purchase of the cycle has brought its commodification to the attention of German critics and magnified its political discourse. Furthermore, the press attracted by the sale in 1995 and the exhibition in 2002 have kept *18. Oktober 1977* and the events it depicts in public discourse far longer than may otherwise have been the case.[31] Thus, this public exposure of the paintings keeps the ambiguity of their significance alive. Their existence in the archives of one of the art world's most conservative art institutions and the political discourses surrounding their acquisition and exhibition open up a whole new set of contradictions. It is easy to criticise Richter's self-interested transaction, and to renounce MoMA's tendency to champion the radicals as martyrs (as Hilton Kramer argues), or bemoan the erasure of German history.[32] However, another approach appreciates Richter's sale and the museum's purchase on the future of these paintings as the engine of a renewed provocation to engage with another historical conundrum from yet another liminal space: the one between 1970s West German political and social institutions and twenty-first-century American cultural institutions. The new context of *18. Oktober 1977* adds another layer of uncertainty and contradiction that fuels the image's revivification of traumatic historical events in the mind of the viewer. In turn, MoMA's gesture furthers the project of interrogating and diffusing the grey space between the state and the revolutionary, between public history and individual life, between viewer and viewed (whether the image or the figure it represents). As long as these interstices are the subject and ground of *18. Oktober 1977*, regardless of context, the image remains a potential agent in the intersubjective process of bearing witness to unresolved traumatic historical events.

Notes

1   Irmgard Möller was also found with four stab wounds to her chest; however, the wounds were not fatal. The authoritative account of these events and the RAF activities is still Stefan Aust, *The Baader-Meinhof Group: The Inside Story of a Phenomenon*, trans. Anthea Bell (London: The Bodley Head, 1985). All of my references to Baader-Meinhof activities are taken from Aust's account.
2   'Photo-paintings' is the term that Richter himself gave to his painted versions of mass-circulated photographs.
3   Looming behind Richter's interrogation of the RAF deaths is the controversial question of the role of the Nazi perpetrator in the Holocaust and acts of violence in the Second World War.
4   See Ernst Piper (ed.) *Forever in the Shadow of Hitler?: Original Documents of the Historikerstreit, The Controversy Concerning the Singularity of the Holocaust*, trans. James Knowlton and Truett Cates (Atlantic Highlands, NJ: Humanities Press, 1993).
5   W. J. T. Mitchell, *What Do Pictures Want?: The Lives and Loves of Images* (Chicago and London: University of Chicago Press, 2005).

6   Ibid., 11 (emphasis in original).

7   Ibid., 25.

8   The paintings inhabit numerous other interstices. Gertrud Koch discusses the paintings' negotiation of the space between modernity and pre-modernity as well as Richter's fascination for the interface of photography and painting. See Gertrud Koch, 'The Open Secret: Gerhard Richter and the Surfaces of Modernity', in *Gerhard Richter*, ed. Gertrud Koch (Paris: Éditions Dis Voir, 1995), 9–27.

9   These events are not really the first and the last of their campaign, but I cite them as bookends here because they mark the span of involvement of those radicals whose incarceration and death provides the subject matter of Richter's paintings.

10 'Die Baader-Meinhof Story: Wie aus einem Angeber der Staatsfeind Nr. 1 wurde', *Stern*, 11 June 1972, 18–30.

11 See Robert Storr, *Gerhard Richter: October 18, 1977* (New York: Museum of Modern Art, 2000), 40.

12 The exaggerated discourses of stigmatisation remind us of the contemporary fear and hysteria around Islamic fundamentalist terrorism. The connection to the contemporary situation is significant insofar as I am interested in shifting the focus away from the myopia of early twenty-first-century understanding of terrorism and perpetration. Terrorism is a historical phenomenon with political and geographical specifics and it must be understood as such, that is, within its unique historical context.

13 These images are often recycled in documentaries about the RAF and the post-1968 student movement in West Germany. Alternatively, the images have also consistently been appropriated by narrative feature films that refer to the events to make a larger point, usually about social injustice. See, for example, *Stammheim* (Reinhard Hauff, 1986), *Starbuck – Holger Meins* (Gerdt Conradt, 2001), and *Baader* (Christopher Roth, 2001).

14 Richter bases *Festnahme 1* and *2* on generic photographs that appeared in much of the sensationalist press at the time.

15 Gerhard Richter, 'From a Letter to Edy de Wilde, 23 February 1975', *The Daily Practice of Painting: Writings, 1962–1993*, trans. David Britt (London: Thames and Hudson/Anthony d'Offay Gallery, 1995), 82–3.

16 See, for example, the many filmic representations of the RAF era in films such as Margarethe von Trotta's *Die bleierne Zeit* (*German Sisters*, 1981) and the collaborative documentary, *Deutschland im Herbst* (*Germany in Autumn*, 1978).

17 The painting could also represent Ulrike Meinhof who was found hanged from a window grating in her cell on 9 May 1976.

18 'Der Fall Stammheim', *Stern*, 30 October 1980, 24–5. These images were released to the press when investigation into the cause of the deaths – assumed suicides – was reopened as evidence demonstrated that it would have been impossible for the prisoners to kill themselves. This was especially the case for Andreas Baader when it was deemed impossible for him to have shot the three bullets found in his cell.

19 See Mitchell, *What Do Pictures Want?*, 39–48.

20 Gerhard Richter, *The Daily Practice of Painting*, 193. This notion of the RAF leader as no more than a generic public image representative of an idea or an illusion is most articulately embodied in *Jugendbildnis* (*Youth Portrait*), a portrait of Meinhof as poised and glamorous; as Robert Storr says, she appears just like a movie star. Storr, *Gerhard Richter: October 18, 1977*, 106.

21 See Allan Sekula, 'The Body and the Archive', *October* 39 (Winter 1986): 3–64.

22 Storr, *Gerhard Richter: October 18, 1977*, 149.

23 On this notion of the modern idolator as attributing the image with a value far beyond its objective worth, see W. J. T. Mitchell, *Iconology: Image, Text, Ideology* (University of Chicago Press, Chicago, 1986).

24 This is a standard way of explaining the obsessive collection of objects for the purposes of cultural domination. See Roger Cardinal and John Elsner, 'Introduction', in *The Cultures of Collecting*, eds Roger Cardinal and John Elsner (Cambridge, MA: Harvard University Press, 1994), 1–6.

25 *Atlas* contains one hundred Baader-Meinhof images. See Fred Jahn (ed.) *Atlas* (Munich: Lenbachhaus, 1990).

26 See Benjamin H. D. Buchloh, 'Gerhard Richter's *Atlas*: The Anomic Archive', in *Gerhard Richter*, ed. Bruno Corà (Prato: Centro per l'Arte Contemporanea Luigi Pecci, 1999), 155–61.

27 Gerhard Richter, *The Daily Practice of Painting*, 203.

28 The German press reported that MoMA paid 3 million Deutschmarks (see 'Baader-Meinhof goes West', *Sueddeutsche Zeitung*, 26 June 1995) and the US press that it paid US$3 million. This is one of many discrepancies in the way the sale was reported in press.

29 Eduard Beaucamp, 'Exportiertes Trauma', *Frankfurter Allgemeine Zeitung*, 8 June 1995, 35.

30 Carol Vogel, 'Inside Art: A Growing Modern', *New York Times*, 16 June 1995, C22.

31 These dates are again significant because they coincide with renewed interest in the ongoing struggle to confront German history and its representation that was raised in 1995 by a controversial exhibition on *Wehrmacht* war crimes. See Hannes Heer and Klaus Naumann (eds) *Vernichtungskrieg Verbrechen der Wehrmacht, 1941–1944* (Hamburg: Institut für Sozialforschung, 1995).

32 Hilton Kramer, 'MoMA Helps Martyrdom of German Terrorists', *New York Observer*, 3–10 July 1995, 1, 25.

8. A Game That Must Be Lost: Chris Marker Replays Alain Resnais' *Hiroshima mon amour*

Jonathan Kear

> That's how History advances, plugging its memories as one plugs one's ears.
>
> CHRIS MARKER

Over the course of his long career Chris Marker's films have provided an examination of the possibilities of cinema as a mechanism for conveying memory and, since the 1990s, the possibilities of new media to create interactive archives of cultural memory. The subject matter of his film essays has focused on the complexities of history and the bringing to light of events buried within the annals of the past, events passed over in silence. In this way, he has remained a jarring witness, questioning and defamiliarising historical narratives of past events, by retrieving the overlooked, the marginalised and the suppressed components of those histories. This chapter explores how Marker engages with the representation of history and his use of montage as a docufictional form in which the history of actual events and the history of cinema are intricately interwoven. Continuing his long preoccupation with Japan, Marker's films since the 1980s have focused on the changes that Japanese society has undergone in the post-war period. His examination of this transition has focused on the events that led to Japan's capitulation during the Second World War and the way this continues to shape its present development. In these later films Marker has returned on a number of occasions to the battle between American and Japanese forces at Okinawa toward the end of the Pacific War and the historical reverberations of the conflict.

By late October 1944 the island of Okinawa, located around 400 miles south of Japan in the Ryukyu Island chain, became a strategic American target for cutting

Japan's sea lines of communication. It was also a platform on which to stage a future American invasion of Japan. The ensuing battle of Okinawa was one of the most harrowing events of the Pacific War.[1] More than 107,000 Japanese and Okinawan conscripts were killed; conservative estimates put the figure of civilians who perished at between 100,000 and 150,000. American casualties in the operation were also substantial and prompted Congressional calls for an investigation into the conduct of the military commanders. The cost of the battle, in terms of lives, time and material, weighed heavily in the decision to use the atomic bomb against Japan just six weeks later. Despite the significance of the battle of Okinawa, a kind of collective amnesia has obscured the events that contributed so decisively to the dropping of the Bomb. Few at the time knew the extent of civilian casualties, as information about the massacre was suppressed in the war correspondence of journalists on both sides of the Pacific. In subsequent years the events at Okinawa received little attention.

Marker reflected on the fate of Okinawa in a brief elegiac passage in *Sans Soleil* (1982), a film that examines the mourning of war victims in commemorative rituals on the island. His feature film *Level 5* (1996) returns to the subject, examining the battle of Okinawa within a multifaceted meditation on the nature of historical representation and the role of the image as testimony. In one of the film's interviews with the Japanese filmmaker Oshima Nagisa, he states that Japanese war films and historical accounts of the war have persistently failed to provide a critical understanding of the war and the underlying ideology that accounted for the sacrifice of so many civilian and military lives. In many respects, *Level 5* continues Marker's long concern with exploring the gap between the official history and the way these events were experienced by those who witnessed them first hand, a concern which unites an otherwise extraordinarily diverse oeuvre. Yet, the film's examination of the battle of Okinawa provides a far from straightforward documentary account of it. Although *Level 5* features newsreel and combat footage taken during the Okinawan campaign, this comprises a comparatively small component of the filmic materials it weaves together into its multi-layered montage. For a film that seeks to unearth a history long buried in Japan's official memory, its reticent use of first-hand testimony has drawn criticism and may seem perverse. Only three witnesses are interviewed in the course of the film, and only one of these, Kinjo Shigeaki, is a native Okinawan who lived through the events. On first viewing, *Level 5* may seem a film more preoccupied with the technical ingenuity of its own formal modes of construction and its metacritical ruminations than with the actual events of its subject matter. In many respects Marker's approach to the events of Okinawa in *Level 5* requires some explanation. How are we to understand the kind of history it presents of Okinawa? In what ways can someone who was not originally involved in the events be a witness to them? And how are we to interpret the relationship between the *discours amoureux* of the film's protagonist and the narrative of the last battle of the Pacific War?

Like much of his later work, *Level 5* is a docufiction, a homage in one respect to his long friendship and collaboration with Alain Resnais.[2] The film is a 'free replay', to use Marker's phrase, of Resnais' *Hiroshima mon amour* (1959). Resnais' intermixing of real historical footage of post-war Hiroshima with a fictional love story scripted by Marguerite Duras may be seen as a forerunner to Marker's self-reflexive docufictional genre. Like Resnais' film, the plot interlaces two parallel storylines: the fictional video diary of Laura (Catherine Belkhodja), a French woman who mourns her dead lover, with the tragic events in the Pacific at the end of the Second World War. But *Level 5* is a replay with a subtle twist, resetting the plot of *Hiroshima mon amour* in the context of the events at Okinawa that preceded the catastrophe of Hiroshima. In doing so, *Level 5* also reframes the film that it remakes. Understanding the role of the battle of Okinawa in the events that led to Hiroshima is crucial to the relationship between Resnais' *Hiroshima mon amour* and Marker's *Level 5*. It was the entrenched bloody resistance the American forces met with at Okinawa that ultimately persuaded the American administration to drop the nuclear bomb on Hiroshima. In this way, the formal resemblance of the two films is overridden by a deeper, more nuanced historical investigation, in which the relationship of original to copy is reversed. *Level 5* thus becomes a supplement which re-enacts the events which led directly to those that formed the basis for Resnais' film.

This reversal of the relationship of remake to source serves to emphasise the continuity between the two films, allowing *Level 5* to operate implicitly as an explanatory text for the earlier film. Through recounting the historical circumstances that led to the bombing of Hiroshima, *Level 5* provides a preface to the film it emulates. But other subtle and crucial distinctions differentiate the two films. While Resnais' movie was set in the immediate wake of Hiroshima's devastation, Marker's is placed in an indefinite time, located somewhere between the present and the future, and as such emphasises the act of reconstructing events long past from a position of belatedness. Unlike Resnais' protagonist who witnesses the aftermath of the carnage in Hiroshima at first hand, Laura's relation to the fate of Okinawa is remote and mediated. Her experience is constructed out of the filmic database her lover was working on before his death and the reminiscences of the journeys across Japan of a filmmaker referred to as Chris.[3] The two strands of the film are interwoven through a computerised hypertext programme, entitled *L'Année dernière à Marienbad Game* (borrowing from the title of Alain Resnais' seminal film). We are told that the object of the game is to reconstitute the battle of Okinawa. Laura operates this mysterious and incomplete game that reconstructs fragments of the history of events that took place at Okinawa in the form of a cubist-like collage. The game presents her, and by extension the viewer, with different kinds of historical evidence and perspectives on the fate of Okinawa. The game's hypertext links interweave archival film footage, citations, interviews, and an array of other visual and textual documents to explore the events that would shape the prosecution of the Pacific War.

The notion of game-playing structures the film on three different levels. On one level, it refers to the gambits of war, to the strategies of the opposing forces in conducting their campaigns and the underlying ideas about nationalism and cultural identity that informed those strategies. Oshima makes this point explicit in *Level 5* when he compares the conduct of the battle to *sure-ishi*, the sacrifice of a piece in the classical Japanese game of Go to save the game. Although Okinawa was strongly defended by more than 100,000 troops, the American invasion initially met with scant resistance. The Japanese chose not to defend the beaches against the overwhelming American forces, but instead to dig into caves and tunnels on the higher ground. This tactic, and the heavy rains which bogged down the offensive, resulted in a protracted and costly campaign. 'Mopping up' operations for the offensive lasted several weeks and, as a result, there was a large number of civilian casualties. During the invasion, many civilians also fled to caves or 'fox holes' where they were subsequently entombed or killed by American forces (an estimated 20,000 were trapped in caves or buried by the Japanese themselves). In sacrificing Okinawa, the Japanese gambled that a costly struggle for the outpost would deter an invasion of the home islands. Okinawan lives were considered expendable by a Japanese administration; they were mere pawns in a fatal endgame. But as *Level 5* makes clear, the sacrifice of Okinawans cannot be separated from a longer history of oppression and imperial occupation, first at the hands of their Japanese colonisers, and later by the Americans. The islanders, a racial mixture of Chinese, Japanese and Micronesian ancestry, had long born the brunt of ruthless subjugation and racial bigotry on the part of the Japanese from the time of its occupation in the seventeenth century. This history contributed significantly, the film argues, to how lightly Japanese commanders regarded the lives of the islanders.

On a second level, the notion of game-playing refers to a range of virtual and actual games that are featured in the course of the film. As a 'latecomer' to the event, Laura has to come to terms with a traumatic historical episode that appears incomprehensible and untellable, as well as a culture that is other to her own. Playing the game of reconstructing the battle of Okinawa provides her with a puzzle; it involves her in a struggle to learn the rules of engagement, to utilise the hypertext programme that does not always cede to her commands and cannot always provide her with the answers she seeks. The problem of accessing the past is played out in *Level 5* by the programme's failure to facilitate particular requests and commands. In one respect this recurring motif reflects back on the terms of the game and, by extension, to the limits of artificial intelligence. *Level 5* explores the possibilities but also the limitations of hypertext programmes (which are unable to make the kinds of imaginative connections or mental synthesis of human intelligence). Hence, in a series of comical sequences, the programme is unable to process a set of absurd commands, instructions that possess a metaphorical or performative meaning in language but not a logical or instrumental one. The phrase 'access denied' takes on deeper meanings as it recurs within the film, linking up with other reflections on the limits to recovering a historical past that is always spiralling further away from us; a historical past that is always already caught in a tangled web of contesting and mutable representations.

The title *Level 5* similarly relates to this imagery of the game, referring to how Laura and her friends would play at giving 'levels' to those they met. Those who introduced themselves as Marxists or Catholics, or displayed '*une bigoterie quelconque*' (a commonplace bigotry), were consigned to Level 1. Those who spurned such categories or who were wittier made it to Level 2. The higher levels were reserved for free thinkers who spurned dogmatism in all its forms, a point that resonates in light of the way imperialist ideology and dehumanising propaganda served to compound the slaughter of innocent lives at Okinawa. No one, Laura remarks, ever made it to Level 5, and the criteria for achieving this is never made explicit.[4]

On a third level, and perhaps most importantly, game-playing functions as a metaphor, as it does in *L'Année dernière à Marienbad* (1961). It is a metaphor for the way component parts or fragments of the historical narrative can be, and indeed always are pieced and re-pieced together in different ways to produce alternative accounts, scenarios and interpretations.[5] The link to *L'Année dernière à Marienbad* is made explicit in a revolving computer graphic on Laura's monitor. The graphic features a match motif superimposed on an image of Delphine Seyrig, the actress who plays 'A' in Resnais' film. Thus, on Laura's monitor we see a reference to the game with matches played in *L'Année dernière à Marienbad*. At one point, Laura speculates on the possibility of imagining alternative ways in which the battle may have been played out, invoking a level of virtuality in which the actual course of events might have changed. It is worth noting that for *Hiroshima mon amour* Resnais asked Duras to write several different endings. While these did not feature in the movie itself, they nevertheless form a level of virtual multiplicity that informs the overall conception and narrative development of the film. The virtual in *Level 5* serves to keep the speculative nature of historical discourse in play. It opens up a space for the counterfactual, for the 'what if' of history, envisaging the past not as a series of actions that have inevitable consequences and that follow an inexorable logic, but as a set of events that contain many possible scenarios and eventualities only some of which are realised.[6]

In this respect, the game metaphor in *Level 5* refers to a mode of engagement with the representation of the past that contests the ground rules of official history, one that is purposely eccentric, heterogeneous, subjective, discontinuous, reflexive, aphoristic and digressional. This mode of operation is questioning rather than conclusive and almost systematically finds a place for everything that traditional rationalised histories regard as a surplus and seek to exclude from their mode of discourse. This playfulness and excess is manifest in the self-parodying approach to classification, with obscure and irrational juxtapositions used to link sequences. At various intervals 'option menus' appear on Laura's internal monitor that take the form of lists of variously numbered alphabetically organised names and places. As with Borges' imaginary classification system of an ancient Chinese encyclopaedia, which subverts rational classification through imitating its form, these lists seem designed to place the very notion of classification, and by implication the modes of knowledge and assumptions about language on which they are based, in question.[7] The *modus operandi* of the game of *Level 5* are chance associations, puns, unlikely and surreal juxtapositions. On closer inspection, these lists invariably reveal hidden and unexpected connections.[8] The list of 'O's that appears on the menu at one point includes Okinawa, Okeechobee (a tribe of native Americans from Florida) and Oklahoma. Although these may seem to have only an arbitrary connection they become concurrent through the film's concern with a history of genocide and the metonymic link between Oklahoma and Pearl Harbor.

A further aspect of this game-playing is found in the self-consciousness apparent in Marker's cinematic essays. *Level 5* presents an intricate *mise-en-abîme* of representations within representations. The studio setting is a performative space where the presence of monitors within monitors creates a continual sense of shifting across different representational registers.[9] Rather than being simply a compositional conceit, the notion of game-playing in *Level 5* carries with it several important principles about historical representation. Playing the game serves to foreground the underlying methods of construction by which we order history and the arbitrariness of that process. It brings on-screen the act of selection, framing operations and the assimilation of diverse materials into a narrative structure. Playing the game thus brings into play a complexity, intricacy and heterogeneity missing from more straight-forward representations of historical events. It presents the capacity of play as a force of subversion, inversion and pleasure, an unpredictable and disruptive force. Hence, in *Level 5* the story of the battle of Okinawa is continually interrupted and its narrative cohesion undermined and never allowed to settle into a stable form. History is the game whose significance is constantly in a state of becoming, the game that continues to be played out in the present.

The historiographical perspective of *Level 5* is taken up most forcibly in relation to the question of the status and conception of witnessing. The film's testimony comprises actual and fictionalised witnesses, and other forms of witnessing. Most notably, the film includes visual evidence in the form of film footage taken during the events of the battle of Okinawa. The role of witnesses and documents has a central role in most historical accounts, and primary source material customarily holds a special status within these accounts. It both grounds retrospective interpretations of the past in the historical context to which they refer, and asserts the reliability, authenticity and authority of the narrative that is relayed of those past events. Such primary source documents, whether visual or verbal, serve as testimony to the 'real'. They are direct evidence of the events and are often presented as simply factual re-cords unmediated by human agency, even by historians well aware of the intellectual limitations of the use of such documents. Photographic records of war, for instance, provide the psychological illusion of unmediated access to the events themselves. Yet such documents are mediated in several different respects, both in terms of their immediate conditions and context of production, and their later history of reception in which such documents are transformed and translated. As the film suggests, such historical documents are always already caught in the web of prior representations. These earlier representations condition how events are perceived, what of those events can be represented, and the form that representation may take.

The question of witnessing in *Level 5* relates closely to the broader issues of his-torical representation that constitute the prevailing structure of the film. In particular, the way history relates to questions about the recovery of memory and the reception of those memories. Here we might make a simple distinction between two kinds of witnessing: *to witness*, in the sense of being present at an event and *to bear witness*, to provide an account of that event. Witnessing in the latter sense must always presume an 'afterwardness'. Hence to see the act of bearing witness to an event as having a self-identical relationship to the event itself elides a complex series of factors that lie between the moment of the event and the later representations of it. This is not simply a matter of factors such as false witnessing, misperception, inconsistencies in testimony, or mistaken recall. It is also a question of the deeper temporal and narrative structures through which memories of the past are organ-ised, relayed and received.

Hayden White has argued for an understanding of history that takes into account the way histories are invariably organised according to dominant literary tropes, such as tragedy, comedy, romance and irony. These tropes serve both a mnemonic role of shaping the events into an ordered and memorable form, as well as attributing particular meanings to the events portrayed.[10] The point could be extended to witnessing. Such tropes play an integral role in processing and configuring contents of experience into coherent and consistent narrative forms of representation and enunciation. It is thus through such tropes that contents of experience are presented as objectively and uniformly accessible to the subject and as uncontaminated by subsequent experience. First-hand testimony of the battle of Okinawa is presented in *Level 5* within a wider autobiographical framework in which the battle itself marks a divide in the subject. The divide comes between the subject who experienced the events and the subject who belatedly bears witness to them. This temporal divide within the subjectivity of the witness points to a deeper division of consciousness, understanding and knowledge of the events witnessed.

Inevitably, within a history that explores its own limits, the question of bearing witness to the past cannot be understood as a matter of recuperation, but rather, it must be approached as a constructive process of re-imagining the past. As such, the act of witnessing implies not time regained, but time re-evoked. Within this framework, remembering and forgetting are not antithetical, but rather, two sides of the same coin. To remember is to remember imperfectly, to recognise that in recalling the past we are recalling also its pastness, bringing to consciousness the meanings and implications related to that pastness.[11] The historical past is therefore not something that is static and complete; it is mutable, something continually remade in the present. Marker's film is concerned as much with the process of (mis)remembering the past as it is with the events themselves. It is only in this context that one can understand why he refers to 'latecomers' to the events at Okinawa as witnesses. Latecomers stand as witnesses not to the event itself, but to the event's later interpretation or misprision which in time, changes the perception of the event itself.

The question of witnessing is complicated still further by what might be construed as an act of witnessing, and by what constitutes witness testimony. In an age of mechanical reproduction, photographic imagery, whether in the form of still or moving images, often plays a powerful role as visual testimony that both documents events and provides images through which our understanding and memory of events are constructed. The role performed by photographic imagery has been a leitmotif in many of Marker's films. A cluster of issues about the witnessing function of photography in historical discourse is pertinent here. There are two that seem of particular importance. The capacity of the cinematic image to outlive the actual event it depicts complicates our ability to discriminate between what occurred and our representations of it. The photographic image as an indexical trace of an event acquires a materiality that substitutes its presence for the contingency of the absent moment it depicts. It substitutes the image of an event for the event itself, reinvents it, creates a legend for it. As it becomes detached from its original context so the capacity for such visual documents to acquire diverse meanings increases as they enter into successive new historical contexts and are used as evidence for different kinds of interpretations. Secondly, any attempt to preserve a simple division between events and the images that represent them has to take into account the presence of technologies such as film or photography at those events and the influence of photographic means of representation on how the event is remembered. In Marker's films we are constantly made conscious of the imbricated relationship of representation and history. In *Sans Soleil* the fictional protagonist is quoted in his letters, 'I remembered that month of January in Tokyo or rather I remember the images I filmed of the month of January in Tokyo. They have substituted themselves for my memory. They are my memory.' Marker's foregrounding of the editorial operations, the frequent discussions in his films of the juxtaposition of particular images, the semantic questions about the act of filming or interpreting film footage, the way we are drawn into the decision-making process of composing his films, all need to be seen as comprising an aesthetic that contests the illusion of film as a transitive instrument of reality. The way that Marker's films bear the imprint of and quote extensively from the work of other filmmakers embeds them within a filmic discourse on visuality that eschews any immanent relation between events and their representations, instead, his practice interrogates its own status as documentary by reflecting back on its relation to other filmic sources and its own modes of filmic construction.

The beguiling power of the image as witness to substitute its reality for the reality of the event, to transform our perception and consciousness of events, and, in turn, to be transformed by the context and framework within which it is seen, is a central feature of *Level 5*. The film's exploration of visual testimony revolves primarily around three archival images that have acquired an iconic status in the historical interpretation of the battle of Okinawa.[12] In each case, Marker probes the complexities and ambiguities of these visual documents, the role they have played as a record of the 'realities' of the war, and the way they have subsequently been used to entrench certain perceptions in the official and unofficial histories of those events. The first is film footage that captures a woman throwing herself off a cliff in Saipan, one of the Northern Mariana Islands, where Japanese soldiers conducted guerrilla operations against American forces. Laura connects this footage with discussions of the last days of the battle at Okinawa when, rather than surrender to the invading troops, many islanders took their own lives. The lucid and moving testimony featured in *Level 5* is that of Kinjo Shigeaki, the only witness featured in the film who experienced the events at Okinawa at first hand. Kinjo, who later became a Christian minister as a result of his experiences at Okinawa, conveys the way imperialist propaganda convinced many to commit suicide or murder their loved ones rather than see them taken by an enemy that had been thoroughly demonised. In his recollection of witnessing a village elder beat his own family to death with a branch, Kinjo recounts how he and his brother realised that it was his duty to do the same to his mother and siblings. Such accounts bring home the full horror of the carnage of the events at Okinawa.

Nevertheless, it is not the horror of the carnage alone that preoccupies Marker. The footage that shows a woman throwing herself from a cliff is paused at the moment immediately before she leaps into the abyss, just as she takes one last glance back in the direction of a cameraman filming the event. A fleeting superimposition montages this still image with famous footage of a man dressed in a bat suit costume who leapt from the Eiffel Tower in 1900 in a vain attempt to fly. Both images capture the moment immediately prior to death and, as Marker puts it, perform 'an act of intercourse with the camera'. While the image of the woman remains suspended on her fleeting glance backwards, Laura's commentary poses the question of whether had the camera not been there to witness the event, both deaths might have been

the image and the witness

averted. Without the camera, each of the individuals might have reconsidered their actions. Instead of being a passive witness of events, the camera's presence exerted a powerful and demanding gaze, stiffening the resolve of those caught in its vision and pressing events on to their fateful outcome.

While the first piece of footage raises consciousness of the constructive rather than passive role of the camera in creating the events it 'records', the second focuses on the selection and manipulation of film footage to fit narrative ends. This footage shows a man, known as Gustave, with his body on fire fleeing a bombing raid in Borneo. In *Level 5*, the footage is first shown as it was in newsreels at the time, ending with the man collapsing and expiring on the ground. Laura's commentary reflects on the power of this image as a haunting symbol of the brutality and inhumanity of war. However, she goes on to point out how the sequence was edited in such a way to suggest the victim's death. The restored footage, screened immediately afterwards, offers a different conclusion; it shows Gustave scrambling to his feet and surviving the ordeal.

The third image in the film's discussion of visual testimony is Jack Rosenthal's famous photograph of the American flag being raised at Iwo Jima, where the Americans suffered terrible casualties in securing the island. In its representation, Marker focuses his commentary on the reception of this image. The publication of Rosenthal's photograph prompted US Senators to commission a monumental bronze memorial to be modelled on Rosenthal's image, which was unveiled by President Eisenhower in 1954. The image was later used on an American stamp and as the promotional poster for the movie *Sands of Iwo Jima* (Allan Dwan, 1949). As part of its fictionalised reconstruction of the Iwo Jima campaign, *Sands of Iwo Jima* predictably featured a restaging of the raising of the stars and stripes banner. This image of the raising of the flag at Iwo Jima has since been reduplicated throughout the world, becoming one of the most famous and emulated war images. The image encapsulates indomitable will, American imperialism and the triumph over adversity.[13] A similar photo of a flag being raised was produced for the taking of Shuri Hill at Okinawa. Comparison with other photographs and film footage from Iwo Jima and the conflicting reminiscences of the soldiers involved reveals the event was far from spontaneous. It was not a moment that by chance happened to be captured on camera; rather, it was a carefully staged event with the original raised flag removed in order for a more choreographed and memorable representation of the event to be recorded for posterity. *Level 5* contests the symbolism and 'truth value' of such images when it juxtaposes the sanitised and glamorised representation of war in *Sands of Iwo Jima*, with a clip from John Huston's disturbing documentary *Let There Be Light* (1944). Houston's film shows a traumatised amnesiac veteran under hypnosis, a clip that was originally cut from the film by censors.

In the analysis of this imagery, Marker assumes the role of a decoder of the coded message and its capacity for generating myth when he probes the layers of meanings such images have acquired. The film becomes a patient and exacting examination of not only of the history of the battle of Okinawa, but also, of its repertory of images and how they connect to a larger history of the representation of war. At stake, however, is more than simply a question of the status of the image as visual evidence. It is also a matter of the photograph as *enigmatic message* and the power of the image to haunt the imagination, even when it has been understood to be framed, staged and constructed. For Marker, the photographic image is marked by ambivalence. On one hand it takes on an almost redemptive role, in so far as its indexical quality recovers something of the event from the oblivion of the past. On the other, the image provides an ambiguous and often distorted form of witnessing, to the degree that it is too often conflated with the totality of the event itself. The examination of these images thus becomes an investigation of the *imaginary* of such war imagery, revealing the way they connect to and inflect other images and events.[14] In each instance, the examination of the iconicity of the image is not merely a reflection on its meanings in relation to the event in question, but on its later historical reverberations. Hence the image of Gustave burning is associated with later imagery of napalm victims in the Vietnam war, in particular Nick Ut's famous 1972 photograph of a young Vietnamese girl, naked and suffering from severe napalm burns, running along a road. The image of the raising of the flag at Iwo Jima is linked through a series of later re-stagings and re-presentations of the original photograph, both satirical and otherwise, to other images of imperial triumphalism.[15]

Beyond the use of first- and second-hand witnesses and the use of visual imagery as a form of witnessing, there is also of course the fictional testimony of Laura; her position as intercessor connects her with this image repertory as a suffering witness and bearer of memory. She is the conduit between two histories: the fictional history of the loss of her lover and the actual history of the tragic events of Okinawa. Her role in the film has, however, evoked much controversy, reminiscent of the criticism of Resnais' protagonist in *Hiroshima mon amour*, in respect of its apparent equation of a fictionalised narrative of personal grief with the collective tragedy of the historical events it portrays.[16] The directness and raw emotion of Laura's discourse, delivered in the first-person while she gazes directly into the camera, draws the viewer into an intimate relationship with her that might seem to affirm this association. But the character of Laura and the role she plays in the film is more equivocal, for it is a role that is continuously questioned, ironised and problematised. In an interview Marker reiterates Resnais' own remarks that the testimony of the actress in *Hiroshima mon amour* recalling her dead lover in Nevers can be read in alternate ways: as a personal trauma or as a complete fabrication.[17] As in *L'Année dernière à Marienbad*, the protagonist in *Hiroshima mon amour* is never given a name. While the protagonist of *Level 5* is given a first name, her identity and status is arguably even more ambiguous. The name Laura is taken from another film. In the middle of *Level 5* the camera catches sight of a video cover for Otto Preminger's film noir *Laura* (1944), the story of a detective who falls in love with a woman whose murder he is investigating. Shortly afterwards, Laura sings the signature ballad of this movie.

Just as Laura enacts a game of historical reconstruction according to a mode of random creative chance, so she herself might be understood as part of this game, part of its puzzle for the viewer to interpret. The connection forged between Laura's identity and Preminger's protagonist draws attention to the fetishised construction of Laura's persona through the longstanding cinematic trope of the mysterious woman, whose alluring identity ultimately seems a projection of male fantasy.[18] For all the intimacy of her confessional monologue, about both her grief and her bewilderment with the game, she remains an enigma. Her spectral identity, caught between reality and fantasy, mythologised and deconstructed in turn, makes her a Clio-like figure, through which the problematic history Marker explores in this film is articulated. In this fashion, Preminger's murder plot becomes a metaphor for the historian's quest for meaning.

Filmed in the approach to the centenary of the birth of cinema, *Level 5* aspires to a conception of film along the lines of the intermedial hypertext programme it simulates, presenting through this template a form of cinematic history that is non-linear and transdisciplinary. This conception of film might be described as a mode of *découpage* in time that cuts away from linear development. As such *Level 5* provides a mechanism that implicitly serves to contest orthodox historicism and those traditional cinematic histories that constrain the constructive potentiality of the filmic apparatus by binding its imagery into a conventionally unified narrative format. In contrast to traditional history's desire to reconstruct and actualise the events it represents, Marker's materialist film history acts as a machine that quotes from the past, interrupts the flow of time, actively combines and recombines images snatched and ruptured from the past. The film assembles these quotations into a form of juxtaposition that provokes questions and thought rather than produces a seamless linear narrative.

To engage fully and constructively with *Level 5* is to participate in its search for meaning, to pursue its trail, to follow-up the links it establishes, in short, to play its game of historical reconstruction and deconstruction. As in Resnais' *Hiroshima mon amour*, we are presented in *Level 5* with a narrative that is incomplete, an open-ended storyline, that yields no final resolution and which mirrors the mysterious un-finished virtual programme of the Okinawa game. Marker's filmic labyrinth, with its infinite array of random pathways, links and traces, present us with fragments of the past, references that lead to other references, but ultimately lead toward neither a final destination nor conclusion. The history of Okinawa remains an incomplete project, not least because the history it concerns itself with is continuous, unresolved, in process.

For all their formal similarities, the ludic dynamics of *Hiroshima mon amour* and *Level 5* are deeply embedded in their radically different historical moments. Made in the immediate post-war intellectual context that was dominated by Sartrean existentialism, Resnais' film was defined by the struggle of its protagonists to come to terms with catastrophe and to live authentically in its wake. In *Level 5* we are instead faced with a melancholy meditation on loss, the loss of a relation to the historical reality of the war that still weighed heavily on Resnais' film and on the memory of its viewers. As a result, *Level 5* is more thoroughly and resolutely pervaded by the spectre of death that hangs over *Hiroshima mon amour*.

Rituals of mourning the dead, especially those who died at Okinawa, but also victims of other battles, wars and genocides, recur cyclically in *Level 5*, with a particular focus on the death of children. This begins early on in the film with footage borrowed from one of Oshima's documentaries about Okinawa, *Shisha wa itsuma demo wakai-Okinawa do sokai-sen no higeki* (*The Dead Remain Young*, 1977), that shows women tipping rice wine, flowers and food onto the waves in the annual pilgrimages to commemorate the children who perished in the initial evacuation of Okinawa when the Americans torpedoed the ship *Tsushima-maru*. Just as women within *Level 5* are charged with the burden of mourning, the constant imagery of the sea comes to take on an associated symbolic meaning, as a metaphor of memory, entropy and death. This spectre of mortality progressively inhabits Laura's words. Initially described by herself as a woman 'happy and in love with life', she becomes drawn into the vortex of mourning and the endgame of *Level 5*. At one point she asks, 'Must one die to reach *Level 5*?' At another, she describes death as stating 'I have won the game, but you may play on if you like.' Laura's unexplained absence from the studio at the end of the film, her computers left on and e-mail box open though empty, intimates that the sacrificial theme elaborated in the course of the film extends also to her. Her disappearance remains an enigma, though one might recall that Preminger's *Laura* is a film about a woman who is already dead. Laura's last action is to adjust the focus of the camera until the perspective through the aperture becomes blurred; the last words spoken by Chris state that he never heard from her again. Indeed, as his commentary suggests, her testimony seems to come from the past: it is a tape replayed in the present of the 'research' she had promised to bequeath to him in order for him to put it into shape. The opening shot of a hand moving a computer's mouse and downloading the files for *Level 5* is thus revealed as that of Chris as he replays her tapes.

If *Sans Soleil* might be said to be organised around a state of mind focused on melancholy, *Level 5* is saturated by an overwhelming and interminable sense of mourning and futility, to the point where knowledge itself becomes placed under the sign of death.[19] In this respect, the spectre of death that hangs over the film contrasts starkly with the imagery of the game, but the imagery of death is, nevertheless, connected to the film's broader historiographical framework. For the death in question is in some respects a death in and of language. It is the ultimate failure of words to adequately describe the event, the event's un-narratable quality, and paradoxically, the way the act of describing must itself at some level negate the particularity of the event. Describing abstracts the event, it distances us from it and replaces its reality with representation. It is in this context that we recognise that, far from suggesting a commensurability between Laura's personal loss and the collective tragedy of Okinawa, the film puts in play two different relations to the experience of loss: the first intimately connected to the personal life of its subject, the other distanced in historical memory, lost in the archives of representation.

This explains some of the differences between Marker's engagement with the events at Okinawa and Oshima's numerous documentaries on the subject. Oshima's primary concern with the transmission of information from one generation to the next in his histories of Okinawa necessitates his use of first-hand witnesses. In contrast, Marker's *Level 5* is focused on the way such witnessing has already shifted into an impersonal context of official commemorations and public museums, including the cavernous subterranean tunnels of the Okinawa War Museum featured throughout the film. Contained within these contexts, the materiality of experience is transformed and translated into historical narratives for mass public consumption. Marker had already touched on this adaptation of the memory of Okinawa in *Sans Soleil*, in a discussion of the replacement of sites of personal mourning by official institutionalised sites of commemoration and their integration into tourism. Resnais too had already posed the same dilemma in the opening sequence of *Hiroshima mon*

the image and the witness

amour where the actress's Japanese lover contradicts her assertion that she has seen and understood Hiroshima. He questions her because her knowledge is based only on the visual evidence of newsreels, newspaper reports and belated visits to the site of devastation. All these signs of loss and death in *Level 5* lead back, by way of a cyclical regression, to Marker's original point of departure in *Sans Soleil*, when he reflected on the forgotten history of Okinawa with film footage of the memorial services on the island. For it is ultimately in the form of a memorial that *Level 5* revisits the battle of Okinawa. But in its sacralisation of the events at Okinawa, Marker's film raises it from a marginal event onto another plane of meaning, using this event to provide a vantage point onto the hidden history of Japan and the Second World War.

Notes

1 Roy Edgar Appleman, *Okinawa: The Last Battle* (Rutland, Vermont and Tokyo: Charles E. Tuttle, 1960), 17–30.

2 Marker and Resnais co-directed *Les Statues meurent aussi* (*Statues Also Die*, 1953) and worked together on *Nuit et brouillard* (*Night and Fog*, 1955).

3 As in *Sans Soleil*, characters in Marker's films often function as surrogates for the director, although always in decentred and deconstructive ways.

4 See Julie Brock's discussion of the levels of *Level 5* in Julie Brock, 'Aperçu du film de Chris Marker *Level 5*: Un parti pris de l'amour,' *Pensée* 312 (October–December 1997): 103–26.

5 See Alain Robbe-Grillet, 'Order and Disorder in Film and Fiction,' *Critical Inquiry* 4, no. 1 (Autumn 1977): 1–20.

6 Niall Ferguson (ed.) *Virtual History: Alternatives and Counterfactuals* (London: Picador, 1997).

7 Borges' fanciful taxonomical 'Chinese Encyclopaedia' divides animals into categories that include among others: belonging to the Emperor; embalmed; tame; sucking; sirens; fabulous; stray dogs; included in the present classification; frenzied; innumerable; drawn with a very fine camelhair brush; et cetera; having just broken the water pitcher; that from a long way look like flies. Quoted in Michel Foucault, *Les Mots et les choses* (Paris: Gallimard, 1966), 7.

8 See Raymond Bellour, 'Le livre, aller, retour', in *Qu'est-ce Qu'une Madeleine?: A Propos du CD Rom Immemory de Chris Marker*, ed. Yves Gevaert (Paris: Centre Pompidou, 1997), 65–108.

9 See Bouchra Khalili, '*Level 5* ou le reposoir', in *Recherches sur Chris Marker*, ed. Philippe Dubois (Paris: Presses Sorbonne Nouvelle, 2002), 146–50.

10 Hayden White, *Metahistory: The Historical Imagination of the Nineteenth Century* (Baltimore: Johns Hopkins University Press, 1973).

11 Elizabeth Cowie, 'Traumatic Memories of Remembering and Forgetting,' in *Between the Psyche and the Polis: Refiguring History in Literature and Theory*, eds Michael Rossington and Anne Whitehead (London: Ashgate, 2000), 196–7.

12 On this see Maureen Turim, 'Virtual Discourses of History: Collage, Narrative or Documents in Chris Marker's *Level 5*', *Sites* 4, no. 2 (Fall 2000): 367–83.

13 See John Lucaites and Robert Hariman, 'Performing Civic Identity: The Iconic Photograph of the Flag-Raising on Iwo Jima', *Quarterly Journal of Speech* 88 (2002): 263–92.

14 On this aspect of Marker's use of images, see Yvonne Spielmann, 'Visual Forms of Representation and Simulation. A Study of Chris Marker's *Level 5*', *Convergence* 6, no. 2 (Summer 2000): 31–40; and Bellour, 'Le livre, aller, retour', 65–109.

15 Turim, 'Virtual Discourses of History', 370.

16 For a critique of *Level 5* along these lines see Ian Hunt, 'Okinawa Replay: Chris Marker's

Level 5', Coil 5 (1997), n.p.

17 Ibid.

18 Marker has frequently used this motif in earlier films such as *Le Mystère Koumiko* (*The Koumiko Mystery*, 1965) and *La Jetée* (1962).

19 Hunt, 'Okinawa Replay', n.p. See also Turim, 'Virtual Discourses of History', 368.

9. The Domestic Vision of *Vietnam Home Movies*

Guy Westwell

As US combat troops packed their kit bags en route to the Vietnam War, many of them added a Super 8mm movie camera and film cartridges to the things they carried. These keen amateur filmmakers who had previously directed their viewfinders at birthdays, weddings and holidays, now found themselves recording the experience of soldiering while on tours of duty in Vietnam. The movies made by these amateur filmmakers provided a way of coping with the experience of the war and, upon returning home, a way of communicating that experience to their friends and families. Stored in box rooms, garages and attics, these amateur films formed a haphazard archive that remained untapped until the mid-1980s when a commercial video production company, Vietnam Archives Inc., collected and distributed them under the title *Vietnam Home Movies*.[1] Each of these Vietnam 'home movies' consists of thirty minutes of Super 8mm film footage roughly edited together. Felt to be too murky and mute to speak for itself, this footage is enhanced and authorised through the addition of the testimony of the amateur filmmaker who talks the viewer through the action shown on screen.

The marketing for the *Vietnam Home Movies* promises to immerse the viewer in the authentic experience of soldiering in Vietnam: 'You are about to witness scenes of war and everyday life in a war-torn country that you have never seen on the evening news. This is the personal, private life experienced by soldiers, sailors, airmen, and marines who fought in Vietnam between 1956 and 1975. This is their story.' These claims are predicated on the powerful reality-effect of the Super 8mm film footage previously unseen in public. The marketing particularly exploits the difference between the amateur footage and the carefully constructed news reportage of the war. It also foregrounds the authenticity of the veterans' experience, especially the heartfelt narration of their own amateur film footage. In the balance of these two key elements – the claimed indexical power of film as historical record and the authority of direct lived experience – the home movies merge their constative and performative elements into an act of witness. This chapter interrogates this specific act of witness. My interrogation leads to a determination of whether or not the claim that the *Vietnam Home Movies* unlock a clearer, more accurate, and more authentic sense of the Vietnam War can be taken seriously. I focus my critical analysis on two representative films from the series, *The Smiling Tiger* and *The Gunslingers*.[2]

The *Vietnam Home Movies* appear to bear out Shoshana Felman's critical conception of witness testimony. Felman argues that witness testimony requires a framework within which listeners can themselves bear witness to the act of witnessing. According to her formulation, to testify is to perform an act of recall within a socially and discursively prescribed scenario, whether it be a court of law, a historical debate or a religious meeting. Felman thus asserts: 'To testify is always, metaphorically, to take the witness's stand, or to take the position of witness insofar as the narrative account of the witness is at once engaged in an appeal and bound by an oath.'[3] This process – the witness in a court of law being the most obvious example – indicates how to bear witness via testimony. Such witnessing also makes a truth claim, the veracity of which others must judge. Thus, of central importance to this notion of the witness is the presence of an audience or listener.

The soldier as amateur filmmaker attempted to record his experience in Vietnam through the widely available medium of Super 8mm film. On returning home, their films were most likely shown to family and friends in a context in which, together, the Super 8mm film footage and the veteran's testimony gave witness to the experience of fighting a war in Vietnam. Viewing these films and listening to the veteran's testimony, the family provided an audience, bringing the testimony to a wider group, corroborating its claims to truth. These intimate and private exchanges within the family group undoubtedly eased the veteran's return home and then with time the film footage was stored away and forgotten.

Twenty years later, the films were unearthed in the 1980s within the context of America's shifting cultural memory of the war, and the activation of discourses specifically designed to rehabilitate both the Vietnam veteran and disruptive memories of the war. Through advertisements in veterans' magazines, the home movies were elicited from soldiers who had fought in Vietnam. The movies were then submitted to a commercial process that reproduced the kind of witnessing framework elucidated by Felman and within which the films had initially been put to use. Together, the different elements of this commercial process forge a synthetic act of witness, a repetition of the original family scenario, and as a result, the films become witness testimony in a wider sense. This next level of witness testimony is realised when they target and engage with a particular imagined audience which itself bears witness to the Vietnam War. True to Felman's notion of the witness, the home movies are 'engaged in an appeal' and 'bound by an oath'. The marketing of the *Vietnam Home Movie* series claims this act of witness will play a crucial corrective role in revising the dominant critical and controversial senses of the Vietnam War within American cultural memory.

the image and the witness

SUPER 8MM

The history of home movie-making and its visual idiom provide some important implications for the use of this idiom in the *Vietnam Home Movies*. Pierre Bourdieu proposes that amateur photography and filmmaking serve what he calls, a *family function*.[4] For Bourdieu, photography 'integrates', that is, pulls into a binding and constitutive relationship, the subject taking the photograph, the subject or object shown in the photograph, and the subject looking at the photograph.[5] The act of taking a photograph, displaying it and viewing it, serves the purpose of allowing an individual family member to locate his or her experience within the context of the family as a whole. For this reason there are strict codes and conventions determining what can and cannot be shown. Amateur photography will not represent any experience that might threaten or destabilise the family. On a personal level, this might include alcoholism, depression, incest or death. On a cultural level, gender or race discrimination, labour exploitation, crime and political conflict (including war) are avoided.

Film scholar Patricia Zimmermann historicises Bourdieu's general claim by examining it in the context of the rise in popularity of amateur filmmaking in 1950s America.[6] This decade saw the return to traditional gender roles after their disruption by war, the shift to suburbia, rising marriage rates and the baby boom, all of which sustained a reconstruction of family life.[7] As a result, a certain family-ideal shaped historical consciousness, encouraging Americans to imagine the social building blocks of their world as the individual and the family.[8] Zimmermann traces the phrase 'home movies' to Kodak's marketing materials of the mid-1950s and examines how home movie-making as a social practice was predicated upon, and sustained, this particular family-ideal. As such, the home movie idiom can be read as the reification, through consumer technology, of the family-ideal so central to the conservative consensus of the 1950s.

Zimmermann charts how the amateur film's integrative function and this historically specific family-ideal remained central to the marketing, consumption and social practice of Super 8mm after its introduction in 1965. Glossy ads showed how Super 8mm could be used to record barbecues, children's parties, family vacations and the enthusiastic performance of household chores, all of which revelled in a sheer physical exuberance that presented the American family as self-confident, open and natural. Consumers of the new technology showed themselves open to suggestion and soon family experience was being shaped to conform to this one-size-fits-all family-ideal, an ideal that soldiers would eventually carry with their Super 8mm movie cameras to Vietnam.

The *Vietnam Home Movies* ask us to accept the Super 8mm film footage as an authentic, indexical representation of the war. As such, they are driven by the constative claim that the Super 8mm film footage, unsullied by the ideological and commercial compromises of the news coverage of the war, shows Vietnam 'as it really was'. The primary grounds for adopting a sceptical attitude toward this claim rests in the films' careful emulation of the home movie idiom. Marketed as such, the films display a certain style that is common to the genre. This style includes shaky camera work, inconsistent and haphazard framing, hastily performed (in-camera) editing and blurred focus. Whip-pans, camera-tricks, close-ups and other contingencies shape familiar home movie subjects such as pratfalls, silly faces and practical jokes. As a result, the visual idiom of the home movie dominates throughout and gives the war a recognisable feel. The familiarity of this film aesthetic cues the viewer to read the event as already known, made safe, domesticated.

The home movie idiom goes deeper than mere formal technique. For example, the *Vietnam Home Movies*, like home movies in general, foreground personal and private space. The institutionalised space of the Army – regimented, strictly hierarchical and bureaucratically impersonal – is de-emphasised in favour of an imaginary space modelled on the family. The Army as structure is replaced with the all-male family unit located around the interior of the helicopter and the tents in which the men live and where they spend most of their non-combat time. This ensures a tight, nuclear-family-sized focalisation for the home movies and acts as a surrogate for a more conventionally conceived home. It is significant that both films I analyse closely show interaction and play with children, the most common subject of the home movie genre. Similarly, in both films the male family unit adopts a dog, and makes this dog a significant character in its home movies. Also, the soldier-filmmakers, Alfred Demalio (in *The Smiling Tiger*) and James 'Bob' Powell (in *The Gunslingers*), clearly attempt to find functional equivalents in Vietnam for the kinds of experiences and activities found in home movies more generally. We see Demalio and Powell relaxing with buddies at base-camp, playing with local children and building a rudimentary house out of rocket pallets. As a result, the comfortable, reassuring activities of life in the suburbs are reproduced in Vietnam – the car as a suburban status symbol is usurped by the helicopter; the house as a source of pride and family togetherness is replaced by the military base customised to be 'just like home'; going on vacation becomes visiting exotic locales. Through this transposition of 'family' to the unit, Demalio and Powell orient themselves to Vietnam, and to war.

Through use of representational strategies familiar to the home movie genre, Demalio and Powell's day-to-day activities of soldiering in Vietnam are naturalised in *Vietnam Home Movies*. Military activities are shown in the films as a kind of monotonous routine much less remarkable than the family-ideal established amongst the troops and this has the effect of stitching the war into a recognisable social universe. Through such representations of the Vietnam War, the soldiers unconsciously filter their experience and, as a result, crucial dimensions of the conflict drop away from the field of vision. Very little attempt is made to identify exact location, to indicate the unique geography of the Vietnamese landscape, to figure the wider military operation, or to locate experience in any contextual framework. The only context given is that of the individual holding the movie camera and the familial space of the surrogate family group that surrounds him. The overall effect here is to produce a representation that shows Vietnam (in reality, a hostile foreign country) to be recognisable and unthreatening. This ensures that upon return home the experience of the war can be presented to the family as simply an extension of normal everyday life. As a result, the initial act of witness, the experience to which the Super 8mm film footage testifies, is only partially sighted, blind to certain aspects of the experience of the war in Vietnam. As Michelle Citron notes: 'By providing the "good" memory, home movies show us an ideal image of family with everyone in his or her proper place: parents in charge, men in control, families together.'[9] Like home movies more generally, the *Vietnam Home Movies* construct just such an ideal image.

Home movie-makers are discouraged from filming anything considered disruptive of the integrative family-ideal, with the soldier-filmmakers no exception. However, as Citron writes: 'In presenting the image of an ideal selective past, home movies announce what is absent. They stand in for what is there *and* what is not there. In their ambivalence, they both confess and hide. The home movies are simultaneously acts of self-revelation, self-deception, and self-conception.'[10] The viewer of *Vietnam Home Movies* could, if he or she wished, call on knowledge that would activate what remains hidden by the film footage – the fact of America's defeat, the massacre of Vietnamese civilians by US troops at My Lai, the devastating effect of carpet bombing and deforestation, and so on.[11] Yet this activity is curtailed in favour of the presentation of recognisable, familiar activities, although something of the difficulty of fighting the war does occasionally find its way into the films.

In one brief sequence in *The Smiling Tiger*, Demalio and his fellow soldiers are shown posing with 38mm handguns. They strike clownish poses and then gesture that they may shoot themselves, or each other, in the foot. This strategy of self-harm became a common way of escaping the difficult experience of the war, but here it is played for laughs. Another sequence shows a series of bullet holes and a large patch of blood sprayed up the side of a helicopter, the aftermath of the death of a door gunner during an encounter with the enemy. The scene is presented as tragic, with Demalio almost breaking down as he gives his voice-over testimony. But it is not dwelt upon and the film moves on, quickly returning to its more upbeat tenor. Like the gaps in family photo albums that signify a divorce or a betrayal, the *Vietnam Home Movies* could be interrogated for evidence of more complex realities hidden beneath the idealised surface. However, due to the brevity of these sequences the viewer is actively discouraged from pursuing these leads, and is quickly sutured into the safely domesticated account of the war.

In general, rather than hard evidence of the war, as claimed by the marketing materials of the *Vietnam Home Movies*, the Super 8mm film footage functions as a domesticating perspective, a robust coping mechanism for the individual soldier. This domestication of an otherwise heinous experience ensures that the veteran and his experience of the war can re-enter American society with as little friction as possible. This coping mechanism constitutes a form of incomprehension, or limited vision, of the war. Just as the macro-structures of society – government, economy and law – rarely feature in home movies, so too here, in the *Vietnam Home Movies*, the war as a violent geopolitical struggle determined by vast cultural, ideological and economic differences is largely absent. As a result, the constative claims made on behalf of the Super 8mm film footage must be met with extreme scepticism. The claimed indexicality of the *Vietnam Home Movies* and their status as unparalleled historical records is problematised by their faithful adherence to the visual idiom of the home movie. Individual soldiers cannot be blamed for using this coping strategy to ameliorate the difficult experience of war and to protect their loved ones from too direct a contact with the traumatic experience of Vietnam. However, far more problematic is the afterlife of these home movies when the incomprehension, or partial-sightedness, is shipped back into the cultural memory of the war. Such was the case with the release of the home movies in the 1980s, when the footage was reproduced and marketed as an authentic act of witness.

TALKING CURE

Having problematised the constative claims made by these films, I will now turn to examine the performative aspect of the *Vietnam Home Movies*, and in particular, the voice-over narration in which the Vietnam veteran responsible for shooting the Super 8mm footage provides a narrative to accompany, corroborate and authenticate the visual image.

The video box blurb to the *Vietnam Home Movies* notes: 'In all cases the narration which accompanies the 8mm film footage was recorded in the home of the contributor. This narration is candid and spontaneous. It was not rehearsed, and no script was written.' Such marketing discourse encourages us to imagine that we are participating in a private screening of the home movies, sitting alongside the Vietnam veteran in his own living room. The voice-over narration is full of warm, nostalgic remembering, a tenor that corroborates the integrative nature of the home movie idiom in general. The organisation of the different elements in this way effectively emulates in the public sphere the act of screening and talking through home movies in the private sphere of the home.

The careful use of language in the talk-through is significant as it demonstrates how combat and death are negotiated without destabilising the idiom of the home movie. Both Demalio and Powell describe the activity of firing machine-guns and rockets at enemy positions in the following ways: 'here we are hosing down the area', 'putting the wazoo on the bad guys', 'we are just softening or prepping the LZ', 'Put it on 'em', 'Get 'em stirred up a little bit', 'Oh Yeah! There we go. Right on! Not bad shooting for a kid.' The use of understatement, simplification and metaphor all serve to evacuate the ethical dimensions of the actions on screen. It allows both home movie-maker and home movie-viewer to remain separate from, and therefore not fully implicated in, the act of killing. As such, the family-ideal is not threatened by any direct contact with the facts of mutilation, dismemberment and death.

Both *The Smiling Tiger* and *The Gunslinger* contain an almost identical sequence that illuminates much about the witnessing dynamics at work in these films. The two protagonists look through the rocket sights of their helicopter gunships and smile and laugh at the camera. In the accompanying talk-through, Demalio states that the shot is simply 'for dramatics', while Powell states that the shot is 'one for Mum and Dad'. In these key scenes both home movies emphasise the image of a young man striking a dynamic and self-conscious pose 'for the folks back home'. These scenes clearly indicate that much in the *Vietnam Home Movies* has been filmed for domestic consumption. Parents, as overseers of the family, are almost always the audience, imagined or real, of the home movie. These clearly staged sequences acknowledge the originary family unit and strive to reconcile this with the slightly odd military version. The primary purpose here would seem to be that of reassuring families anxious that their sons might be physically or psychologically harmed by their experience of serving a tour of duty in Vietnam. The narration draws attention to this fact, corroborating it as the preferred reading.

Significantly, the series producers chose not to show the Vietnam veteran giving his testimony. In their present-day identities as veterans, Demalio and Powell remain continually off-screen as disembodied voice-overs. This has the effect of protecting the integrity of their identities as constructed by their film representations. The image preserves their youth, their dated clothing, their hair-cuts and, above all, their exuberant physicality. The possibility that we conflate their present and past identities becomes all the more probable, and while there is obviously continuity between these two, the conflation helps to suture together the potential discontinuities between past and present. It is crucial that neither veteran refers explicitly to either contemporary events or to the passing of time. The home movie replaces the experience of Vietnam by providing a ready-made family-ideal, and thereby effaces key aspects of the experience of war. This results in the elision of the time that has passed between the shooting of the footage and its incorporation into the *Vietnam Home Movies*. The processes of ageing, reflection and remembering are elided, as is any recognition of the cultural and political fractures of the 1970s. This conflation confirms the sense of Vietnam produced by the home movie idiom and its elision of the complex experience of fighting the war.

In her analysis of Claude Lanzmann's documentary of Holocaust testimony, *Shoah* (1985), Shoshana Felman claims that what a witness does not remember, or indeed, chooses to forget, is as significant as what he or she recalls.[12] Any sophisticated representation of witness testimony, of which Lanzmann's film is exemplary, will draw attention to the process of inclusion and omission, of remembering and forgetting, that figures any act of witness testimony. *Shoah* does this through its forensic attention to the human face as the witness testifies. Ironically, by absenting the veteran's face from the scene, the *Vietnam Home Movies* deter their viewers from focusing their critical attention on the veteran's testimony as a speech act that is being performed in the present. The decision not to show the Vietnam veteran's face in the present also refuses the viewer the chance to test the veracity of the words spoken against the physiognomy of the witness. A shot of the face would signify time passing, as the soldier is now older, and therefore, its omission makes the absence of any reference to the passing of time more noticeable. Also, if the face were depicted, when the testimony breaks down the viewer would have further evidence with which to read the silence. Ultimately, viewers of the *Vietnam Home Movies* are discouraged from any examination of the aporias, deceits and blind spots intrinsic to the veteran's act of witness and his home movie footage.

The idiom of home movie-making provides a script of sorts for the encounter between the veteran and his Super 8mm film and, as noted, almost without exception the veteran's reminiscences corroborate the domesticating perspective through which the war is seen in these films. Bourdieu describes the family photograph as a 'pure sign' that is 'intelligible only to someone who holds the key to it'.[13] The *Vietnam Home Movies* can be understood similarly. Here, the veteran's narration provides the key to intelligibility, however, it is a key that can only unlock meaning of the most limited kind. In particular, the meaning of these documentary images does not venture into the territory of the violence, devastation and bloodshed of the battlefield.

Michelle Citron describes how during the viewing of home movies 'Time folds back on itself. Two places on the time line of our life meet. In this moment of superimposition, a space is created from which insight can arise. This is the latent hope in all home movies.'[14] Citron also notes how 'The home movie opens a potential space where we can enter either its affirmations or its silences. What we experience in this ambiguity is determined at the moment of reading.'[15] Through the presentation, reworking and analysis of her own family's home movies, Citron's work in film and book forms explores the gaps between past and present and between a 'safe' version of family history and a more truthful version that admits to secrets, incest and sexual abuse. The kind of reflective, unflinching, analytical engagement with her past self, as embalmed in her family's home movie footage, is precisely the kind of dialectical relationship between past and present that the *Vietnam Home Movies* elide. In her work, Citron explores a personal history as well as the discourses that occlude, illuminate and complicate knowledge of that history.[16] This level of self-reflectiveness, tied to an intellectual and artistic tradition of feminist distrust, appropriation and recuperation of forms that subordinate and compartmentalise female experience, has no counterpart in the determinedly ego-driven narratives of the *Vietnam Home Movies*, whereby the male subject is represented as in control of the experience of war, and then twenty years later, remaining similarly in control while reflecting back on the experience of war.

Memory-work closer to that conducted by Citron (and Marianne Hirsch in the realm of family photographs) does exist in relation to the Vietnam War. During and immediately after the war films such as *Interviews with My Lai Veterans* (Joseph Strick, 1971) and *Hearts and Minds* (Peter Davis, 1974) showed veterans reflecting on their experience of war. In one particularly moving sequence in *Hearts and Minds*, a pilot tries to imagine how he would feel if someone dropped napalm on his own family. These veterans, and the films in which they bear witness, acknowledge and explore what John Carlos Rowe calls, the 'equivocal realities' of the Vietnam veteran.[17] Through a brave engagement with the traumatic and difficult experience of the war these films acknowledge the 'ambivalent location of the GI as simultaneously the agent and victim of imperialist politics'.[18] These American soldiers bear witness to their experience in Vietnam in ways that acknowledge the complexity of the war, allowing a nuanced, more profound sense of the war to emerge. It is possible to imagine a different kind of narration, running counter to the image in *Vietnam Home Movies*, a narration in which the veteran acknowledges experiences that are not captured on their Super 8mm footage or that were particularly difficult to reconcile. However, this is a terrain of experience and memory that the *Vietnam Home Movies* assiduously avoid.

DEAR AMERICA

The blend of elements that make up the *Vietnam Home Movies* – especially the primacy of a family-ideal and the use of this family-ideal as a way of understanding the war in Vietnam – have obvious roots in the cultural context of the mid-1980s, when the *Vietnam Home Movies* were first commercially distributed. The 1980s were governed by the neo-conservatism of the New Right, a dynamic political movement that presented itself as an alternative to the political culture that had shaped the 1960s and 1970s. Under the leadership of President Reagan, the New Right drew strong, self-conscious parallels with the 1950s, and relied heavily on the key issue of 'family values', a term which marked out the family as of central symbolic importance to the construction of a particular conservative ideal of individual, state and nation. 'Families', repeated Reagan many times, 'are the basic unit that hold our society together.'[19] The popularity of television series such as *Family Ties* (1982), *The Cosby Show* (1984), *Who's the Boss* (1984), *Growing Pains* (1985) and *The Wonder Years* (1988), which all contributed to what Andrew Ross has termed the 'reinforced familialism of the 1980s', confirm the profound ideological investment in this particular way of thinking about society.[20] It is perhaps no surprise then that the 1980s saw a massive boom in home movie-making, especially after camcorder sales took off in 1982.

This commitment to the family dovetailed with a process of considerable historical revisionism at the centre of which were a series of moves to recuperate American credibility in the wake of the unsuccessful and divisive war in Vietnam. The war remained a strongly contested and politicised event that sat uneasily with the New Right's forceful conservative and nationalist agenda. The logic of revision was laid bare in a 1980 campaign speech to the Veterans of Foreign Wars in which Ronald Reagan stated that 'It is time we recognised that [in Vietnam] ours, in truth, was a noble cause.'[21] One of the primary means to recuperate credibility for American involvement in Vietnam lay in the focus on the experience of the veteran, who, according to revisionist logic, had merely done his patriotic duty in difficult circumstances. America was asked to extend understanding to these soldiers, and insomuch as they could be helped and healed, the war itself could be rendered less divisive. Reducing the war to individual experience rendered it more difficult to level criticism at the conduct of the military, the state, or even America itself during and after the war. The primacy of the Vietnam veteran's role in remembering the war was particularly foregrounded in 1985 when the Vietnam Veteran's Memorial was unveiled on the Mall in Washington DC, and also through the organisation of a welcome home parade in New York on 7 May of the same year. As Fred Turner notes, 'healing the wounds' became the dominant metaphor for understanding the war a decade after its end.[22] This move represented a turn away from the angry protests, cultural contestations and politicised silences that shaped the experience and debate of the war in the 1970s. *Vietnam Home Moves* chime with this cultural context as, in contrast to films such as *Hearts and Minds*, memory-work became more conciliatory and therapeutic, governed by a general rhetoric of the Vietnam veteran's sacrifice and of healing, national unity and the family.

The New Right's disavowal of all those aspects of the 1960s and 1970s deemed incompatible with its emergent conservative value system – antiwar protest, feminism, civil rights, the acknowledgement of military incompetence and corruption – is evident in the way in which the *Vietnam Home Movies* effect a tight fit between the Super 8mm footage and the Vietnam veteran's narration. This marriage between the veteran's narration and home movie-making results in the drawing together of two historical moments: the 1980s, and its imagined precedent, the 1950s. The *Vietnam Home Movies* make no reference to the political upheavals and disturbances of the late 1960s and 1970s, either in their recording of the war, or in the testimony of the veterans made from the historical vantage point of the 1980s. This move neatly elides a twenty-year period when Americans, in imagining themselves not solely in relation to family, but also, as members of ethnic groups, religious communities and political parties, chose to question some of their nation's most powerful vested interests and succeeded in effecting considerable progressive change.

This elision can also be found across a whole range of representations in the 1980s. Indeed, it is particularly marked in Hollywood movies about the war. The difficult and controversial Vietnam War movies of the late 1970s, such as *Coming Home* (Hal Ashby, 1978), *The Deer Hunter* (Michael Cimino, 1978) and *Apocalypse Now* (Francis Ford Coppola, 1979), gave way to a distinct 1980s cycle, which included *Platoon* (Oliver Stone, 1986), *Gardens of Stone* (Francis Ford Coppola, 1987), *Hamburger Hill* (John Irvin, 1987) and *In Country* (Norman Jewison, 1989). Less allegorical, and with a firm focus on the individual, the military unit and the family, these films activated a similar sense of the Vietnam War to that found in *Vietnam Home Movies*. The marketing campaign for *Platoon*, for example, included posters showing amateur photographs of director Oliver Stone and other GIs taken while on active duty in Vietnam. By foregrounding the director's own experience of war as a component part of the film itself, the film generates a series of expectations in its audience very similar to those activated and given structure by the *Vietnam Home Movies*. In both cases, the veteran's experience is privileged as authentic and his voice is seen to speak with authority.

Like the *Vietnam Home Movies*, the narrative of *Platoon* functions according to a particularly limited frame of reference which reduces the war to a purely American experience. The film's central protagonist, Chris Taylor, describes his tour of duty in Vietnam through voice-over in the most insular way. At no point is there any reflection on the historical context of the war or the motivations of the Vietnamese; they are reduced to an enemy that is rarely seen. The letters that Taylor writes home to his Grandma signal a problem with the basic structure of the family as it indicates the 'folks back home' are somehow absent. The film's narrative then resolves this problem through an epic struggle between two father figures: one violent, repressive and militarist, the other, nurturing, feminised and a peacenik. By the end of the film, Chris has chosen the latter father figure (solving the 'problem' identified in the film), and is able to return home with greater insight, presumably to some process of rehabilitation to which the family will be key. The marketing of the film's video release, as Keith Beattie notes, further extended the tendency to activate the family as a structure of therapeutic forgetting:

> An advertisement accompanying the video release of the film features a woman sitting in her kitchen speaking to the camera, informing the spectator that initially she could not understand her husband's refusal to discuss the war. Having seen *Platoon* she now understands not only the experience of the war but also her husband's reluctance to talk.[23]

The tendency is even more marked in the narrative resolution of *In Country*. The film tells the story of Vietnam veteran Emmett whose war experiences have left him suffering from Post-Traumatic Stress Disorder. He has withdrawn from the family in order to build a military bunker underneath his house and occasionally dresses in women's clothing. Once again, the war is posited as a narrative about the family-ideal and its disruption; the experience of war has led to Emmett's inversion of that ideal, which the narrative eventually resolves through a family trip to Washington DC to see the Vietnam Veteran's War Memorial where Emmett is able to retrieve his role as patriarch of the family. As the film closes, we see the reflections of the characters in the polished black granite of the memorial, almost as if their story was now inscribed in the memorial, and the experience of this American family now echoes across all the names on the wall. Beattie concludes that representations such as these conduct memory work whereby 'the once inexplicable war – "radically ambiguous, undecidable, and indeterminate" in the words of one observer – was rendered intelligible through the structure of the family and home'.[24]

John Carlos Rowe identifies the same tendency at work in Bernard Edelman's, *Dear America: Letters Home From Vietnam* (1987), a collection of letters written by US troops while on tours of duty in Vietnam, which was produced for the New York Vietnam Veteran Memorial Commission.[25] In an echo of the marketing of the *Vietnam Home Movies*, a national advertisement for *Dear America* introduced the book as 'The Vietnam correspondents who got the story right.' Marketing materials and reviews claimed that the book unlocked a more truthful understanding of the conflict gained through unprecedented access to the experiences of those most intimately involved in the fighting.[26] Edelman's book was followed in 1987 by an eponymous television adaptation, which J. Hoberman describes as 'a sort of transpersonal home movie'.[27] It is a film in which letters, photographs and home movies are placed alongside more familiar news coverage to construct an allegedly more complete account of the war, an account underscored and authenticated by the personal experience of the Vietnam veteran. Rowe is critical of this over-arching tendency:

> Sentimentalizing the war and thus remystifying the political questions posed by it, these personal mementos serve as chimerical forms of 'understanding', always framed already by familiar myths of American individuality and the family as *alternatives* to the interrogation of those American socio-political attitudes (including the individual and the bourgeois family) that contributed to our involvement in Vietnam.[28]

Rowe's critique holds particularly true of the *Vietnam Home Movies*. The screening of the experience of the Vietnam War through the domesticating perspective of the home movie requires key aspects of that experience to be filtered out, in particular the motivations and struggles of the Vietnamese. It transforms the complex history of international relations into individual experience and then integrates this individual experience into an American family-ideal. The effectiveness of this process in stabilising and silencing potentially disruptive private experiences and memories of the Vietnam War cannot be over-emphasised and has allowed a certain clear consensus to take hold with regards to Vietnam. This consensus figures the war as a wholly American event, entered into for noble reasons and overcome through the reinforcement of a particular family-ideal. Moreover, this family-ideal as it continues to define the fabric of American life is the enabling force of a therapeutic forgetting.[29]

CONCLUSION

In her influential 1972 account of the war, *Fire in the Lake*, Frances Fitzgerald argues that US policymakers and the military did not understand the history, politics and culture of Vietnam, and thus, consequently adopted tactics and strategies that were ill-advised and often counter-productive. This lack of understanding made itself apparent in an inability to see the architecture of the revolution being fostered by the National Liberation Front (NLF) in South Vietnam and, in particular, the failure to comprehend the profoundly strong and deep-rooted individual, family and community relationships – quite different from the US – that constituted Vietnamese society. 'In raiding NLF villages', contends Fitzgerald, 'the American soldiers had actually walked over the political and economic design of the Vietnamese revolution. They had looked at it, but they could not see it, for it was doubly invisible: invisible within the ground and then again invisible within their own perspective as Americans.'[30] They were thus not able to win the hearts and minds of the Vietnamese people and were forced to resort to ever more extreme levels of violence.

The manner in which the *Vietnam Home Movies* filter the war through the idiom of home movies constitutes an integral part of the structural blindness described by Fitzgerald. This partial way of seeing is embalmed in the 8mm footage and reinforced twenty years later through the veteran's affirmative narration. The structural blindness that precipitated such a calamitous event in the first instance is therefore reproduced in the cultural forms used to remember the war in the 1980s. We have come to expect such blindness from the Hollywood studios, and much has been written about the industry's problematic relationship to the war in Vietnam. However, it is more disappointing to recognise the same structural elisions and obstructions to cultural memory perpetuated in the ostensibly more personal, private and richly ambiguous medium of the home movie. Such a recognition serves to underline the pervasive tendency for the forms of memory that hold together America's sense of the both the Vietnam War, and war in general, to replicate the very blindness that made the Vietnam War such a catastrophe for both Vietnam and the US.

Notes

1   Vietnam Archives Inc. released twelve separate films in the collection.
2   *The Smiling Tiger* consists of amateur film footage produced by Capt. Alfred Demalio, a helicopter pilot based at Bong Song, LZ English, Hue and Camp Evans from 1967–68 and from 1970–71. *The Gunslingers* consists of amateur film footage produced by Capt. James R. Powell, a helicopter pilot based at Phu Loi from 1968–69.
3   Shoshana Felman, 'In an Era of Testimony: Claude Lanzmann's *Shoah*', *Yale French Studies* 79 (1991): 39.
4   Pierre Bourdieu, *Photography, A Middle Brow Art* (Cambridge: Polity Press, 1990), 19.
5   A similar economy of looks is mapped by Marianne Hirsch, *Family Frames: Photography, Narrative and Postmemory* (Cambridge, MA: Harvard University Press, 1997), 48–97.
6   Patricia R. Zimmermann, *Reel Families: A Social History of Amateur Film* (Bloomington: Indiana University Press, 1995), ix.
7   Steven Mintz and Susan Kellogg, *Domestic Revolutions: A Social History of American Family Life* (New York: The Free Press, 1988), 180.

8   Zimmermann uses the term *familialism* to describe this dimension of Kodak's marketing strategy; I prefer Lynn Spigel's formulation, 'family-ideal'. See Lynn Spigel, *Make Room For TV: Television and the Family Ideal in Postwar America* (Chicago: University of Chicago Press, 1992).

9   Michelle Citron, *Home Movies and Other Necessary Fictions* (Minneapolis: University of Minnesota Press, 1999), 15.

10 Ibid., 20 (emphasis in original).

11 For a sense of the complex and contradictory experiences of fighting in Vietnam including war crimes committed by American troops, antiwar protests within the armed forces and mutinies against military authority, see Bruce H. Franklin, *Vietnam and Other American Fantasies* (Amherst: University of Massachusetts Press, 2000), 32–40 and 61–2.

12 Felman, 'In an Era of Testimony', 41.

13 Bourdieu, *Photography*, 27.

14 Citron, *Home Movies*, 25.

15 Ibid., 21.

16 A similar journey into her family's photographic archive is undertaken by Marianne Hirsch.

17 John Carlos Rowe, '"Bringing It All Back Home": American Recyclings of the Vietnam War', in Nancy Armstrong and Leonard Tennenhouse (eds), *The Violence of Representation: Literature and the History of Violence* (London: Routledge, 1989), 197–219, 214.

18 David James, 'Presence of Discourse/Discourse of Presence: Representing Vietnam', *Wide Angle* 7, no. 4 (1985): 42.

19 Ronald Reagan quoted in Keith Beattie, *The Scar That Binds: American Culture and the Vietnam War* (New York: New York University Press, 1998), 138.

20 Andrew Ross quoted in Beattie, *The Scar That Binds*, 135.

21 Ronald Reagan quoted in Fred Turner, *Echoes of Combat: Trauma, Memory and the Vietnam War* (Minneapolis: University of Minnesota Press, 2001), 15.

22 Ibid., 142.

23 Beattie, *The Scar That Binds*, 146.

24 Ibid., 145.

25 John Carlos Rowe, 'Eye-witness: Documentary Styles in the American Representation of Vietnam', *Cultural Critique* 1, no. 3 (1986): 126.

26 Ibid., 140.

27 J. Hoberman, 'Vietnam: The Remake', in *Remaking History*, eds Barbara Kruger and Phil Marians (Seattle: Bay Press, 1989), 193.

28 Rowe, 'Eye-witness', 148.

29 As *Shoah* indicates, the human face can tell a great deal of truth, even without or in contradiction to words. As such, the Americans soldiers shown in the *Vietnam Home Movies*, in their partial-sightedness, in their refusal of responsibility, in their adherence to robust coping mechanisms that effectively produce silence, revision and incoherent cultural memory, share much in common with Lanzmann's bystanders and perpetrators.

30 Frances Fitzgerald, *Fire in the Lake: The Vietnamese and the Americans in Vietnam* (New York: Vintage Books, 1989), 179.

PART IV | TEMPORAL AND SPATIAL DISPLACEMENTS

10. Constructing the Image of Postmemory

Tina Wasserman

Two contemporary media artists, Daniel Eisenberg and Rea Tajiri, have produced work that revisits the past by investigating the representational complexities of history and memory in relation to their respective family histories, each of which was formed by traumatic historical events. In his experimental film *Cooperation of Parts* (1987) Eisenberg confronts his parents' experience of the Nazi Holocaust, while in her video essay *History and Memory: For Akiko and Takashige* (1991), Tajiri excavates the history of her mother's relocation to Japanese-American internment camps during the Second World War. Through their respective investigations of their family histories, each artist develops a unique language of moving images that explores the complexity of historical trauma, the processes of intergenerational memory, and the profound representational impasses encountered through these interrogations.

Part of the difficulty in revisiting the past for both Eisenberg and Tajiri lies in the very nature of traumatic experience. As Cathy Caruth points out, traumatic experiences 'are experiences not of wholly possessed, fully grasped, or completely remembered events, but more complexly, of partially unassimilated or "missed" experiences'.[1] To reposition such incomplete memories back into new historical narratives, Eisenberg and Tajiri must discover a critical language of images that allows them to 're-encounter' the traumatic past within the context of the present. They accomplish this through their return to and representational engagement with the specific landscapes and sites from their parents' pasts. In *Cooperation of Parts* Eisenberg journeys to Europe to witness and record the places that signify his parents' catastrophic past. In *History and Memory*, Tajiri journeys to Arizona to witness and record the ruins of the internment camp to which her mother was relocated.

Although they work in different media, Eisenberg and Tajiri adopt similar objectives and strategies to interrogate their difficult yet distinct pasts. At the same time, the differences of their work are equally provocative. While both historical events – the Holocaust and the internment of Japanese-Americans during the Second World War – bear the weight of their own terrible and disturbing specificity, they are nevertheless very different. Viewed and analysed here together, Eisenberg's film and Tajiri's video provide insight into both the problems encountered when revisiting the past, and the capacity of visual representation to address these issues, even as they are confronted in relation to diverse traumatic historical events.

Eisenberg and Tajiri access the past by returning to its sites and interrogating its landscapes. Both artists navigate complex philosophical terrain when they link a place that exists in the present with a time that has already passed. Each artist acknowledges that the past itself can never be precisely located, neither as a 'there' nor as a 'then'. Instead, the differing levels of time and space, self and other, history and memory that are excavated through the artists' encounters with their family histories collide to underscore the representational impasses and tensions in any act of conveying the past. As a result of these collisions, instead of reconstructing the past, Eisenberg's and Tajiri's work explores the tangled relationship between history and memory, self and other, then and now. These two media artists recognise the impossibility of accessing the past unadulterated, and therefore opt to reveal all that stands in the way, namely, the relationship between the *outside* of events and the *inside* of remembrance.

Through their formation out of the residue of the past, history and memory are inextricably linked. Both are constituted through a process of transcription from an original occurrence in the past, and yet each returns to the past in a different way. History is the transcription of public events connected to the external world, and memory is an internal, subjective transcription of experience connected to the individual self. But the distinction between the two is often more porous and slippery than this straightforward definition would imply: what is subjective memory for one generation is not necessarily just public history for the next. Past events that produced personal memory for one generation may, in fact, affect the next generation in deep and personal ways. Eisenberg and Tajiri explore the relationship between history and memory by tracing a line from the self and their own personal memory, through the intergenerational memory passed down by their parents, and out into the public sphere where history is made and written. Both artists explore the point where history and memory overlap, become entangled and spill into one another. Their work thus demonstrates that while the memory of one generation may become history for the next, intergenerational memory can also transform into new forms of personal remembrance.

And yet, when they imagine the past in the present, when they give voice to a past that was never articulated in its moment, their respective images also work differently. Eisenberg explores his own memories as they are formed by the non-present memories of his parents who suffered in Nazi Germany. Tajiri, however, creates the images of her mother's experience. Each work thus enables different solutions to the problem of how to represent the absence experienced by the second-generation witness.

Like other experimental media artists in the 1980s and 1990s, Eisenberg and Tajiri were influenced by the radical paradigm shifts of historiography inaugurated by Michel Foucault. For these artists, history no longer has one single, official narrative but can, instead, accommodate multiple narratives. Citing such fellow film and video artists as Su Friedrich, Alan Berliner, Abigail Child, Rea Tajiri, Jay Rosenblatt and Isaac Julien, Eisenberg connects their 'free-ranging, subjective investigations of history' through their shared interest in the archive:

> Either as a redress to official histories or as a means of producing documentary histories for marginalized or dehistoricized groups, the archive, the family home movie, and the trash heap have been raided for images and raw material. The point of this immense body of activity, far from the goals of the formal experiments of the 1970s, is to directly counter authorized histories, to recuperate lost or subjugated history or to provide new working historical documents for political purposes.[2]

To produce these 'new working historical documents', Eisenberg and Tajiri focus on the permeable space between history and memory. Their interest in the reinvestigation of the past lies not just in examining gaps in their own family narratives or in challenging official history, but also in exploring the very effect such histories and memories have had on the construction of their own respective identities. Their lifelong reaction to their parents' memory is an example of what Marianne Hirsch identifies as 'postmemory'. Hirsch characterises postmemory as 'the experience of those who grow up dominated by narratives that preceded their births, whose own belated stories are evacuated by the stories of the previous generation shaped by traumatic experiences that can be neither understood nor recreated'.[3] Originally developed in relation to children of Holocaust survivors, Hirsch contends that such a term 'may usefully describe other second-generation memories of cultural or collective traumatic events and experiences'.[4]

While memory is itself subjective, it is 'more directly connected to the past'; postmemory, Hirsch writes, is 'distinguished from memory by generational distance and from history by deep personal connection'.[5] Thus, for Hirsch, though direct, or first-hand, memories of traumatic experiences may vary from subject to subject, they are nevertheless connected to specific events in the past. Postmemory, though still deeply felt, does not stem directly from experience of the historical events in question. Rather, it is formed through close familial ties with those who have experienced such events directly.

While Hirsch's term is useful, she points to its possible shortcomings when she admits that the prefix 'post' suggests postmemory to be a secondary form of memory, one that takes shape only after some original form of memory has already occurred – a kind of 'after' memory effect.[6] Although these intergenerational postmemories are affected by, but separated from, the original events, they do however represent new forms of remembrance. Although produced at a 'generational distance' from the original trauma, second-generation memories are authentic. Likewise, as *Cooperation of Parts* and *History and Memory* illustrate, they generate their own forms of existential and epistemological crisis.

Both memory and postmemory are inevitably connected to various acts and degrees of witnessing. Witnessing here is a direct and original occurrence of seeing and experiencing, connected in a primary and unmediated way to the original time and place of a specific event. It results in direct personal memory. Thus Eisenberg's and Tajiri's parents witnessed the events that were the source for not only their own trauma, but also the subsequent secondary trauma of their family members. And in the formative process of postmemory, both Eisenberg and Tajiri bear witness to their parents' memories of those events.

Direct memory and Hirsch's concept of postmemory are thus paradoxically removed from each other, but also simultaneously connected: they are separated by lived events and experiences, but linked by the way trauma threads itself through generations. As the next generation, Eisenberg and Tajiri are temporally and spatially removed from the event that produced their parents' trauma. Eisenberg's and Tajiri's second-generation memories are thus unhinged: they have no 'original' mental images to anchor them back to real 'lived' events: they are memories of memories. It is this divide in the registers of memory and experience that inaugurates a crisis in the process of postmemory. And yet, Eisenberg and Tajiri are able to resolve this potential crisis through an access to their respective parents' memory, an access that was not possible for the parents themselves. As imagemakers, Eisenberg's and Tajiri's methods are similar through their ability to bear witness where their parents could not. For Eisenberg, resolution of the crisis comes through a self-exploration, and for Tajiri, through a giving to her mother, thus her family, the 'gift' of representation that had been officially and psychically denied them.

As the son of Holocaust survivors, Eisenberg's identity is inextricably connected to a catastrophic history and its memory. And yet the event of the Holocaust has created a deep sense of rupture between him and the personal history of his parents. Eisenberg has stated that as he grew up his parents' memories of the Holocaust were conveyed to him through 'complicated, disrupted narratives', told with 'repeated details of some stories', and the omission or compromise of others due to 'the inability to express certain experiences'.[7]

In response to the unsatisfying nature of these narratives, Eisenberg set about representing the memories that were never accessible to his parents. In *Cooperation of Parts* Eisenberg relinquished his ongoing interest in the archive to investigate the past his parents were never able to articulate.[8] Eisenberg shot his own footage, and began to examine 'how the Holocaust had defined him personally'.[9] He acknowledges that it had already become common practice among his generation, as the children of Holocaust survivors, to travel to Europe and enact some sort of homage to one's parents and their traumatic experience. He also contends that 'no one that I know of took on the task of their own process, their own experiences, their own way of dealing with history and I felt that was an important thing to do'.[10] But Eisenberg's focus on his own process is not meant to reconstruct a more coherent self, but rather, to meditate upon a fluid, forming self, one that is situated within the vicissitudes of history and memory. His own definition of identity attests to its inherently provisional nature when he says: 'I think identity, or one's definition of oneself, is a moving target and I think it's also contingent on whatever necessities there are.'[11]

To interrogate the past, Eisenberg travelled to Europe to record various sites that signified his parents' past. The most significant of these were Berlin, Auschwitz, Dachau, the Jewish Cemetery in Warsaw and his mother's native town, Radom, in Poland. The resulting images of landscapes, sites and cityscapes, as well as a section of the film composed only of a darkened image-less screen, are accompanied by Eisenberg's voice-over narration and on-screen text drawn from a variety of sources. These include Eisenberg's own writings, various proverbs, phrases of folk wisdom and quotes from Roland Barthes, Theodor Adorno and Franz Kafka, among others. 'Happy is the country that has no history' reads one title while Eisenberg utters the ominous motto of the concentration camp: 'Work makes you free.' The verbal narration and written titles that accompany the images or the darkened screen are elliptical and abstract. Even material that suggests more deeply personal facets of Eisenberg's life and history is treated in a similarly oblique manner.

Eisenberg approaches his visual material in an equally elliptical way. He avoids any kind of straightforward declarative style, and he underscores his unwillingness to suggest any sense of closure or conclusiveness to his investigation. These strategies express Eisenberg's self-consciousness that such a history will never, as Saul Friedlander notes, 'surrender a fully comprehensible text'.[12] Through much of the film, Eisenberg uses long, hand-held takes, choosing a shaky, unsteady swish-pan style of recording, rather than cutting between different angles and views. Eisenberg rejects a self-conscious montage style of editing, and instead, adopts a restless observational camera style that not only preserves the actual pattern of his agitated looking, but also gives the impression of preserving its real time. Eisenberg creates a responsive immediacy to these images: it is as if his hand-held style documents his embodied experience, as though it is a visual record of his presence at the scenes he observes.

In the cityscapes, people vaguely move in and out of the frame. In one sequence, small abstract specks of humans and their elongated shadows move about a plaza as Eisenberg shoots the scene from above. In another, we are presented with a distant view of the city, a view partially blocked as the camera looks from behind the back of the standing figure of an unidentified man. In other sequences, he shoots buildings from a position closer to the ground, as random tourists and pedestrians move about. Darting from building facade to window to rooftop, Eisenberg's camera is constantly in search of something. It is as if he is interested in depicting something that cannot be seen, something that lies beneath the benign scenes he captures. His agitated style of shooting along with his evocative voice-over narration suggests that something *is* there, that these sites are still saturated with the past and weighted with a terrible history. Thus, a tension created between sound and image generates an uncertainty about the past. 'Yesterday is already here', he says, 'under our feet, above our heads.' But the seemingly ordinary surface of the contemporary quotidian scenes works to undercut any specific assignment of blame, guilt, responsibility or judgement for what happened there in the past. He says on the soundtrack:

It's a place of disasters, of the failure of will
A foreign terrain, at once familiar and exotic.
I have the illusion that nothing of great importance will be revealed.

How can I describe this place?
The rules are the same, the distances equivalent,
Privacy is respected.
Commerce is the common language.
Its an average state of existence, a state of undifferentiated exchanges.

Eisenberg also travels away from the cities to more specific sites of his parents' Holocaust past. He composes many of his shots through the windows of moving trains en route, drawing our attention to the landscapes in motion and also to the trains themselves. The visions of landscape in motion remind us that as the mode of transport to the extermination camps, the train is still an icon of the Holocaust. At the concentration camps, Eisenberg circles outside the barbed-wire gates with hand-held, tracking shots. He continues to shoot in this vein as he moves through the grounds of the concentration camps, and again, when he forays into their dark interiors, past ovens and starkly empty barracks.

While the film is the result of his own journey to these sites, he is nowhere identifiable on the image track. With his body 'displaced', it is through voice and camera movement that Eisenberg asserts his presence, making his film more than just a record of the places he encounters. He writes:

> I tried to use the camera not only to record what I was seeing, but also to register my own physical responses to what was seen. The camera is truly a medium here – a giving back takes place; automatic, unrehearsed, irregular. The sites themselves were of course indifferent and impervious to my presence, so film became a way to both inscribe them with meaning and the imprint of my presence.[13]

The self-inscribing movement of his camera is evident in footage Eisenberg shot of the Jewish Cemetery in Warsaw. In this more expressive sequence, he leaves behind the agitated, observational style and adopts one that is more fluid, though still gestural. As he moves through the brush and undergrowth that has taken over the slanted and crumbling stone grave markers, it is as if he is etching out a path, or leaving an engraving of his own movement through such a ruined, but clearly, evocative place.

The inscription of Eisenberg's presence is most evident in the final scene of the film when he encounters the Polish apartment building where his mother lived before the Holocaust. The treatment of this scene is lighter than the others as he captures a group of children playing in the courtyard through a suite of images that are cut to emphasise what seems to be a moment of acute awareness and sensation for him. Indeed, each moment captured by his camera is so swiftly cut and intercut, that images flutter across the screen as if this encounter with such a place was too much for Eisenberg to take in through one unblinking look. The scene is especially poignant because it reminds us that for Eisenberg, 'yesterday is already here' – that is, for him, the courtyard still remains a sign of the Holocaust. Clearly for the children, there is no such remnant of the past in their present acts of play. Indeed the past is only present to us in this scene through the filmmaker's own awareness of the history he seeks, a history which he has communicated to us throughout the film in a fractured and elliptical narration.

In taking this journey to Europe, Eisenberg returns to the past. Yet how does he return to a past in which he did not participate, but which has nevertheless deeply permeated his own sense of identity? In a strange way, it is his own past for which he searches. These places he now physically observes have had a presence in his past. However, their presence is only ever an immaterial presence, in the form of fragments and mental images: it is the memory of his parents to which he bears witness; it is his parents' memory that he himself remembers. As he approaches this final scene, the very site of his mothers' past home, he asks on the soundtrack:

What is it about the streets, the shutters, the lamp posts,
that brings me to the thought of these memories?
Where have I seen this place before?

How can one access the temporal past by confronting a place? What can a place reveal? In many ways, nothing is revealed. A place cannot be interrogated. The landscape is mute. If Eisenberg seeks evidence, it is buried, transformed or returned to nature. He notes in the voice-over: 'Perhaps the ruins are necessary, perhaps only absence has the power to endure.'

Yet a landscape can be physically investigated and examined, and Eisenberg does so in a manner that reveals both the power of a place, a site, to metonymically stand in for an event and, at the same time, to reveal its imperviousness. In a sequence that follows his arrival at the Dachau train station, Eisenberg's camera moves across the ground. It appears as though he is looking for something. The search yields nothing but small white flowers, ground and grass. No answers are revealed. Yet Eisenberg insists that something does indeed persist:

The feeling is this: an anxiety ... a phantom pain.
Something unseen yet intensely present.
How can I describe this feeling to you?

Indeed, these very ordinary images of the ground draw our attention to a kind of representational impasse. While Eisenberg may be looking for history, his filming demonstrates that a mute physical site can no longer precisely mean the absent catastrophic history that took place there. And yet, landscape and site are concrete remnants of the past that continue to exist in the present. Thus, they have the capacity to be powerful visual surrogates for a time that no longer exists. The landscape, therefore, is a marker of the temporal past and, as such, can be a place to encounter history.[14]

Eisenberg states that the impulse for the trip 'was the need to provide the image of real "sites" for all the imagined locations of the story: the sites of my parents' childhood, the sites where they were imprisoned, the place they met'.[15] These sites then, for Eisenberg, represent something that remains 'real'. His desire to witness remnants of the 'real' from the Holocaust past is a particular existential and aesthetic problem for postmemory work. Dealing with such an overwhelming, but nevertheless 'vicarious past', James Young has noted a tendency within the postwar generation of artists to be preoccupied 'with not having been "there" but still being shaped by the Holocaust'.[16] Such a gap in experience has brought to bear upon this generation what Dora Apel identifies as a 'compulsion toward forms of re-enactment by those who did not experience the original events',[17] even though such re-enactments 'end in a kind of crisis, a greater sense of traumatic history's elusiveness, but also its pervasiveness and its imminence'.[18]

It is true that Eisenberg, like other children of survivors, faces the Holocaust in a different way than survivors do, because for him, it is a vicarious past. He also faces it differently from those of his generation who are not the children of survivors. Indeed, Hirsch's theory addresses these differences by emphasising postmemory as an effect of trauma that occurs within the close contact of family relations and family structure. Hirsch's term can be distinguished from other concepts of second generation witnessing, such as Dora Apel's 'secondary witnessing' or Andrea Liss's 'retrospective witnessing' and 'indirect witnessing'.[19] While these other modes of witnessing speak of the Holocaust funnelled through larger generational and temporal divides, Hirsch connects her concept of postmemory specifically to the children of survivors. Children of survivors have a different relation to the past than that of the general population because they have gained knowledge of the Holocaust not just through public and collective means, such as archival film footage, documentary photography and museum exhibitions. The children of survivors experience the Holocaust through intensely private and often unspoken communication within their own family.

Our identity is strongly connected to experiential and mnemonic continuity. The paradox for children of Holocaust survivors is that they construct their identities through powerful, disturbing events that were, for them, 'events without experience'. Encounters with the real landscapes and sites of the past that occur in Eisenberg's film connect his 'memory without experience' to some form of lived experience. Eisenberg's impulse to seek out the reality of his family's Holocaust past is an impulse to connect and anchor what he remembers of his parents' memory to his own embodied experience *in situ*.

Many of the same concerns that surface in *Cooperation of Parts* can be found in Rea Tajiri's video *History and Memory*, in which she investigates the relationship between history and memory as they relate to an event that ensnared her family: the internment of Japanese-Americans during the Second World War. In events that remain on the margins of US history, the internment forced Tajiri's American-born family and 100,000 other Japanese-Americans into camps as 'enemy aliens', even while other family members were fighting the war in the US army. She pays particular attention to her mother's memory of the internment – a memory that is so incomplete it approaches the condition of amnesia. Her mother's compromised memories are further enhanced by an insufficient family archive of images: cameras were illegal in the camps and her family has very few images available from that time in their possession. Because of this deficiency, Tajiri finds evidence of the events primarily in public records and documents.

Through this process of 'returning' to her family's past in the present Tajiri also investigates larger questions around the image itself. She asks how the dissemination of images constructs both personal and public meanings and why some are suppressed while others come to signify official emblems of history. She also examines the cultural status of images and establishes their profound impact on the creation of various histories and identities. Because taking pictures in the camps was illegal, it is difficult for Tajiri to locate images from that time. When she does eventually find official images of the internment, they fail to articulate its profound impact on her family. Consequently, her objective is to create images that will reframe and reclaim this absent part of her family's history. As she tells us on the soundtrack, her video is thus constructed out of 'the search for an ever absent image' of her family's past 'and the desire to create an image where there is none'.

In her search for her family's 'ever absent image', Tajiri presents us with heterogeneous material 'raided' from various sources. As she begins this search, officially archived photographs of the internment, archival film footage and even enemy alien identification cards act as surrogate images for her family's history. These archival images become her strongest visual recourse to the past. While she appropriates these public documents to reconstruct her family's history, she also challenges their authority. When she presents archival footage that depicts a War Department official justifying the internment in 1942, Tajiri counters by interjecting a title over the image: 'Who chose what story to tell?'

Tajiri examines the status of the image as a reliable source of history through disembodied voice-over narration with occasional off-screen commentary and recorded conversations involving other family members. In contrast to Eisenberg's elliptical, fragmented use of film form and imagery, Tajiri's video essay relies more on the presentation of research, facts and visual information. Found footage, personally-shot footage, documentary and feature-film clips, graphics, vignettes, rolling text and more make her video less a mediation on representational impasses. It is more a video essay on history and memory that actively, analytically and, at times, poetically investigates the relationship between ideology, images and constructed meanings.

Tajiri also turns to American popular culture, another kind of public repository of images and meanings, to examine these issues. She is particularly concerned with how culturally-constructed images might contribute to identity formation. In one section, her investigation is personal as she points to the photographs of Hollywood stars her sister collected when they were children. She asks how the movies might have influenced her sister's life, as well as her own, particularly because all the photos were all 'of white people'. In so doing, Tajiri addresses the ironies and inequities of racial difference and idealisation as it constructs identity.

By incorporating film clips from Hollywood films she extracts other ideologically framed readings of race. She presents a series of clips from John Sturges' film *Bad Day at Black Rock* (1955) in which Spencer Tracy plays a war veteran who travels to a small California town to present a posthumous Congressional Medal of Honor to the father of his fallen Japanese-American comrade. But the father he seeks, Komoko, is nowhere to be found and Tracy soon uncovers the town's dark secret: Komoko's murder and its cover up. While a film about a minority veteran might exhibit some altruistic, progressive tendencies in Hollywood, Tajiri challenges such claims by pointing to the complete and total absence of Japanese-American characters from the entire film. Although they are the centrepiece of the story in *Bad Day at Black Rock*, both Japanese-American characters, Komoko and his son, are physically absent from the film: the war hero is dead and his father is missing, only later to be found dead. Even the place where Tracy finally finds Komoko's grave remains unmarked and anonymous. 'There's something buried up there', he says, 'wildflowers ... that means a grave ... I figured it wasn't a human grave because it wasn't marked. Kind of a mystery ... isn't it?' *Bad Day at Black Rock* is punctuated with such symbols of absence and Tajiri keeps returning to clips of this film throughout her video to underscore her theme of 'missing' images. What is missing for Tajiri is not just the character's marked grave but the presence of all that he signifies in American history.

She also presents a series of clips from Alan Parker's *Come See the Paradise* (1990), a contemporary film which directly represents the Japanese-American internment. Nevertheless, the internment is presented through the point of view of a white character, while at the same time pushing the Japanese-American characters to the background. As clips are presented from this film, we hear a family member off-screen denouncing the movie as 'sentimental mush', with Dennis Quaid playing the lead so that there is a 'virtuous white guy the audience can relate to'.

Tajiri's engagement with American popular culture allows her to underscore the relationship created between culturally-constructed images and their powerful contribution to the formation of history and identity.[20] This is important because the presence or absence of images, both within the public archive as a form of history and as they are manifest in personal memory, are the discursive centrepiece of *History and Memory*. Indeed, the entire structure of the video rests on Tajiri resolving the meaning of a persistent but enigmatic mental image in her memory:

> I don't know where this came from but I just had this fragment, this picture that has always been in my mind. My mother, she's standing at a faucet and it's really hot outside and she's filling a canteen and there is this dust everywhere.

Complementing this narration is one of the more evocative and mediated images in the video. In it, a woman fills a canteen with water. However, the image is fleeting in its appearance, slightly overexposed and manipulated to run at a slower speed, evoking the imprecise nature of memory. Tajiri alters and denatures this image to mark its difference from the rest of the imagery in her video. Even though the image is carefully manipulated in post-production, it clearly complements and 'performs' this particular act from her mother's past. It is only at the end of the video that we will come to understand its significance.

In other sequences, Tajiri turns to historical and archival footage to examine how the construction of images contributes to ideologically-framed readings of history. In one scene, archival footage of the Japanese attack on Pearl Harbor in 1941 is attached to Tajiri's following observation: 'There are things which happened in the world while there were cameras watching. Things we have images for.' Here Tajiri points to the way in which camera recordings are used to produce official, 'objective' documents of history. And yet, something is missing from these official documents, there is something we cannot or are not allowed to see. In another sequence, what is clearly the staged footage of an American propaganda film depicts a Japanese

the image and the witness

'kamikaze' pilot – rendered in a blatantly racist caricature – descending on his target during the Second World War. In tandem with this footage, Tajiri narrates: 'There are other things which have happened while no cameras were watching which we restage in front of the camera to have images of.' And still, there is something we cannot see in these restagings, something outside of the viewfinder.

Later in the video she states: 'There are things which happened for which the only images that exist are in the minds of the observers present at the time.' Here Tajiri opens up her investigation of the relation between images and history to include memory itself. She turns to her mother's memory of the internment. Leading up to this moment in the video, Tajiri has already demonstrated the incomplete manner in which the events surrounding the internment had been transmitted to the next generation. Off-screen commentary between family members attests to this: a niece says of Tajiri's mother: 'She always says that she didn't remember'; and a grandson says, 'I never understood what happened.' Even Tajiri's mother herself claims complete amnesia of the relocation process, when she says, 'I don't even know how I got there.'

Familial omissions, amnesia and missing images lead Tajiri to the National Archives to fill in these gaps. At the National Archives, a strange connection occurs: she finds a picture of her grandmother in a bird-carving class in the internment camp in 1942. The picture is not just material evidence of her grandmother's past, but also a strange link to an object, a small, carved wooden bird that Tajiri knew her mother kept in her jewellery box. Tajiri knew her grandmother had made this object, but she did not know about the historical circumstances attached to its making. Like the small wooden bird, locked away in her mother's jewellery box, this uncanny sequence of events attests to the way traumatic events within family histories can become severed, set-off and sealed away from a sense of temporal and generational continuity. These gaps in her family's history demonstrate how things and events can simply disappear and leave no trace: the rupture of the internment was so removed from any sense of generational continuity in her family that it simply fell away from the family chronology.

Knowing that archival film footage and photographs only provisionally addressed her family's past, Tajiri, like Eisenberg, embarked on a journey to the site of internment, saying:

I began searching for a history, my own history, because I had known all along that the stories I had heard were not true and parts had been left out … There was this place that they knew about. I had never been there, yet I had a memory of it … I had no ideas where these memories came from, yet I knew the place.

Like Eisenberg, she has a memory of a place that is familiar to her but to which she has never been. In April 1988, Tajiri rented a car and drove to Poston, Arizona to witness and record the remains of the Japanese-American internment camp (constructed inside the Colorado River Tribal Reservation) to which her mother had been relocated in 1942. Like Eisenberg, Tajiri focuses on trains, their tracks and stations as a meditation on disruptions and deportations. And like Eisenberg, she also searches for and finds the exact address and place of her mother's internment: Block 213, 11a, Poston 2. She shoots extensive footage of the remains of the internment camp and the surrounding desert landscape. Similar to the mediated image of the woman filling a canteen with water depicted earlier in the video, the footage of the site of the internment camp and its surrounding landscape is altered, slowed down and denatured. Its grainy texture and slow speed also mark it as decisively different from the other parts of the video.

Tajiri's engagement with a disappeared past, through this journey to a place she remembered but had never been, allows her to resolve the mystery of the fragment, the picture that was in her memory, but which she did not understand. The image of her mother filling a canteen with water is, in fact, the only story Tajiri remembers of her mother's memories of camp: it is her mother's fractured memory that she remembers: 'I have been carrying around this picture for years. It is the one memory I have of my mother speaking of the camp when we grew up … for years I've been living with this picture without the story.' We understand now the importance of the 'performed' image that re-enacts this memory. Its fleeting presence doubly inscribes the two timeframes of intergenerational memory: that of her mother's memory and that of Tajiri's postmemory. Tajiri's video is a project of making what was invisible in history and memory visible again: 'I can forgive my mother her loss of memory', she says on the soundtrack, 'and make this image for her.'

Both Eisenberg and Tajiri turn to the physical site of trauma to reactivate their relationship to the past. Place functions as a surrogate, yet nonetheless manifest link for a discursive and embodied engagement between the memory of one genera-tion and the postmemory of the next. Hirsch contends that such links are important in connecting generations, and she uses the photograph to provide that connec-tion: 'Photographs in their enduring "umbilical" connection to life are precisely the medium connecting first- and second-generation remembrance, memory and post-memory.'[21] Without recourse to the past through sufficiently meaningful and per-sonal photographs, Eisenberg and Tajiri turn to the physical sites of trauma and the imaginative capacities of their cameras for such a connection. Engagement with site functions as a mechanism to connect their 'unanchored' memories – those inherited from their parents – to their own lived, embodied experience.

Eisenberg's engagement with place is an encounter with absence and loss. While he witnesses and records what is there, it only reminds him of what is already gone and vanished from view. Eisenberg does not produce images of the past, however he does produce images that are *encoded* with the past, even while this past can-not be imaged. They are encoded with the past through the very dialectic of his acts of witnessing and recording paired with remembering his parents' memory. It is ultimately through the filmmaker's consciousness of the past and the capacity of his camera to materialise that consciousness that images infused with history can be produced. Tajiri also focuses on the absence of images and memories. However, her goal is not to make an image of that absence, but to construct a new presence and to 'create an image' for her family where there was none. To reinstate what was miss-ing, what was invisible, Tajiri must make visible what has not yet been sufficiently im-aged, which, as part of traumatic memory, has been barely allowed to be imagined. Tajiri creates such images when, for example, she produces that of the canteen at the tap as a kind of gift to her mother, as a way of witnessing the traumatic memory of the camp that her mother could not herself possess as her own. It is precisely through her purposeful construction of a new, alternative image produced within the critical context of the present that Tajiri is able to reframe and reclaim the past for herself, her mother and the public. Both artists have produced interventionist images that act, as Eisenberg states, 'to recuperate lost or subjugated history' through the production of 'new working historical documents'. Part of their interventionist tactics lie in their purposeful acts of witnessing, in their direct, original acts of seeing. For, in doing so, Eisenberg and Tajiri can now reframe their parents' compromised or partial witnessing of the original traumatic events with their own historically conscious acts of witnessing. Added to their acts of witnessing is the act of recording. And recording, as such, implies the involvement of not just the parents' original, compromised acts of witnessing and the children's postmemory witnessing, but other acts of public seeing and viewing. Indeed, the act of recording, and the subsequent film and video, assume the presence of a potential and implied audience. And it is this viewing audience that can now participate in reinstating those original traumatic events in history that were so compromised by incomplete memories.

Cooperation of Parts is distributed by Canyon Cinema, 145 Ninth Street, Suite 260, San Francisco, CA 94103, USA (www.canyoncinema.com). History and Memory is distributed by Women Make Movies, 462 Broadway, Suite 500W. New York, NY 10013, USA (www.wmm.com).

Notes

1   Cathy Caruth, *Unclaimed Experience: Trauma, Narrative and History* (Baltimore: Johns Hopkins University Press, 1996), 124, n. 14.
2   Daniel Eisenberg, 'The Authority of Site/The Site of Authority: Cinematic Observation and the Discourse of Documents'. Paper presented to the Chicago Film Seminar, The School of the Art Institute of Chicago, November 1996.
3   Marianne Hirsch, *Family Frames: Photography, Narrative and Postmemory* (Cambridge, MA: Harvard University Press, 1997), 22.
4   Ibid.
5   Ibid.
6   Hirsch writes 'the prefix "post" could imply we are beyond memory and therefore perhaps, as [Pierre] Nora fears, purely in history' (22).
7   Eisenberg, 'The Authority of Site', n.p.
8   Eisenberg's earlier film *Displaced Person* (1981) is composed entirely of archival imagery and examines the dissemination of history solely through the use of the public record. He explains this archival 'obsession' as a compensatory act to address the traumatic gaps in his own familial archive: 'There were no images from my parents life before the war, no landscapes to refer to or see. The maps, historical images, newsreels and films that constituted the official record of the war were my only visual links to those stories' (Eisenberg, 'The Authority of Site', n.p.).
9   Mark McElhatten, 'Dan Eisenberg's *Cooperation of Parts*', *Kinemathek* 77 (January 1992): 28.
10 Alf Bold, 'Daniel Eisenberg in Conversation with Alf Bold', *Kinemathek* 77 (September 1991): 9.
11 Ibid.
12 Saul Friedlander, *Memory, History and the Extermination of the Jews of Europe* (Bloomington and Indianapolis: Indiana University Press, 1993), 134.

13 Eisenberg, 'The Authority of Site', n.p.

14 Arguably the most powerful cinematic use of landscape as a means to confront the past can be found in Claude Lanzmann's *Shoah* (1985). Resisting the use of archival images and insisting that the framework of his film remains firmly rooted in the present, Lanzmann nevertheless creates the framework for a spectral temporality to unfold. This occurs in the film's opening scene, a scene in which Lanzmann has convinced a survivor from Chelmo, Poland to return to the place of his catastrophic past. And it is in this precise movement toward returning – both to a 'there' in space (to the place where it happened) and to a 'then' in time (through anamnestic testimony) – that creates the representational force of the scene, and allows for a kind of damaged time to erupt; one that is still infused with the Holocaust past.

15 Eisenberg, 'The Authority of Site', n.p.

16 James Young, *At Memory's Edge: After-Images of the Holocaust in Contemporary Art and Architecture* (New Haven and London: Yale University Press, 2000), 9.

17 Dora Apel, *Memory Effects: The Holocaust and the Art of Secondary Witnessing* (New Brunswick, NJ: Rutgers University Press, 2002), 3.

18 Ibid., 188.

19 See Andrea Liss, *Trespassing through the Shadows: Memory, Photography and the Holocaust* (Minneapolis: The University of Minnesota Press, 1998). Liss also employs the term 'postmemory', but applies it to the general population rather than to children of survivors.

20 Tajiri's ironic use of popular culture further differentiates her method of investigation from that of Eisenberg. Saul Friedlander provides a possible explanation for this differentiation in *Memory, History and the Extermination of the Jews of Europe* when he writes that there is a 'moral imperative' which the Holocaust seems to claim within the public sphere that ultimately works to 'impose limits' on its representation. This limitation, he writes, inevitably 'creates a major obstacle to the representation of the Shoah within the main components of present-day cultural sensibility: the ironic mode and postmodern aesthetic' (53). Such a restraint, he continues, 'seems particularly at odds with what may sometimes appear as the playful experiments of post-modernity' (55).

21 Hirsch, *Family Frames*, 23.

11. Haunting Absences: Witnessing Loss in Doris Salcedo's *Atrabilarios* and Beyond

Edlie L. Wong

While the grandmother floated through the swamps of the past, Eréndira busied herself sweeping the house, which was dark and motley, with bizarre furniture and statutes of invented Caesars, chandeliers of teardrops and alabaster angels, a gilded piano, and numerous clocks of unthinkable sizes and shapes.

GABRIEL GARCÍA MÁRQUEZ

Since her first solo exhibition, *Atrabilarios* (1991), at the Boston Institute of Contemporary Art, Colombian sculptor Doris Salcedo has garnered international acclaim for her long-standing commitment to a politicised art practice. Born in Bogotá, Salcedo studied at the Universidad de Bogotá Jorge Tadeo Lozano before receiving her graduate degree in sculpture from New York University in 1984. After returning to Colombia to take up positions at the Instituto de Bellas Artes, Cali (1987–88) and the Universidad Nacional de Colombia, Bogotá (1989–91), Salcedo has chosen to continue living in Bogotá, and exhibiting selectively in her native country. In *Atrabilarios*, Salcedo used an article of clothing – women's shoes – to address the haunting depersonalisation of violence in Colombia.[1] Female *desaparecidos* or disappeared, as she discovered in her research, were usually subjected to prolonged periods of captivity before execution, and clothing was often the only object remaining to identify those discovered in common graves.[2] Inset into niches covered with translucent animal fibre, coarsely stitched with thick black surgical thread into the white gallery walls, the shoes in *Atrabilarios* refer the viewer to the absent owner: they suggest the body

173

rather than attempt its direct representation. These worn shoes, caught somewhere between fetish and relic, serve as a material signifier and metonymic displacement for the absent body.[3] Unlike the piles of shoes and other personal items displayed in the United States Holocaust Memorial Museum, these do not function simply as mementos of the dead. Like the work of contemporary sculptors Mona Hatoum and Maya Lin, they challenge the commemorative function of monuments and memorials.[4] Salcedo's sculptures transform ordinary household objects into powerful sites of transmission that align viewers with witnesses and survivors. These objects of 'bizarre furniture' evoke the lived experiences of traumatic loss and its memory.[5]

In contemporary Colombia, the complex and persistent legacies of conflict among the *narcotraficantes* (Cali and Medellín drug cartels), leftist guerrillas (the long-standing Fuerzas Armadas Revolucionarias Colombianas and Ejercito Liberacion Nacional), right-wing paramilitaries (Autodefensas Unidas de Colombia) and armed security forces converge in a repressive state government that uses state-of-siege legislation in a 'war of silencing'. In a country where multiple constituencies vie for political power and violence atomises communities, the disappearance, death and displacement of civilians have become, as a result, a frequent occurrence. As a technique of social control, disappearance renders its victims anonymous and leaves an ever-present and haunting absence in its wake. Those who witness and survive continue to suffer psychic violence as they are forced to occupy a paralytic state in between knowing and not knowing. Their loss remains inarticulate. There are few precedents, as some art critics have noted, for Salcedo's type of socially and politically informed art in her native Colombia.[6] Exhibitions spanning *Atrabilarios* and *Neither* (2004) contemplate how these overlapping mechanisms of repressive power establish systems of public record and memory, both locally and globally. Many of her sculptures develop collaboratively from personal interviews with survivors gathered from the interior of Colombia and take their form from specific words used in the storytelling. The *Atrabilarios* pieces, according to Salcedo, 'rely heavily on the words the victim used while telling his or her experiences, in some instances, and on objects given to me in others ... The work is defined by the nature of the victim's ordeal.'[7] These sculptures become sites of transmission for those witnesses from whom both the social rituals of mourning – burying the dead and public speech – are withheld. While personal testimony endows these sculptures with their peculiar form, Salcedo openly resists narrativisation in her working method. She has maintained in interviews that words 'are no longer possible ... when you deal with violence' and she is 'not interested in telling stories'.[8] This refusal to narrativise functions as a political strategy to immerse the exhibition visitor in the confusing and empty spaces that are the sites or non-sites inhabited by Salcedo's survivor-witnesses.

If narrative or story-making necessarily mediates the cognitive passage from witnessing to knowing or processing a traumatic event, then what does Salcedo's working method convey about the condition of traumatic loss, its aesthetic translation and the act of witnessing? In seeking to represent subjects who fall outside of established systems of representation, she purposely moves away from narrative, which organises unfolding events along a teleological or etiological continuum. Narrative, in this sense, imposes an artificial order upon experience in the effort to rationalise or 'make sense' of loss by turning it into story. In keeping with Salcedo's working method, personal testimony undergoes a radical transformation into material image, as the artist becomes, in her words, 'a witness of a witness, loyally reproducing the victim's experience'.[9] Her artwork refuses simply to give voice to the victims of political violence; rather, it captures the magnitude and duration of suffering in the material image as it simultaneously positions the viewer as witness to traumatic loss. Installations such as *Atrabilarios*, furthermore, intensify the internal contradiction of trauma, which Cathy Caruth describes as a 'breach in the mind's experience of time, self, and the world [that] suggests a certain paradox: that the most direct seeing of a violent event may occur as an absolute inability to know it'.[10] The carefully placed shoes in *Atrabilarios*, for example, present an alternative mode of representing violence that recognises the limits of the visual field. The shoes translate testimonial experience through complex processes of substitution, association and incorporation. Salcedo formally shifts away from mimetic representation *and* testimonial writing, both inadequate to the task of representing such loss, as it seeks to convey what art critic Euridice Arratia describes as the 'power of memory to recover the effaced body', a disappeared body effaced from Colombian national history.[11]

While works of visual analogy such as the atrocity photograph emphasise the numbing hypervisibility of violence and elicit the immediate shock of recognition in its viewers, Salcedo's sculptures organise a very different experience of seeing. Her sculptures offer a language of grief that expresses the diffuse melancholic temporality of traumatic loss, the lived circumstances, as she notes, of 'those who have suffered violence … ongoing displacement as individuals, families and entire communities' in Colombia.[12] Disappearance operates strategically within the realm of representation to destroy the quantifiable 'evidence' of crime, and it takes the form of erasure and occultation: there is no material or historical record of the deceased. A representational project confronting the particular violence of disappearance must negotiate this constitutive indeterminacy or absence. Salcedo's working method recognises how violence often defies visual representation and statistical measurement. She works at the limits of the visual field by making art that addresses certain forms of unquantifiable loss: the absent body, a body that is in fact 'disappeared'. Under such conditions, her sculptures provide an alternative mode of seeing that acknowledges the presence of those absent, yet not definitively dead. The non-documentary format of her artwork establishes a politics of memory that seeks to redeem the dead from their enforced anonymity. Those left behind cannot recover or recognise the violated body, bury the dead and begin the work of mourning. In the melancholic refusal to let go, these witnesses and survivors refuse to forget the dead as they desperately hold onto a past that otherwise has no place in history or public memory.

FURNITURE WITH NO MEMORIES: THE AFTERLIFE OF LOSS IN *UNLAND*

In solo exhibitions ranging from *La Casa Viuda* (*The Widowed House*, 1994) and *Unland* (1998), Salcedo sought to capture women's experiences of political violence and the spatial and temporal dimensions of their loss. *La Casa Viuda*, which opened at the Brooke Alexander Gallery, New York, refers not only to the houses of women left widowed by ongoing violence in Colombia, but also a phrase indicating a home whose inhabitants have 'vanished'.[13] In the attribution of 'widowhood' to the archi-

tectural space of the home, Salcedo offers *La Casa Viuda* as an intersubjective encounter in which the viewer is positioned as witness to a violence that ruptures the
exterior materiality – the façade – of the home. With found doors as its central objects, *La Casa Viuda* transforms entryways into free-standing skeletal assemblages
that, like the *Untitled* armoires and oddly distorted chairs of *Tenebrae*, physically
block the viewer's passage through the gallery space. By placing art as an obstacle
to movement, perception and cognition, Salcedo challenges the viewer to acknowledge the limits of viewership while attending to that which the work cannot say.
Her sculptures evoke the bewildering experience of living on the blurred boundaries
of the rational and fantastic more frequently associated with Latin American literary
magical realism. They capture a life, as she describes it, 'constantly interrupted by
acts of violence ... that disrupt the way you wish to live'.[14]

Salcedo's almost exclusive use of abandoned and discarded objects of furniture
stands in an intimate referential relation to the absent occupants displaced by political violence. Many families from Colombia's rural areas resettled – both voluntarily
and involuntarily – on the peripheries of metropolitan centres. These communities
constitute the 'dispersed sector' of the urban poor.[15] The past two decades alone
have seen more than 350,000 deaths and about two million internal refugees, most
frequently *campesinos* (subsistence farmers) and indigenous peoples, who have begun to spill over into neighbouring Venezuela, Ecuador, Peru, Brazil and Panama.[16]
In Salcedo's efforts to seek an aesthetic mode of address for those dislocated and
historically without access to representation, she, like other contemporary artists
and scholars of the dispossessed, has sought to delineate the social meaning and
effects of repressive power. Her art explicates the mundane yet no less violent and
deforming effects of this power.

In *The Bluest Eye* (1970), Toni Morrison portrays how regimes of modern bio-
political power transform an inanimate article of furniture into a source and trans-
mitter of pain. 'The furniture', she writes, 'had aged without ever having become
familiar. People had owned it, but never known it ... There were no memories among
those pieces. Certainly no memories to be cherished.'[17] In her novel, social violence
quite literally marks the furniture – the contested split, 'which became a gash, which
became a gaping chasm that exposed the cheap frame and cheaper upholstery'.
Ownership becomes an ever-present shameful reminder of the quotidian ways in
which power shapes their lived social relations. Such a 'hated piece of furniture',
according to Morrison, 'produces a fretful malaise that asserts itself throughout the
house and limits the delight of things not related to it'.[18] Salcedo, likewise, works
upon the proximity of furniture, the body and the lived intimacy of violence. Destroy-
ing the false divisions between private and public, interior and exterior, her art reveals
the particular ways in which repressive state power penetrates and disfigures the
intimate spaces of the home.

Unland (1998) opened at the New Museum of Contemporary Art, New York, and
its simple title gestures towards the sitelessness of peoples displaced by the ongoing
political violence of Colombia's decades-long civil war. In Salcedo's artwork, the site-
less are those who have lost both home and nation. They are denied the recognition
necessary to enter the life of a legitimate community for they live anachronistically in
a modern state that denies them full citizenship while their legal status remains in a

state of suspension.[19] Political violence makes the home into an uninhabitable place that can no longer function properly as a refuge or domestic sanctuary. The grafting of organic materials closely associated with the human body onto household objects, such as wooden tables in *Unland*, defamiliarises these everyday artefacts. Salcedo describes in an interview one particularly affective testimonial encounter:

> There was one widow, the widow of a political leader, who told me how difficult it was to continue living with objects that are reminders of her husband. Every morning you open the closet and the clothing is there. Everyday you sit at the dining table and the empty chair is there, screaming the absence of that person. It can be a very difficult object to live with.[20]

Salcedo's pervasive use of found objects alludes both to the forced abandonment of home and the subjective experience of this loss – the *unheimlichkeit* or uncanniness, that is, of a suddenly vanished relation and the haunting quality of this absence.

Unland consists of three sculptures that are variations on a common theme that offers the most distinct articulation of her earlier working method.[21] Salcedo joined wooden tables of differing proportions and then drilled hundreds of tiny holes into the wood fibre to resemble epidermal pores, which she then threaded with dark human hair. In *irreversible witness* (1995–98), single strands of knotted hair are almost imperceptible under a membrane of cloudy silk fabric, while the remains of a rusted metal baby crib are fused into one end of the joined table segments. In the second sculpture, *audible in the mouth* (1998), strands of hair that resemble dark veins or scratches cover two nearly equal table segments of blond wood. These visual details are virtually imperceptible – unless one is positioned within inches of the textured surface – and suggest the radical insufficiency of sight. These structured relationships between viewer and material image frustrate the easy appropriation of the place of the 'other', the survivor-witness. They preserve the difference between viewer and survivor-witness rather than encourage acts of voyeuristic identification. Salcedo invites the viewer to enter into an intimate relation with the material image, to draw close, but stop just short of contact. Her painstakingly wrought details resist an encompassing or dominating gaze. The subtle traces of home and intimacy with the lost loved one – a zipper, lace ruffle, flannel shirtsleeve or button – impose a relation of silent, yet attentive proximity. This relation maintains the integrity of the dead when it requires the viewer to forgo a vision of the person in favour of a contemplation of a metonymic possession, an object that once characterised the bereaved.

Unland is a work of translation that acknowledges the mediating hand of the artist. It enables a representational practice that does not re-enact the very vio-

Figure 1: Doris Salcedo, *Unland, the orphan's tunic*, 1997, wood, cloth and hair. Courtesy of Alexander and Bonin, New York.

lence that it attempts to disarticulate. The third sculpture, *the orphan's tunic* (1997), bears a title alluding to the poetry of Holocaust survivor Paul Celan (figure 1). In Celan's poem, the 'orphan's tunic' functions as a 'flag', in the sense of an emblem that stands for a loss which becomes embodied as 'his/ first/ birth-marked, se/ cret-speckled skin'.[22] *Unland*'s pervasive use of skin-like membranes, like *Atrabilarios*, references Celan's expression of somatic experience. *the orphan's tunic* also questions the meaning of survivorship and the qualified life it promises. The *Unland* tables are all sized to the length of an adult body and act as object surrogates for the disappeared body. Salcedo based *the orphan's tunic* upon her encounters with a 6-year-old girl who witnessed the slaying of both her parents and remained unable to articulate her loss in language. Throughout the course of their interactions, the young girl returned each day wearing the same garment: a dress, as Salcedo discovered, made by the girl's mother.[23] This dress, the orphan's tunic, acquires meaning in its ha-

Figure 2: Doris Salcedo, *Unland, the orphan's tunic*, 1997 (detail). Courtesy of Alexander and Bonin, New York.

bitual wearing and intimate contact with the body: the tunic becomes, as in Celan's poem, a skin that envelops and defines the orphan. Elongated cracks resembling open wounds split the wooden surface of *the orphan's tunic*, which appears tenuously held in place by the weave of hair and silk (figure 2). Salcedo's substitution of human hair for thread alludes both to the gendered labour of weaving or mending torn garments and the figurative act of working through and coming to terms with traumatic loss. This reference to the simple tasks of domestic labour also indicates how women and children are often left behind, in such instances, as the unacknowledged victims of ongoing psychic violence.

The *Unland* tables manifest the atomising and deeply embodied experience of individual loss through the re-presentation of objects rooted in the home, in order to address the epistemic violence of disappearance. While some thinkers have conceived of the 'home-place' as a site resistant to pervasive forms of dehumanisation, Salcedo's critical engagement with the architecture of domestic space questions exactly *how* the home can exist independently from the state when political violence disfigures it into an ever-present reminder of repressive power.[24] Political violence, as Salcedo notes, deforms the home into a 'non-[site], a space impossible to inhabit because transformed into a sign for the disappearance of loved ones'.[25] Salcedo positions her artwork as witness to this alienation associated with place: 'The marks left behind by the violent act in these places are sometimes evident and sometimes imperceptible although, in any case, indelible. My task is to transform these traces into relics that enable us to acknowledge other people's experiences as our own, as collective experiences.'[26] Salcedo inscribes individual memories of traumatic loss onto the object-form in a process described as 'relic making'. The dynamic interplay of tactile material including animal fibre, hair, silk and cloth with found objects of furniture marks her labour and intervention as an artist and the fetish-like quality of these assemblages. Caught somewhere fluctuating between spirit and thing, Salcedo's sculptures embody a form of cultural transmission that mediates subjective experience through the art-object. They are, perhaps, best described as composite fabrications of found objects and personal artefacts. In *Atrabilarios* and the *Untitled* furniture, for example, articles of clothing once belonging to the victims and given to Salcedo by her interviewees are woven into her sculptures. These physical traces of the dead are found in all the sculptures marking the period of artistic production through *Unland*. They express the materiality of a loss that, while ephemeral, is experienced as weightiness for those who witness, survive and bear the burden of history.

Unland asks viewers to enter the intimate space of violence, the 'non-site' of the installation, which becomes the site of a collective remembering that actively works against the alienation of a state-imposed silence seeking to disfigure personal memory into prohibitory nightmare.[27] The ongoing civil war in Colombia is a war of silencing that uses memory against itself to further forms of political repression. Michael Taussig elaborates: 'The point about silencing and the fear behind silencing is not to erase memory. Far from it. The point is to drive the memory deep within the fastness of the individual so as to create more fear and uncertainty in which dreams and reality commingle.'[28] This is a repressive silence that is, as in *Unland*, only 'audible in the mouth' – a suspended speech in the moment of subalternised articulation that cannot be released as social communication. Rather than posing speech against silence, Salcedo explores the productive power of silence to evoke the particular experience of witnessing disappearance. Silence, for Salcedo, becomes a site of shared collective engagement that preserves the painful inarticulateness of loss: 'The silence of the victim of the violence in Colombia, my silence as an artist, and the silence of the viewer come together during the precise moment of contemplation and only in the very space where that contemplation occurs.'[29] Her work recontextualises and, thereby, critically transforms repressive silence into a publicly acknowledged intersubjective engagement with the victims' experiences. In sharing this silence, a community of witnesses emerges that addresses the repressive fragmentation of collective memory by redirecting silence from the privacy of the individual or the family into the shared public spaces of the museum.[30]

Installations such as *Unland* seek to mitigate the depersonalising anonymity of violence through the critical process of bringing insider and outsider together at the traumatic event. Salcedo recounts meeting with a mother of the disappeared whose life was irrevocably marred by her loss:

I remember I met a very beautiful woman two years ago. A mother who had been waiting for ten years for her son to appear. In ten years she has never come out of the house in fear that her son might call or come to knock at the door when she is not around. She is a person caught in her own jail. His dish is always on the table. There are hundreds of cases like hers. It is then that one realizes how these persons have been marked by violence, although they were never the direct recipients of it.[31]

The home, in this encounter, summons the affective qualities of *La Casa Viuda* and the furniture of *Untitled* where Salcedo encased ponderous mahogany armoires, china cabinets, chests and chairs in grey cement to suggest how violence muffles and immobilises the household. This encounter also summons the image of the 'spiteful' house in Morrison's *Beloved* (1987), where traumatic memories of loss threaten identity rather than reconstituting it in the present. Such stories of haunting loss also inhabit Salcedo's sculptures; they produce a space of pregnant silence, an expectant inarticulateness that gives a home to pain.[32] Salcedo describes in an interview this particular effect of loss: 'When a beloved person disappears, everything becomes impregnated with that person's presence. Every single object but also every space is a reminder of his or her absence, as if absence were stronger than presence.'[33] The mother's embodied memories of loss are physically marked by the habitual placement of 'his dish' upon the kitchen table and her melancholic attachment to place. She simply cannot leave the home: even as her continued contact with his personalised objects reaffirms the futility and hopelessness of her expectations. She is psychologically – and physically – trapped as she desperately awaits her son's endlessly deferred return. Objects such as 'his dish' serve as repositories for violence they puncture the moribund normalcy of 'terror as usual', and they animate this scene with an affective power of address.

In the conceptual framing of memory through the trace object, Salcedo's sculptures materialise what Caruth describes as the 'profound link between the loved one and the ongoing life of the survivor'.[34] Memory must work, according to Salcedo, in this shadowy realm 'between the figure of the one who has died and the life disfigured by the death'.[35] These installations translate testimony into material images that make palpable the afterlife of loss. As a material object invested with a signifying or symbolic aura created in the play of history and memory, the collective and individual, Salcedo's artwork reconfigures the art gallery into what Pierre Nora describes as the *lieu de mémoire* (place of memory). As a 'mixed, hybrid, mutant' place bound 'intimately with life and death … the collective and the individual', the *lieu de mémoire* functions in ways similar to Salcedo's installations to 'block the work of forgetting, to establish a state of things, to immortalise death, to materialise the immaterial'.[36] Her art practice forges intimate connections between the individual experience of loss and the depersonalising act of terror by giving a material object-form to traumatic memory within the bounded *lieu* of the installation space.

A HOME IN THE WORLD: AFTER *NOVIEMBRE 6*

In a one-year period spanning November 1992–93, the Colombian government enacted 32 emergency decrees that, according to Santiago Villaveces-Izquierdo, severely limited and modified, 'individual liberties, *habeas corpus*, freedom of the press, freedom of speech, and the right to privacy'.[37] The country's periodic use of state-of-siege or state of emergency legislation banishes the critical alternatives and transformative possibilities of a dissenting public sphere. Such state-enforced silences repress the ability of imagining oneself as integrated within a larger political or social community, either locally or globally. Similarly, global news media all too often perpetuate and amplify this sense of atomisation with its almost exclusive focus on sensational images of violence and abjection in Colombia. Given these local and global dynamics, the transnational circulation of Salcedo's work offers an essential form of publicity designed to counter that of the mainstream media. This alternative sphere of publicity allows those delegitimated from participation in dominant society – the disenfranchised – to reinhabit the liminal spaces of their marginalisation with the force of a critical perspective. Salcedo's artwork reconstitutes the institutional site of the US art museum into an alternative space that enables the production of critical counter-histories of loss. The art gallery is thus far from its conventional perception as an apolitical realm for aesthetic appreciation.

Even as Salcedo re-circulates Colombian violence within the US art world, she is wary of how these institutional sites often perpetuate the history of US neo-colonial relations. Art historian Mónica Amor, for example, argues that US museum curatorial practices towards Latin American art unconsciously partake in neo-colonial relations by facilitating the conflation of cultural identity and art object. She criticises the homogenising Euro-American tendency to limit 'Latin America's artistic critical discourse to a subject that so far seems to be the only one permitted for it, namely cultural identity'.[38]

Despite her growing international acclaim, Salcedo continues to resist the cultural homogenisation of Latin American difference and the over-determination of her artwork as simply an instance of the turmoil popularly associated with Colombia. US neo-colonial relations with the country have often taken the insidious form of international narcotics-control legislation. Two past incidents have confirmed this pervasive image of Colombia as social threat and contamination. At JFK International Airport, New York and Barajas Airport, Madrid, customs officials needlessly destroyed sculptures destined for the 1995 Carnegie International in Pittsburgh while searching for narcotics.[39] For Salcedo, these events entered into the very cycle of national violence that her work sought to interrogate:

> The pieces were the object of the same violence that they were referring to. … No matter the place, the attitudes towards the pieces would have been the same … They were not just looking for drugs inside the pieces because they literally destroyed them. One single cut would have done the job, but they had five, six, seven cuts. It was an act of brutality. It was something redundant. The piece had already gone through all that; the piece came from an act of brutality and they returned it to that.[40]

These excessive acts of US and European border-policing demonstrate the convergence of neo-colonial forms of violence with Colombian state violence couched in a flexible discourse of counter-narcotics regulation. They illustrate the vicious effects of a US foreign policy that intensifies a repressive Colombian government even as it vigilantly polices its border against contamination. Such acts mobilise an authoritative discourse of policing the Westernised nations' social health as they seek to distinguish violence as the distinct product of a third world nation-state.

As testimonial-based installations such as *Unland* and *La Casa Viuda* circulate within these Euro-American national contexts, they continue to struggle against the damaging assumption that political violence constitutes and is coextensive with Colombian national identity. Installations such as *Tenebrae* (2000) and most recently *Neither* have moved more explicitly towards the disarticulation of victim communities from national boundaries. Salcedo, as some art critics note, has begun to argue *against* the national specificity of her work which, nevertheless, has returned time and again to the effects of political violence in her native Colombia. Building on the earlier themes of sitelessness and displacement, her new work dwells on the detachment of traumatic loss from personal testimony and location. In fact, there are no more individual signifiers or traces of witnesses and survivors. This recent work evokes a range of experiences that, according to art historian Jill Bennett, are no longer rooted in a singular national identity, but engaged with the trauma of others in various nations around the world.[41] This noticeable shift in Salcedo's art practice also unsettles the coherence of local meaning found in past work. Moreover, the transnational circulation of recent work further de-localises the specificity of her geopolitical references. *Tenebrae*'s temporal markers, *Noviembre 7, 1985* and *Noviembre 6*, for example, forego their mooring to a determining national event and a localised frame of intelligibility once they are placed within a transnational circulation. The title, with no narrative accompaniment or extra-textual explanation, holds no meaningful reference for those unfamiliar with modern Colombian history. Thus, nation may be erased, but it is, at the same time, vehemently reinforced in these works. *Noviembre 6* displays an open-ended temporality where the past seems persistently alive in the present and in history.

While installations such as *Tenebrae*, first exhibited at Alexander and Bonin, New York, seek to prevent collective amnesia, they continue to offer a form of social memory that refuses to historicise or memorialise the event. War and history, for Salcedo, are both struggles to control geopolitical space and mechanisms of public record.[42] *Tenebrae* marks the infamous then-active M-19 (19 April Movement) seizure of Bogotá's Palacio de Justicia on 6 November 1985 where magistrates and civilian visitors were taken hostage.[43] Over one hundred hostages including all the guerrillas were killed in the ensuing two-day military attack upon the occupied building, and records of this event were subsequently effaced from public history. This event coincided with Salcedo's homecoming to Colombia after completing her graduate studies in Europe and the US. She witnessed the event directly, and her first untitled works in 1987 and 1989 were her attempts to come to terms with these deeply personal embodied memories.[44] While *Tenebrae* marks an

Figure 3: Doris Salcedo, *Tenebrae, Noviembre 7, 1985,* 1999–2000, lead and steel. Courtesy of Alexander and Bonin, New York.

the image and the witness

autobiographical homecoming of sorts, it also presents a significant departure from the techniques used in her previous work. Unlike *Unland*'s emphasis on painstaking detail, *Tenebrae, Noviembre 7, 1985* and *Noviembre 6* use methods of casting, which remove the impress of the personal from the work. Salcedo casts wooden chairs – reminiscent of destroyed office furniture – in lead and stainless steel. She then assembles them into large amalgamated structures that, as in past work, continue to define space through their relation with the absent body (figure 3). While *Tenebrae* is part of Salcedo's longstanding exploration of the temporal as well as the spatial dimension of loss, the personal artefacts – the ruffle, shoe or sleeve – are no longer in evidence.

Trauma studies generally emphasise the significance of returning to the site of original trauma to confront and 'work through' the past.[45] However, these installations and their transnational circulation pose provocative challenges to this understanding of traumatic resolution and re-negotiation. For Salcedo, the original site of trauma – the disappeared body and its historical record – is radically inaccessible. Her turn towards an aesthetic principle of re-contextualisation was emergent in *Unland*, and its return in these later works marks her renewed endeavours to address traumatic loss, not simply as individual and isolated process, but as a global one. Salcedo's material images offer their own dynamics of witnessing, a dynamic which is enhanced by transnational circulation rather than experienced as a loss of local meanings and contexts. The new work, dating from *Tenebrae* on, begins to conceptualise more explicitly the agency of the material image in facilitating the act of witnessing.

Increased attention to the placement of art objects and the transformation of gallery space in these installations open up a space of encounter for a viewer who is actively positioned as participant in, and therefore, witness to the unfolding of a world trauma or what some scholars in the fashion of political philosopher Giorgio Agamben have begun to theorise as the global refugee crisis.[46]

These recent installations are increasingly attuned to forging particular spatial relations between viewer and material image that dictate the experiential conditions of their viewing. They ask the viewer to enter into a different, more active level of engagement. An installation such as *Tenebrae* abruptly re-channels the flow of museum visitor traffic; and *Neither* beckons the viewer to enter the installation space physically. Salcedo's contribution to the Eighth Istanbul Biennial (2003) carried only one identifying mark: the address 'Yemeniciler Caddesi

Figure 4: Doris Salcedo, Installation for the Istanbul Biennnial 2003. Courtesy of Alexander and Bonin, New York.

No. 66' where she filled a three-story gap in a row of buildings with 1,600 wooden chairs (figure 4). The chaotic lattice-like arrangement of brown and tan chairs appear fused to the worn façades of its neighbouring buildings. In turn, they draw the viewer's attention to the former building it replaced. Situated in a still-active commercial quarter filled with hardware stores and small ironmongery businesses, the installation became an unavoidable aspect of the daily context of those who lived there and frequented its establishments. In another public installation that was only exhibited in Bogotá, Salcedo staged a two-day event recognising the newly reconstructed Palacio de Justicia destroyed seventeen years earlier. It involved the lowering of 280 wooden chairs over the eastern side of the exterior wall, the ornamented façade of the new building. The installation was designed to correspond with the exact hours of the M-19 attack and military response: the chairs gradually descended to hang in an asymmetrical pattern just above the anonymous pedestrians, onlookers and the curious who happened to be strolling in the Plaza de Bolívar below. Not only do these later installations mark a progressive shift in Salcedo's work from inside to outside spaces, private to public objects, they also fashion a much more dynamic relationship between the material image and the imagined, and often accidental, viewer.

These new works have explicitly moved away from representing the intimate spaces of the home to dwell upon public sites of state violence. While public and private spaces in past installations have been intimately related, she now transforms a Bogotá courthouse, city plaza and an Istanbul neighbourhood into unlikely 'homes' for her art objects. While Salcedo cites the influence of Joseph Beuys' concepts of 'social sculpture' and 'social architecture', she takes his ideas one step further: she also seeks to emphasise the blurred distinction between the unidirectional communication of art and the participatory use of architecture. While the inset niches of *Atrabilarios* extend the sculpture into the architecture of the gallery, *Tenebrae* actively reconfigures the gallery space to draw the viewer into an experiential relation with the material image.[47] In *Tenebrae*, bizarrely elongated chair legs extend over and pierce the gallery walls to block the narrow entryway into the installation space. The sculpture functions both as an obstacle to the viewer's passage through the gallery space, and as an integral part of the room's structure. Even the most transient and disinterested of viewers is forced to confront the material image and sheer physical intransigence of traumatic loss. This loss becomes, in a literal fashion, a part of the gallery space into which the viewer steps.

These recent installations continue to refuse narrativisation, both in terms of the production and reception of the material image (such as the narrative impulse in museums to supplement artwork with explanatory text) even as they mark the historical force of memory. *Neither* opened at London's White Cube to reveal a dark heavy-duty diamond-patterned metal fencing that Salcedo had painstakingly fitted within the gallery's white plaster walls (figures 5 and 6).[48] The installation (which is permanently housed in Belo Horizonte, Brazil) transforms the gallery into nothing but empty space, a transformation that vaguely recalls a military containment centre. While *Neither* contemplates the ambivalent workings of enclosures and boundaries, belonging and exclusion, this new project continues to move viewers away from the domestic spaces of *Atrabilarios*, *La Casa Viuda* and *Unland*. It offers an interrogation of the public and institutional places of sitelessness, such as, in Salcedo's words, 'the camps in Australia and Nauru where asylum seekers are held. In Guantánamo. For those awaiting deportation from the United States.'[49] Viewers must enter a space that resembles a chain-link-fenced refugee camp or detention centre in order to view the installation, an imperative that transforms viewing into a physical immersion in the experience of the prisoner. The distinctions between viewer, participant and witness break down when the gallery is turned into the non-site or 'no-man's land' of imprisonment and dislocation and the viewer is, consequently, compelled to experience how state power defamiliarises life. Salcedo has long probed the geopolitical and phenomenological boundaries of trauma, and *Neither* delineates, as in earlier work, political communities beyond the borders of a given nation-state or territory. Unlike the grisly and often shocking explicitness found in certain works of political critique such as those of Colombian artist Fernando Botero's Abu Ghraib paintings (2005), *Neither* radically reorganises the gallery space to make the collective experience of imprisonment and displacement the work of the material image.[50] The viewer cannot turn away from this artwork, and becomes, upon entering the space, a living part of the installation.

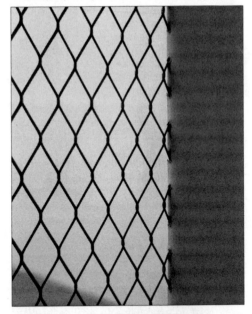

Figures 5 and 6: Doris Salcedo, *Neither*, 2004 (detail). Courtesy of Alexander and Bonin, New York.

Salcedo's installations work against forms of historical narration when they evacuate the bodily evidence of violence and offer a representation of traumatic loss that addresses those silenced and effectively rendered invisible within public history and social memory. Violence, according to Salcedo, 'has always been present, one just needs a certain way of looking, of seeing certain things in order to unveil this presence'.[51] Her installations orchestrate a participatory spectatorship where aesthetic interpretation requires the viewer to literally enter into and share the space of the 'other'. She defines her art practice as a process of continual recontextualisation in the passage from individual to collective signification:

As an artist, I do not try to control the experience of the viewer. I simply reveal
– expose – an image. I use the word expose (*Exponer*) because it implies vulnerability. The image is not finished in my studio; I complete it in situ, in the
very space where the viewer will encounter it.[52]

While her sculptures acknowledge the limits of representing traumatic loss, they
offer an opportunity for collective engagement that does not end with reconciliatory
closure. They recognise the urgent need to hold onto the past by disseminating it
to audiences, locally and globally. In the melancholic refusal to relinquish the loved
object, Salcedo discovers a political and social commitment not to forget those for
whom memory remains the only record of life and death. Her art practice moves
towards forging critical transnational communities that work against the Colombian
government's war of silencing whereby witnessing means inhabiting, if only for a
brief moment, a space among furniture *with* memories.

Notes

1   The title *Atrabilarios* derives from a Latinate word expressing a melancholic state. See
    Nancy Princenthal, 'Silence Seen', in *Doris Salcedo*, eds. Doris Salcedo, Carlos Basualdo,
    Nancy Princenthal and Andreas Huyssen (London: Phaidon Press, 2000), 53–4.
2   Princenthal, 'Silence Seen', 49; and idem, 'Carlos Basualdo in Conversation with Doris Sal-
    cedo', in *Doris Salcedo*, 17.
3   Charles Merewether, 'To Bear Witness', in *Doris Salcedo* (New York: New Museum of
    Contemporary Art, 1998), 19.
4   Jill Bennett, 'Art, Affect, and the "Bad Death": Strategies for Communicating the Sense
    Memory of Loss', *Signs* 28, no. 1 (Autumn 2002): 344.
5   Ibid., 345–6.
6   Joshua Mack, 'Violent Ends', *Modern Painters* 17, no. 4 (2004–05): 54–6.
7   'Carlos Basualdo in Conversation', 18.
8   Katya Garcia-Anton, 'Silent Witnesses', *Art Newspaper* 10, no. 94 (1999): 21.
9   Ibid.
10 Cathy Caruth, *Unclaimed Experience: Trauma, Narrative, and History* (Baltimore: Johns
    Hopkins University Press, 1996), 4, 91–2.
11 Euridice Arratia, 'Doris Salcedo', *Flash Art* 31, no. 202 (1998): 122.
12 Bennett, 'Art, Affect, and the "Bad Death"', 345; and Garcia-Anton, 21.
13 Dan Cameron, 'Absence Makes the Art', *Art Forum*, 33, no. 2 (1994): 89.
14 'Carlos Basualdo in Conversation', 13–14.
15 Charles Merewether, 'Zones of Marked Instability: Woman and the Space of Emergence',
    in *Rethinking Borders*, ed. John C. Welchman (Minneapolis: University of Minnesota Press,
    1996), 103-4.
16 Nazih Richani, *Systems of Violence: The Political Economy of War and Peace in Colombia*
    (Albany: State University of New York Press, 2002), 1.
17 Toni Morrison, *The Bluest Eye* (New York: Plume, 1994), 35-6.
18 Ibid., 36.
19 See Judith Butler, *Antigone's Claim: Kinship Between Life and Death* (New York: Columbia
    University Press, 2000), 81; and Giorgio Agamben, *Homo Sacer: Sovereign Power and Bare
    Life*, trans. Daniel Heller-Roazen (Stanford: Stanford University Press, 1998).
20 Anastasia Aukeman, 'Doris Salcedo: Privileged Position', *ART News* 93, no. 3 (1994): 157.
21 Rhea Anastas, 'Doris Salcedo: A Tour of the Borderland of *Unland*', *Art Nexus* 29 (1998):
    104–5.
22 Paul Celan, *Poems of Paul Celan*, trans. Michael Hamburger, rev. edn. (New York: Persea

Books, 2002), 275.

23 Merewether, 'To Bear Witness', 22.
24 bell hooks, for example, argues for what she terms 'home-place', the African-American domestic space, as a historical site of resistance against racist structures of economic and political domination. See *Yearning: Race, Gender, and Cultural Politics* (Boston: South End Press, 1990), 46–7.
25 Doris Salcedo, 'Doris Salcedo', *Flash Art* 171 (1993): 97.
26 Ibid.
27 Michael Taussig, *The Nervous System* (New York: Routledge, 1992), 45–6.
28 Ibid., 27.
29 Charles Merewether, *An Interview with Doris Salcedo* (San Francisco: Museum of Modern Art, 1999).
30 Taussig, *The Nervous System*, 48.
31 Santiago Villaveces-Izquierdo, 'Art and Media-tion: Reflections on Violence and Representation', in *Cultural Producers in Perilous States Editing Events, Documenting Change*, ed. George E. Marcus (Chicago: University of Chicago Press, 1997), 241.
32 Veena Das, 'Language and Body: Transactions in the Construction of Pain', in *Social Suffering*, eds Arthur Kleinman, Veena Das and Margaret Lock (Berkeley: University of California Press, 1997), 85.
33 'Carlos Basualdo in Conversation', 16.
34 Caruth, *Unclaimed Experience*, 8.
35 Merewether, *An Interview with Doris Salcedo*.
36 Pierre Nora, 'Between Memory and History: Les Lieux de Mémoire', *Representations* 26 (1989): 19.
37 In the early 1990s, the popularly elected National Constituency Assembly established a permanent *estado de excepcion* (state of emergency) over an *estado de derecho* (state of law) as the most expedient mode of governance. See Villaveces-Izquierdo, 'Art and Media-tion', 235.
38 Mónica Amor, 'Cartographies: Exploring the Limitations of a Cultural Paradigm', in *Beyond the Fantastic Contemporary Art Criticism from Latin America*, ed. Gerardo Mosquera (Cambridge, MA: MIT Press, 1996), 248.
39 See Ann Landi, 'Demolition Men', *Art News* 95, no. 1 (1996): 25; and Brooks Adams, 'Domestic Globalism at the Carnegie', *Art in America* 84, no. 2 (1996): 32–7.
40 Villaveces-Izquierdo, 'Art and Media-tion', 249.
41 Jill Bennett, 'Tenebrae after September 11: Art, Empathy, and the Global Politics of Belonging', in *World Memory: Personal Trajectories in Global Time*, eds Jill Bennett and Rosanne Kennedy (London: Palgrave, 2003), 177–94, 193.
42 Audrey Walen, 'Doris Salcedo: Alexander and Bonin', *Sculpture* 20, no. 44 (May 2001): 69–70.
43 As with *Atrabilarios*, the title *Tenebrae* comes from a Latinate word signifying darkness. It is most commonly associated with the Roman Catholic Church's highly stylised liturgical candle ceremony symbolising the passion of Christ during Holy Week.
44 In an interview with Carlos Basualdo, Salcedo describes in a speech where ellipses mark the difficulty of verbalising memory how the event was 'something I witnessed for myself. It is not just a visual memory, but a terrible recollection of the smell of the torched building with human beings inside … it left its mark on me' ('Carlos Basualdo in Conversation', 14).
45 Bennett, 'Art', 340–1.
46 Erin K. Baines, *Vulnerable Bodies: Gender, the UN, and the Refugee Crisis* (Aldershot: Ashgate, 2004); and Giorgio Agamben, 'We Refugees', trans. Michael Rocke (1994). Available <http://www.egs.edu/faculty/agamben/agamben-we-refugees.html> (accessed 14 December 2005).
47 Ivonne Pini, 'Doris Salcedo', *Art Nexus* 3, no. 56 (2005): 144–5.
48 Mack, 'Violent Ends', 55.

49 Ibid.

50 In a series of 48 paintings and sketches completed in 2005, Fernando Boteros explores in graphic detail the gruesome torture of Iraqi detainees held by US forces at Abu Ghraib prison. He did not base these images on the now publicly recognisable and well-circulated documentary photographs of the tortures, but on news reports of these crimes.

51 Villaveces-Izquierdo, 'Art and Media-tion', 238.

52 Merewether, *An Interview with Doris Salcedo*.

12. Picturing Ruinscapes: The Aerial Photograph as Image of Historical Trauma

Davide Deriu

Trauma is constituted not only by the destructive force of a violent event but by the very act of its survival.

CATHY CARUTH

Photography not only documents destruction, it frames and represents its subjects in order to create a distance between beholders and the events to which the photographs bear witness.

CHARLES MEREWETHER

In January 2004 the Aerial Reconnaissance Archives at Keele University (TARA) announced the completed digitisation of their collections, which comprise approximately five and a half million photographs taken by the Allied Air Forces during the Second World War.[1] While this vast body of images has long been accessible to the public, it gained an unprecedented degree of exposure when it was made available on the Internet.[2] When promoting the launch of the web archive, the project head asserted that 'these images allow us to see the real war at first hand as if we are RAF pilots'. He made specific reference to images of bombed-out German towns as scenes of ruination: 'It is astounding to see the pictures of Cologne before and after bombing. It's like a live-action replay.'[3] This and other reports indicated a renewed interest in the spectacular evidence of wartime aerial photographs, overshadowing deeper questions about our ability to confront the documents of some of the more ruinous acts in modern history. The case of TARA suggests that, while the ongoing proliferation of web archives is bound to expand the accessibility of photographic collections, it also exposes the weakness of the critical tools with which these historical images, and thus the histories they narrate, are comprehended.

With this event in mind, this chapter reassesses the problematic status of the aerial photograph as a document of mass ruination. I shall discuss the ways in which this imagery records and reiterates the destructive effects of modern industrialised warfare, with particular regard to the Second World War. To explore this issue I pursue three lines of inquiry. First, I consider the implications of aerial photography for the representation of ruinscapes in the wake of the First World War. Second, I examine the production of aerial reconnaissance photographs taken by the Royal Air Force during the Second World War. I focus on how these images functioned differently in the domain of military intelligence and in the contemporary press. Third, I draw upon recent literature on trauma studies and photographic theory to pose an alternative reading of the aerial photograph of ruins. In particular, I argue for the agency of this imagery as witness to traumatic historical events.

THE PHOTOGENIC RUINSCAPE: AERIAL IMAGES AND INSCRIPTIONS OF WAR

The history of aerial photography reflects, to a significant degree, the deeper tension between surveillance and spectacle that Jonathan Crary argues has defined modern visuality.[4] Since the early developments of aerostatic photography in the mid-nineteenth century, this medium has been used for a broad range of documentary and aesthetic functions.[5] After the advent of powered flight, the increasing production and circulation of these images blurred the demarcation line between the two functions. This ambivalence has haunted the aerial photography of ruinscapes since the First World War, when the medium became an essential tool of military reconnaissance.[6] The bird's eye view offered an unprecedented documentary perspective on the battlefields. This perspective subsequently gained wide public exposure through the industrial reproduction of photographs. Paul Virilio points out that the military 'observation machine' was directly implicated in the new 'perceptual logistics' that drastically redefined the techniques of modern warfare.[7] Since the airborne camera was integrated into the military apparatus, it left a unique visual testimony of war devastation.[8] In pinpointing bombing targets and subsequently recording the destruction of bombardment, aerial photography functions, according to Charles Merewether, as both 'an instrument of war and a witness to its effects'.[9] Merewether thus contends that 'the illusion of veridical documentation and the ideological function of instrumental and aesthetic realism create a blind spot, obscuring the complicity of technologies of representation in technologies of destruction'.[10]

This complicity was recognised early on by Ernst Jünger, who investigated the impact exerted by the First World War on modern structures of perception. In his 1930 essay, 'War and Photography', Jünger (himself a war veteran) remarked that the medium employed to document the conflict was coterminous with the military apparatus:

A war that is distinguished by the high level of technical precision required to wage it is bound to leave behind documents more numerous and varied than battles waged in earlier times, less present to consciousness. It is the same intelligence, whose weapons of annihilation can locate the enemy to the exact second and meter, that labors to preserve the great historical event in fine detail.[11]

Jünger's belief in the 'preservative' power of technology led him to formulate the concept of 'second consciousness' to describe the impact of photography on human perception. He praised the camera's 'insensitive and invulnerable eye' as a synthetic organ of perception that could toughen people's resistance to the experience of pain.[12] Accordingly, shock photographs could neutralise the effect of their traumatic contents by inuring their viewers to scenes of violence and horror.[13] A desensitised realm of experience was further invoked by Jünger in his short essay 'On Danger', where he articulated an aesthetic appreciation of photographs depicting traumatic events.[14] For Jünger, photography, 'the artificial eye of civilisation', distanced contemporary man from the distressing effects of modern warfare: the 'dangerous moment' was frozen in a still image, and the viewer was accordingly 'hardened' to the chaos of the battlefield. Jünger equated this psychological response with the fundamental nature of modern experience. He argued that the 'zone of danger' established by industrialised warfare had extended beyond the boundaries of the battlefield and encompassed the technological sphere in its entirety. In his later essay, 'On Pain', Jünger pondered the consequences of this phenomenon: 'As the process of objectification progresses, the amount of pain that can be endured grows as well. It almost seems as if man had an urge to create a space where ... pain can be regarded as an illusion.'[15] However contentious these ideas may have been, due to their ideological overtones, they held a significant import in inter-war Europe.[16]

In keeping with Jünger's logic, if action photographs published in the press could numb their viewers to the violence of war, aerial images introduced a new perceptual distance between beholders and the scene of ruination. The airborne camera, with its detached and disembodied gaze, normalised the scale of devastation by producing an abstract representation of landscapes scarred by combat. As Bernd Hüppauf points out,

> From such a perspective, scenes of destruction may be seen as grandiose spectacles or places of pure horror, but they no longer arouse feelings of empathy, pity, or sorrow ... The war killed the natural landscape and replaced it with highly artificial and, within its own parameters, functional spatial arrangements. Aerial photography then, creating a metalevel of artificiality, further abstracted from the 'reality' of this artificial landscape.[17]

Owing to their abstraction, aerial photographs displayed a peculiar aesthetics in which the picturesque contemplation of decayed buildings was rekindled by an appreciation of non-figurative patterns, giving a distinctly modern expression to the 'puzzling pleasure of ruins'.[18] This phenomenon informed the reception of aerial photographs in the post-war period, when reconnaissance images were traded on the art market due to their aesthetic qualities (which transcended the instrumental order of their production). According to Allan Sekula, the appreciation of military photographs as works of art revealed an 'unqualified beautification of warfare'.[19] Sekula also indicates that the responses elicited by aerial views varied considerably according to their vantage point. While 'high verticals' reduced the field of vision to the abstract patterns of a planar image, 'low obliques' reproduced the customary space of perspectival vision: 'Each of the two types gravitates toward a different kind of aestheticised reading; one tends to deny, the other to acknowledge the referential properties of the image.'[20]

During the 1920s and 1930s, airpower acquired a decisive role in the apparatus of modern warfare and, consequently, aerial photography became increasingly involved in the record of ruination.[21] The Spanish Civil War, which precipitated the indiscriminate bombing of urban areas, was marked by a widespread use of aerial imagery to record, and to report, the destructive effects of air raids. Caroline Brothers questions the sanitised image of Spain's ruinscapes as it was presented by these photographs in the international press.[22] According to Brothers, the public conscience potentially stirred by aerial photographs was eased by their removal of 'everyday human concerns'. These images performed a crucial denial of experience by keeping the viewer at a safe distance from the scene:

> Its artificiality, its 'rationally structured order', its elimination of the appallingly sensory aspects of warfare, the sense of all-seeing power it conferred on the viewer, and above all its eschewal of empathy in recording war's most devastating deeds as abstractions – all these characteristics of the aerial photograph were normalised in the pages of the press.[23]

Along similar lines, Karen Frome discusses the use of aerial photography and its ethical implications during the Italian colonial enterprises of the 1930s. As Frome succinctly remarks: 'The aerial perspective, like that of the cartographer, objectifies the target, making mass destruction psychologically viable.'[24] In a manifesto singing the praises of war's alleged beauty, the Futurist poet Filippo T. Marinetti famously rejoiced in the orgy of destruction caused by Italy's military campaigns in East Africa. This celebration of industrial warfare and its unparalleled degree of destructiveness prompted Walter Benjamin's riposte in the epilogue of his Artwork essay:

> Instead of draining rivers, society directs a human stream into a bed of trenches; instead of dropping seeds from airplanes, it drops incendiary bombs over cities ... Mankind, which in Homer's time was an object of contemplation for the Olympian gods, now is one for itself. Its self-alienation has reached such a degree that it can experience its own destruction as an aesthetic pleasure of the first order.[25]

Benjamin condemned the Futurists' aestheticisation of violence as an integral component of fascist culture. His indictment of industrial warfare, and the beautification thereof, openly rejected the 'anaesthetics' of violence that Jünger had advocated.[26] Benjamin's words were prophetic: shortly after his essay written in 1935, the complicity of technologies of representation and destruction reached a new peak in the Second World War. Benjamin hinted at an altogether different contemplation of ruins when, only a few months into the war, he invoked the allegorical image of the 'angel of history' whose face is turned back toward the past as 'the winds of Paradise' propel him forward: 'Where we perceive a chain of events, he sees one single catastrophe which keeps piling wreckage upon wreckage and hurls it in front of his feet.'[27] The angel's gaze, transfixed on the unfolding scenery of debris, invites us to revisit the aerial imagery of ruination and explore its potential historical value. If we take Benjamin's insight as a springboard, then the aerial photograph is not only historically significant, but it also engenders a particularly provocative example of the image as witness to traumatic historical events.

EVIDENCE IN CAMERA: THE CITY AS SCENE OF RUINATION

The oscillation between photography as authentication and aestheticisation continued to characterise the production and reproduction of aerial photographs during the Second World War. As cities worldwide became the target of air raids, aerial imagery was instrumental in maintaining a record of ruinscapes. Britain's involvement in the war, in particular, produced not only an unprecedented display of airpower, but also a unique documentation of urban devastation. Military writers and historians have elucidated how the development of photographic reconnaissance, along with sophisticated methods of interpretation, played a key role in the achievements of British and Allied intelligence.[28] However, the instrumental and aesthetic functions of aerial photographs have seldom been investigated. That is to say, the complex layers of the images themselves have not yet been given sustained critical attention. Through an examination of a range of archival and published sources, I shall explore how wartime reconnaissance photographs operated within different discursive spaces, ranging from the domain of military intelligence to the public press.

The operational use of aerial photography was deemed a strategic priority in Britain by the end of the First World War, when the Royal Air Force was established as a merger of the Royal Flying Corps and the Royal Naval Air Service. After minor developments, the Air Ministry formed independent squadrons for air reconnaissance in 1937 amid the fears raised by the war in Spain. The following year, a photo-interpretation unit was finally created by the Directorate of Intelligence. When the Second World War broke out, a special section was set up at Wembley, which was then reorganised as the Central Interpretation Unit (CIU).[29] Millions of photographs were catalogued by the CIU throughout the war: they constitute an incomparable survey of aerial photography which extends across Western Europe and the theatres of war overseas. While it would be an impossible task to scrutinise this enormous body of images, we may nonetheless subsume them under three main categories: general survey; records of operations; and damage assessment.[30] This taxonomy, however simplified, identifies distinct classes of images on the basis of their instrumental uses. These uses were bound to the strategy of visualising the enemy's territory before, during and after military campaigns.

Archival files show that comments annotated by photo-interpreters, far from being merely factual, were often inflected by aesthetic considerations.[31] Interpreters singled out, in particular, vertical survey images for their puzzling abstract geometries. They frequently remarked on the sensational contents of photographs taken during night raids. These images were marked by a wide array of overlap-

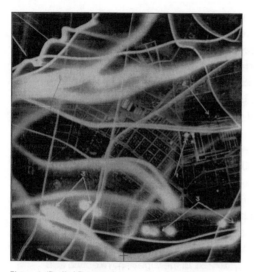

Figure 1: 'Berlin.' Reconnaissance photograph taking during a bombing raid, n.d. Copyright: The Imperial War Museum. Negative number: C.3044.A.

ping patterns generated by various light sources – such as flash bombs, tracer bullets, searchlights, anti-aircraft artillery and fires burning on the ground (figure 1). A shell-burst recorded during a raid over Hamburg in July 1943 was annotated as follows: 'One of the most extraordinary night air-war photographs yet taken ... To the uninitiated it is a complete puzzle-picture, with a curiously fascinating beauty in its flowing light pattern.'[32]

A different kind of spectacle was offered by damage assessment photographs which ranged from high-altitude views of urban areas to close-ups of specific targets. Intelligence staff often resorted to metaphoric language in attempts to describe the uncanny sights of ruination. The consequence of incendiary bombs on residential areas, in particular, prompted terms such as 'premises being open to the sky' (referring to 'gutted buildings') and the oft-cited 'honeycombing effect' formed by the patterns of roofless houses. A common procedure that allowed interpreters to plot the location and scale of destruction was the juxtaposition of vertical photographs taken before and after air raids. These sequential images validated the effects of bombing by charging otherwise dormant photographs with a new forensic value. A pair of photographs depicting a central district of Cologne, for instance, allowed interpreters to estimate that about two thousand acres of this densely built-up area had been 'totally devastated' during heavy raids in the spring of 1943 (figures 2 and 3).

The weekly publication *Evidence in Camera*, which was issued 'for official use only' by the British Air Ministry between October 1942 and March 1945, constitutes

Figures 2 and 3: 'Cologne: Before and After Photographs' (Neumarkt square is visible at the bottom), n.d. Copyright: The Imperial War Museum. Negative number: C.5028 and C.5027

the image and the witness

a unique historical source for understanding the wartime uses of aerial reconnaissance.[33] The chief aim of this publication was to keep military personnel up to date with the CIU's latest findings. Over the years, the tone and contents of *Evidence in Camera* changed somewhat, from a bare display of photographs with minimum commentary to an ever more assorted range of texts and pictures. From 1944 onwards, its editors adopted a layout typical of illustrated magazines at the time and began alternating reports of war incidents with articles on the cultural and historical aspects of aerial photography. The published photographs, which spanned the entire gamut of reconnaissance imagery, aimed to inform, and possibly entertain, the journal's readers. Several texts and captions suggest that intelligence staff were captivated by the visual appeal of aerial views. A case in point is the weekly column 'What are these?', which presented a 'problem picture' or 'puzzle

Figure 4: 'Puzzle Pictures'. Reconnaissance photograph of a prison building in Milan, n.d. Copyright: The Imperial War Museum. Negative number: C.4065.

picture' selected from regular operational photographs. The image in question challenged readers to make out unusual patterns detected from the air (figure 4).

Aerial photographs of ruination were a recurrent feature of *Evidence in Camera*. The first issue opened with a series of vertical views of industrial sites before and after bombing.[34] Reconnaissance images were subsequently used to illustrate the damage inflicted by air raids on various kinds of targets, from strategic installations to residential districts. In addition, *Evidence in Camera* documented the state of what might be called *un-ruined* buildings. An article published in the summer of 1943 claimed: 'Photographs taken after the first attack on Rome (19/07/43), by American bombers, prove that all targets were severely damaged and few bombs fell elsewhere.'[35] Towards the end of the conflict, these images of ruination were evidence to the argument that the Allied liberation of Europe had caused limited damage to its architectural heritage. An issue published in early 1945, for instance, carried a series of aerial photos of French cathedrals taken during the retreat of German occupation forces months earlier.[36] This feature was the prelude to an article entitled 'Paris from the Air', which proposed a sightseeing tour of the liberated French capital from an aerial perspective.[37] As the conflict neared its dénouement, reconnaissance photographs had all but exhausted their role as operational documentation and were taken up to meet a wider range of needs.

While the circulation of *Evidence in Camera* was restricted to military circles, newspapers and magazines disseminated aerial photographs to the British public.[38] In summer 1943, the *Illustrated London News*, one of the most popular periodicals of the time, took on the task of instructing its readers on how to decipher aerial images. An article on 'How to read air photographs of destruction caused by bombing' introduced the public to a visual practice that can be considered a form of 'spec-

Figure 5: Cover page of
The Illustrated London News, 17 July 1943.

tatorial reconnaissance'.[39] Shortly before that, the magazine had reported on the devastation inflicted by heavy air raids over of the city of Cologne. A double page spread image showed a large residential district razed to the ground, and was accompanied by the caption: 'A magnificent RAF photograph of the extensive damage caused by the June raid on Cologne.'[40] As well as giving legitimacy to acts of destruction, the rhetoric of propaganda promoted the public consumption of their spectacular sights.

The same issue of the *Illustrated London News* is a remarkable example of the press' documentation of *un-ruined* monuments, in particular religious architecture, used as war propaganda. The front page of the magazine carried an aerial photograph of Cologne Cathedral and the adjacent railway station amidst their bombed-out neighbourhood (figure 5). In the lower-right corner, a smaller inset photograph of the still-standing Cathedral taken in the aftermath of the '1000-bomber raid' of May 1942 documented the precision which had consistently enabled bomber pilots to spare the building. An editorial explained that aerial photographs were an efficient means to invalidate the Nazi propaganda about 'British criminality'. The article dismissed allegations that the RAF had deliberately targeted historical monuments in Germany:

> The sober truth is that the Cathedral was scarcely touched. RAF reconnaissance photographs, as they have so often done in the past, have nailed the German lie. They show the Cathedral standing among acres of devastation ... Indeed, it seems to have suffered no more – possibly less – damage than was sustained by St Paul's Cathedral during the German blitz on the City.[41]

The shadow cast by the twin spires of the Cathedral confirmed the seemingly intact appearance of the building: this trace was an index of survival amidst a scene of urban devastation. While the Cathedral had been a useful landmark for bomber pilots, it had also simultaneously become a symbol of German resilience.[42] Its imposing figure surrounded by ruins left an indelible mark on the iconography of the *Trümmerzeit*, as it was documented by reporters who flew over German cities at the end of the war.[43] Those eyewitness accounts were mostly illustrated with oblique photographs (images produced with the camera on a lateral axis), which provided the public with a picture of urban devastation at a glance. In comparison, the overhead shots taken by RAF reconnaissance planes throughout the war offer a more ambivalent testimony.

196

The apparent abstract quality of photographs taken from overhead makes it more difficult to retrieve a connection with their referents. When shot from a vertical point on high, the landscape, whether natural or manmade, lost all of its undulating definition. In post-bombardment photographs, the already patterned appearance of urban spaces became further abstracted through the craters, razed city blocks and skeletal structures left by the bombing. Although these reconnaissance images were primarily operational – intended to measure, compare and validate the effects of bombing raids – they also subsequently acquired unintended historical significance as traces of wartime events and conditions.

While the above examples offer only preliminary and partial insights into a complex history, they nevertheless help us to understand further how air-reconnaissance photography realised a new phenomenology of ruination in the Second World War. The significance of aerial imagery in relation to various spaces of publication and dissemination sheds light on its status as public currency within the vocabulary of wartime visual representation. The unique documentation gathered by reconnaissance missions provides a valuable contribution to the historical reassessment of the effects of airpower on civilian populations, in Germany as well as elsewhere.[44] This attempt to historicise the production, reproduction and consumption of aerial photographs raises questions regarding the present currency of wartime aerial photographs. What is the historical significance of these images? How do we confront their visual records of ruination? What is their involvement in the formation of collective memory and trauma? Through consideration of these questions, it is possible to explore alternative interpretations that resist the aestheticisation of aerial photographs as spectacular evidence and appreciate their potential witnessing function.

IMAGES OF TRAUMA: TOWARDS AN ARCHAEOLOGY OF PHOTOGRAPHIC RUINSCAPES

In spite of the imbrication of aerial photography in the representation of traumatic events, its testimonial capacity has gone largely unrecognised. So far this hybrid medium, based on the integration of camera and aircraft technologies, has been confined to a specialist field within photography studies.[45] In contrast to the flood of literature linking photography with practices of memory and forgetting, the aerial photograph is commonly denied any memorial value. We intuitively refrain from associating this imagery with our experiences, identities and memories because its field of vision transcends our everyday habits of human perception. The familiar signs of life and movement recognisable at the so-called 'human scale' disappear within the abstract visual space of the aerial photograph, especially the 'high vertical' image. However, critiques that merely reiterate the abstract, artificial and detached properties of this imagery fall short of acknowledging its dynamic potential as a trigger for the kind of ethical response central to the act of bearing witness. Given the urge to interrogate the historical significance of the aerial photograph as an image of traumatic historical events, its latent agency is illuminated by contemporary debates on trauma and photography.

During his pioneering research into the experience of trauma, Freud discovered that the 'wound of the mind' caused by the psychological shock of life-threatening events can never be thoroughly healed, for the traumatic event is bound to resurface to the subject's consciousness after a latency period.[46] This deferred action, what Freud calls *Nachträglichkeit*, signals that the momentary danger has been shielded from consciousness at the time of its occurrence.[47] Cathy Caruth has underlined an important consequence of this phenomenon: 'Trauma is not locatable in the simple violent or original event in an individual's past, but rather in the way that its very unassimilated nature – the way it was precisely *not known* in the first instance – returns to haunt the survivor later on.'[48] This paradoxical structure, which makes traumatic experience essentially unintelligible, and yet, unforgettable, Caruth calls the 'enigma of survival'.[49] Beyond the realm of individual consciousness, this enigma also applies to the collective experience of traumatic events and the possibility (and limits) of their historical representation. As Mark S. Micale and Paul Lerner insist in their historiography of trauma in the modern age, 'trauma turns out to be not an event per se but rather the experiencing or remembering of an event in the mind of an individual or the life of a community'.[50] An emphasis on historical time opens up the possibility of understanding traumatic experience as the enigma of collective survival.

How are photographs involved in this process? A particularly accomplished study of the relationship between trauma and photography is provided by Ulrich Baer in his book *Spectral Evidence*. Elaborating on Benjamin's notion of the 'optical unconscious', Baer argues that the camera works like traumatic memory by recording momentary occurrences that escape the subject's consciousness and by keeping them in store for deferred legibility:

> Photography can provide special access to experiences that have remained unremembered yet cannot be forgotten … Because trauma blocks routine mental processes from converting an experience into memory or forgetting, it parallels the defining structure of photography, which also traps an event during its occurrence while blocking its transformation into memory.[51]

By giving access to the 'explosive' and 'instantaneous' time of experience, the photograph reproduces the incomplete and fundamentally unknowable nature of trauma. With reference to Caruth, Baer points out that trauma theory helps us to 'grasp how a particular photographic image can show a scene that becomes meaningful only in and as its representation'.[52]

Eduardo Cadava similarly compares the delayed experience of trauma with the deferred action by which the image may arouse historical consciousness. Taking inspiration from Benjamin's writings on history, Cadava proposes an analogy between the photograph and the ruin. Accordingly, while every photograph can be regarded as a ruin, in that it bears the trace of a past presence, the photographic 'image of ruin' doubles this general quality and can therefore be considered a 'ruin of ruin':

> This means … the emergence and survival of an image that, telling us it can no longer show anything, nevertheless shows and bears witness to what history has silenced, to what, no longer here, and arising from the darkest nights of memory, haunts us, and encourages us to remember the deaths and losses for which we remain, still today, responsible.[53]

The memorial quality of the image of ruin derives from the camera's power to capture what Benjamin called the 'posthumous shock' of historical experience: that is, the momentary emergence of a historical object from the continuum of the past in the form of a dialectical image: 'effecting a certain spacing of time, the photograph gives way to an occurrence: the emergence of history as an image'.[54] In other words, it is the survival of the image *as* ruin that enables its deferred legibility.[55] These theoretical propositions help us to recognise the aerial photograph as an image of traumatic historical events. The airborne camera has a unique capacity to detect the scale of phenomena that are unintelligible to a 'terrestrial' eye. In Baer's words, it 'can show a scene that becomes meaningful only in and as its representation'.[56] This applies to traumatic events of mass destruction, such as wholesale urban ruination, of which aerial photographs produced extensive and detailed coverage. If a host of visual documents have preserved the traces of war ruination, air reconnaissance imagery produced a distinct space of representation in which those traces were systematically visualised, on a large scale, from the vantage point of the military apparatus.

The inspection of archival images prompts us to reconsider the ambivalent meaning of the very term *ruination*, which denotes both the act of ruining and the state of being ruined. Both definitions are covered by a specific typology of reconnaissance: action photographs taken during air raids and 'damage assessment' photographs taken afterwards. How can we interpret these distinct classes of images beyond their original function as documentation? A clue is given by the critic Max Kozloff who points out that, although war photographs usually shield the viewer from their traumatic contents, images of violent events command entirely different reactions from those of their aftermath:

> There is a distinction to be made between being excited and being moved by war photographs. Action excites response, but the fatal aftermath of action invokes emotion. With the first, I am caught up in an exhilarating incompletion; with the second, I meditate on something terribly consummated. The moment I am excited I forget everything but present sensation. When I am moved, I am reminded of who I am in relation to others or of what I might be in a broader range of human possibilities.[57]

This argument moves beyond Jünger's *anaesthetics* of representation. Kozloff suggests that our ability to develop a reflective, ethical response to war photographs might actually be awakened by images of ruins and devastation. Accordingly, while action photographs create an 'aesthetic distance' between the viewer and the subject, in the images of the aftermath 'appearances intimate something about our historical fortune', so that we 'perceive and reflect upon them as such, in grief, astonishment, anger'.[58] Hence, the proximity to the heat of action is inversely proportional to the emotional temperature of the photograph – what Kozloff calls its 'affective tone'. The aerial photograph of ruinscapes is particularly provocative here, because it combines its perceptual distance from the scene of violence with its capacity to encompass a wide field of vision, and therefore, to visualise the full extent of mass devastation. The 'affective tone' of this imagery can thus inflect the responses and reflections of viewers after a latency period.

In questioning the conditions of legibility of air reconnaissance photographs, we should also recall the distinctive use of these images as diachronic records of destruction. The sequential arrangement of photographs validates the process of ruination by showing evidence of what has vanished from sight. It might be said, paraphrasing Roland Barthes, that these images conjugate their subject in the past perfect tense. If every photograph is the 'certificate of presence' of a reality 'that-has-been', then the evidential force of sequential images intimates a 'certificate of absence' for a reality 'that-had-been'.[59] And yet, this absence, which is to be inferred dialectically from the pair or sequence of before-and-after images, is never completely erased from historical consciousness. The traumatic event is inscribed in the visual traces of material destruction that are bound to reappear in the mind of the spectator as lingering images. Releasing paired photographs of this kind from their authentication of a *fait accompli* means to recognise the photograph's capacity to embody 'a potentially open-ended form of testimony'.[60]

As Barthes also remarked, the bird's eye view enables us to decipher the separate yet familiar elements we see on the ground and, through the 'power of *intellection*', to reconstitute a larger whole; in other words, panoramic vision allows us 'to see things *in their structure*'.[61] It follows that aerial photographs of ruinscapes may be read not only as documents of mass destruction but also as images that bear witness to a city's survival from the threat of urbicide. The forensic records gathered by reconnaissance planes reveal the traces of this survival, which can be found in the persistence of urban structures such as street patterns, landmarks, edges and other features. In this context, the image of the *un-ruined* buildings acquires particular meaning, for it signals the obstinate permanence of architecture amidst transient ruinscapes. As the case of Cologne has shown, the photographs of the extant Cathedral bear witness to the surrounding devastation as well as to the building's enigmatic survival, and ultimately, the city's own endurance. Through its deferred legibility, its transmutation of destruction to survival, of the past to the present and the future, the photographic image of ruinscape may therefore acquire a memorial value and trigger personal as well as collective recollections of traumatic events.

One way of overcoming the impasse determined by the rigid categories of the photograph as either authentication or aestheticisation is to propose an 'archaeological' approach that turns the photographic documents of ruination into visual monuments. This approach seeks not only to contextualise images as illustrations of historical facts but also to interrogate the specific cultural conditions in which such images are viewed and the memorial practices they activate. This operation of 'damage reassessment' would recover the original function of photographic *reconnaissance* and bring it to bear on a spectatorial practice of historical *recognition*. In addition, an archaeology of ruinscapes ought to recognise that aerial photographs bear witness not only to their subjects but also to their own conditions of existence. By exposing the supposedly ideological function of aerial images that, as Merewether would have it, instrumentalise through their claim to veracity and objectivity, it is possible to consider reconnaissance photographs as a distinctive form of evidence: they are evidence of the complicity between apparatuses of representation and apparatuses of destruction that is their historical *raison d'être*.

the image and the witness

CONCLUSION

This chapter has provided a preliminary critical framework for the reassessment of aerial photographs of ruinscapes. This proposition is urged by the momentous changes that are currently taking place in the structure of image archives. The Internet is destined to have a profound impact on the status of the technical image in the age of its digital reproducibility. As museums and collections around the world embrace new media technologies, the traditional barriers that used to restrict the accessibility of visual documents are increasingly breaking down. It might be argued, paraphrasing André Malraux, that the modern project of re-housing the world of art in a 'museum without walls' has given way to a systematic re-storing of visual heritage in archives without shelves.[62] The changed modalities of preservation and circulation of visual documents are bound up with new conditions of viewing that can have an effect on the reception of historical images. The accessibility of wartime reconnaissance photographs, in particular, is likely to receive a significant boost from digitisation projects such as the one undertaken by the archives at TARA. However, a critical approach is required to foster the comprehension of this historical imagery.

Critical theories of photography informed by psychoanalysis have indicated some possible implications of this specific imagery in the aesthetics and politics of imaging and imagining historical trauma. Arguably, the recognition of the testimonial agency of aerial photographs can trigger recollections of specific and localised traumatic experience, besides more universal reflections about the destructiveness of war. The project of memorialising aerial photographs therefore needs to be corroborated by further research, especially on the relationships between historical images and the specific 'sites of trauma' they might represent.[63] An archaeological approach can bring out the redemptive potential of aerial photographs, so long as they are regarded not only as documents of specific places and incidents, but also as images that witness the depth of historical trauma in their midst.

Research for this chapter has benefited from a grant by the Arts and Humanities Research Board of the United Kingdom.

Notes

1 TARA archives hold a major collection of the Allied Central Interpretation Unit (ACIU), which was loaned by the UK Ministry of Defence to Keele University in 1962–63.
2 The public demand was so overwhelming that the service had to be suspended shortly after the launch of this web resource: http://www.evidenceincamera.co.uk.
3 Allan Williams, quoted in the *Times* (London), 'Web Archive Offers New Perspective on the War', 17 January 2004.
4 See Jonathan Crary, *Techniques of the Observer: On Vision and Modernity in the Nineteenth Century* (Cambridge, MA: MIT Press, 1990), 17–18.
5 Charles Waldheim, 'Aerial Representation and the Recovery of Landscape', in *Recovering Landscape*, ed. James Corner (New York: Princeton Architectural Press, 1999).
6 See Andrew J. Brookes, *Photo Reconnaissance* (London: Ian Allan, 1975); Peter Mead, *The Eye in the Air, History of Air Observation and Reconnaissance for the Army, 1785–1945* (London: Her Majesty's Stationery Office, 1983).
7 Paul Virilio, *War and Cinema: The Logistics of Perception* (London: Verso, 1989).

8   Paul Virilio, *The Vision Machine* (London: British Film Institute, 1994).

9   Charles Merewether, 'Traces of Loss', in *Irresistible Decay: Ruins Reclaimed*, eds. Michael S. Roth, Claire L. Lyons and Charles Merewether (Los Angeles: The Getty Research Institute for the History of Art and the Humanities, 1997), 29.

10 Ibid.

11 Ernst Jünger, 'War and Photography', *New German Critique* 59 (1993): 24.

12 See Anton Kaes, 'The Cold Gaze: Notes on Mobilization and Modernity', *New German Critique* 59 (1993): 105–17.

13 See Brigitte Werneburg, 'Ernst Jünger and the Transformed World', *October* 62 (1992): 54.

14 Ernst Jünger, 'Über die Gefahr', in *Der gefährliche Augenblick*, ed. F. Bucholtz (Berlin: Junker and Dunhaupt, 1931). The photographs published in this picture book depicted a broad range of events, including war explosions, earthquakes, public riots, train and car crashes.

15 Ernst Jünger, 'Photography and the Second Consciousness: An Excerpt from "On Pain"', in *Photography in the Modern Era: European Documents and Critical Writings, 1913–1940*, ed. Christopher Phillips (New York: The Metropolitan Museum of Art, 1989), 209–10.

16 Andreas Huyssen, 'Fortifying the Heart – Totally: Ernst Jünger's Armored Texts', *New German Critique* 59 (1993): 3–23.

17 Bernd Hüppauf, 'Experiences of Modern Warfare and the Crisis of Representation', *New German Critique* 59 (1993): 56–7.

18 Linda E. Patrik, 'The Aesthetic Experience of Ruins', *Husserl Studies* 3, no. 1 (1986): 31–56.

19 Allan Sekula, 'The Instrumental Image: Steichen at War', *Artforum* 14, no. 4 (1975): 26–35.

20 Ibid., 29.

21 See Sven Lindqvist, *A History of Bombing* (London: Granta, 2001).

22 Caroline Brothers, *War and Photography: A Cultural History* (London: Routledge, 1997).

23 Ibid., 103.

24 Karen Frome, 'A Forced Perspective: Aerial Photography and Fascist Propaganda', *Aperture* 132 (1993): 77.

25 Walter Benjamin, *Illuminations* (London: Fontana, 1973), 235.

26 Susan Buck-Morss, 'Aesthetics and Anaesthetics: Walter Benjamin's Artwork Essay Reconsidered', *October* 62 (1992): 3–41.

27 Benjamin, *Illuminations*, 249.

28 See Ursula Powys-Lybbe, *The Eye of Intelligence* (London: Kimber, 1983).

29 The CIU was established in Medmenham in 1941. It was renamed ACIU (Allied Central Interpretation Unit) in 1944, after the RAF liaised with USAAF photo sections.

30 A special sub-category of 'general survey' reconnaissance concerned the detection of camouflage. See Davide Deriu, 'Between Veiling and Unveiling: Modern Camouflage and the City as a Theatre of War', in *Endangered Cities: Urban Societies and Military Powers in the Age of the World Wars*, eds Roger Chickering and Marcus Funck (Boston: Brill Academic, 2004).

31 The materials examined here belong to the Photograph Archives of the Imperial War Museum, London (henceforth, IWMPA), which is one of the most comprehensive repositories of wartime British reconnaissance. Unlike the TARA archives, the IWMPA allow direct access to open-shelf files, affording greater insights into the classification of photographs and their captions.

32 Source: IWMPA, File No. C3879.

33 This publication inspired the name of the web service linked with TARA. It had previously been adopted in the 1950s as the title of a popular account of wartime intelligence: Constance Babington-Smith, *Evidence in Camera: The Story of Photographic Intelligence in the Second World War* (Harmondsworth: Penguin, 1957).

34 *Evidence in Camera* 1, no. 1 (1942): 2–5.

35 *Evidence in Camera* 4 [n.a.] (1943): 178–9.

36 *Evidence in Camera* 8 [n.a.] (1944–45): 125–31.

37 Ibid., 145-7. An earlier article entitled 'Week-end in Paris' showed aerial views of public places in which Parisians spent their Sunday afternoons. *Evidence in Camera* 7, no. 1 (1944): 10–1.

38 Reconnaissance photographs released by Bomber Command had to be scrutinised by the Security Branch and the Ministry of Information before they were published in the Press.

39 *Illustrated London News*, August 7, 1943.

40 *Illustrated London News*, July 17, 1943.

41 Ibid.

42 See Toni Winkelnkemper, *Der Großangriff auf Köln: Ein Beispiel* (Berlin: Franz Eher, 1942).

43 See Margaret Bourke-White, *'Dear Fatherland, Rest Quietly': A Report on the Collapse of Hitler's 'Thousand Years'* (New York: Simon and Schuster, 1946). See also Dagmar Barnouw, *Germany 1945: Views of War and Violence* (Bloomington: Indiana University Press, 1996).

44 See Jörg Friedrich, *Der Brand: Deutschland im Bombenkrieg 1940–1945* (Munich: Propylaeen, 2002).

45 Beaumont Newhall, *Airborne Camera: The World from the Air and Outer Space* (London: The Focal Press, 1969).

46 Sigmund Freud, 'Beyond the Pleasure Principle', in *The Standard Edition of the Complete Psychological Works*, ed. James Strachey, 18 (London: Hogarth, 1953–74).

47 See Ruth Leys, *Trauma: A Genealogy* (University of Chicago Press: Chicago, 2000).

48 Cathy Caruth, *Unclaimed Experience: Trauma, Narrative, and History* (Baltimore: Johns Hopkins University Press, 1996), 4 (emphasis in original).

49 Cathy Caruth, 'Violence and Time: Traumatic Survivals', *Assemblage* 20 (1993): 24.

50 Mark S. Micale and Paul Lerner, 'Trauma, Psychiatry, and History: A Conceptual and Historiographical Introduction', in *Traumatic Pasts: History, Psychiatry, and Trauma in the Modern Age, 1870–1930*, eds Mark S. Micale and Paul Lerner (Cambridge: Cambridge University Press, 2001), 20.

51 Ulrich Baer, *Spectral Evidence: The Photography of Trauma* (Cambridge, MA: MIT Press, 2002), 7–9.

52 Ibid., 12.

53 Eduardo Cadava, '*Lapsus Imaginis*: The Image in Ruins', *October* 96 (2001): 36.

54 Ibid., 53.

55 Eduardo Cadava, *Words of Light: Theses on the Photography of History* (Princeton: Princeton University Press, 1997).

56 Baer, 12.

57 Max Kozloff, *The Privileged Eye: Essays on Photography* (Albuquerque: University of New Mexico Press, 1987), 207.

58 Ibid.

59 Roland Barthes, *Camera Lucida: Reflections on Photography* (London: Vintage, 1993).

60 Baer, *Spectral Evidence*, 182.

61 Roland Barthes, 'The Eiffel Tower', in *The Eiffel Tower and Other Mythologies* (Berkeley: University of California Press, 1979), 9 (emphasis in original).

62 André Malraux, *The Voices of Silence* (London: Secker & Warburg, 1954).

63 Dominick LaCapra, *History and Memory after Auschwitz* (Ithaca: Cornell University Press, 1998).

PART V | WITNESSING THE WITNESS

13. Not Looking at Lynching Photographs

James Polchin

I want a History of Looking.

ROLAND BARTHES

NOT LOOKING

In her history of lynching imagery, Dora Apel begins with the problem of looking at lynching photographs. Apel writes: 'When we look at lynching photographs today, we try not to see them. Looking and seeing seem to implicate the viewer, however distanced and sympathetic, in the acts that turned human beings into horribly shamed objects, as if viewing itself were a form of aggression. Most of us would prefer not to look.'[1] These images provoke our shock and foster an anxiety through their depictions of graphic violence as well as how they turn human victims into visual objects. We struggle with where we should look – at the barely recognisable corpse, at the white bystanders who, in many images, crowd around the body like satisfied hunters, or at the incomprehensibility of these two elements existing in the same frame. The images arrest us precisely because they challenge our assumptions about how to look at a photograph.

Apel directs her comments to the travelling exhibition 'Without Sanctuary: Lynching Photography in America', which attracted unprecedented numbers of museum patrons across four different venues in the US between 2000 and 2002. Displaying items from the collection of James Allen and John Littlefield, antique collectors from Atlanta who purchased these photographs over several decades, the show began as 78 framed images without explanatory texts in a tiny, one-room art gallery on the Upper East Side of Manhattan in the winter of 2000. The exhibit became increasingly

207

wrapped in historical and cultural context as it moved to the panelled halls of the New-York Historical Society, then to the contemporary glass and steel space of the Andy Warhol Museum in Pittsburgh. In 2002, the exhibit moved south to the Martin Luther King, Jr. Center in Atlanta, Georgia, the heart of the New South. While the Warhol Museum expanded the exhibit to nearly one hundred images, by the time it arrived in Atlanta in the Spring of 2002, it displayed only 42 photographs, but included an expanded historical context, a two-day academic conference and a number of public programmes.[2]

These exhibits confronted patrons with an archive of small, almost delicate half-tones and picture postcards depicting a legacy of brutal and racist murders enacted as public spectacles mostly in the American South and Midwest in the late nineteenth and twentieth centuries. The images had never before been gathered and displayed as museum objects. Rather, they were originally circulated locally in small towns, displayed on parlour mantle pieces and family albums, as well as more public venues, such as barber shops and store windows (sometimes along with 'souvenir' remains of the victim). The ones made and sold as postcards were sent to friends and family around the country until such mailings were banned by the postal service in the early twentieth century.[3] Their genesis was often in the backwoods clearings or the town squares where the torturous lynchings took place. Professional photographers from local studios would capture the proceedings and then print and sell postcard mementos to attendees. Or, armed with the new Kodak cameras that used easy-to-handle film rolls, onlookers and participants alike took their own photographs of the lynchings. The photographs were usually taken at the end of the violence, when the victims, hanged or burned, or both, were displayed as a grotesque public spectacle. While some photos show only the body of the victim, others take a more expansive view showing us the large crowds of onlookers. More often than not, the photographer, a complicit if not active participant in the murder, captured a highly-posed tableau of white spectators – men, women and children – calmly standing around the expired black victim. The bystanders sometimes smile, sometimes point at the burned or beaten corpse and sometimes just stare blankly at the camera. It is this juxtaposition between corpse and crowd, between victims and violators, that strikes us most with feelings of disgust and rage, and yet, also unnervingly, encourages our sense of wonder. These average-looking townsfolk, often dressed in suits and ties, look so respectable, smiling or staring with gazes that both hypnotise and horrify.

In his essay that accompanies the published monograph to the exhibitions, a grisly tome of images oddly resembling an art book, writer Hilton Als writes: 'What I see in those pictures ... is a lot of crazy-looking white people, as crazy and empty looking as the white people who stare at me. Who wants to look at these pictures? Who are they all? When they look at those pictures, who do they identify with? The maimed, the tortured, the dead, or the white people?'[4] The question of identification gets at the heart of the problem of looking at these photos, for Als' question does not direct itself merely to a concern over the content of these historical images. His question differs from the one Susan Sontag raises in her distrust of these photos when she asks: 'What is the point of exhibiting these pictures?'[5] Rather, Als' question raises the problem of how we ought to look rather than why we look.

The history of 'Without Sanctuary' demonstrates the struggle between written and visual representations in the witnessing of historical violence. This struggle manifests in how each incarnation of the exhibit attempted to mediate this question of 'how to look'. Indeed, the burden of mounting these shows rested on how to display such images of racist violence for contemporary public consumption. As museum display, the photographs in 'Without Sanctuary' held a particular force as historical objects. The challenge lay in not reproducing the images' original intent to assert white power through the objectification of black victims. Indeed, organisers and curators faced a particular conundrum: how do you display photographs of racist violence without replicating the spectacle of that violence?

The history of this exhibition as it travelled from city to city illuminates a deep anxiety about the act of historical witnessing – an anxiety that manifested precisely around the question of how to look. Each show had to transform the experience of looking so as to reappropriate the photographs from their original intent. This reappropriation I am calling 'an act of not looking'.[6] By this, I do not mean the ways these images were literally hidden or ignored. Rather, the act of not looking refers to ways each show transformed the spectacles of violence into visual documents of the past. In this sense, I am interested in the particular epistemological concerns that looking at these photographs engendered and how the shows confronted these concerns by shaping a context for looking that countered the photographs' original intent. In considering this problem, the historical and cultural contexts that accompany the act of looking become clear. Indeed, the different approaches to viewing these photographs, and the commentaries about each show, reflect the difficulties and contradictions of transforming these historical artefacts of white supremacy into useful objects for historical witnessing.

WITNESSING

In the winter of 2000, when the Roth Horowitz Gallery on Manhattan's Upper East Side mounted the initial show, entitled 'Witness', it was not prepared for the crowds of patrons that came to look at the 78 photographs. Shortly after its opening, and following several reviews in the New York Times, the gallery had to organise a viewing schedule, passing out two hundred free tickets each day, with patrons queuing up in the cold. Writer and scholar Patricia Williams was one of the many who waited in line. In the Nation, Williams wrote of her experience in the gallery: 'The Roth Horowitz itself is the tiniest of rooms, to which only a few spectators can be admitted at a time.' Williams found the gallery an appropriate space to view the photographs for the intimacy of the gallery stood in stark contrast to the 'large, mob-driven, spectacle events' that fuelled the lynchings themselves.[7] Ironically, the show would soon gather its own large crowds, drawing nearly 5,000 people in its one-month showing, and foreshadowing even larger crowds in other venues over the next two years.[8]

The show's title explicitly defined and shaped the patron experience. Like a holy pilgrimage, the patrons came to witness historical realities and be transformed by what they saw. They were coming to the scene of a crime, many crimes, conducted over several decades. The crimes they saw were rarely if ever investigated when the actual lynching occurred. 'Killed by person, or persons, unknown' was the usual, official resolution by the white legal system to these murders. No witnesses were called. No trial was conducted. While the title 'Witness' rests on a belief in the veracity of these photographs, translating the viewing into an encounter with real historical events, the word elides the complicated layers of witnessing that rest with each photograph. The whites who crowd around the corpse represent the immediate witnesses to the event, although many commentators refer to them as 'spectators' rather than witnesses. The photographer may be the most apparent and troubling witness for he or she is not simply recording the act but constructing a way of memorialising the violence of white supremacy, complicit in the act of violence through the image's objectification. The role of the photographer was not simply to capture but also to shape a view of the murderous spectacle. 'The immorality' of these photographs, writes Apel, 'resides not only in the execution itself and in the attitude of the participants but also in the role of the photographer, whose ostensibly neutral position is not neutral but appears to sanction the acts he records by declining to oppose them in any way. We, as viewers, are invited to occupy the photographer's viewing position.'[9] If we are witnesses, we look through a complicit lens, which captured a scene meant to promote an idea of white superiority and black inferiority. Yet Apel rejects the notion that we passively subscribe to the symbolic or iconic power of these images. She argues that we 'recognize a much different issue at stake today in this legacy of representation, namely, the responsibility of historical witnessing'.[10] How do we reject the position of the photographer? Of the white mobs? How do we become witnesses and not simply spectators?

To witness is to participate, to experience the event in some way, and then to testify to what you saw. John Durham Peters examines the concept of witnessing as it has come down to us through religious and juridical traditions, and, more recently, through survivor narratives most poignantly exemplified in Holocaust testimonies.[11] For Peters, the act of witnessing has two faces: 'the passive one of seeing and the active one of saying'. I would refine these terms further between (passive) spectator and (active) witness for, as Peters contends: 'In passive witnessing an accidental audience observes the events of the world, [while] in active witnessing one is privileged possessor and producer of knowledge in an extraordinary, often forensic, setting in which speech and truth are policed in multiple ways. What one has seen authorizes what one says; an active witness first must have been a passive one.'[12] Passive witnessing equates with the experience of a spectator, defining a much different experience of looking. Indeed, while these words are often synonymous they hold profoundly different connotations. A spectator defines a viewer who is unable, or unwilling, to speak about what she has seen. Indeed, the difficulty of becoming an active witness rests in being able to translate what one sees into language – to testify to one's experience by communicating personal knowledge to a larger public. The move from spectator to witness 'involves an epistemological gap whose bridging is always fraught with difficulty'.[13] As Peters argues: 'Witnessing is a discourse with a hole in it that awaits filling'.[14] The act of witnessing, then, coheres around both looking and speaking since looking alone presumes a position of spectator.

Consequently, the word 'witness', as we have come to define it in the latter half of the twentieth century, is more readily equated with the experiences of surviving trauma, investing the act of witnessing with an ethical responsibility, something the white mob clearly lacked. To witness, especially in the context of historical visual documents, demands not only a speaking but also a speaking out. In naming the mobs as spectators, we are comfortably distanced from them. The Roth Horowitz show needed this distance between viewer and image. In this space the show, lacking much context about any one image, raised not only the difficult question of how to look, but the much more mysterious question: what are we looking at? This question holds a constellation of responses that both defines and makes the act of witness an even more problematic matter. If we are witnesses, what are we witnesses to?

In her reflections on the archive of lynching photographs, Susan Sontag criticises our passive witnessing: 'The lynching pictures tell us about human wickedness. About inhumanity. They force us to think about the extent of the evil unleashed specifically by racism. Intrinsic in the perpetration of this evil is the shamelessness of photographing it … The display of these pictures makes us spectators, too.'[15] Dubious of the viewer's ability to transform the power of the photographer's gaze that participates and implicates the viewers in the violence, Sontag's critique indicts us all as spectators, resisting any notion that these photographs can be reappropriated by the modern viewer. Sontag's claims not only question our approach to the photographs, but also the evidentiary nature of the images themselves. Her claims lead to a particular relationship between the image and the witness in these shows: defining the status of these photographs (the question of what we are looking at) relies precisely on shaping the experience of looking (the question of how we look at these images).

WORDLESSNESS

The problem of this relationship between the visual object and the act of looking is precisely a problem of the photograph as a document of reality and historical truth. The Roth Horowitz show rested on a tradition of photographic objectivity where the image itself commands a truthfulness through its verisimilitude. The photographs were meant to speak, to inform and to educate us in historical facts. Yet the language they spoke more often than not left patrons speechless. Indeed, the effect of this visual language, so often commented upon by writers and journalists, was a profound silence.

Patricia Williams begins her essay about the Roth Horowitz show with a memory of her late aunt sharing with her a few 'small possessions' that included 'photographs of black men hanging from trees'. Williams writes: 'I am not even sure why my aunt showed them to me so wordlessly. I did not ask. I had only wordlessness to give her in return.'[16] This wordlessness underscores a particularly deep anxiety about the act of looking for African-American patrons. As Williams shows, at times these photographs also circulated within African-American communities as both warnings of white power and memorials of loved ones. Yet the experience of looking at them today confronts such patrons with a history to which they have been (and continue to be) subject. Not only are African-Americans subject to violence and victimisation within a racist society, but also to a history of images that have promoted the marginality of blackness while constructing an imagined whiteness.[17] The wordlessness that Williams relates comes out of an experience of looking that confronts the viewer with her own subjugation to these histories. Indeed, these images confront us with the ways that the tools of photography participated in such scenes of violent subjection. The photograph, as an instrument of nineteenth-century, empirical rationality, emerged as a populist tool precisely when lynchings became spectacle events in the South of the 1890s.[18] By turning the subject into a visual object, photography furthered the precise project of lynchings: a powerful visual symbol that helped to rationalise white supremacy.[19]

The conundrum for curators of the Roth Horowitz show rested with the utter irrationality of these scenes that were made to look normal and rational through the photographic lens. In a gallery space on Manhattan's Upper East Side, known for its shows of fine art and photography, these images do not fit into either category. Or, at least, we do not wish to approach them as objects that fit within either tradition. Confronting them in the Roth Horowitz unsettled patrons not only with scenes of violence, but more significantly, with an unrecognisable visual archive. 'They refute the notion that photographs of charged historical subjects lose their power, softening and becoming increasingly aesthetic with time', writes *New York Times* critic Roberta Smith, adding that these images 'send shock waves through the brain'.[20] The visceral effect of looking at these images takes hold in this conflicted experience of looking, such that the mystery of the images limits our ability to recognise, to speak about or to interpret.

How ironic that the display of these images as valuable historical documents elided the fact that the camera itself was part of the subjection, capturing the final scenes of the lynching.[21] In fact, these photographs do not contemplate or ponder the spectacle of violence. They are not part of a documentary tradition that has evoked strange and sentimental scenes of suffering, such as we confront in Jacob Riis's Lower East Side of the 1890s or Walker Evans' Alabama farmlands of the 1930s. Rather, these photographs, to borrow Roland Barthes term, 'prick' us and disturb precisely because we cannot define them.[22] In confronting them as framed gallery images, we struggle with this naming, with placing them within a photographic tradition. While the gallery may define them as historical records of social realities, their more racist intentions keep cutting at us, silencing us in the very mystery of the image itself. It is not so much the gory details of the images that provoke our horror and the wordlessness that accompany this horror. It is not that these images shock us solely in their offering up historical realities to witness. Rather what pricks us in the 78 images of the 'Witness' show is how they confront us with a deeply felt confusion about the photograph itself.

EMOTIONWISE

In this confusion and shock, we are left with the emotional experience of seeing. The show 'evoked emotions as varied as the people who had come to see it', commented *New York Times* reporter Somini Sengupta. Patron Marvin Taylor, whose family is from Jamaica related: 'I don't know these victims, but I feel a connection, emotionwise.'[23] The contradiction between the photographs' depiction of historical realities and their inability to help us understand or integrate these events into our rational thinking provokes a cognitive dissonance that is filled in through an appeal to emotions.

This emotional response continued to shape reviews of the show in its subsequent incarnation, 'Without Sanctuary: Lynching Photography in America', even though the new exhibition offered far greater historical context. When 'Witness' closed in February of 2000 it moved across Central Park where, in March, the New-York Historical Society mounted a much more contextualised exhibition, but with fewer photographs than the Roth Horowitz show. The Historical Society displayed 65 lynching photographs in its large central gallery. Each photograph had explanatory wall texts that offered information about the specific lynchings displayed. The exhibit provided computer stations with links to an on-line exhibition where patrons could post comments.[24] In the centre of the gallery stood waist-high glass cases displaying artefacts from anti-lynching crusades. The organisers also held a series of public lectures and talks. In contrast to 'Witness', where the images were presented with little comment, 'Without Sanctuary' grappled with the tensions between passive and active witnessing by giving us fewer images to look at, but mediating those images with more words than any one patron could absorb in an afternoon.

While art critic Sarah Valdez validates the photographs' veracity when they 'make the abomination of lynching appear real in a way that textbook history cannot', she acknowledges that 'though historical realities are documented by means of these texts, objects, and photographs, the show's impact was primarily emotional'. These emotions provoke for her a rush of adrenaline, making it impossible for her to think at all since 'the images function, in a way, as a catalyst for rage release, addressing the inner "other" in all of us ... The intensity of violence, visual and textual, makes the events mind-numbing.'[25] This separation of emotional and intellectual responses, feelings and words, also cuts the complicated experience of looking into a binary process. Interpreting how these images are constructed slips us too close to the photographer's perspective – too close to the complicity of the spectators. Thinking about these images compositionally, or reflecting on the ways these photographs objectify the victims and validate the bystanders, pulls us closer to the white mobs. Feeling emotions, on the other hand, allows us to identify with the victims and empathise with their fate, distancing ourselves from those white onlookers.

Ultimately, through this emotional response, the show promoted a more universalising experience. The 'inner other' that is supposedly in all of us suggests how this emotional response mediated the hole between active and passive witnessing. The Historical Society show encouraged our emotional reactions in shaping the experience of looking. In this effort, the show implicitly turned patrons away from a contemplation (or interrogation) of the images themselves, toward a broader historical narrative of racist violence. In doing so, the show transformed the problem of looking into an exploration of our own emotional responses to violence. To mediate the shock and horror of the images, and the mysterious ways they prick us, the show fostered a different kind of looking: an introspective view of ourselves grappling with images of racist violence.

L. J. Krizner, Director of Education for the Historical Society, organised a series of staff meetings, which included everyone from directors to gallery security guards, to discuss the show even before it opened. 'We wanted everyone to feel that they knew why the institution was installing the exhibition', relates Krizner. 'By listening to the staff', Krizner concludes, 'we learned in advance the range of reactions that we would later experience from the general public.'[26] A similar approach was used with patrons. The Historical Society worked with Facing History and Ourselves, a national educational organisation, to develop 'a conversational format for interpretation', in which facilitators would be available to moderate a conversation for school and tour groups after they had completed an unguided visit to the exhibition. Stewart Desmond, Director of Public Affairs and Public Programs for the Historical Society, explains that 'facilitators would provide some historical background but the main role would be to help visitors work through the meaning of the photographs together.'[27] In fact, such efforts, along with a series of public programmes, were meant to resist the powerful silencing effect of these images through a shared experience of looking. While the gallery itself was presented as a contemplative space with a sign at the entrance requesting only hushed conversation, the exhibit countered this near silence through patron forums that encouraged a release of words and feelings. The fear of the photographs' power to silence, to move us to wordlessness, structured the context of the show – the literal movement from seeing to speaking shaped the patron's experience. In fostering this movement, the show asked patrons to become active witnesses of their own experiences of looking.

Through their shared experience of witnessing, patrons were encouraged to look beyond the photographs towards the contemporary moment. While displaying a history of lynching, the show encouraged an experience of looking that focused on the legacy of this history such that the patrons were asked to look at themselves in the contemporary moment. Indeed, the intent of the show was deeply shaped by a series of violent incidents involving the New York City Police Department and the black community, including interrogation abuses and random violence such as the highly publicised death of Amadou Diallo, an unarmed African immigrant shot 41 times by police officers outside his Bronx home in February 1999. The organisers of 'Without Sanctuary' viewed the show as a forum to give historical perspective to these events, thus providing a space for interracial dialogue that moved beyond the invective impulse of the moment. By the time the show closed at the New-York Historical Society in October 2000 (after two extensions), nearly 50,000 patrons had come to share in the experience of looking, more patrons than any other exhibit in the Society's long history.

QUOTATION

In considering the relationship between images and memory in an era of information overload, Sontag contends that 'the photograph is like a quotation, or a maxim or proverb'.[28] As quotations, photographs act as metonyms, carving out a split second of time as a signifier of larger events or historical experiences. As Sontag notes, 'the problem is not that people remember through photographs, but that they remember only the photographs'.[29] The metonymic quality of the lynching photographs was crucial in visualising racist ideologies. In lynching, the act of violence was a literal breaking down of the black male body, turning the individual into an unrecognisable beast that fit within the racial and sexual ideologies defining the boundaries between

the image and the witness

whites and blacks. As Wood indicates, 'To take a picture of the victim in this state of debasement reinforces this process of representation by freezing the moment in time. The photographic image therefore transformed the lynching, itself a signifying ritual, into a symbolic form.'[30] As quotations, these photographs furthered a racist imagination through their continued ability to objectify and signify racial supremacy. As mementos of the event, the photographs' metonymic power furthered the lynching spectacle by circulating it to the larger society as well as future generations.

Through their collection and archiving as museum objects, these photographs signify a different social experience. While their original intent is difficult to ignore, the exhibitions reinscribed them precisely through the archive. Each photograph evidences a particular event that happened within a precise time and place (some known, others unknown). As a series of lynching photographs from different places and time periods, when displayed together, the images take on new meanings through the visual relationships that this gathering fosters. Indeed, the archive transforms the lynching photographs beyond the specific denotative qualities of each image towards the connotative force of the archive. The archive organises a range of murderous events, conflating time periods and geography, such that each photograph builds towards a larger meaning of the archive as a whole. Furthermore, the archive mediates the gaze of one complicit photographer through the act of repetition. In their original production and consumption, each photograph or postcard circulated independently of each other at different times and in different places, existing alongside other racist images in local and popular culture. The contemporary archive confronts us with the collage of historical moments, pulling out those connected events from Indiana in 1894 to Florida in 1910, from Texas in 1923 to Virginia in 1937 so that they are one stream of historical consciousness. This museum archive transforms the way we look at these images for while each photograph's denotative power rests within its frame, it depends on the other photographs (and artefacts, narratives and images) in the archive to tell its story.

Noting a particular historical context that was absent in the Historical Society's show, Valdez comments: 'The lynching photographs are contemporaneous with the dawn of the yellow press [and] were hardly on their own as graphic evidence of real-life mayhem.'[31] While this is true, lynching photographs were rarely published in newspapers and anti-lynching crusaders were loathe to use such images in their publications. For most Americans, the confrontation with lynchings occurred through narrative representations in newspapers and magazines.[32] Even in 1935, when the NAACP mounted an anti-lynching art exhibition in New York City, organisers, while initially planning to present an award for the best lynching photograph, ultimately decided on leaving out all photographs. Though it is unclear exactly why this award was dropped, it would certainly seem problematic for an award to recognise such 'achievement' and suggests the very problem of situating these images within any visual aesthetic or documentarian tradition. 'Though photographs were omitted in the end', writes Apel, 'the influence of lynching photographs is seminal in the production of anti-lynching artwork in the 1930s, not only because of specific photographs that served as departure points for artworks, but more fundamentally as the images to which all other images necessarily responded.'[33] For Apel, the paintings, drawings and sculptures of this earlier show transformed the gaze of the white supremacist into the complex perspectives of the artists whose works valorised the subjectivity of the black victim. The art transformed and countered the objectifying views of the photographs. Indeed, whereas photographs document through the eyes of the complicit spectator, art can testify and criticise, fostering different ways of humanising what the camera objectifies. How differently would we look at these photographs if they were displayed next to artworks that countered such images? Art can resist quotation, and perhaps because of this, the organisers in the 1930s found that the art better represented the truth of lynching.

However, the photographic archive of 'Without Sanctuary' transforms in a different way. Through the museum archive, each photograph refers to and builds upon the other, turning these images into quotations of a brutal past – transforming each image into a metonym of racism and turning us away from any one image. The archive mediates the images' paradox – a trust in their veracity coupled with an anxiety over how to look at them. Indeed, in these exhibitions, lynching photographs sit within a constellation of quotations (from historians, commentators, anti-lynching crusaders, newspaper accounts and patrons themselves in the comment books and on the website), and their meanings emerge from how they signify, and memorialise, a more general, historical experience of white supremacy and black victimhood.

NORMALISING

Writer and journalist Brent Staples reminds us that just as the white mobs were photographing these scenes of violence, anti-lynching crusaders were cautious in the use of such images. Staples recalls the efforts of Ida Wells-Barnett, one of the most vocal anti-lynching activists at the turn of the twentieth century, who preferred to use forensic descriptions rather than pictures or even illustrations. In relating this difference, Staples fears our own repeated exposure to them would inure us to their effect. This repeated exposure would turn these photographs from shocking events to iconic images, integrating themselves into our collective imaginary, discarding their potential to provoke and shock. 'With these horrendous pictures loose in the culture', argues Staples, 'the ultimate effect could easily be to normalize images that are in fact horrible.'[34]

We cannot see these images at the end of the twentieth century the way they would have been seen in the 1930s when the NAACP omitted photographs in their anti-lynching art show. We are perhaps too far removed, both in time and sensibility. Unlike those earlier generations, we have decades of images of violence that, for many, have shaped our understanding of the world and recent history. Holocaust photographs, images of war, famine and genocides have all entered our visual consciousness and, more often, our domestic spaces through photojournalism and television newscasts. In his discussion of the news representations of the 1994 Rwandan genocide, David Levi Strauss argues for the impossibility of photographing genocide for such images transform the suffering of individuals into the suffering of masses of peoples, and more often, masses of bodies. 'As we become subject to images, the subject of any image becomes less and less available to us', writes Strauss.[35] But he is not content to leave the image behind, to bury it and forget it.

Instead, for Strauss, a writer and visual artist, the problem is one of perspective, and the ability of a photograph to document individual experiences and not simply events that abstract individuals into objects. Quoting writer Fergal Keane, Strauss notes: 'In our world of instant televised horror it can become easy to see a black body in almost abstract terms, as part of the huge smudge of eternally miserable blackness that has wormed in and out of the public mind through the decades: Biafra in the 1960s; Uganda in the 1970s; Ethiopia in the 1980s; and now Rwanda in the 1990s.'[36] To look at lynching photographs today, framed in museums and galleries, reflects a kind of looking that characterises late twentieth-century Western culture where the visuality of Black suffering fits into a constellation of images, each quoting others, each shocking in their own way.

Today, the experience of looking coheres around this experience of being shocked. Images of grotesque violence, obscene encounters, deviant or pornographic acts have come to shape our definitions of visual reality. Arguments of the lynching photographs' veracity define this quality through the images' graphic depictions. Indeed, the lynching photographs strike us as truthful because we have come to understand graphic and shocking images as qualities of reality and truthfulness.[37] This graphic imperative foregrounds shock as the conditioned response to such images and shapes our interpretation of them.[38] To be shocked and horrified by the lynching photographs is the whole point of the Historical Society's show in edifying the crowds of museum goers who paid the price of admission. The accompanying catalogue offers pages of lynching images, neatly bound in a tastefully crafted coffee-table art book. Our horror has the effect of distancing us from these photographs and situating them within a stream of shocking images that stand in for truthfulness.

But to normalise this stream is to evacuate the images' content. This, as Sontag has warned us, is to replace the image for reality itself, conflating the historical experiences of lynching with the photographs and avoiding other ways of knowing. Perhaps it is not that repeated looking at these photographs may ultimately come to 'normalize images that are in fact horrible' as Staples contends, but rather, this normalisation occurs when we stabilise the complexities of the photographs by reducing them to simple documents of historical realities. If we are to avoid normalising these images, then we need to resist this slippage between reality and image, between experience and representation, such that the photographs are understood as windows into the past.

DOCUMENTING

This transformation of images into experience became particularly acute when the show moved to the Andy Warhol Museum in Pittsburgh, opening eleven days after the attacks on the World Trade Center on 11 September 2001. Seeing the lynching photographs amid the constant flow of images of destruction shaped the experience of looking and not looking. Through photographic and video footage captured by journalists and amateurs, the events of 9/11 deepened long-held beliefs that the image and the experience of an event are analogous. 'Photography', Sontag writes, 'has become one of the principal devices for experiencing something, for giving an appearance of participation.'[39] Today's digital technology has given this experience of participation even greater immediacy. In reflecting on the visual records of 9/11, Barbara Kirschenblatt-Gimblett argues:

> Digital photographs, viewable on the spot, occupy the same moment and place as the event they record. They become part of the event in the very moment of their creation. The sheer volume of testimony and images in the months that followed [9/11] make the documentation seem as if it were conterminous with the disaster. Documentation anticipates a future looking back.[40]

Conflating the time between photographing and looking, the immediacy of capturing and transmitting images furthered a faith in photographic truth, transforming documenting into experiencing. Within this logic, we can avoid dealing with the complexities and anxieties of what the image is or how we ought to look at the image. Within this faith in the veracity of the photograph, images no longer stand in for the events, but rather stand as the events themselves.

While expanding to nearly a hundred photographs, the Warhol Museum approached the show in much the same way as the New-York Historical Society, wrapping the photos in even more context, including performances, video diaries, daily patron conversations and talks. However, the events of 9/11 shaped a new approach to these photographs by situating them within a constellation of terror and violence that effectively removed the historical specificity of lynchings. For example, Mary Thomas, the *Pittsburgh Post-Gazette* art critic, commended the museum 'for having the courage and the leadership to take on this important humanitarian task, made all the more urgent in light of this month's equally incomprehensible terrorist attack on civility and moral order.'[41] In his review of the subsequent Atlanta exhibit, Charles Nelson writes: 'To see the documentation of what these people did to fellow human beings is to come to grips with the terrorism that occurred in America prior to September 11, 2001.'[42] What gets lost in such analogies between 9/11 and lynching is precisely the specificity of racism in the United States. More significantly, the image itself gets lost within a set of historical and contemporary quotations that all signify a generalised violence inside and outside the borders of the nation. Within this cultural narrative of terror, the question of 'what we are looking at?' in the lynching photos can be more readily explained away within a legacy of violent human practices. Not only does the content of the photographs lose specificity in such analogies, but also, and more importantly, the practices of photography lose all historical context.

HAUNTING

While the events of 11 September 2001 certainly influenced the experience of seeing these images, the exhibitions themselves were more profoundly shaped by the local histories and contemporary concerns that informed each exhibition site. Curators and directors at the New-York Historical Society mounted 'Without Sanctuary' with an interest in intervening in the conflicts arising from police brutality against black New Yorkers. Yet the exhibit's historical force was still somewhat removed from New York City in both time and place when compared with Atlanta in May 2002.

After troubled negotiations with both Emory University and the Atlanta Historical Society, organisers opened 'Without Sanctuary' at the Martin Luther King, Jr. National Historic Site. While the images were born in the South, this was the first time these photographs were displayed together in the centre of the New South. James Allen would later call the experience of finding a venue in Atlanta a 'painful and bruising' one. Quoting Allen, Apel notes: '"Most of the institutions weren't even willing to look at the images," said Allen, "They didn't want to even crack the book. They didn't want to discuss it." The initial caution is unsurprising; the memories of the past tread on "graves dug just a while ago," with the last lynching on record in Georgia taking place in 1965.'[43] Displaying these images in the South demanded new responses to the troubling questions of how we look and what we look at, questions which had shaped the exhibition since its inception.[44]

To address these concerns, Allen asked his friend, artist Joseph Jordan, to curate the Atlanta show. Jordan selected only 42 images, the fewest of any of the exhibitions. In an interview, Jordan relates: 'What I wanted to do is first of all trust the eyes of the people who would see this. And having done that, to paint a sort of portrait in time of what lynching looked like. And my feeling was that if I could do that, then people would see what needed to be seen.'[45] Jordan's approach crafted the show as an artistic space, where the photographs were but one part of this visual and aural story. Not only were detailed explanatory texts used with each photograph, but there were also quotations and poems by African-Americans painted on the walls, a map of the South that marked the locations of specific lynchings, and well-known spirituals filling the air of the gallery. With its black painted walls and lyrics of spirituals haunting the air, the gallery space solemnised the experience of looking, making explicit a respect for the victims. Yet this space also asked patrons not to look at the dead, to look elsewhere at words and poems, to close our eyes and listen to the music. The show memorialised the dead, by telling their stories, and, more profoundly than any earlier exhibit, Jordan situated the photographs amid a host of musical and poetic quotations that spoke against the violence.

Within this memorialising atmosphere, the photographs embodied the stories of victims, asking patrons to reflect and remember their deaths, in a similar manner that the black community would have used these photographs at the time of the lynchings. While Jordan claims he did not want the show to focus only on the victims, the effect of the gallery experience fostered this memorialisation. Unlike the Historical Society's show, which used the photographs to promote conversations about current-day racism, the Atlanta show sought to create a mournful space to witness a kind of exhumation of the past. In reflecting on the show's significance in Atlanta, Jordan stated:

> There is a haunting sensibility that comes when people are able to say, 'This happened right over there, or this happened in Marietta, or this happened right down here in Thomasville.' I would always say to folks, 'OK, when you drive home now and you look over to the side of the road, you're not just looking at a patch of the Interstate, you're looking at a place where the grass is growing on somebody's body.' In New York or in Pittsburgh, for example, you generally don't say that.[46]

Similarly, at one of the conferences held during the Atlanta show, Allen commented that if he could find 'every victim that lies pasted in some racist family's photo album' or elsewhere, so as 'to place their photos in an accurate, respectful context', then he would feel 'some awareness of what is meant by resurrection'.[47] In this way, the photographs become a kind of embodiment of the victim. As memorial, the show asked patrons to witness absence, with the hope that the experience of looking would enact a presence. Indeed, in the show's efforts at resurrecting the buried past, the photographs stood like ghostly penumbra, haunting the gallery experience as much as the victims haunt the geography of the South.

The emphasis on memorialising the dead released the viewer from looking at the living. After her walk through the Atlanta exhibit, historian Grace Hale asked: 'Why do we learn the names of the dead in those images and not the names of the living? Why do we learn very little about the people who participated in the tortures, took the photographs, and sent the postcards?' These questions were rarely addressed in any of the shows, if they can in fact be answered. As a memorial, the Atlanta show pays respects to the dead, and asks us to look beyond the whites who point at corpses, who stand by staring at us. It is not their lives that the show is memorialising. It is not their actions that the show questions. As Hale concludes:

> How much does our moral revulsion change the fact that these photographs still, as their creators and original purchasers intended, present victimization as the defining characteristic of blackness? A much more accurate exhibition, far closer to Wells-Barnett's challenge to (white) America, would foreground violence as a defining characteristic of whiteness.[48]

The history of the 'Without Sanctuary' exhibitions reflects as much on the conflicts over race at the end of the twentieth century as it does the history of lynching at the beginning of that century. In raising questions about how to look and what we are looking at, the exhibitions presented a more profound, though implicit, distrust in images themselves. Tied into a constellation of definitions – as art, as historical document, as memento – the archive of lynching photographs presents an uncomfortable display where the complexities of photographic representation and historical witnessing challenge our assumptions about what an image can actually tell us. In their efforts at defining the images, each show also defined the viewers themselves, suggesting the intricate dependency between viewer and photograph. While each show asked patrons to look, they more importantly shaped an experience of not looking, of filling that ambiguous and complicated space between event and representation, between witness and image.

Special thanks to Frances Guerin and Roger Hallas, who encouraged this chapter with insight and patience. Additional thanks to Janet Burstein, who read and commented on an earlier version with enthusiasm and thoughtfulness.

Notes

1   Dora Apel, *Imagery of Lynching: Black Men, White Women, and the Mob* (New Brunswick,

NJ: Rutgers University Press, 2004), 9.

2 'Without Sanctuary' has continued to tour the United States, including exhibits at the Charles H. Wright Museum, Detroit (2004) and the Chicago Historical Society (2005).

3 See Amy Louise Wood, 'Spectacles of Suffering: Witnessing Lynching in the New South, 1880–1930' (PhD diss., Emory University, 2002).

4 Hilton Als, 'GWTW', in Without Sanctuary: Lynching Photography in America, ed. James Allen. (Santa Fe, NM: Twin Palms, 2004), 40.

5 Susan Sontag, Regarding the Pain of Others (New York: Farrar, Strauss, and Giroux, 2003), 91.

6 I borrow this phrase, and its intended irony, from E. M. Forster's essay 'Not Looking at Pictures', Two Cheers for Democracy (New York: Harcourt, 1951), 130–4.

7 Patricia Williams, 'Without Sanctuary', The Nation, 14 February 2000, 9.

8 Somini Sengupta, 'Racist Hatred in America's Past Stirs Emotions at Exhibition', New York Times, 24 January 2000, B1.

9 Apel, Imagery of Lynching, 8.

10 Ibid.

11 John Durham Peters, 'Witnessing', Media, Culture and Society 23 (2001): 707–11.

12 Ibid., 710.

13 Ibid., 711.

14 Ibid.

15 Sontag, Regarding the Pain of Others, 91.

16 Williams, 'Without Sanctuary', 9.

17 In reflecting on the struggle between racism and images, bell hooks argues: 'Before racial integration there was a constant struggle on the part of black folks to create a counter-hegemonic world of images that would stand as visual resistance, challenging racist images.' See bell hooks, Art on My Mind: Visual Politics (New York: New Press, 1995).

18 Wood, 'Spectacles of Suffering', 143.

19 For a consideration of the symbolic force of these images, see Grace Hale, Making Whiteness: The Culture of Segregation in the South, 1890–1940 (New York: Pantheon, 1998).

20 Roberta Smith, 'An Ugly Legacy Lives On, Its Glare Unsoftened by Age', New York Times, 13 January 2000, E1.

21 There are no known photographs that capture the lynching in process, and in fact, there is evidence that such photographs were aggressively discouraged by the white mobs. See Wood, 'Spectacles of Suffering', 147.

22 Roland Barthes, Camera Lucida: Reflections on Photography, trans. Richard Howard (New York: Hill and Wang, 1981), 51.

23 Sengupta, 'Racist Hatred in America's Past', B1.

24 The website is available at <http://withoutsanctuary.org>.

25 Sarah Valdez, 'American Abject', Art in America 88, no. 10 (October 2000): 88.

26 Stewart Desmond, 'Risk and Rewards: The Story of 'Without Sanctuary', Museum News 80, no. 2 (March–April 2001): 45.

27 Ibid., 45–6.

28 Sontag, Regarding the Pain of Others, 22.

29 Ibid., 89.

30 Wood, 'Spectacles of Suffering', 143.

31 Valdez, 'American Abject', 89.

32 See Fitzhugh Brundage (ed.) Under Sentence of Death: Lynching in the South (Chapel Hill: University of North Carolina Press, 1997); and Jaquelyn Dowd Hall, Revolt Against Chivalry (New York: Columbia University Press, 1993).

33 Apel, Imagery of Lynching, 129.

34 Brent Staples, 'The Perils of Growing Comfortable with Evil', New York Times, 9 April 2000, A23.

35 David Levi Strauss, Between The Eyes: Essays on Photography and Politics (New York: Aperture, 2003), 102.

36 Ibid., 82.

37 Hall defines these images as 'folk pornography' in their representations of sexual and racial violence. However, Wood rightly points out that the term suggests that the photographs were hidden or forbidden, problematically eliding 'the ways ordinary people celebrated these images publicly.' See Hall, *Revolt Against Chivalry*, 150; and Wood, 'Spectacles of Suffering', 136, note 8.

38 I draw here from Joel Black's work on how film has shaped our conceptions of reality. See Joel Black, *The Reality Effect: Film Culture and the Graphic Imperative* (New York: Routledge, 2002).

39 Sontag, *On Photography*, 10.

40 Barbara Kirshenblatt-Gimblett, 'Kodak Moments, Flashbulb Memories: Reflections on 9/11', *Drama Review* 47, no. 1 (Spring 2003): 26.

41 Mary Thomas, 'Without Sanctuary Digs Deeply into Painful Issues of Inhumanity', *Pittsburgh Post-Gazette*, 29 September 2001, B2.

42 Charles H. Nelson, Jr., 'Atlanta', *Art Papers* 27, no. 1 (January–February 2003): 35.

43 Dora Apel, 'On Looking: Lynching Photographs and the Legacies of Lynching after 9/11', *American Quarterly* 55, no. 3 (2003): 464–5.

44 Currently the Atlanta History Museum includes a small display to the Ku Klux Klan that includes one lynching photograph, which is mounted six feet high and is covered by a square of black felt that hangs over the image and can be raised for viewing. A note next to the image warns patrons that the photograph may be disturbing for some viewers. This pornographic quality effectively heightens the image as spectacle.

45 Olufunke Moses, 'Bearing Witness', *Independent Weekly* (Durham, NC), 11 July 2002. Online. Available <http://indyweek.com/durham/2002-07-10/ae.html> (accessed 15 June 2005).

46 Ibid.

47 Quoted in Apel, *Imagery of Lynching*, 14.

48 Hale, *Making Whiteness*, 995.

14. Here and Then: The Act of Remembering in Richard Dindo's Documentaries

Marcy Goldberg

> As a documentary filmmaker who works with the past, I am constantly confronted by the impossibility of representing it.
>
> RICHARD DINDO

Tlatelolco, Mexico, 2002: Plaza de Las Tres Culturas. A white-haired man walks across the square where, on 2 October 1968, riot police opened fire on student demonstrators. A young professor at the time, he had been among the demonstrating crowd. The man's posture is stooped, he is shuddering inwardly. 'It was here', he says, points and crouches down. This is the spot, he explains, where a bullet aimed at him killed a student instead: the spot where he too could have been killed, but was not. The camera moves discreetly over and down, framing the concrete paving stones with streaks of dirt that suggest bloodstains, in spite of the intervening years. It then moves back up to the man's face, showing the muscles working around his eyes and mouth. The film cuts to a few brief, silent images, in the washed-out reds and greens of 1960s television footage, of soldiers with drawn rifles advancing on the screaming and fleeing masses of demonstrators. Then the scene shifts back to its present time, to the stooped figure of the professor set against the wide, nearly empty square.

TESTIMONY ON LOCATION

This scene is typical of documentary testimony: a survivor, standing at a historical site, recounting memories, accompanied by archival images. It appears in *Ni olvido, ni perdón* (*Neither Forget, Nor Forgive*), Swiss filmmaker Richard Dindo's 2003 documentary about the brutal crushing of student-led protests for democracy and civil rights in Mexico in October 1968. This massacre took place under the orders of Mexican Prime Minister Diaz Ordaz, who did not want demonstrations to interfere with the summer Olympic Games which would take place in Mexico City later that month. Several hundred demonstrators were killed at the square; others were arrested, and ultimately, disappeared.

Until the late 1980s, the events of October 1968 had been a repressed chapter in modern Mexican history. Official accounts of the period, based on misleading government information and the skewed newspaper coverage of the time, either did not mention the massacre, or blamed the violence on the demonstrators rather than the police. The Mexican people, however, never allowed the events to be completely forgotten. In dissident circles the government's betrayal of the students fueled a permanent, underlying mistrust of authority. In 1989 Jorge Fons made a fiction film based on the events, and in the early 1990s a monument was placed on the square in Tlatelolco commemorating those who died there. The mass grave where murdered demonstrators were dumped remains unmarked to this day. It was not until 2001, when the Institutional Revolutionary Party (PRI) was voted out of power after seventy years in rule, that the massacre was officially recognised by the government and discussed in the mainstream press.

Dindo shot his film in Mexico in 2002. Many of the witnesses who share their memories in front of the camera are thus remembering them publicly for the first time, after years of silence. These scenes, in which survivors of the massacre relive their experiences, are among the most moving in the film. Dindo's camera captures the middle-aged men and women as they return, individually or together, to the Plaza de las Tres Culturas, to the exact spot where they stood on 2 October 1968 (figure 1). No scripted or acted scene could achieve the same effect as the words and gestures of their testimony or the emotions triggered by their presence at the site of their

Figure 1: Richard Dindo, *Ni Olvido, ni perdón* (*Neither Forget nor Forgive*, 2003).

the image and the witness

traumatic experiences. *Ni olvido, ni perdón* seems to invite the viewer to come as close as anyone could to sharing someone else's memories. And yet, if the viewer happens to be familiar with documentary theory, these scenes may also provoke a feeling of discomfort. Do they not also recall the formulaic 'it-happened-here' testimonies so familiar to us from television? And have film theorists not demonstrated that the conjunction of testimony and location is a rhetorical device or trope that in no way guarantees the truth of what is being recounted?[1]

QUESTIONING THE 'FILM OF MEMORY'

David MacDougall's ironic rendering of 'films of memory', in his essay of the same name, helps to understand the disquieting aspects of the abovementioned scene for the documentary film theorist.[2] MacDougall characterises the 'conventional film of historical reminiscence' as 'a cinematic subgenre whose ritual ingredients are aging faces (usually of interviewees), fetish-objects from the past, old photographs, archival footage and music'; a sub-genre which purports to tell us our '"true", unwritten history'.[3] MacDougall expresses the frustration of a filmmaker who aims to 'record memory itself', but ends up reproducing nothing but unreliable signifers. 'We end by filming something far removed from memory as it is experienced, but instead a mixture of dubious testimony, flawed evidence and invention ... If memory itself is selective and ideological, films of memory redouble this and add further codes of cultural convention.'[4]

Such mistrust of documentary codes and conventions has no doubt been nourished by the clichés of television reportage and the excesses of a certain kind of didactic filmmaking practice, both of which tend to appeal to the naïve truth claims problematised by MacDougall and other theorists. But the body of critical theory calling into question the ability of the 'film of memory' to provide authentic and meaningful accounts of historical events poses a serious challenge to the scholarly analysis of films like *Ni olvido, ni perdón*. How can documentary witnessing be analysed as a distinct practice, when what seemed both informative and genuinely moving is dismissed as a mere reality-effect?

This dilemma is at the heart of ongoing debates about the documentary representation of reality. On the one hand, developments in semiotics, historiography and narratology have shown that there can be no unmediated access to the real. Scholars in these fields have demonstrated that historical accounts necessarily consist of processes of exclusion and arrangement which make objectivity impossible, and that discourses which present themselves as non-fictional share narrative forms with the writing of fiction.[5] On the other hand, a number of documentary theorists continue to insist on the specificity of documentary as a distinct mode of representation of the historical world, and as a potential instrument of political critique and social change.[6] If MacDougall outlines so precisely the problems associated with attempting to capture memories on film, he surely does not mean to discourage documentarists from making the attempt, but rather, to alert them to the potential pitfalls they face. In this context, it becomes useful to examine how a filmmaker who is aware of these dilemmas integrates them into filmmaking practice, while continuing to use the documentary form to as a tool to analyse and commemorate past events.

DOCUMENTARY FILM AS EPISTEMOLOGICAL TOOL

In his 1968 essay 'On the Impression of Reality in the Cinema', Christian Metz contrasts the fundamental pastness of the photographic image with the projective power of the film medium, which stems from the cinematic image's perennial message of 'there it is'.[7] The cinema spectator, says Metz, 'always sees movement as being present'. The 'then' of photography is transformed into the 'now' of the motion picture. This is what makes films convincing: 'Films speak to us with the accents of true evidence, using the argument that "It is so". With ease they make the kind of statements a linguist would call fully assertive and which, moreover, are usually taken at face value. There is a filmic mode, which is the mode of presence, and to a great extent it is *believable*.'[8]

However, for Metz, the 'filmic mode of presence' is an illusion; he insists on film's power to *seem* real while remaining unreal: 'There, on the screen, is a large tree, faithfully reproduced on film, but, if we were to reach forward to grasp it, our hands would close on an empty play of light and shadow.'[9] Metz is not interested in the content of the images, but the phenomenon of an impression of reality across film genres: 'The *subjects* of films can be divided into the "realistic" and the "non-realistic", but the filmic vehicle's power to make real, to *realise*, is common to both genres.'[10]

Metz's remarks here are part of the larger project of a semiotics of the cinema developed in the 1970s, and they are meant to emphasise the fundamental codedness and constructedness of 'film language'. However, the cinema's ability to turn the 'pastness' of the photograph into a perennial present has other important implications when its content has been 'indexed' as non-fictional. In his essay 'Moving Pictures and the Rhetoric of Nonfiction: Two Approaches', Carl Plantinga takes up this concept of indexing formulated by Noël Carroll:

> According to Carroll, we typically view a film while knowing that it has been indexed, either as fiction or nonfiction. The particular indexing of a film mobilizes expectations and activities on the part of the viewer. A film indexed as nonfiction leads the spectator to expect a discourse that makes assertions or implications about actuality. In addition, the spectator will take a different attitude toward those states of affairs presented, since they are taken to represent the actual, and not a fictional, world.[11]

Thus, the film medium's perceptual illusion of presence is linked with the viewer's cognitive recognition of the factual content of the images, creating the impression that the film has temporarily conjured up the historical past, or, as some would have it, resurrected the dead. The late Dutch filmmaker Johan van der Keuken put it best in his essay-documentary *The Filmmaker's Holiday* (1974). In a sequence concerning film's ability to move back and forth across the barrier that separates life from death, the filmmaker-narrator comments, 'Film is the only medium that can show the transition from life to death ... Showing the transition from death to life is harder.' As an example of the cinema's power to bring things back to life, he reworks images he had shot in 1967 for *Big Ben: Ben Webster in Europe*, his portrait of the jazz saxophonist. 'Last year Ben Webster died', says van der Keuken in voice-over. 'Here he lives again, as I filmed him seven years ago.'

This temporary forcing together of 'here' and 'then' is volatile, but therein lies its power. Fredric Jameson has characterised the oscillation between artifice and insight as the 'constitutive tension' of the realist aesthetic and its claim to an 'epistemological function' which positions art as a form of knowledge.[12] As Jameson points out, classical theories of filmic realism have, seemingly paradoxically, tended to ascribe the epistemological function to fiction film, not documentary.[13] And yet, in emphasising both its own constructedness (artifice) and its testimonial potential (insight), a film like van der Keuken's shows that documentary realism can be deployed as an epistemological tool that is particularly potent for the purposes of remembrance.

AN 'IMPURE' DOCUMENTARIST

In a career spanning 35 years, Dindo has developed a distinct set of strategies for handling the fundamental impossibility of representing the past. He has achieved this in part by including reflections on witnessing into his work. In interviews and essays he has also provided a highly articulate account of his method and the philosophy that informs it. In a 1994 interview for German television, Dindo emphasises the problem of representing a past which is always already irrecoverably lost:

> All my work revolves around the problem of re-producing the past. That's why I'm an impure documentarist. Documenting essentially means filming what is taking place in front of the camera at a given moment. That's how the documentary film came into being. But I am a documentarist of the past. When I arrive at the location, the event has already occurred. I can no longer film it; my protagonist is no longer there.[14]

Thus, Dindo chooses to structure his films around the fundamental absence of the event, or the absence of its original witness, with the aim of stimulating the viewer to participate in the process of recalling the past:

> So the first thing I must do is bring the event back to life. But since I'm not making a fiction film, I can only recreate the event in the viewer's imagination. The viewer must be able to picture events and people that are no longer visible. That means, the film constructs itself shot by shot in the face of an absence. And I try to render visible – through speech, through story-telling – what is essentially absent.[15]

Dindo knows that the film image alone 'proves' nothing. He is entirely aware that accounts of the past must remain fragmentary, subjective and contingent. And yet, in more than twenty films, he has continued to use the film medium to treat subjects drawn from history and biography, developing formal strategies for deploying the documentary potential of the cinema in ways that admit the limits of what can be known or shown. Dindo's films continue to insist on the possibility, and the political necessity, for the present to encounter the past.

Dindo's method is closely linked to his choice of subjects. Nearly all his films are biographies: of artists, revolutionaries or both. Alongside world-famous rebels with cult status, such as Che Guevara (*Ernesto 'Che' Guevara, The Bolivian Diaries*, 1994), Jean Genet (*Genet à Chatila*, 1999) and Arthur Rimbaud (*Arthur Rimbaud, A Biography*, 1991), Dindo has also devoted a number of films to lesser-known, but no less intriguing, characters from modern Swiss history, each a rebel and a victim of injustice in one way or another. In his 1975 film, *Die Erschiessung des Landesverräters Ernst S.* (*The Execution of the Traitor Ernst S.*), the villain/victim of the title, a petty thief, was shot for collaborating with the Nazis while leaders of Swiss industry did the same with impunity. And in *Verhör und Tod in Winterthur* (*Inquiry and Death in Winterthur*), his 2002 re-examination of police brutality during the 1980s youth movement, Dindo maintains his commitment to exposing some of the more unsavoury episodes in his country's recent past. Whether local heroes and rebels, or internationally-known artists, his protagonists are often utopian dreamers. In most cases their dreams – and often they themselves – have been brutally crushed. Since history is usually written by the winners, Dindo's portraits of his protagonists' lives often involve setting the record straight. His films are not only about representing history, but also about supplementing and amending established accounts of it. Thus, it is essential to his project for these accounts to be recognised as authentic and credible.

RE-PRODUCING THE PAST

Dindo's use of film images to conjure up the past is a cornerstone of his method for what he calls 're-producing' history.[16] Like van der Keuken, Dindo is interested in exploiting Metz's 'filmic mode of presence' as a means to recall the past. Unlike the example cited by van der Keuken, however, Dindo rarely has film footage of his subjects at his disposal, thus he must find other means for re-producing or reconstructing the events he is attempting to portray.

In Dindo's films the practice of re-producing the past is usually based on one of two types of testimony. Either Dindo uses his protagonist's own account of events, as preserved in diaries, memoirs and other texts – or, in the case of the visual artist Charlotte Salomon, in her paintings – to create what he calls a 'filmic adaptation' (*Verfilmung*) based on the writer's autobiographial material. Or he may gather witnesses to testify to a past event or an absent protagonist. The films often begin with an announcement of the protagonist's death, before proceeding to recount the events leading up to it. By structuring a film as a 'chronicle of a death foretold', Dindo casts the story in an elegiac mood and invites the viewer to participate in reconstructing a protagonist's life.

The journey to the authentic location – to what Dindo calls, in German, the *Schauplatz*, the scene of the action – is a crucial component of Dindo's method. This journey is necessary, but it is not sufficient, as Dindo explains in this vivid statement inspired by his 1973 film *Schweizer im Spanischen Bürgerkrieg* (*The Swiss in the Spanish Civil War*):

Let's say I'm standing at a crossroads outside Madrid and filming a shot. It's a beautiful landscape, and with any luck the sky clouds over and the sun shines through. That's beautiful, but it's not moving. It becomes moving when I know that a Republican fighter was killed here – and I share this knowledge with the viewer. Then the viewer will take a new look at the shot of the crossroads, and will also be moved. That emotion is what I try to convey with my films. The emotion is transmitted through the authentic location, and through language. And the image of the location is linked with a human voice, with a narrative.[17]

The image, Dindo knows, is not enough: hence the importance of language as a second strategic element; most particularly, the statement 'this is where it happened' (*hier ist es geschehen*). There are several ways to convey what happened via language: eyewitness testimony, voice-over commentary, a quotation from the memoirs of his dead protagonists read off-screen or filmed off the page. Theorists of photography have often commented on the need for a caption to counteract the 'polysemy' of the image and anchor it within a specific context.[18] In a sense, this is what these constant juxtapositions of the image and the spoken or written word are doing. Supplementing and extending the Metzian illusion of presence, these linguistic counterpoints to the image anchor its content within the viewer's knowledge of history. At the same time, this appeal to the viewer is also meant to trigger an emotional insight.

Alongside language, Dindo also uses images to comment on other images: juxtaposing photographs, paintings or scenes from fiction films with shots of the authentic *Schauplatz*. Dindo emphasises documentary's ability to make these materials speak as documents, to include and borrow from all other forms of artistic expression:

The real *Gesamtkunstwerk* is the documentary. Only the documentary can assimilate other materials to approach its reality. Documentary incorporates theatre, feature film, photographs, music, as well as documentary images, the locations where the story happened, and the witnesses telling the story. All these elements can be used to approach the subject, circle around it repeatedly, out of the same things said in different ways. That's how the memory is created.[19]

In other words, Dindo, somewhat playfully, calls the documentary 'the true *Gesamtkunstwerk*' because it can incorporate all other art forms for its own purposes. In doing so, he is not invoking the high-modernist totalising practice often associated with the concept of the 'total work of art'. Rather, his stance here is closer to that of the ethnographer or archaeologist, in understanding that essentially non-documentary elements, such as paintings, or scenes borrowed from fiction film, may also become artefacts, documents from the historical world. In other words, the documentary genre is expanded to include fictional materials, which are then inscribed as documents and read for their testimonial potential. With his expanded definition of documentary, Dindo is deliberately reversing the more common practice of subordinating documentary to fiction within the hierarchy of film genres. Rather than emphasising the 'fictive' nature of documentary's formal structures, he is making a claim for documentary authenticity.[20]

This is a particularly interesting move with regard to the concept of documentary witnessing. The strength of the documentary, according to Dindo, is that it can position the most diverse objects as documents and interrogate them accordingly. Dindo may arrive too late to document the original event, but he can still stage an encounter with the document. The notion of the object as witness within Dindo's work can be seen as a practical application of 'thing theory', the interdisciplinary conjunction of anthropology, history, archaeology and critical theory, which analyses objects as a means of understanding the culture or society which created them.[21] In his introduction to *The Social Life of Things: Commodities in Cultural Perspective*, Arjun Appadurai invokes the ability of 'things-in-motion' to 'illuminate their human and social context'.[22] The choice of the word 'illuminate' is significant. As we will see below, Dindo's citations of poems, paintings and music turn these elements into witnesses and help to evoke the momentary flashes of insight into the past that are at the core of his project.

Although Dindo foregrounds his role in selecting and shaping the films' elements, he is reticent about appearing within the frame himself, and tends to restrict his presence to questions asked off-screen or the reading of brief voice-over texts. Instead, he often introduces a stand-in, a figure who visibly conducts the film's research or supplies a subjective point of view. Very occasionally, he introduces an actor into a documentary situation, such as the young Frenchwoman of North African descent who retraces Jean Genet's Middle Eastern journeys in *Genet in Chatila*. In *Arthur Rimbaud, A Biography* he goes even further. The film is composed entirely of staged scenes in which actors, dressed in period costume and playing Rimbaud's relatives and friends, visit key locations from the poet's life and speak or read authentic texts, such as journal entries or letters, evoking key moments from Rimbaud's biography.

In sum, four main formal strategies feature in Dindo's filmic reconstruction of events: the return to the authentic location; the use of spoken or written language to supplement or contrast the film image; the integration of artefacts or objects functioning as silent witnesses; and the introduction of a real or fictive stand-in who sifts through and examines these remaining traces. All these devices testify to the difficulty in bridging the gap between 'here' and 'then'; as a result, they convey information about the past while simultaneously pointing to its fragmentary, elusive character.

The 1981 documentary *Max Frisch, Journal I–III*, which combines all these elements, provides the most extensive demonstration of Dindo's filmmaking method, and could even be considered his signature film. At the same time, it represents an important exception within his filmography because Frisch was still alive at the time the film was made (he died in 1991). True to form, however, Dindo structures the film around Frisch's absence, allowing the writer to appear only in the past tense, in a few brief clips of old television footage and a sound recording of a 1974 speech. As its title indicates, *Max Frisch, Journal I–III* is the filmic adaptation of Frisch's autobiographical writings, taken from both his diaries and the memoir *Montauk* (1975). In these texts, Frisch ponders the limits of language and representation, and comments repeatedly on the difficulties of writing truly authentic and honest autobiography, although he also praises literature for its ability to 'preserve' moments of existence for the sake of memory.

Dindo's film extends these musings by juxtaposing text and images, contrasting Frisch's prose with footage of the things and places it describes. Frisch's doubts as a writer, his evocation of the gap between life and literature, find their parallel in Dindo's inconclusive search for the traces of Frisch's experiences in New York, as chronicled in *Montauk*. Dindo's assistant, an American student named Alexandra, appears in the film. As the researcher, she is a stand-in for the filmmaker himself; at the same time, she recalls the figure of Lynn, Frisch's young American lover in *Montauk*. In one scene, Dindo has Alexandra run up and down a flight of stairs on the beach. In the book, Frisch had described Lynn stumbling on the narrow staircase, but Alexandra disagrees: no one could have tripped here. When the film cuts from a close-up of the book page with the printed word 'Montauk' to footage of the actual location, each shot serves to both anchor and question the other. Is this the place? Is this how it looked when Frisch saw it in 1974? Here Dindo builds the *work* of tracking down the past – and the doubt which accompanies this work – into the actual structure of the film.

STRATEGIES OF WITNESSING

In her discussion of Claude Lanzmann's *Shoah* (1985) as 'a film about witnessing', Shoshana Felman has pointed out that the film's witnesses – victims, bystanders and perpetrators – all provide different performances of the act of seeing.[23] Dindo's films can be said to provide performances of the act of remembering. The fact that these performances are deliberately filmed and presented as such saves them from accusations of being 'dubious testimony' and mere 'external signs of remembering'. As we have seen (and will see again below), Dindo's documentaries not only portray witnesses, they also reflect on the question of the witness, and the ground of possibility of witnessing, as one way of avoiding the naïve approach to portraying history against which MacDougall warns.

This is perhaps most clear in *Grüningers Fall* (*Grüninger's Case*, 1997), Dindo's homage to Paul Grüninger, the Swiss border policeman who was dishonourably discharged for illegally allowing Jewish refugees to enter the country during the Second World War. Grüninger died in poverty in 1972; the Swiss government only rehabilitated him posthumously in 1993. The film is intended as a further, definitive act of rehabilitation. Dindo sets the bulk of *Grüninger's Case* in the St. Gallen district courthouse where Grüninger was convicted in 1940. But now the courtroom is the scene for testimony about Grüninger's heroism and his courage in obeying his own conscience against the unjust laws of the time. Former refugees, mostly living far away, return to Switzerland at Dindo's request and take the stand, as it were, to share their memories of how Grüninger saved their lives. Their wartime documents are piled in file folders on the courtroom tables, as in a trial.

'Is this you?' Dindo asks the elderly Yetty Tenenbaum, as an identity photo of a young woman is shown. 'Yes', replies the old woman sitting in the witness stand. In an ironic voice she continues: 'I was young and beautiful then. I don't know what's happened.' In this context, the humour comes as a surprise, but Mrs Tenenbaum's wry jest points to the film's declared goal: to collapse the gap between 1940 and the present time. Once again, we are in the paradoxical Metzian situation of finding ourselves both 'here' and 'then'. Here, in the courtroom in 1997, but also in the same place where Grüninger stood then. Here, with Mrs Tenenbaum as she is today, but also reliving with the elderly woman her memories of how she was then. If, for Mrs Tenenbaum, the intervening years have gone by 'in a flash', as the stock phrase would have it, we, the audience, have been transported by a similar flash in the opposite direction.

The fundamental absence of Grüninger himself at the core of the film is emphasised, rather than resolved, by a brief clip from a television interview done shortly before his death, in 1971. This material too is 'cited' as part of the symbolic trial,

Figure 2: Richard Dindo, *Grüningers Fall* (*Grüninger's Case*, 1997).

and introduced as a document. It is screened in the courtoom as the surviving witnesses watch (figure 2). Later they will comment on it. Images of the aged Grüninger walking with the aid of a cane along the bridge marking the Swiss-Austrian border, his old-fashioned hat, coat and glasses, all testify to a past time that is irrecoverably lost. The grainy black-and-white of the vintage television images creates a further contrast to the present time, which is filmed in crisp colour. Through their presence and their ability to testify, the refugees Grüninger saved embody the results of his actions. But Grüninger's absence from the courtroom, and his brief 1971 statement upholding the rightness of his choices, point to his status not only as a hero, but also, as a victim.

It is also significant that the *Schauplatz*, or traumatic location, is doubled. Both the border and the courtroom are the 'scenes of the crime'. The crime is Grüninger's conviction, and also, in a larger sense, the official Swiss refugee policy that closed the country's borders to Jews persecuted by the Nazis. It is crucial to point out here that Dindo's decision to set the bulk of his film in the St. Gallen courthouse is more than just a canny piece of documentary staging or an easy bridge between 'then' and 'now'. It is also a device for incorporating the motif of the witness into the very structure of the film. The courthouse provides a temporary stage upon which the survivors can perform their testimony, and renders them witnesses in Dindo's 'case' against the Swiss state.

In *Ernesto 'Che' Guevara, the Bolivian Diaries*, the return to the *Schauplatz* plays an equally important role. In this film, interviews with eyewitnesses who fought with Che are conducted in the countryside where the battles took place. A statement from the woman who was the last person to see him alive is recorded in the same village schoolhouse which was the scene of their meeting. However, once again, the main witness being 'interrogated' is the absent Che himself. The film includes scenes shot from his imaginary point of view, as his diary entries are read off-screen. Thus the character of Che becomes a kind of virtual witness who offers the viewer a brief glimpse into his own subjectivity.

The 1966–67 diaries of Che's final campaign and the last days of his life chronicle the decline of his revolutionary project. Under siege in the forests and hills of Bolivia, his last soldiers deserting or dying, Che's dream of a more just political system is reduced to a struggle for survival, a struggle he ultimately loses when his whereabouts are betrayed. In his documentary, Dindo attempts to resurrect this atmosphere, projecting Che's chronicle of the death of a utopian political dream onto contemporary forest paths. The written chronicle of Che's last, doomed, military campaign in the forests of Bolivia is read off-screen and accompanied by subjective camera footage, shot by Dindo and his crew, of rambles through those same forests. This footage functions simultaneously as an illustration of Che's diary and a counterpoint to it. On the one hand, the viewer is shown things and places resembling those mentioned in Che's account. But, on the other, these colour images also emphasise Che's absence, as well as the gap in time between Che's last days and the present time of Dindo's film. For the potential tension between Che's words and Dindo's images, or between the past and the present, to be realised, it is necessary for the viewer to adopt an active role. But as we will see, this is both a potential weakness as well as a potential strength of Dindo's method.

> When I'm shooting a film, I ask myself two questions. First of all: who is speaking in this film? And then: who is looking? When I film a shot, I always need to know whose gaze it represents. I try not only to film as if my dead protagonists were watching: I also try to bring their extinguished gaze back to life. That is why I go to the important places from their lives, the authentic locations, and try to film these places with their eyes, to reproduce their gaze. In the Che Guevara film, I go by foot along the paths he once walked, using a subjective camera perspective – as if he himself were looking. And then off-screen there is the voice reading from his diary, telling the story of his gaze. One of the reasons why language is important for me is because it helps define the image, because it helps to explain what the image reveals. This may sound funny coming from a filmmaker, but I don't believe one can express very much through images.[24]

This is one of Dindo's most revealing statements, expressing his fundamental scepticism regarding the truth content of the film image. However, *Ernesto 'Che' Guevara* also points to the limits of the use of language to clarify or define the image and thus to the limits of Dindo's intentions as a filmmaker. Although he means to portray Che Guevara as a tragic hero, some viewers may see him as a misguided bumbler, or worse. Seeing what Che saw, and hearing what he thought, viewers may not necessarily adopt Che's perspective as their own. The choice to accept or reject Che's point of view is the productive result of the tension between 'then' and 'now', between the image and text of Dindo's film.

Dindo's explanation for his deliberate doubling or juxtaposition of image and text may not always be satisfying. His trademark style runs the risk of being criticised as illustrative or tautological: naming a thing, showing that thing. But as the gap between Dindo's view of Che and a potential viewer's perception indicates (as does the *Montauk* example), this seeming redundancy is actually a means for highlighting the deliberate artificiality of this method. And it is a formal manipulation that finds its ultimate meaning in the choice given to the active, thinking viewer.

If the films about Che Guevara and Paul Grüninger explicitly address the difficulty of recapturing the past, Dindo's documentary about the Mexico City massacre forcefully catalogues potential strategies for doing so. *Ni olvido, ni perdón* not only documents what actually happened in October 1968, thereby setting the historical record straight. It also examines the multiple ways that the events of the time are being remembered today. Alongside clips from Jorge Fons' fiction film *Rojo amanecer* (*Red Sunrise*, 1989), which dramatises the bloody events of 2 October 1968, Dindo's documentary also catalogues a whole spectrum of strategies for representing and commemorating the past. Discussions between survivors, and their testimony at the site, represent the most basic and direct form of performing the act of remembering. In addition, the film explores the use of other, more symbolic strategies. 'Official' memory is represented in the film by the recently-erected monument on Tlatelolco square, as well as by memorial services in Mexican schools where the story of Tlatelolco had only recently been added to history lessons at the time the film was shot. A more anthropological gaze is represented in footage capturing the reactions of random visitors of various ages and political persuasions to the monument. The film also visits the more private ritual of a graveside ceremony for a survivor of the massacre, who was mysteriously killed in 2001 after sharing his story with a news magazine. Talks with the man's young daughter introduce the question of the transmission of memories to younger generations. This issue is reinforced by the school scenes, and most particularly, by scenes from a 2002 play about the massacre performed by contemporary students as part of their commitment to carrying on the work of remembrance.

In one telling scene, a veteran of the 1960s protests goes through the newspaper coverage of the time, pointing out how it was distorted to reflect the government's official and blatantly untrue version of events. The ongoing political significance of setting the record straight is emphasised repeatedly by Dindo's interview subjects. It is hoped that spreading knowledge of what really happened under PRI rule will help inspire contemporary youth to continue the struggle for full democracy and human rights. Scenes like these make clear that *Ni olvido, ni perdón* is not simply a film about the event itself or how it is remembered. It is also, most importantly, about the political aspects of remembrance: about how corrupt power holders attempt to distort the historical record to their own advantage, and about the possibility of resisting or combatting such distortions.

THE 'PRODUCTION' OF MEMORY

'All these elements can be used to approach the subject, circle around it repeatedly, out of the same things said in different ways', notes Dindo in his reflections on the *Gesamtkunstwerk*; 'that's how the memory is created.' This statement might, at first glance, seem to contradict the emphasis on authenticity at the core of Dindo's work in particular and the documentary project in general. So what does he mean?

> Instead of turning documents of everyday life into memories, I try to restore the actuality of memory itself. By doing someone's portrait, you bring that person back into the present, even if he's already been dead a long time. And

that's how one creates one's own actuality and tries to convey something beyond the daily news … For me that means: thinking things anew, making a new start.[25]

Dindo recognises the artifice involved in conjuring up the past, and the instability of the moments he produces. Yet it is the very volatility of these moments that makes them convincing and powerful:

When I produce memories I'm also producing a truth – which exists only for the space of my film, flaring up in Rimbaud's sense of the word, like an illumination. The truth flares up for a few moments, is perceived by the viewer, and then forgotten once again. I don't believe in absolute truths. I believe in truth only as an intellectual and artistic process of re-creation. My viewers are the witnesses to this process.[26]

Dindo's account of truth as unstable, as a momentary flash, may have been inspired by the poet and rebel Rimbaud, who was also the subject of one of his filmic biographies. However, both the filmmaker's practice of conjuring up images of the past in the present, and the paradoxical idea that his viewers may be transformed through viewing his films into witnesses of past events, are also directly connected to an understanding of history best expressed by Walter Benjamin in an oft-quoted passage from his 'Theses on the Philosophy of History': 'The true picture of the past flits by. The past can be seized only as an image which flashes up at the instant when it can be recognised and is never seen again.'[27] In his account of the historian's activity, Benjamin makes explicit the political implications of keeping memory and testimony alive. He also emphasises the importance for historians of the present to recognise the concerns of the past as their own. 'Only that historian will have the gift of fanning the spark of hope in the past who is firmly convinced that *even the dead* will not be safe from the enemy if he wins', writes Benjamin.[28] Thus, as long as viewers continue to witness the filmic 'resurrection' of past events, the lessons of history may not be lost. Or, as the narrator of *Ni olvido, ni perdón* puts it, flatly but no less powerfully: 'So that these events are not forgotten, they must be recounted.'

Dindo has referred to the viewer as a potential witness to his conjuring up of past events. But for Dindo's method to be successful, the viewer must also take the role of active participant. This necessity represents both a strength and a weakness of this method. On the one hand, by inviting the viewer to assume an active role, and by baring the film's devices in order to encourage viewers to participate knowingly in the reconstruction of events, Dindo's films adopt a progressive, open approach.[29] On the other, the films' effectiveness depends on the viewer's willingness to take up the role offered. In addition, their open construction allows viewers to develop interpretations different from, or even at odds with, Dindo's intentions as filmmaker and chronicler. And yet, it would be impossible for Dindo's films to fulfill their political project of remembrance without addressing their viewers as autonomous and active. As Dindo puts it: 'For me, remembering is not nostalgia. Remembering is also the critical reappraisal of politics and history. My task is politicising memory – and drawing memories out of politics.'[30]

CONCLUSION: MEMORY AND UTOPIA

Dindo's attitude, as expressed in his assertion, 'I don't believe one can express very much through images', separates him from the mainstream of historical documentary filmmakers whose practices are not otherwise fundamentally different. Dindo knows that what he is trying to do is impossible. And yet he continues to use images to evoke the historical past, stubbornly insisting on the necessity of remembrance. Thus, his work constantly reflects the tension between the inadequacy of the image and the need to illustrate the past. The combination of Dindo's scepticism about the image and his commitment to explore the past as a form of remembrance makes his treatment of witnessing particularly nuanced. His work is strongest, and most convincing, where witnessing and its implications are also treated as an explicit theme; in films such as *Ni olvido, ni perdon* and *Grüninger's Case*. Setting the Grüninger film in a courtroom, or filming the Mexican survivor's deconstruction of the false newspaper coverage, does not simply produce 'the external signs of remembering' as MacDougall fears. Rather, the uncertainties and challenges of documentary remembrance, and remembering more generally, are built into the very structure of the film and the content of the images. Scenes such as those discussed reveal themselves to be part of the continuing struggle against forgetting and against injustice.

If Benjamin emphasises the importance for historians of the present to recognise the concerns of the past as their own, Dindo attempts to bring this message to a wider audience of cinema viewers and ordinary citizens. His films reposition remembrance as an activity which is primarily about the present rather than the past, and they create an active role for the spectator through re-presenting historical events. In doing so, they approach the ultimate goal of Benjamin's historical 'flash': aiming for an accurate understanding of the past in order to keep utopian hopes alive. It is a goal which is both impossible, and necessary.

Richard Dindo's films are distributed by Filmcoopi Zürich AG, Heinrichstrasse 114, CH-8005 Zürich, Switzerland (www.filmcoopi.ch).

Notes

1   Michael Renov argues that 'all discursive forms – documentary included – are, if not fictional, at least fictive, this by virtue of their tropic character (their recourse to tropes or rhetorical figures)'. Michael Renov, 'Introduction: The Truth About Non-Fiction' in *Theorizing Documentary*, ed. Michael Renov (London: Routledge, 1993), 7.
2   David MacDougall, 'Films of Memory', in *Transcultural Cinema*, ed. Lucien Taylor (Princeton: Princeton University Press, 1998), 231–44.
3   Ibid., 235.
4   Ibid., 232.
5   See Hayden White, *The Content of the Form: Narrative Discourse and Historical Representation* (Baltimore: Johns Hopkins University Press, 1987) or William Guynn, *A Cinema of Nonfiction* (Rutherford, NJ: Fairleigh Dickinson University Press, 1990).
6   The most sustained argument on this subject has been made by Bill Nichols, particularly in his *Representing Reality* (Bloomington: Indiana University Press, 1991) and *Introduction to Documentary* (Bloomington: Indiana University Press, 2001). See also Linda Williams, 'Mirrors Without Memories: Truth, History, and the New Documentary', *Film Quarterly* 46,

no. 3 (1993): 9–21; and Philip Rosen, 'Document and Documentary: On the Persistence of Historical Concepts', in *Theorizing Documentary*, 58–89.

7   Christian Metz, *Film Language: A Semiotics of the Cinema* (Chicago: University of Chicago Press, 1974), 3–15. Metz emphasises the 'believeable' element of the 'mode of presence' in his original.

8   Ibid., 4 (emphasis in original).

9   Ibid., 8.

10 Ibid., 5. (emphasis in original).

11 Carl Plantinga, 'Moving Pictures and the Rhetoric of Nonfiction: Two Approaches', in *Post-Theory*, ed. David Bordwell and Noël Carroll (Madison: Wisconsin University Press, 1996), 310–11.

12 Fredric Jameson, *Signatures of the Visible* (New York: Routledge, 1990), 158–60.

13 Ibid., 186.

14 Published as 'Richard Dindo: Alles ist Erinnerung', in *Dokumentarisch Arbeiten*, ed. Christoph Hübner and Gabriele Voss (Berlin: Verlag Vorwerk 8, 1996), 28–63. The translations are mine.

15 Ibid., 33.

16 Dindo uses the word *wiederherstellen*, which can also be translated as 'reconstructing' or 'reactualizing'.

17 Ibid., 34.

18 See Roland Barthes, 'The Photographic Message', in *Image, Music, Text*, ed. and trans. Stephen Heath (London: Fontana, 1977), 15–31; Walter Benjamin, 'The Author as Producer', in *Reflections: Essays, Aphorisms, Autobiographical Writing*, ed. Peter Demetz (New York: Harcourt Brace Jovanovich, 1979), 220–38; and Victor Burgin, 'Photographic Practice and Art Theory', in *Thinking Photography* (London: Macmillan, 1982), 39–83.

19 Unpublished interview with Richard Dindo, Zürich, June 2003.

20 See Renov, 'The Truth About Non-Fiction'.

21 See, for instance, *Critical Inquiry* 28, no. 1 (Autumn 2001), a special issue edited by Bill Brown titled 'Things'.

22 Arjun Appadurai, 'Introduction: Commodities and the Politics of Value', in *The Social Life of Things: Commodities in Cultural Perspective*, ed. Arjun Appadurai (Cambridge: Cambridge University Press, 1986), 3–63.

23 Shoshana Felman and Dori Laub, *Testimony: Crises of Witnessing in Literature, Psychoanalysis and History* (New York: Routledge, 1992), 204–83.

24 Dindo, *Dokumentarisch Arbeiten*, 39.

25 Ibid., 37.

26 Ibid., 35.

27 Walter Benjamin, 'Theses on the Philosophy of History', in *Illuminations*, ed. Hannah Arendt (New York: Schocken Books, 1968), 255.

28 Ibid., 255. (emphasis in original).

29 See Umberto Eco, *The Open Work* (Cambridge, MA: Harvard University Press, 1989).

30 Dindo, *Dokumentarisch Arbeiten*, 37.

15. Megatronic Memories: Errol Morris and the Politics of Witnessing

Devin Orgeron and Marsha Orgeron

Since his 1978 film *Gates of Heaven*, documentary filmmaker Errol Morris has repeatedly returned to the scene of the crime. Though not always concerned with criminality per se, his work focuses on sites of trauma, micro- and macroscopic in magnitude, ranging from the humane slaughtering of farm animals to the Vietnam War. Built around an aesthetic of expressive re-creation, Morris's documentaries reveal an ongoing obsession with the relationship between memory, which forms the thematic centre of his work, and image. Morris's films transcend the quest for access to 'the event itself' and expose the imperfect process of recollection. Though he resists the term 'documentary', or at least he did before winning an Academy Award in this category, we might consider Morris's filmography an ongoing documentary on the ways human beings document their own experience. In this way, his collected work functions like a large, highly inclusive, sometimes travelling 'witness stand'. Morris has claimed that 'people construct for themselves some kind of world they live in that they reveal through language'.[1] Language, or to be more specific, testimony, is Morris's perpetual subject. His spectators are figured as part of the director's large collection of witnesses and not, as our legal metaphor of the witness stand and several generations of documentary production might imply, as jurists. When we watch an Errol Morris film, we become witnesses to the process of witnessing.

At the heart of Morris's linguistically-based process is his cinematic apparatus, which has evolved considerably over the years. The technological developments in Morris's cinema have been motivated by his desire to allow self-knowledge and self-narration to materialise on-screen: from a stationary camera trained on talking heads in *Gates of Heaven* and *Vernon Florida* (1981); through the Interrotron, a dual-teleprompter, two-camera system that physically separates interviewer from interviewee but retains mediated eye contact between them, used in *Mr. Death* (1999); to his post-*Mr. Death* creation, the Megatron, which adds to the Interrotron system multiple, strategically placed cameras which record the interviewee.[2] The multiple cameras provide Morris with a vast amount of footage from a wide range of angles and allow him to create striking formal sequences atypical of the mainstream documentary form. As his layering of apparatuses has increased, so too have the intrusions of the filmmaker's voice and image. Compounded by the insistent presence of Morris's hand in the form of dramatic camera angles and lighting effects, altered projection rates, and the inclusion of eccentric found footage, these indices of authorial presence lend a considerable degree of metaphorical weight to his subjects' words. Perhaps more critically, these intrusions serve to remind the viewer of the filmmaker's guiding presence, his role in the process of creating memory.[3]

The aggressive presence of multiple optical devices in Morris's recent work destroys any illusion that the films are unmediated windows into history, in part because they dramatise, in near Brechtian fashion, the inherent unknowability of human psychology. This is amplified by Morris's mechanically saturated system of capturing and scrutinising the documentary subject, his focus on technological quantity and simultaneity, and even the inventive, sci-fi naming of these devices. Within Morris's system, multiple and simultaneously filming cameras articulate the slipperiness of human character, forcing the viewer to reconcile both the unreliability of Morris's many witnesses as well as his/her own perceptual deficiencies. The accretion of visual signs – the apparatus, found footage and authorial intrusion – leads to a documentary form that foregrounds multiplicity and does not disavow its ties to the fictional world; rather, Morris's films suggest (and even embrace) the degree to which memory has been shaped by mediated and often fictionalised images, as well as the degree to which the documentarian is responsible for this transformation.

In *Representing Reality* Bill Nichols, in a section titled 'The Elusiveness of Objectivity', enumerates the three distinct valences of documentary objectivity:

(1) An objective view of the world is distinct from the perception and sensibility of characters or social actors. The objective view is a third-person view rather than a first-person one. It corresponds to something like a normal or commonsensical but also omniscient perspective. (2) An objective view is free from personal bias, self-interest, or self-seeking representations. Whether first- or third-person, it conveys disinterestedness. (3) An objective view leaves audiences free to make their own determination about the validity of an argument and to take up their own position in regard to it. Objectivity means letting the viewer decide on the basis of a fair presentation of facts.[4]

In his obsession with the process of witnessing, which is itself defined by the subject's position in relation to the memories in question, Morris seems to have taken Nichols' primer as a guide for what is essentially a career-long move away from each of Nichols' three categories. First, Morris's films rely precisely on (rather than deny) the perception and sensibility of his subjects. Second, in this reliance, they cannot possibly escape the effects of personal bias, self-interest or self-seeking representations. In fact, Morris never attempts to conceal that his subjects narrate themselves, that their own biases are bound to materialise. Morris's carefully crafted formal arrangement, which includes his distinctive *mise-en-scène*, editing structure and cinematography, belies, almost in spite of itself, the filmmaker's own objectives. Third, the layering of Morris's various witnesses becomes vertiginous. Morris always suggests his own presence as guiding witness, largely through the formal and technological intrusions that recur in his work. His films also routinely point out the ways that the concept of witnessing itself is virtually all-inclusive: his camera, the films' spectators, and the films' subjects all operate as witnesses with varying degrees of investment and credibility. And although his films are often 'about' the judicial process, they complicate the notion of judgement. Morris's non-objective formal manoeuvring compels the viewer to indulge in the spectacle of witnessing: his subjects are often observers of the same event, though they perceive and consequently narrate this same event differently. By layering these narratives, Morris creates documentaries that seek out less a thing, an event or a person, than the many acts of remembering and retelling, and the repercussions of such acts.

NARRATING MEMORY

> For many, many years I have been in search of what I would call the absolutely clueless narrator, the narrator who has absolutely no perspective about himself, whatsoever.
>
> ERROL MORRIS[5]

Morris situates himself and his recording apparatus as witnesses to the secondary event of narrating memory. This event is most interesting when Morris's machinery allows for brief glimpses into the not-altogether-even surface of recollection, when he renders memory and its articulation through visual signs such as re-enactments, found footage or newspaper clippings. Creating a parallel universe in which memory is made observable, Morris's practice resembles that of other documentary filmmakers who deploy re-enactment footage and photographic evidence to allow the spectator to witness that which is otherwise unwitnessable. Unlike the majority of his contemporaries, however, Morris frees documentary conventions from their ties to objective realism. Stylish recreations, expressive editing, emotive musical scores and sound effects distance the films from the fact-finding missions that motivate other documentary projects.

While Morris de-authenticates the image as document in its conventional sense, his subjects frequently provide photographic evidence to underscore the relationship between memory and image. In *Gates of Heaven*, interviewees repeatedly hold photographs during interviews, have their departed pets' images emblazoned on their diminutive tombstones, and decorate their homes with formally arranged photographic representations. Their memories of their lost companions are accessed and allowed to enter the public sphere through the presentation of the photograph as evidence. Talking head-style images of one couple who share their memory of their deceased 'Trooper' are intercut with Polaroids of Trooper taken during the Christmas holiday.

The images sanctify and authenticate the memories. Morris trains his own cinematic gaze upon individuals who cling hard to the photograph to suggest the ways in which images – whether still, remembered, moving, fictive or borrowed – accrue meaning to become what appears to be a coherent story.

First-person testimony and narration are always key elements of Morris's films. His work suggests the degree to which images cannot act as witnesses in their own right without the intervention of words, and vice versa. Images are, at best, ambiguous without words, and yet words consistently fail to do justice to images. Morris's films frequently focus on multiple subjects whose perspectives are as distinctive as their voices. This is apparent as early as his first feature documentary, *Gates of Heaven*, in which pet owners, a rendering plant operator, pet cemetery owners, employees and business partners all discuss, in very different ways, the subject that connects them: the mortality of the animal kingdom and its consequences. The end result in Morris's work is, more often than not, a collection of competing subjective views.

In 'The Hybrid Metaphor' John Dorst writes that 'Morris has said that he is after a truly "first-person" documentary, an appropriate linguistic characterisation because it is in the first-person pronoun that the inherent doubleness of subjectivity, the simultaneity of the speaking subject and the object of speech, is closest to the surface of language'.[6] Morris's characteristic accumulation of voices, however, complicates this linguistic pattern. Often his subjects narrate not just themselves but each other, switching between a first- and third-person voice, in which they tell their versions of another's story. Their stories do not exist in isolation; they are in competition with each other. The 'conflict' of these stories – the rupture that alerts us that witnessing is a fraught and imperfect process – typically occurs at points of disagreement, points where the witnessed moment is narrated differently by different parties. Morris creates first-person images to accompany the narrated memories – images that often support but occasionally undermine the utterances of the speaking characters – and suspends them in a visual and auditory environment that signifies something other than historical truth. In so doing Morris rejects the documentary form's longstanding commitment to the mimesis of the image and achieves the 'first-person' form argued by Dorst, but only by insisting on an expressive and palpable third-person role in the process.

Morris has allowed his frustration over the 're-enactment debate' surrounding his work to surface in recent interviews. This debate rarely moves beyond claims of truth or accuracy, claims which place his work alongside other mainstream documentarians in the business of making historical truth-claims. Brian Winston has argued convincingly that the acceptance of Direct Cinema's 'fly-on-the-wall' aesthetics as 'the only legitimate documentary form' is deeply uncritical.[7] In discussing the history, ethics and multiple layers of documentary 'fakery', Winston introduces the notion of 'sincere and justified reconstruction'. He uses the term to remind us of how difficult it is to shake the old adage that 'the camera cannot lie'.[8] Morris's re-enactments may well lie, but their aim is the 'sincere and justified reconstruction' of subjective truth.

In *Mr. Death* these questions of subjective truth revolve around expert witnesses, authorities in their field who are called upon to confirm or deny the validity of evidence disproving the Holocaust. This film interrogates the role of the image in the process of legal, intellectual and emotional quests for proof. At one critical moment, we see an image of Fred Leuchter, an expert in execution devices, whose expertise has been called on by Holocaust deniers to 'prove' them right. Leuchter emerges from what he keeps referring to as an 'alleged' crematorium, and the image is rewound and revised (re-narrated, re-witnessed) by Holocaust historian Robert Jan van Pelt. The images themselves are identical, but are assigned different meanings by their narrators. Their divergent first-person narrations compete so that the very process of witnessing, remembering and interpreting is made into a tangible dialectic. That these issues arise in a film focused, at least partially, on the Holocaust seems especially appropriate. Marianne Hirsch has written about the handful of images from the Holocaust that are 'used over and over again iconically and emblematically to signal this event'.[9] Memory, she argues, has been reduced to a set of widely circulated photographs. Morris, like Hirsch, points to the iconic weight of images, especially contested images, and indicates, in this film and elsewhere, the degree to which images create memory, create the illusion of 'having witnessed'.

This emphasis on the visual vocabulary of memory is made evident from the start of *Mr. Death*. Following the expressionistic, mad-scientist-style credit sequence, the film begins with a black and white long take of Leuchter's bespectacled eyes in the rear-view mirror of the car he's driving (figure 1). Already, the film suggests the degree to which we are entering the personal vision of a narrator who looks back while moving forward. Leuchter begins to narrate his career as a designer of execution devices over a montage of black and white close-ups of car and body parts, some dramatically canted. These are followed by an extreme close-up of Leuchter's face that places the audience almost behind his glasses. This image fades out as Morris incorporates colour talking-head footage of Leuchter actually speaking what was previously the voice-over, intercut with images of blueprints and plans for the devices and structures he is discussing. In these opening moments, Morris dramatises and abstracts the process of his subject narrating his own history. In its alteration of film stock, camera angle, framing and location in a fashion one expects from the likes of contemporary fiction filmmakers like David Fincher or Oliver Stone, Morris's eccentric formalism indicates the complexity and cinematic quality of both narrative and memory as processes.

Figure 1: In this carefully composed long take from the beginning of *Mr. Death*, Morris allows Leuchter to reflect upon his own story.

In Morris's world, there is no such thing as a straightforward narration of history, personal or otherwise. Leuchter's first-person narration is, a mere four minutes into the film, already framed by devices that work to highlight his idiosyncrasies, his propensity to remember and perceive in his own peculiar way. When we are placed into a position nearly behind Leuchter's glasses in the opening sequence, the film suggests the degree to which we are all beholden to the lens through which we happen to witness and conceive history. We are plunged into darkness through a fade-out that prefaces the familiar conventions of the talking-head documentary format. This editorial act functions as a reminder of the power of the image by virtue of its awkward, momentary absence; it is also a reminder of the power of the image-maker. Such heavy-handed and highly-mediated moments are more than the stylish obfuscation of some knowable 'truth' that Morris's detractors claim them to be. Rather, they remind the viewer that the witnessed event is only made tangible through the act of narration and that verbal or visual narration is itself a form of re-enactment.

This culturally-reflexive process forms the core of *The Thin Blue Line* (1988), a film overtly concerned with crime, punishment and a miscarriage of justice following the shooting of Texas police officer Robert Wood. The film is replete with depictions of its subjects' competing stories. In the opening sequence, opposing and highly subjective interviews are intercut with each other. The film goes on to weave together divergent re-enactments of the same event accompanied by different voice-over narrations.[10] Morris seems intent on depicting the process by which his witnesses remember the variants of their perspectives. For example, the woman officer who witnesses Wood's shooting fails to remember the make, model and licence plate number of the murderer's car. Her story is told by a fellow officer, who describes his understanding of the events that took place on the night of the shooting and his frustration at extracting information from this sole eyewitness. His narration is accompanied by images that represent events precisely as he describes them, including the wrong car (a blue Vega). The murderer's car turned out to be a blue Comet and the licence plate number 'JNA 890' was different from that originally reported in the press as having the letters 'HC' in it.

Shortly after this sequence, the same officer is intercut with expressive images of a swinging pocket watch as he describes attempts to hypnotise the female officer in order to get at the recesses of her memory. According to his account, the hypnosis allows her to recall a licence plate from an event earlier in the day. At this point the camera zooms in to a licence plate number, reproducing her recollection as told by the officer in third-person narration. Despite this third-person narration, and the fact that the female officer here never speaks for herself, her first-person perspective is nonetheless represented on the film's image track. This first-person mimesis is at least twice removed, but its presence is part of the larger aesthetic of witnessing that allows Morris's spectators to witness the process of narration, to see 'through' the eyes of the witnesses themselves even when their voices are absent.

These different forms of first-person narration place the spectator in the position of being a first-hand witness, even when the memories being represented are Morris's created fictions. By virtue of watching the re-enactments, the spectator is transformed into an eyewitness and must question her own capacity for remembering and narrating. Would we remember the licence plate number or even a few of its components? Even those within the film who are critical of the female officer's faulty memory are guilty of inaccuracy. Morris subtly points this out when he includes the narration of yet another officer: 'There's a difference between a Vega and a Mercury Comet ... So you know in reality in regard to cars every piece of information that was called in they were calling in regard to a Comet ... I mean, or a, a Vega.' The slipperiness of memory and of the narration of that memory is here made auditory, while elsewhere it is visualised. Throughout, these elisions are achieved through a layering of memories and the presentation of an array of often-contradictory first-person perspectives.

In a film in which almost all of the witnesses seem to be either accidentally unreliable or to possess ulterior motives for their erratic testimony, the decision to provide visual evidence to accompany each story reveals the pitfalls of personal testimony while also underscoring its persuasiveness. We must not forget that as a result of this film a man was absolved of murder. One interviewee describes his memories of driving past the scene of the crime and we witness him trying to remember the details, stumbling over the accuracy of his own memories. As we observe him there is a cut-in to a close-up of his eyes just before Morris transitions to yet another re-enactment of the crime scene. As in *Mr. Death*, this close-up signals our entrance into the world of a subjective perspective. Here we witness the flaws of memory, dramatised through images both of the present real testimony and of the fictional but nonetheless material recreation of that memory. We are often reminded that Morris's films are not only first-person; they are past tense.[11]

Perhaps Morris's most telling story of memory appears in one of his *First Person* episodes, *The Parrot: A Story About Max*.[12] Max is an actual parrot with a limited, if fascinating, vocabulary. He is also the sole witness to a brutal murder, and may be Morris's dream subject/witness/narrator. Less a clueless narrator – for he does, it seems, have a clue – Max is a narrative-less narrator upon whom a variety of competing narratives are pinned. His words and perhaps memories, limited as they are, are open to even more explication than usual, and the witnesses to Max's speech are all too willing to offer their interpretations for his behaviour. In addition to Max's own witnessing act, several witnesses to the parrot's post-murder conduct claim that he mimics his murdered owner's voice, especially the repeated refrain of 'Richard, no, no, no'. In the name of self-interest others claim that, perhaps, the parrot's former owner was a man named Richard and his utterances have nothing to do with the recent traumatic event.

This 30-minute study includes a complex layering of witnesses who perform interpretive acts. Re-enactment footage of the murder is intercut with what might best be described as parrot point-of-view shots, including close-ups of the parrot's eye and corresponding reverse-shots of the imagined murder scene (figures 2 and 3). The re-enactment footage is distorted; it would not be mistaken for an authentic,

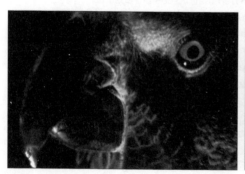 

Figures 2 and 3: Shot/reverse-shot. Max from Morris's *First Person* series and his privileged, if distorted, point of view.

the image and the witness

surveillance-like capturing of reality. Rather, it is a formal acknowledgment of the need for a visual counterpart to Max's inarticulate testimony, an imagining of what Max might or might not have seen. Max poses a series of challenges for the spectator as well as for the legal and judicial system, most especially: can a parrot, one of the great mimics of the natural world, testify in a court of law? Ultimately, Max helps Morris present his overarching thesis: that testimony and memory are always already forms of mimicry.

The episode posits that Max's testimony is as reliable as that of the other people who populate this story, many of whom have rather transparent motives for making claims about the murder, its investigation and Max's words. This episode reminds us of the degree to which the language of memory is the perpetual subject of Morris's work; the idea of parroting words and images exists in all of Morris's films. Max's status as a non-human who is incapable of being asked to remember in the same ways as Morris's usual subjects makes his perspective, as it is represented by the re-enactment, a simulation of witnessing, a re-enactment of remembering. Max's testimony does not differ substantially from Morris's other treatments of human memory. Morris does not make an argument about guilt and innocence but rather about the modes of representing the past, the complexity of bearing witness. His spectator, here and elsewhere, is invited to witness the camera's attempts to see what the documentary subject sees, even when that subject is feathered and caged.

THE ACT OF WITNESSING IN THE AGE OF MECHANICAL REPRODUCTION

We built a piece of Auschwitz.

ERROL MORRIS[13]

Morris's formal conventions ensure that the spectator is witness to the imperfect process of bearing witness, a notion that resonates with what Marianne Hirsch, in the context of her work on Holocaust imagery, refers to as 'postmemory'. Hirsch defines postmemory as 'the response of the second generation to the trauma of the first'.[14] Morris is similarly fascinated with the various methods by which memory is absorbed, intuited and 'passed along'. Morris's films are about the universal act of spectatorship; they are about the process of seeing and the complexity of acting as a conduit for that information, as is made absurdly clear in the episode from *First Person* explored above. Although Morris rather famously resists the label of postmodernism – making him, we would argue, his own 'clueless narrator' – his ongoing collection of witnesses is a decidedly postmodern curatorial act.[15]

Morris believes in the potential for the documentary genre and expressive style to function in a complementary fashion. His oft-discussed stylistic overload is an attempt to debunk the notion of innocent images, but is not an attempt to purge them. In fact, Morris's films appear to celebrate the postmodern status of images despite his coy claims about that concept. Morris's formal approach is to intersperse images of the interviewed subject – sometimes framed within a provocative *mise-en-scène*, as in *Gates of Heaven* or *A Brief History of Time* (1991) – with what we might call 'breakaway metaphorical moments', which are always staged and comment to varying degrees on the given subject's idiosyncratic worldview. In *A*

Brief History of Time, a computer-generated Rolex watch spins through a computer-generated representation of space as Stephen Hawking discusses the mysteries of the space-time continuum. In *Mr. Death*, the imagery alternates between Leuchter as talking head, Leuchter as living, breathing participant in the historical world and

a series of highly stylised and metaphorically remarkable images of Leuchter's personal dreamscape: he chips away at rocks in a *mise-en-scène* of utter emptiness (at times in an Auschwitz re-created in Cambridge) (figure 4); he sips coffee before a series of mirrors endlessly reflecting into the distance; and at times, he walks towards the camera operator's telephoto lens and falls out of focus. These moments all attest to the filmmaker's guiding presence. Like his menagerie of witnesses, Morris himself always functions as a narrator.

Figure 4: A recreated, expressionistic examination of Leuchter at work in *Mr. Death.*

Mr. Death, like *The Thin Blue Line*, concerns a legal case and relies heavily upon a key element of the judicial system: the witness. In both films, narrated, recreated and videotaped images are consulted to explain events. A key moment early in the film addresses acts of imagistic interpretation when Leuchter discusses a particularly haunting photograph. As Leuchter's reputation as an expert in execution devices was growing, he was contacted by the state of Tennessee to inspect and reconstruct their antiquated and, for reasons only the state of Tennessee can explain, sentimentally valuable electric chair. As Leuchter narrates, Morris provides grainy, expressive images, alternating between black and white and colour, of Leuchter and his step-son in their basement workshop. The images are highly stylised, their angles eccentric. When the cinematographer shoots a television screen playing previously recorded images of Leuchter in his workshop discussing his own amateur photography, the images shift to highly degraded, blown-up and pixilated video images. As Leuchter explains it, in order to facilitate his reconstruction of the chair, he had to photograph it in detail. One photograph, however, catches his attention, because it appears to contain, he says, two images. Leuchter offers the following interpretation of the photograph:

> As far as I understand it, certain objects give off auras. And some objects that have been exposed to high intensity electromagnetic fields absorb some of that energy and will give off an aura. I don't know what we photographed. We don't know if we photographed an entity, I mean we don't know what's there. It may still reside in the parts that are in Tennessee ... But when I tore the chair apart, maybe it was freed. I don't know ... that's assuming that there was something there to start with.

The image in question, a detail of the chair's seatback and straps, does indeed also seem to contain the diaphanous image of a face. Coming just after the hyperbolically grainy and pixilated footage of Leuchter, Morris offers us a reminder of the inadequate transparency of any photographic images, his own included. Here, Morris facilitates spectatorial scrutiny by providing close-ups of the photograph's details. We find ourselves seeking out what Leuchter has told us that he sees: is there really a face in the photograph, or do we just see what we have been told to see? This is a highly self-conscious moment of directorial commentary, suggesting Morris's own scepticism toward the ability of images to depict truth in any reliable way. What appears to be the not-so-mysterious phenomenon of double-exposure eludes Leuchter. At least, this is the impression Morris gives us as Leuchter spins out his theories about aura, accidentally echoing Walter Benjamin's important ideas about the age of mechanical reproduction.[16] This segment of *Mr. Death* offers a concise lesson in both the primacy of the photographic image and in the vagaries of photographic interpretation, points Morris's films return to repeatedly.

For Benjamin, the loss of aura brought about by the proliferation of the mechanical arts resulted in the potential liberation of art, enabling it 'to meet the beholder halfway'.[17] Wrested from its specificity in time and space, the aura-less object was not beholden to a notion of the 'original' for its value. In contrast, Leuchter imagines a photograph so representative of the object's specific time and place that it carries upon its surface 'entities' from the past, ghosts of the original. This unquestioning belief that a photographic surface carries traces of the past is central to the film's larger questions about the image as witness. The use of photographic materials without Morris's consistently interrogative form leaves us all, to borrow Leuchter's words, wondering if 'there was something there to start with'. Morris does not suggest that events never happened, but that all attempts to recover them – via photography, narration or re-enactment – are imperfect, removed from the so-called original moment. As Robert McNamara's seventh lesson in *The Fog of War* (2003) instructs, 'seeing and believing are both often wrong'. Morris quips back at McNamara in a manner perfectly relevant to the present discussion, saying 'we see what we want to believe' and, we should add, we narrate accordingly.

Morris both relies upon images and also tests their stability, calling into question our faith in them as a source of indisputable knowledge. In *Mr. Death*, Leuchter's scientific journey to the concentration camps in Poland is scrutinised in just such a fashion. His trip, the subject of the second half of the documentary, was recorded by a videographer who accompanied him on his evidence-gathering mission. Leuchter, as Joel Black has argued, is himself a deluded documentarian.[18] His footage is convincing to himself and to Holocaust deniers in part precisely because of its amateur aesthetic. Shaky hand-held cameras, grainy video stock and generally poor lighting combine to create a sense of 'realism', a sense so overbearing that its 'reality effect' spills over into Leuchter's specious and often childlike narration. This video footage of Leuchter at work at Auschwitz provides Morris's audience with a twice-removed test of the camera's capacity for witnessing. The images themselves appear to support the tenuous science they uphold, but only until they are scrutinised by Morris as editor or by alternate narrators, such as historian Robert Jan van Pelt. They may at first appear to present the 'facts' of Leuchter's evidence-gathering unproblematically, but these facts only take us so far.

At one point Morris slows down footage of Leuchter as he collects samples by chiselling into what we assume to be a wall at Auschwitz. As if to prove his commitment not to the integrity of the image but to its pervasive capacity to mislead, Morris presents mock footage of Leuchter at work in a recreated Auschwitz. As Morris's work continually demonstrates, all images have a questionable past, a dubious relationship to their subject. But the act of Leuchter's chiselling has a dual function: Leuchter wishes to carve his name into the annals of history and, in so doing, ends up eroding the history that he hoped would support him.[19] When these images are slowed down, the invisible reveals itself: Leuchter's tragically and falsely heroic self-image is elongated and exaggerated, placed in relief. And yet, Morris, like Leuchter, is also collecting and manipulating samples. Morris, however, collects behavioural, not archaeological samples; his tool is an editing table rather than a chisel. Thus, for Morris, the conception of the camera as an impartial witness is debunked; it is always a functionary of subjective human desire.

The penultimate images in *The Thin Blue Line* formalise the degree to which Morris comments upon his own highly mediated role. Within Morris's oeuvre, this extended sequence is unusual. It contains a series of shots not of re-enactments or interviews, but of a hand-held tape recorder (figure 5). For the first time in the film, the soundtrack introduces us to Morris's voice as he questions and gets answers from David Harris, the man not convicted of Wood's murder. Here Morris intrudes from outside of the diegesis, making an important first- and third-person foray into the world of the story. Shot from a variety of different perspectives and distances – medium shot, extreme close-up, canted angles – images of a tape recorder mimic the rhythm of shot/reverse-shot editing as each cut initiates another framing of

Figure 5: In their compositional eccentricity and title placement, Morris's shifting images of the tape recorder at the end of *The Thin Blue Line* look like advertisements for the multiple truths his film presents.

the device. While the editing is evocative of a conversation, the disembodied voices tell the most crucial story of the film: David Harris, in essence, confesses that he fingered Randall Adams for the murder of Officer Wood to a police force desperate to solve this high-profile crime.

When Harris speaks about why he implicated Adams in Wood's murder, he uses the third-person present tense to refer to himself instead of the more appropriate first-person past tense: 'Scared sixteen-year-old kid. He sure would like to get out of it if he can.' Morris is highly aware of the linguistic structure of Harris's narration, making his auditory appearance in this final scene the film's most revealing moment. Harris's adoption of the third-person, perhaps equally calculated, rhetorically removes him from himself, from his own personal history. In adopting this position, Harris becomes a spectator and narrator to his own acts. This process of removal is made all the more palpable in Morris's refusal to show us anything but the device that records and subsequently plays back this transformation. This is not to say that

Morris refuses the primacy of the image. On the contrary, he effectively implies its sway over human experience. However, Morris focuses our attention equally upon the apparatus and what it has the potential to capture: the process of memory, history and, on occasion, even truth.

Morris's style, here and elsewhere, forms a long-running commentary on our cultural faith in images, our desire to believe what we see, our hope that not all cameras lie. It is no coincidence that Morris's own cameras find themselves gazing most often upon individuals in legal or personal battles for the truth. Morris's awareness of and insistence on his own mediating hand makes for more than self-conscious images; the films make the viewer conscious of the manner by which truth, history and the witnessed moment are always reproductions.

FOR YOUR CONSIDERATION: OF MEMORIES AND MOVIES

Nichols provides the following sketch of realism and its function within three broadly conceived cinematic categories or types:

> In classic Hollywood narrative, realism combines a view of an imaginary world with moments of authorial overtness (commonly at the beginning and end of tales, for example) to reinforce the sense of a moral and the singularity of its import. In modernist narrative (most European art cinema, for example), realism combines an imaginary world rendered through a blend of objective and subjective voices with patterns of authorial overtness (usually through a strong and distinctive personal style) to convey a sense of moral ambiguity. In documentary, realism joins together objective representations of the historical world and rhetorical overtness to convey an argument about the world.[20]

It should come as no surprise that Morris's place within this schematic is problematic at best. Morris's work would seem to share much in common with Nichols's ideas about modernist narrative. The chorus of visual and aural, objective and subjective voices is in fact a product of Morris's own authorial overtness. Except for his interest in 'the historical world', however, Morris seems to exist outside of Nichols's documentary domain. Morris often uses clips from feature films in his attempt to visualise his subjects' own cinematically-informed dreamscapes. In fact, this interest in the fictional world as a catalyst for understanding the historical world, and the hold that the former has over it, has been a longstanding feature of Morris's work.

Perhaps no Errol Morris piece addresses the cinematic nature of memory more directly than his 2001 documentary short made for the ABC broadcast of the Academy Awards Ceremony.[21] The ceremony itself occurred at a moment in American history when national viewing habits were being called into question. Americans puzzled over their own relationship to and reliance on the broadcast images of the September 11 'events', and the celebration of something as frivolous as 'going to the movies' appeared suspect, at best. The ceremony began with Tom Cruise assuring his celebrity audience and those at home that movies were okay, even important as a reassurance that life continues despite the threat of political events. The introduction was followed by Morris's contribution, a short film documenting people's responses to the following general question: 'What do movies mean to you?' The exercise itself was undertaken in the spirit of Edgar Morin and Jean Rouch's popular ethnography in *Chronique d'un été* (*Chronicle of a Summer*, 1960), although the resulting film is something else entirely.

Morris's Academy Awards' film is, on the one hand, a thoroughly entertaining celebration of cinephilia. It got laughs. Judgement is not passed in any clear way: Morris slaps no hands for the crime of cinephilia, nor does he make claims about film's inherent value. However, the film's timing, its subject matter and its placement within Morris's career would suggest that within these several minutes resides a subtle questioning of our love affair with images, our chronic spectatorship, our cinematic relationship to reality, and the role that movies and other mass-produced images play in the articulation of our own memories. Morris is committed to exposing witnesses to the process of witnessing. However, in this short film, he calls both terms into question. His Academy Awards' short represents the process of spectatorship via a series of spectators-turned-spectacle.

Subject after subject, some famous, others unknown, offer cinematic soundbites against the stark white background that has become the hallmark of Morris's advertisements, a background that replicates the scope and emptiness of the silver screen itself.[22] Wavy Gravy attempts to find cinema's use-value when he claims that Peter Davis's *Hearts and Minds* (1974) ended the Vietnam War, to which Morris playfully asks 'Can movies do that?' Mikhail Gorbachev, an apparent Russell Crowe fan, likes *Gladiator* (Ridley Scott, 2000). Laura Bush is a fan of *Giant* (George Stevens, 1956). Occasionally Morris's voice is audible on the soundtrack, teasing, provoking and asking additional questions. But the overall structure of the piece is a steady stream of individuals whose very individuality is accentuated by the emptiness of the space that contains them, the space that cuts between them and their freedom to narrate themselves.

Morris has repeatedly suggested that all human beings live in their own self-created dreamscapes. His films argue, however, that these dreamscapes are often cinematically derived. Film is our mythology, providing us with images that function as our collective memory. This is an idea reiterated in *Fast, Cheap and Out of Control* (1997) where characters directly express the manner in which films have influenced their career choices and their lives more generally. Morris's expressive techniques, which have on occasion been faulted for being 'too cinematic', are self-consciously so. Cinema and its grip on the imaginative life, in fact, are what these images express. The canted framings of Fred Leuchter are not simply the product of Morris's cinematically-informed mind, though they are certainly this as well; they are expressive of Leuchter's own cinematically-informed worldview.

The idea of film spectatorship is also central to *The Thin Blue Line*, which swerves into a curious 'film within a film' when Randall Adams narrates the portion of his encounter with David Harris that found them at a drive-in movie theatre watching a double feature. This unusually long narrative detour (the sequence lasts a full two minutes) shows a re-enactment of the seemingly mundane event of going to a drive-in movie, including extended footage from *Swinging Cheerleaders* (Jack Hill, 1974) and *The Student Body* (Gus Trikonis, 1976), the films that Adams and Harris had been watching on the fateful night. The camera is parked at the drive-in along with Adams and Harris and the resulting images shift between long shots of the movie screen and glimpses inside the car where we see actors playing Adams and Harris drinking beer and smoking marijuana. Adams's narration guides us through this entire sequence, and includes his own spectatorial evaluations: he does not like the second cheerleading film and wants to leave but Harris wants to see the film through to the end. In a film about who saw what on the night Robert Wood was shot, this lengthy and seemingly inconsequential sequence offers an important reminder: every spectator sees, perceives, reacts to and evaluates things differently.

This sequence illuminates both the culture's incessant desire for spectatorship and its need to narrate and evaluate what it sees. Morris's insistence on aestheticising first-person narrations, on creating reproductions of the real in order to point out the degree to which we rely upon the fictional, suggests that remembering is, indeed, a process of re-creation. His films envision the many literal and metaphorical lenses through which we perceive: the windshield at the drive-in movie, Leuchter's spectacles, the side windows of passers-by, rear-view and side mirrors, as well as the lenses that record and project images. Morris's films offer a primer on the variable functions of memory and narration, as well as a compelling argument about the great necessity of examining the multiple layers embedded within the process of witnessing.

We would like to thank Ellen Harrington of the Academy of Motion Picture Arts and Sciences for providing us with a copy of Morris' Academy Awards' segment and Sarah Loffman for introducing us to First Person.

Notes

1   Quoted in Joel Black, *The Reality Effect: Film Culture and the Graphic Imperative* (New York: Routledge, 2002), 151.
2   Morris has discussed the Interrotron and Megatron on his website: 'Since the Interrotron makes use of two-way mirrors and television monitors, it is possible using lipstick cameras to add additional cameras behind the two-way mirrors.' Morris also explains that the Megatron adds a minimum of twenty cameras to the Interrotron. Online. Available <http://web.archive.org/web/20040204132401/http://errolmorris.com/conversations.php> (accessed 31 May 2003).
3   Morris descends in some ways from John Grierson who, as Brian Winston points out, opted for a documentary practice grounded in 'poetic image-making' that 'claimed all the artistic licence of a fiction with the only constraints being that its images were not of actors and its stories were not the products of unfettered imagining'. Brian Winston, *Lies, Damn Lies and Documentaries* (London: British Film Institute, 2000), 20.
4   Bill Nichols, *Representing Reality* (Indianapolis: Indiana University Press, 1991), 196.
5   Errol Morris, Interview with Ron Rosenbaum, Museum of Modern Art, Fall 1999, reproduced on Errol Morris' website. Available <http://www.errolmorris.com/content/interview/moma1999.html> (accessed 31 May 2003).
6   John Dorst, 'Which Came First, the Chicken Device or the Textual Egg?: Documentary Film and the Limits of the Hybrid Metaphor', *Journal of American Folklore* 112, no. 445 (Summer 1999): 279.
7   Winston, 5. Winston also points to Errol Morris' *The Thin Blue Line* (1988) as a point where these aesthetic prejudices began to shift.
8   Ibid., 132–3.
9   Marianne Hirsch, 'Surviving Images', *Yale Journal of Criticism* 14, no. 1 (2001): 7.

10 Morris's interest in multiplicity would seem to link him to currents in postmodern thinking, with which he is clearly familiar. At the same time, Morris, with his ever-present sense of irony and calculated humour, claims distance from this thinking, as he indicates in a fall 1999 interview with Ron Rosenbaum conducted at the Museum of Modern Art: 'Yes, I believe there is such a thing as real, historical truth. I am no post-modernist. I live in Cambridge, Massachusetts. And one of the nice things about Cambridge, Massachusetts is that "Baudrillard" isn't in the phone book.' Online. Available <http://www.errolmorris.com/content/interview/moma1999.html> (accessed 31 May 2003).

11 Even this is somewhat misleading, since the films are both diegetically first-person and yet necessarily third-person.

12 *First Person*, part of Bravo's so-called 'Counter-Culture Wednesday' line-up, was a series of 30-minute Megatron-heavy interviews. Airing for two complete seasons (2000–01), this innovative series focused on Americans with eccentric careers: the highly educated and articulate autistic designer of more humane slaughtering devices, a lifelong Giant Squid follower, a crime-scene cleaner, the curator of a museum of medical curiosities in Philadelphia, and the like.

13 Errol Morris interview, 'Mr. Death: The Executioner's Song', *Filmmaker Magazine*, Fall 1999, 85.

14 Hirsch, 'Surviving Images', 8.

15 Morris occasionally acknowledges this curatorial connection. 'Smiling in a Jar', an episode of *First Person*, focuses on Gretchen Worden, curatorial director of Philadelphia's Mütter Museum, a museum of medical curiosities and atrocities. Not only are the similarities between Worden and Morris drawn out comically in the episode but, at one point, Worden, making a joke about Morris's teleprompter system and its effect, suggests that the filmmaker's head would look interesting in a jar. Worden states that, staring as she has been at his disembodied face on a screen, it does not seem to be too much of a stretch. Morris takes the opportunity, in his editing of the piece, to rather forwardly 'expose' the apparatus, giving the viewer a glimpse at said teleprompter and said head smiling wryly. As the series continued through its second season, these self-reflexive moments occurred with greater frequency.

16 Walter Benjamin, 'The Work of Art in the Age of Mechanical Reproduction', reprinted in *Film Theory and Criticism: Introductory Readings*, eds Marshall Cohen and Leo Braudy, 6th edn. (New York: Oxford University Press, 2004). 791–811.

17 Ibid., 793.

18 Black, *The Reality Effect*, 151–4.

19 James Roth, the chemist who tested the samples Leuchter brought back, explains in the film that cyanide does not penetrate more than ten microns beyond the surface and that Leuchter's samplings were therefore improperly gathered.

20 Nichols, *Representing Reality*, 166.

21 The ceremony was broadcast on 24 March 2002.

22 Morris has had an active career in advertising, making commercials for such companies as Miller High Life, Adidas, Nike, Levis, and Volkswagen. The composition, editing, soundtrack, and overall sensibility of this work is almost instantly recognisable. A sample of his work can be seen on his website. Available <http://www.errolmorris.com/commercials.html> (accessed 31 May 2003).

Index